JEFF CIOLETTI

THE

Drinkable
Globe

The Indispensable Guide to the Wide World of Booze

TURNER

Turner Publishing Company
Nashville, Tennessee
New York, New York
www.turnerpublishing.com

Cover design: Maddie Cothren
Cover photo: ©Phillip Fryman, All Rights Reserved.
Book design: Maddie Cothren and Tim Holtz
All interior images courtesy of Jeff Cioletti, except the following: page 62, Dreamstime.com; page 92, courtesy of Simon Fenton; pages 136 and 240, iStock by Getty Images; page 210, courtesy of Lucas Bols; page 247, courtesy of Glencairn Crystal

Library of Congress Cataloging-in-Publication Data is available via the Library of Congress

Printed in the United States of America
17 18 19 20 10 9 8 7 6 5 4 3 2 1

For my wife and thirsty travel companion, Craige

CONTENTS

LIST OF COCKTAIL RECIPES

ix

xi

FOREWORD

"ALWAYS BE CURIOUS ABOUT HOW THE

REST OF THE WORLD TASTES."

—JEFF CIOLETTI

Jeff has dropped a lot of great information, advice, and even philosophy on us in this latest book. Where did local drinks get their character? What can you do with them? Where are the places to go that you might overlook? It's all in here, and it's fun—much like drinking with Jeff is fun. (Been there, done that; kind of unclear on where I lost the T-shirt.)

But tucked into Jeff's incisive warning of global booze homogenization—and look, global cultural homogenization of all types is one of the worst nonphysical threats going on right now, because you don't want everyone to *be like you*—is that particularly, wonderfully useful thought: *Always be curious about how the rest of the world tastes.*

Why would you travel to Chile and then want to drink beers that are just more attempts to be like Stone IPA? Why travel to China and have Jack Daniel's? Hell, why go to California and drink what the local brewer thinks is a New England–type IPA? What's the point, when there are local drinks and ways of drinking them that you cannot find at home?

If you're somehow worried about getting something you don't like, you're probably buying this book for someone else. Jeff's advice is for the girl who's getting this book because she wants to find new drinks—yes, you!—and the guy who knows that even Lonely Planet doesn't dive this deep into booze tourism.

Get the most out of your travel, open your mouth, and order off the locals' menu. What's the worst that could happen?

You might find something you just love, and can't get at home. In which case, you had a beautiful experience, and you'll always have that, and you may come back.

You might have something you just don't care for at all. Okay, now you have an amusing story to tell, complete with shuddering and sound effects.

You might actually become ill. Well, as they say, you could get hit crossing the street, or fall off the couch. Life is inherently risky, and at least you're out doing something.

Always be curious about how the rest of the world tastes. Be fearless. Do the vodka shot. Have the shochu. Grab the honey wine. Taste the dung-smoked beer. Other people have done it and lived; and some of them loved it. Doesn't that make you curious?

There are only so many days each of us has, wedged in between work, and sleep, and doing laundry, and driving to band practice, and mowing the damned lawn. Do you want to spend all of your bonus days doing the same thing, eating the same foods, drinking the same drinks?

I don't, and that leads to a bit of advice I have to add to Jeff's: You'll never ever find your favorite thing if you don't try as many things as you can. Food, drink, places, friendships . . . you name it. Variety is the road to discovery.

I'd write more, but I've got a plane to catch, menus to read, local folks to meet, new bars to find. Let's spin the globe, and have a drink. First round's on Jeff.

Lew Bryson
June 2017

INTRODUCTION

Planet Earth is a paradoxical place. The more I see of it, the bigger and smaller it gets. Stay with me on this.

When I was a kid living on the East Coast, California seemed like the most distant place in the world. The fact that I didn't set foot on an airplane until the tail end of my senior year in high school certainly didn't help (and that trip was only to Orlando, Florida, barely a two-hour flight from my home state of New Jersey), nor did the fact that it would be another three years before I boarded another plane.

But as my personal and professional travel accelerated, I realized that getting from A to B—even when B might be four-thousand-plus miles away—was really no big deal. Six continents and scores of international acquaintances and social media connections later, New Zealand feels as close to Washington, DC (where I write these words), as, say, Asheville, North Carolina.

On the other hand, the more cities, states, and countries I visit, the more I discover how little I know about those specific places, the world, and anything, really. The globe just gets that much bigger—or maybe my perceived place in it just becomes smaller. I guess it's a version of the sense of insignificance in the universe that astrophysicists feel when they see more of it. Fortunately for space scientists, they're really good at calculus and all sorts of higher, esoteric, hard-to-pronounce forms of arithmetic, and that enables them (and ultimately us) to make a little more sense of how the cosmos operates.

I'm not as well equipped. I got a C in calculus in college and now, decades removed, I would likely flunk.

But one thing I do know is booze. So whenever some corner of our beloved Earth needs figuring out to make it feel a little less big, the first thing I want to know is what people are drinking there.

For all of humanity's countless differences, one of the common threads that crosses oceans, forests, deserts, and tundras—and in the best way possible—is our relationship to alcohol.

Entire countries may have gone dry for religious or other reasons, but there are, at the very least, centuries within the histories of even the most teetotally of nations that are awash in alcohol. There's a certain irony in the fact that intoxicating beverages are illegal in much of the Middle East and North Africa, considering that it's there where brewing and distilling were born.

Getting to know the diverse peoples of the world means getting to know what and how they drink. The best travel vessel is a glass. So, all aboard!

First, a little about the itinerary. Our voyage includes stops in most regions of the world, on every continent. And yes, that includes Antarctica (and beyond—you'll have read on to learn exactly what I mean).

I focus mainly on regional groupings of countries, as many customs and traditional tipples overlap across national borders. However, I stop to explore many individual countries in detail, depending on the richness and scope of their beverage heritage.

Many regions have equally prominent traditions of fermenting (beer and wine) and distilling (spirits like whisky and vodka), which takes the fermentation process one step further. Wherever possible, I delve into both of those. In other countries, where those processes are a bit out of balance, I give preferential treatment to one over the other.

Now, a bit about the structure of this book: For a brief moment, I entertained the notion of organizing the book alphabetically by country or region, formatting it in an encyclopedic manner. But then I decided that doing so would be completely bonkers. We don't travel in alphabetical order. (Okay, maybe some people who want to make a game out of globetrotting do, but it's definitely not the norm.) When we visit multiple countries on a single trip, we usually choose those destinations based on their proximity to each other.

If we had unlimited riches and free time (which I'm going to daringly assume applies to virtually no one reading this) and were about to leave for a real trip that took us to every time zone on every continent of the world, how would we plan our trip? I flipped a coin and decided to go east to west, beginning at the international date line. In other words, we'll be drinking sake and shochu in Japan long before we have our first sip of Tennessee whiskey. And we'll never lose our bearings, as each section will feature a map of exactly where we are.

I've included personal observations and anecdotes wherever I could. I've been to most of the *regions* detailed throughout the book, but not every *country* within those regions. In many cases, I've encountered the beverages that originated in one country in a completely different part of the world. I've also relied on locals—whether they're brand reps, bartenders, or fully immersed enthusiasts—to fill in some of the blanks for places I've yet to visit.

Although cocktails aren't the traditional method of consuming spirits in many of the countries across the globe (neat or on the rocks tends to be the norm), the worldwide craft cocktail scene is booming, and innovative mixed drinks have become the entry point to many of these exotic liquors for a whole new generation. So you'll see that I've included cocktail recipes that use many of the local tipples found in the different regions of the world. Renowned bartenders from across the globe, as well as representatives of the international brands themselves, have graciously contributed most of the recipes.

Think of this book as a series of happy hours and geography lessons rolled into one. Call it The Geography of Drinking 101. There are no exams in this class, though. The only thing getting tested will be your palate.

Are you ready to spin the drinkable globe? Let's go.

AUSTRALIA AND
NEW ZEALAND

Our first stops are in the far southeastern reaches of the planet: New Zealand and Australia. One of the legacies left over from the imperial age has been a taste for fine whisky.

NEW ZEALAND

In New Zealand, alcohol consumption by the indigenous population was virtually nonexistent before the Europeans came. (The same is true of its large continental neighbor—if a place that's a three-hour flight away can be called a neighbor—which we'll get to in a moment.) Alcoholic drinks simply weren't part of the Maori culture, and the industry today is based mostly on production traditions that settlers brought to the double-island nation in the nineteenth century.

Back in those days, the British Empire was using most of its colonies for various raw materials. The Brits would ship these materials back to the United Kingdom, process them into commercial products—food, beverages, what have you—and ship them out into the world.

As those involved in the modern beverage-making industry like to tell it, Scottish settlers started turning some of the barley grown on the islands—particularly in the South Island's Otago region—into whisky in the middle of the nineteenth century. A man named Owen McShane has been widely credited as the father of New Zealand distilling. McShane produced what was essentially moonshine, with the label Chained Lightning.

Naturally, the desire for tax revenue reared its ugly head, and the government passed the Distillation Act of 1865, which made it illegal for distilleries producing less than five thousand gallons a year to operate. And that meant that McShane and others of his ilk had to close up shop. However, two distilleries, one on each island, did manage to meet the criteria: New Zealand Distilling Co., in the South Island city of Dunedin, and Crown Distilleries, based in the North Island's Auckland, the country's largest city. Both distilleries gained a reputation for producing some pretty A-list whisky, which, the story goes, could have held its own against proper Scotch (that is, the type of whisky actually produced in Scotland).

But by the end of the 1870s, the government had increased the duties on local production to match those of imports from the UK, which forced those two distilleries to close. There's been a bit of conjecture (whispers and innuendo, really, no true documented evidence) that Scottish banks may have put the screws to New Zealand's government, withholding loans for building the country's railroads if locally produced whisky continued to compete with Scotch.

It wasn't until the 1950s that legal distilling returned to the country. The most iconic of New Zealand producers, Willowbank (also known as Wilson's Distillery), opened in 1974. Willowbank was able to expand production in the 1980s when Seagram's acquired it. But then Australia's Foster's Group bought it and shut down the distillery permanently in 1997. For the twenty-three years of its operation, Willowbank enjoyed the distinction of being the southernmost distillery in the world.

But that wasn't the end of the whisky story in New Zealand—not by a long shot. At the turn of the millennium, consumer tastes began to change and ushered in a global whisky renaissance. A small craft distilling industry started to bloom in the country, much as it had in Australia and the United States, but on a much smaller scale. (New Zealand has a significantly smaller population, after all.)

And the leaders of New Zealand whisky's third epoch have their forebears to thank for their first products. Mathew and Rachael Thomson opened Thomson Whisky in 2010, blending some of Willowbank's old barrels that they bought at auction when Foster's shuttered the distillery. They've come up with some award-winning expressions in the process.

Thomson Whisky's business model initially was that of independent bottler (those that source spirit from a third-party distillery, tweak it to their own specifications, then release it), but it's evolved to include an operating distillery of its own (though spirit-making activities happen courtesy of Auckland's Hallertau Brewery, from which Thomson borrows space).

Of course, in the inaugural years of its production activities, none of the distillate the new facility actually produced was on the market as whisky, as it typically takes three years before it achieves full whisky-hood. But, in addition to its bottlings of Willowbank-produced whisky, Thomson marketed limited quantities of new-make single malt straight from the still, as well as the aptly named Progress Report line, which is just that: Thomson takes young, partially matured spirit and bottles it while it's still on its coming-of-age journey. An update from the road, if you will.

New Zealand's distilling history has been bumpy, to say the least. But it seems that the demographic stars are at last starting

3

to align to produce a solid, sustainable consumer base for whisky output—both on its home islands and abroad. There are only a few whisky makers sparsely scattered across the two islands, but as more get into the business, a full-fledged industry will emerge to elevate New Zealand in the eyes of the whisky world. It will also facilitate collaborations between distillers, something that's common among craft brewers.

Kiwis may lack in numbers, but certainly not in thirst. The demand among New Zealand drinkers far outstrips supply, and Mat Thomson is always running out of his spirits. There just aren't enough local producers to serve the market. Thomson concedes that distilling—especially whisky distilling—is a tricky racket to get into, which likely gives many potential producers pause. "Whisky is one of the hardest businesses you can start," he admits. "You've got to make it, put it in the barrel, age it for a long time, and then you may or may not be able to sell it at the end of that. You've got this big stock of whisky, the market for which may change."

And, thanks to high taxes and virtually no economies of scale, local spirits can be quite pricey. I had to be extremely selective when I went whisky shopping in Auckland, where a bottle cost upward of US$100.

As more New Zealand producers get in the game and start putting more product on the market, the next hurdle will be to establish a whisky tradition and style unique to the nation, independent of the Scottish tradition that so directly influenced it. If Thomson has his way, that moment will come sooner rather than later.

Thomson has been experimenting a great deal to produce a New Zealand–specific flavor profile. The key element is manuka wood, native to New Zealand, which he uses to smoke the barley used in some of the distillery's products. This produces a flavor profile that other countries can't claim, one that is distinct from the peat-smoked spirits of Scotland and Australia. "By default, we came up with a new whisky that you couldn't get elsewhere," Thomson says. "The holy grail for me is a New Zealand style in its own right that we can be proud of."

The distillery is also experimenting with New Zealand's most famous alcoholic beverage on the world stage: wine. Thomson has been aging some whisky in casks that previously held the reds and whites produced by nearby wineries, giving it a more subtle taste of the regional terroir. He's even playing around with the manuka-smoked spirit in those barrels, which is a complicated flavor combination to get just right. That's all a bit of a work in progress—just as Kiwi distilling has been for two centuries.

⋈ A Trail of Grapes

Though there are burgeoning whisky distilling industries in both Australia and New Zealand, these countries are much more famous on the world drinking stage for their wines. New Zealand Sauvignon Blancs, in particular, are legendary, especially for their earthy and fresh-mown-grass notes. The white varietal becomes much more prominent the farther south you go. (You're moving farther from the equator, so think of it as a climate similar to Germany, Austria, or France's Alsace region, where the cooler temperatures are more suited for whites and lighter reds like Pinot Noir.) For greater diversity, at least as far as a red-white balance is concerned, the area around Auckland, far north on the North Island, offers an amazing cross section of everything from world-class Cabernet Sauvignons and Montepulcianos to Bordeaux-style blends. A great day trip from New Zealand's largest city is a ferry ride to nearby Waiheke Island, home to about two dozen vineyards. As soon as you disembark, you can rent a bike and pedal on both pavement and gravel from winery to winery, sipping the temperate region's finest. (Or, if you want to get more bang for your buck, and less exercise, you could always rent a car.)

5

KIWI COCKTAILS

☞ BIRDS OF PARADISE

I met up with Mat Thomson from Thomson Whisky at a Brooklyn-esque brick-and-stone bar called Bedford Soda & Liquor in the fashionable Auckland district of Ponsonby. The place more than delivered—I immediately knew I had to get some of the pub's stellar whisky cocktails into these pages. Here's one of its fine liquid lovelies.

⇢ DIRECTIONS ❧

Combine all ingredients in a shaker with ice and shake vigorously.

Double-strain into a chilled absinthe-rinsed coupe or martini glass and garnish with edible flower.

⇢ INGREDIENTS ❧

30 ml (1 ounce) Thomson Two Tone Whisky

15 ml (½ ounce) Aperol

15 ml (½ ounce) Fruitlab Hibiscus Liqueur

20 ml (⅔ ounce) fresh orange juice

10 ml (⅓ ounce) fresh lemon juice

Edible flower, for garnish

☞ WHITE WHISKY COBBLER

Here's another drink from the good folks at Bedford Soda & Liquor, using Thomson's unaged white whisky to fantastic fruit-and-honey-accented effect.

⇢ DIRECTIONS ❧

Build cocktail in a highball glass and top with crushed ice.

Garnish with large mint sprig and soaked berries (don't drain the syrup—make sure it's still stuck to the berries).

⇢ INGREDIENTS ❧

30 ml (1 ounce) Thomson White Malt New Spirit

30 ml (1 ounce) fresh lemon juice

15 ml (½ ounce) honey syrup (a honey-fied version of simple syrup: 2 parts honey, 1 part water)

Mint sprig, for garnish

Mixed berries soaked in Shott black currant and honey syrup, for garnish

☞ TWO TONE GINGER

This gingery delight comes from Auckland's Peach Pit—think of it as a boozier version of the diner of the same name on Beverly Hills, 90210.

⇢ DIRECTIONS ⇠

Muddle fresh ginger with smoked ginger syrup.

Add whisky and Chambord.

Top with ice and shake for 10 seconds.

Double-strain into a tall glass full of ice.

⇢ INGREDIENTS ⇠

Fresh ginger

15 ml (½ ounce) smoked ginger syrup

60 ml (2 ounces) Thomson Two Tone Whisky

15 ml (½ ounce) Chambord

☞ OIL RIG

This formidable drink comes courtesy of the Auckland bar Golden Dawn: Tavern of Power!

⇢ DIRECTIONS ⇠

Combine all ingredients in a cocktail shaker, and shake.

Serve in an ice-filled tumbler and garnish with a strip of orange peel.

⇢ INGREDIENTS ⇠

30 ml (1 ounce) Thomson Two Tone Whisky

15 ml (½ ounce) Pedro Ximénez sherry

15 ml (½ ounce) Campari

2 ml (about ½ teaspoon) caramel syrup

Orange peel, for garnish

☞ THOMSON PRESBYTERIAN

Our final Thomson Whisky cocktail is a tall refresher.

⇢ DIRECTIONS ⇠

Build cocktail over ice in a tall highball-type glass and garnish with spent lime wedge and mint sprig.

⇢ INGREDIENTS ⇠

150 ml (5 ounces) soda or sparkling mineral water

45 ml (1½ ounces) Thomson Two Tone Whisky

30 ml (1 ounce) ginger and black pepper syrup

15 ml (½ ounce) fresh lime juice (about ¼ lime; reserve squeezed wedge for garnish)

Mint sprig, for garnish

◄ The Highland Clearances

Want to know who gets the most credit for New Zealand's whisky-making history? Sheep. From the late eighteenth century through the mid-nineteenth century, mass evictions drove many Scottish farmers from their highland homes. Turns out that the wealthy landowners realized they could make a lot more money running sheep across the land—they were far better at scaling hills than, say, cows. The Highland Clearances, as they came to be known, peaked around 1850. With nowhere else to go in Scotland, massive waves of Scots immigrated to the United States, Australia, and, yes, New Zealand. The new arrivals brought their whisky-distilling expertise with them, and the rest is history. (In the States, they're the ones responsible for what came to be known as bourbon.)

AUSTRALIA

Australia has one of the most storied drinking cultures in the world, for better or for worse. It's no accident that Eric Idle and the rest of the Monty Python crew sang their famous "Bruce's Philosophers Song"—an ode to history's great thinkers and drinkers—in stereotypically exaggerated Australian accents. It probably has something to do with Australia's history as a British penal colony. For their hard labor, convicts frequently were paid in rum rations.

However, the country's relationship with alcohol is one of earth's great paradoxes. Believe it or not, Australia has historically been one of the driest places on earth outside of the Middle East.

The temperance movement in Australia mirrored the Prohibition movement of the 1920s in the United States. Although alcohol was never outlawed nationally in Australia, it was prohibited between 1910 and 1928 in the Australian Capital Territory—a region in the southeast that's essentially Australia's Washington,

DC. Referenda for national Prohibition came up every decade or so for the first half of the twentieth century. A couple of those instances resulted in majority votes in favor of alcohol bans, but each occasion fell short of the three-fifths majority required to make the ban a law.

Alcohol has been banned outright at various points in many of Australia's indigenous communities, due to what was perceived as excessive drinking. However, European colonists are largely to blame for any intemperate consumption aboriginal populations were alleged to have engaged in: Prior to the colonists' arrival, traditional indigenous beverages were low-alcohol liquids fermented from various plants. The inebriated aborigine is an unfair and unfortunate stereotype whose perpetuation does little more than stoke racial tensions.

For as long as alcohol has existed on the mainland, however, the epicenter of Australian distilling activities has been Tasmania, an island off the south coast of the continent. Tasmania's geography and climate are particularly conducive to whisky making. Barley fields are abundant, soft (read: distillery-friendly) water is plentiful, and Tasmanian (or "Tassie") peat bogs—the sort that impart that desired smokiness—rival those of Scotland, which has of course been known to dabble a bit in distilling.

In the eighteenth and early nineteenth centuries, whisky producers enjoyed quite the heyday—until 1838, when everything came crashing down. Sir John Franklin, lieutenant governor of Van Diemen's Land—later renamed Tasmania—banned distilling on the island; the ban eventually spread to the whole country. As local whisky lore goes, Franklin decided to wipe out the industry when his wife, Lady Jane Franklin, reportedly said, "I would prefer barley to be fed to pigs than it be used to turn men into swine." (Ouch!)

There was probably more anti-alcohol hysteria than there needed to be at the time. Remember, there were criminals lurking about. When convicts completed their sentences, they usually

9

stuck around and became part of the general population. You can probably surmise that they weren't exactly welcomed with open arms by the stodgy ruling elite, who thought giving ex-cons easy access to booze was a recipe for disaster.

At the time the ban was enacted, there were sixteen legal distilleries (and lots of not-so-legal ones as well) on the relatively sparsely populated island, all of which had to immediately shutter their operations.

And that didn't change for more than a century and a half.

The godfather of Tasmania's modern craft distilling movement is Bill Lark, who, in 1991, marveled at the island's soil, climate, and pristine water and decided it would be the perfect place for a distillery. So, like any good entrepreneur, he applied for a license. Little did he know, however, that the archaic Franklin Law was still on the books. Bill worked with his local representative to petition the federal customs minister about the matter. Eventually, the longstanding legislation was repealed, and Bill and his wife, Lyn, founded Lark Distillery.

Since then, the number of distilleries in Tasmania has grown to exceed the nineteenth-century heyday tally of sixteen. There are in the neighborhood of sixty distilleries across Australia— roughly one for every 383,000 people in the country.

The development of Australian craft distilling got a bit of a head start on the parallel phenomenon in the United States.

While a few small distilleries set up shop in the States in the 1980s and early 1990s, the American craft spirits boom didn't begin in earnest until about 2010. Most distillers had their hearts set on producing whiskey—which has enjoyed a worldwide renaissance in the twenty-first century—but whiskey, of course, takes time. While the spirit is sitting in barrels, waiting years to reach the requisite age to be marketable, distillers have had to turn to unaged spirits like gin, vodka, and rum to make ends meet. But because Tasmanian distillers got a head start in the '90s, many of them already have a rolling stock of whiskies of various ages. So, in that sense, the Australian craft spirits industry has a bit of an edge on its counterpart in the United States.

And the stuff is pretty world-class to boot. Tasmanian single-malt whisky is a bona fide category—and many distilleries have the international awards to prove it. In addition to those from Lark, some standout whiskies have emerged from other distilleries:

* Belgrove
* Heartwood
* Hellyers Road
* McHenry
* Nant
* Old Hobart (makers of Overeem)
* Redlands
* Sullivans Cove
* Trapper's Hut

High(-priced) Spirits

You know how you can tell when a region's whisky-making tradition has truly arrived? When a distillery has the clout to release a bottle that retails for a cool AU$10,000 (about US$7,200). Sullivans Cove, based in the town of Cambridge—a suburb of Tasmania's largest city, Hobart—turned heads back in 2015 when it released Manifesto, a bottling of very rare single malt pulled from the distillery's most prize-winning casks (its French oak single malt was named the planet's best single malt at the 2014 World Whisky Awards). Such a high price tag demands an upscale package; Sullivans Cove commissioned Tassie glass sculptors to design a decanter, complete with a hand-molded bottle stopper crafted from Tasmanian pine and Portuguese cork. Only two bottles were made, and both sold immediately. (I'd personally be afraid to open it.)

An Angel in Reverse

If you've been anywhere near a bottle of whisky, you've probably heard the term "angel's share" kicked around. That's the portion of

11

alcohol that evaporates in the barrel—a hefty percent at that. In Scotland, Kentucky, Tennessee, and most other places known for whisky making, it's an accepted fact of life. There are numerous bars (and even a movie) called Angel's Share to celebrate this phenomenon.

But things are a little different down in Tasmania. The island may share many climatological features with Scotland—not to mention DNA, since a lot of the early settlers of Tasmania were Scottish—but the air is considerably different. When one thinks of Scotland, the term "damp" comes to mind (Scottish comedian Craig Ferguson has said that in his home country, damp is a color); Tasmania is considerably drier. So while the Scots lose alcohol to the angels, the Tassies lose only water. Water evaporates much more quickly in dry temperatures. When it's damp, water doesn't evaporate as easily (as you've probably experienced when you've tried to hang-dry laundry on rainy days). But alcohol doesn't have as much trouble evaporating in damp conditions, especially since its evaporation point is at a significantly lower temperature than water's.

Days get hot in the middle of a Tasmanian summer, but they don't stay that way for too long. At night, there can be a drop of nearly thirty degrees. The massive fluctuations in temperature, pressure, and humidity give Tasmania some of the best conditions in the world in which to age whisky. Such an environment forces the barrels to work really hard, expanding and contracting, thereby giving the spirit an intensity of character in a short period of time that even the Scots (very quietly) envy.

⚔ Tasmanian Distilling's Mad Scientists

As a whisky producer in the far-flung reaches of the world, you can't make a name for yourself simply by copying what the folks in Scotland and Kentucky are doing. Some of Tasmania's greatest spirits' personalities have appeared on the global radar because they're . . . well, personalities. Chief among those is Peter Bignell, founder of Belgrove Distillery in rural Kempton.

{ BELGROVE DISTILLERY'S PETER BIGNELL, AN ICON OF TASMANIAN WHISKY MAKING }

Bignell's entry into the spirits-making realm was a purely logical progression. He's a sixth-generation farmer who had an over-abundance of grains. What else are you going to do with it?

In 2010, he launched Belgrove on the grounds of his farm. Kempton's an idyllic sort of place, with acres and acres of unspoiled land. The sunset over rows of golden grain is like something out of a Terrence Malick film. So why would anyone want to spoil that with industry?

That's essentially Bignell's philosophy. He touts his operation not as carbon neutral, but rather carbon *negative*, as far as fossil fuels are concerned. In other words, he doesn't use any, instead powering Belgrove with used cooking oil. He feeds all the spent grain to sheep, which dutifully convert it to fertilizer, and the cycle continues. "The whole thing's a closed loop," Bignell raves as he gives me the cook's tour. "It's actually been improving the soil. The soils here are a lot better now than when I started."

Even when he constructed his distillery, Bignell expended no carbon. He just converted an old horse stable—it's a farm, after all!

A tinker at heart, Bignell malts his own grain outdoors in a repurposed clothes dryer with a stainless-steel mesh and a sprinkler, which gradually does the job over the course of two and a half days. If he wants a smokier expression, akin to an Islay Scotch whisky, he simply burns some peat underneath the malter.

13

And though Tasmania has much in common with Scotland, Bignell's spirits are a little closer in production technique to the Irish tradition, insofar as he combines malted with unmalted grain.

Another aspect that sets Bignell apart from his Tasmanian distilling peers is that his grain of choice is rye—a true rarity in those parts. His flagship is an unaged white rye, which pays the bills while he waits for the latest batches of his barrel-matured products to come of age. But it's not just grain-based spirits Bignell's making. He'll distill anything that's not nailed down, from apple and pear cider to ginger beer and Sauvignon Blanc.

A stroll through his barrel room—an admittedly brief journey, as Belgrove really puts the "micro" into micro-distillery—reveals the collegiality of the Tasmanian distilling scene. Wooden casks read "Overeem," "Lark," and "Sullivans Cove." It's like a small town where neighbors lend and borrow from each other—but instead of cups of sugar and power drills, it's oak cooperage.

"Enthusiastic" doesn't begin to describe Peter Bignell's demeanor. When he guides guests through his distillery, he is like an effusive seven-year-old showing off all the neat toys he got for Christmas.

Another prominent Tassie who knows his way around a barrel is Tim Duckett, founder of Heartwood Malt Whisky. Unlike Bignell, Duckett doesn't actually distill his own spirits; he's an independent bottler who buys whiskies fresh off the still from the likes of Lark and Sullivans Cove and turns them into something magical—and, frequently, award-winning. At any one time, Heartwood has some forty-five to sixty barrels with whisky maturing in them. Duckett spends much of his time mixing and matching, blending whiskies in ways they've never been commingled before.

"We mature it the way we want to," Duckett proudly declares as we chat over a couple of drams in his Hobart headquarters. "We produce a product that people either love or hate."

This might sound strange, but whisky drinkers can be a passionately polarized bunch. Consider Jim Murray, author of the

annual *Jim Murray's Whisky Bible*. I know as many people who worship at his altar as I do those who'd sooner tar and feather him.
Many might find such an intense emotional disparity off-putting,
but Duckett seems to revel in it, harnessing its energy to release
truly inspired whisky expressions.

One such love-it-or-hate-it offering is Four Corners of Ross,
named for a crossroads in the center of the Tasmanian town of Ross.
Duckett recalls, "I had one guy tell me, 'Four Corners of Ross . . .
best whisky you've ever made!' Another guy said, 'You know Four
Corners of Ross? Sucks!' That's good. As long as we've got people
talking about it. It's better than no one talking about it."

The passions of whisky drinkers may be extreme, but extreme
is exactly what Heartwood's whiskies are. "That's 65.4," Duckett
says, gesturing toward my glass, noting the alcohol by volume
(ABV) of the whisky I'm sipping. In proof terms, that's 130.8. Pretty
potent stuff, in line with the rest of Heartwood's output, give or
take a few percentage points. Everything the company releases
is barrel proof—that is, no water is added before bottling. "Our
point of difference is strength," Duckett proudly reveals.

So, if you ever find yourself drinking a Heartwood whisky,
make sure you're walking, taking public transportation, Uber-ing,
or employing the services of a reliable designated driver. One
glass is likely to push you over the legal limit, which in Australia is
a paltry 0.05 blood alcohol concentration (BAC). It always seems
that the countries with celebrated spirits-making heritages get
penalized. Scotland's BAC was lowered in 2014 to 0.05 as the
rest of the United Kingdom held on to 0.08. Even in the puritan-
ical, post-Prohibitionist land we call the United States, the BAC
threshold remains (in most states) 0.08.

✛ Chapter 2 ✛

SOUTHEAST ASIA

Let's jump north of the equator to the Asian continent proper, many of whose member states managed to retain their indigenous beverages even as explorers and colonial forces integrated their own into those societies. Just as rice is a central component of mealtime across much of Asia, so it is with many of the adult beverages Asians consume. Most countries in this part of the world have some variation of a fermented rice beverage—and many take the fermentation a step further into distillation.

The history of Western imperialism in Asia really began with Europe's desire to establish trade routes to China in the Middle Ages (Marco Polo did his gallivanting in the thirteenth century), and the following centuries were a cocktail of commerce, colonization, and combat, involving imperialist powers that included the likes of the British, French, Spanish, Portuguese, Dutch, and, much later, the Americans.

From the middle of the twentieth century up through the first decade of the twenty-first century, whenever Westerners heard about one or more of the countries in Southeast Asia, it was often in the context of social strife or war. We rarely heard about the people themselves or their fascinating ancient cultures. With many of those conflicts behind them and relations with the Western world normalized, these countries are eager to welcome a new generation of foreign travelers to experience—and taste—those cultures firsthand.

INDONESIA

We'll start our tour of Southeast Asia in the island nation of Indonesia. This may at first seem an odd destination for us on our global drinking adventure—as alcohol isn't exactly embraced in Indonesia these days. Let me explain.

The populous archipelago—more like a mega-archipelago, with some seventeen thousand islands—has been a popular region throughout history, given its strategic location between Asia and Australia. Over the centuries, it has incorporated the cultures and customs of many of the foreign traders who passed through. Perhaps the greatest legacy that outsiders left in the expansive collection of islands was religion. Ultimately, Islam became the dominant religion—nearly 90 percent of Indonesia's 250 million citizens are Muslims—which, naturally, has an impact on Indonesian alcohol consumption, or lack thereof. Alcoholic beverages are legal, but, as in many Muslim countries, there's been a bit of a crackdown as of late. (We'll explore this more when our journey takes us to the Middle East and North Africa.) In 2015, the Indonesian government banned the sale of alcohol in small retail establishments, restricting it to supermarkets, hotels, and restaurants. This sounds reasonable relative to the much stricter restrictions in other nations, but keep in mind that the ban means that strong beverages now cannot be sold in the more than seventy thousand convenience stores, neighborhood markets, and other small establishments.

Then, in 2016, members of two of Indonesia's conservative Islamic parties proposed a complete ban on production, distribution, and consumption across the country. The prospect of such an absolute restriction doesn't sit well with those on the island of Bali, a predominantly Hindu part of Indonesia for which foreign tourism—largely from nearby Australia—is a huge source of income.

It would also spell the end of Bintang, a European-style lager produced by a subsidiary of Heineken, and the biggest beer brand across the archipelago. Additionally, a ban would force a range of traditional indigenous beverages underground—well, in some cases *further* underground. A popular homemade and sometimes commercial concoction, particularly on Bali, is a mild fermented rice beverage known as brem. Unlike the world's best-known alcoholic rice beverage, Japan's sake, brem is brownish. It gets its dark tint by combining white and black glutinous rice. With an ABV of about 5 percent, brem is also far lower in alcohol than the average sake, which is usually around 15 percent.

Palm wine, which we'll dive into later in our journey, is prevalent in many tropical cultures in Asia and Africa. The Indonesian version, tuak, is practically required drinking at festivals among the Batak people of the northern part of the island of Sumatra. Its makers draw the sap from the palms, mix it with the bark of the raru tree, and let it ferment for just a few hours. The resulting beverage is quite sweet. Typically, it's homemade and sold at Sumatran street stalls to be consumed with snacks (anything from local nuts to grilled reptiles).

On the spirits side of things, the go-to among imbibing Indonesians is arrack, which has a name similar to that of a certain Middle Eastern spirit (more on that later), but has little else in common. Batavia arrack, as the Indonesian liquor is known, is sugarcane-based and, therefore, a close relative of rum. (Batavia

19

was the old Dutch name for what is now Jakarta.) There's no anise in it, which distinguishes it from the Middle Eastern arak (the preferred spelling of that particular beverage, though it's also frequently spelled "arack"). There's a bit of a misconception about Batavia arrack; some have erroneously called it a rice-based spirit. The grain is involved, but it is not the spirit's main source of fermentable sugars. Rice plays a role similar to its function in the early stages of sake and shochu production in Japan. A rice mold, not unlike Japanese koji, helps kickstart the fermentation process in Batavia arrack.

Distillation technology came to Indonesia by way of China; the first Batavia arrack distillers in the archipelago were Chinese. Today, commercial Batavia arrack producers continue to use sugarcane as their base, but home producers use whatever is available to them to create a decidedly moonshine-ier version. That could mean that they use rice or perhaps the fruit of the same palms that are used to make tuak; there really are no rules—just as with moonshine.

The alcohols of Indonesia often play central roles in religious celebrations. It's common across many global cultures to offer up a drink to the gods, and it's no different in Bali and other parts of the country. Hopefully, such customs can continue without fear of government reprisals. Only time will tell whether the country's Prohibition wave is a sign of permanent things to come.

SINGAPORE

There's no such trouble finding a drink in Singapore. You might pay a bit more than you're used to, because there are some hefty import duties on spirits, but there are plenty of places to sit down with an adult beverage.

The strategic location of what's now a self-governing island city-state attracted much international attention over the centuries. Its existence was on mariners' (figurative) radars as early as the third century, when it became a hotbed of commercial activity among Chinese, Arab, Indian, and other civilizations in the region. By the early sixteenth century, Europeans had begun to take a keen interest in the port. First it was the Portuguese, and then, in 1819, Sir Thomas Stamford Raffles arrived, ushering in nearly a century and a half of British colonization (save for a three-year period of Japanese occupation during World War II).

Singapore achieved full independence in 1965, and today it's a global commercial and financial hub and one of the wealthiest countries in the world, with a melting pot of cultures. The Chinese represent the largest ethnic group in Singapore—nearly three-quarters of Singaporeans are of Chinese descent—followed (distantly) by the Malay and Indian people. There's a small minority of other ethnicities, mostly from Asia and Europe (a sizable number of Brits still live there). Most of the drinks you'll find on the island borrow from these many cultures.

The cocktail that nearly everyone has heard of is the Singapore Sling, whose origin is tied to the aforementioned Sir Thomas Raffles—or, more precisely, to the hotel that bears his name. The Raffles Hotel, with its striking colonial-era architecture, carved out its place in cocktail history when, around 1915, bartender Ngiam Tong Boon created a concoction of gin combined with Bénédictine, bitters, grenadine, lime juice, triple sec, pineapple juice, and sometimes additional alcohols like cherry brandy.

Many perceive having a Singapore Sling at the Raffles Hotel (which still exists, its nineteenth-century colonial façade in stark contrast to the ultramodern skyscrapers in the city center) as the "thing to do" when visiting Singapore. It is—but only if your bucket list is simply a succession of the most touristy activities imaginable on planet Earth. My advice: Don't. You likely won't find a single local drinking one. It's a fine drink, but you're better off having it at your favorite tiki bar than in the country after which it is named.

Most often, you're going to find Singaporeans drinking the beverages you're most familiar with: beer, wine, spirits, and cocktails. Tiger Beer, first launched in 1932 and now a product of Heineken Asia Pacific, is the most pervasive brew across the island. Heineken also owns the Archipelago Brewery, which opened a year after Tiger produced its first batch. And although you'll find a host of upstart craft breweries in Singapore, I wouldn't exactly call it a beer town.

In my experience in Singapore, I've found that the food elevates whatever it is you choose to drink. A plate of Hainanese chicken rice or the über-spicy chili crab at one of Singapore's ubiquitous hawker centers—think food court with street-style stalls—will make a bottle of Tiger taste like fine champagne. I'm an even bigger fan of the alcohol-free options in Singapore, particularly the freshly pressed watermelon juice, lime juice (more of a limeade), and sugarcane juice.

The Marina Bay Sands, a triple-towered upscale hotel with what looks like a colossal surfboard resting atop its three identical buildings, has a trendy bar on its top floor, with the best view on the island after dark. But you're going to pay for the privilege of sipping against that backdrop; expect a gin and tonic, with a not-so-fancy base spirit, to liberate the equivalent of US$20 to $25 from your wallet. Consider it an admission fee for the stunning vistas and the people watching, which is a theatrical experience in itself.

THE PHILIPPINES

Any time a country emerges from a clash of cultures over the centuries, you can bet that country's fine beverage traditions will draw from an eclectic array of influences. Portuguese explorer Ferdinand Magellan in 1521 claimed the Philippines on behalf of the Spanish Empire—it was named for Spain's King Philip II—and a little more than thirty years later, the first waves of Spanish settlers arrived. Spain controlled the archipelago for more than three centuries before the United States took over after defeating the Iberian conquerors in the Spanish-American War in 1898.

Filipinos weren't exactly happy with that arrangement and fought the three-year Philippine-American War, which ended in another US victory. Next, World War II brought Japanese occupation. Finally, following this war, the Philippines gained recognition as an independent sovereign nation.

Not surprisingly, Western influences have played a substantial role in Filipino drinking habits. As is the case in much of the world, beer is a big deal among local drinkers. San Miguel is the dominant brand produced in the Philippines, and it's also a popular export product—it's got a huge presence in Hong Kong, for instance. Spanish brewer Mahou acquired the brand in 2000 to form Mahou San Miguel, enabling San Miguel to widen its footprint around the world. (Mahou San Miguel is now even playing in the US craft beer market. In 2014, it bought a 30 percent stake in Founders Brewing Company, based in Grand Rapids, Michigan.)

23

But it's in the gin category that Filipinos have really made their mark. The Philippines is the largest consumer of the botanical spirit in the world; according to International Wine & Spirit Research (IWSR), the country consumes nearly half of the world's total gin volume—nearly twice that of the Netherlands (gin's birthplace) and more than four times as much as the United Kingdom (which adopted and popularized the spirit on the world stage). Additionally, Filipinos consume 50 percent more gin than Americans do.

Ginebra San Miguel (a subsidiary of San Miguel Corporation, the owner of the beer of the same name) is the brand responsible for most of the gin produced in the Philippines—and thus the world. The brand has roots dating back to 1834, when Destileria y Licoreria de Ayala y Compañia became the first commercial distillery in the Philippines. There have been the usual mergers and acquisitions over the course of two centuries, but Ginebra

San Miguel has more or less stayed the same. Its juniper-forward spirit is based on the Dutch tradition and made from a sugarcane base—no surprise there, as this is the tropics of Southeast Asia we're talking about.

Ginebra San Miguel is fairly inexpensive; those with a little extra to spend can splurge on the premium version. And those who don't want to spend much at all can always opt for the locally produced "bathtub gin," but it's rarely advisable in a country where it's easy to access reputable products at reasonable prices.

Beyond gin, if you are seeking a bit of indigenous flavor in the Philippines, you have several ways to experience the complex tropical terroir:

Tuba: Sometimes referred to as coconut wine, tuba is produced from the sap of the coconut flower rather than the milk of the coconut itself. In another Southeast Asian country, Myanmar (formerly Burma), a similar tipple goes by the name of htan yay. In both instances, the producer collects the sap with a tapper that extracts about a gallon a day from a single tree. Both tuba and htan yay tend to be classified under the broader heading of "palm wine," also sometimes known as toddy.

Lambanog: Lambanog is to tuba what brandy is to wine. That is, it's a distilled version of tuba—if you're looking for a bit of a kick with your indigenous drinking experience.

Tapuy: The local rice wine, tapuy, never had much of a presence as a mass-distributed product, mostly because its flavor wasn't stable. Then the Philippine Rice Research Institute stepped in and invested time and money in studying the dynamics of the beverage. The result was a clear product, simply called PhilRice Tapuy, that comes in an attractive, premium-skewing bottle.

Game On!

Ginebra San Miguel is so ingrained in Filipino culture that it's also the name of a basketball team. Barangay Ginebra San Miguel is one of the most popular teams in the Philippine Basketball Association. The owners didn't choose the team's name just because they like to drink gin; the team is actually owned by Ginebra San Miguel Inc.

Grounded

With such an active drinking culture, it's only natural that the Philippines has a few customs associated with imbibing—and you'd be wise not to deviate from them. The traditional way to kick off a drink-related gathering is to pour a shot on the ground. The ritual is known as "alay sa demonyo," or an offering to the spirits—a custom that occurs in many cultures throughout the world.

LAOS

Most who have visited Laos, or any Southeast Asian country for that matter, have encountered the Beerlao line from the major national producer, Lao Brewery Company. It may not be a world-class lager, but it's all about the context. It hits the spot alongside traditional Laotian fare, typically involving a healthy helping of sticky rice eaten with one's fingers.

Being a mass-produced adjunct lager (in this case, the adjunct is the rice) that uses some foreign-grown ingredients (the hops and yeast are imported from Germany), it's hard to make a case for it being a "traditional" or "indigenous" beverage in Laos, despite the fact that most adults you encounter will likely be drinking it.

A slightly more homegrown representation of Laotian drinking culture can be found in the form of a beverage called lao-Lao. It may look redundant written out, but speakers articulate each syllable with a slightly different intonation, giving them two completely different meanings. The first, pronounced with a sort of downward tone, means alcohol, while the second, annunciated in a type of up-talk, signifies that it is Laotian (hence the second word's capitalization). Lao-Lao is a type of moonshine, but it's derived from rice rather than the corn that's the usual base of American moonshine. Corn's not nearly as easy to come by in that part of the world as it is in the United States; rice, of course, is the staple food of Asia and likely to be found not just at every meal, but in most traditional drinks as well.

Distilleries are frequently dilapidated shacks in small Laotian villages, where visitors and locals can drink right from the source. Typically, a heaping portion of rice is boiled and then allowed to cool and ferment for nearly a week. The lao-Lao maker then boils the fermented mash in a copper kettle, condenses the steam, and recaptures the concentrated alcohol in liquid form. Lao-Lao is also shipped off to cities, where it's a staple of bars in more populous areas.

THAILAND

Thailand's most famous spirit is Mekhong "whisky." Those quotation marks are deliberate, as Mekhong would more accurately be categorized as a rum than a whisky. (We'll revisit this phenomenon later in our journey, when we look at the "whiskies" of India.) Most of Mekhong's fermentable base is molasses and/or pure sugarcane. A minuscule amount—roughly 5 percent—is rice; technically, the rice would make it whisky, but the grain's presence is negligible. Then again, who really cares? The spirit is a source of immense Thai pride and has taken on a life of its own that defies categorization.

Mekhong first came on the scene in 1941, just as most of Asia was embroiled in global warfare. The name, of course, comes from Southeast Asia's most famous river. The spirit's distinctive flavor

MEKHONG COCKTAILS

The team at Mekhong recommends these simple classic cocktails to experience the full flavor of the spirit.

☞ MEKHONG CLASSIC

So quick to mix and so refreshing!

➤ DIRECTIONS ⟵	➤ INGREDIENTS ⟵
Fill a rocks glass with ice.	1 part Mekhong
Pour Mekhong and soda water over ice.	3 parts soda water
Stir well, then squeeze and drop in lime slice.	Lime slice, for garnish

☞ THAI SABAI

Many consider the Thai Sabai to be the signature drink of Thailand. It's a real crowd pleaser—almost like the Thai version of a mojito.

➤ DIRECTIONS ⟵	➤ INGREDIENTS ⟵
Muddle basil leaves in a shaker.	4 or 5 Thai sweet basil leaves
Add ice cubes and Mekhong, lime juice, and simple syrup and shake.	45 ml (1½ ounces) Mekhong
	25 ml (¾ ounce) fresh lime juice
Double strain into a glass over ice.	30 ml (1 ounce) simple syrup
Top with a splash of soda water.	Soda water

derives not from the base itself but from the combination of local herbs and spices (the exact combo, as you'd expect, is a secret). Notes of ginger, toffee, citrus, and vanilla are most apparent on the palate. Mekhong's 35 percent alcohol content is a bit lower than is common among most whiskies—and rums, for that matter—but it doesn't make it any smoother to drink. Often, drinkers will mix it with plain soda or with soda, lemon juice, and Thai basil in a cocktail called the Thai Sabai.

The brand also revived an old tradition it calls Siam Legacy: Chill five shot glasses of Mekhong until frosted and pair them with typical Thai snacks. Snack types vary, but they usually include one sour, one salty, and one spicy item.

The country's other prominent spirit, SangSom (which means "moonlight"), arrived thirty-six years after Mekhong and quickly became the best-selling spirit brand in all Thailand, commanding about 70 percent of the market. The main difference between SangSom and Mekhong—which now share a parent company, ThaiBev—is that SangSom is fine calling itself a rum, as its base is all molasses, not a molasses-rice blend. SangSom is also slightly higher in alcohol, with a 40 percent ABV that is more in line with conventional spirits. Beyond those relatively minor details, Sang-Som and Mekhong have more in common than they don't—particularly in that they both use a blend of indigenous herbs and spices to achieve their signature flavors. And they're both a bit on the sweet side.

ThaiBev also markets the molasses-rice spirit blends Hong Thong and Mangkorn Thong, both with a 35 percent ABV.

That's not to say that Thai producers aren't making proper whisky—or semi-proper whisky, anyway. Red Bull Distillery (also part of ThaiBev) offers Blend 185 and Blend 285, which combine oak barrel–aged malt whisky with some neutral spirit—you can think of them as whisky-vodka hybrids.

Any of those products can be used interchangeably as the core ingredient of a communal oddity known as the Thai bucket (or "whisky bucket"), a big attraction in nightclubs in Thailand and other Southeast Asian countries. Recipes vary, but basically you take a bottle of Mekhong, SangSom, Hong Thong, or whatever else is available, pour it into a bucket, add ice, and then pour in either four cans of Coke or two cans of Coke and two of Red Bull (or any combination thereof—there's no hard-and-fast recipe). Insert multiple straws and enjoy with friends. It's not as crazy as it sounds, when you think about it. If you've ever been to a tiki bar, there's likely some version of a shareable bowl on the menu—and few ever bat an eye at that.

VIETNAM

I don't think I've ever had a drink in a more exciting place than Ho Chi Minh City (previously known as Saigon). That doesn't necessarily mean it was the tastiest, or even the most strikingly noteworthy—far from it. But I could have been sipping a glass of tap water with a squirt of lemon in it (though I'd advise against the tap water, by the way) and it probably would have been one of the top drink experiences of my life. Here's where that context thing comes in—though in Vietnam, it's like context on steroids. A recurring theme of this book is the "how" versus the "what" to drink. The dynamic varies from country to country, from continent to continent, and it's frequently lopsided in favor of one over the other. The "how" is the hands-down, runaway favorite in Vietnam.

When the sun goes down on Saigon (which I prefer to call it—I'm old school that way), a wild sort of electricity animates the city. Swarms of motor scooters buzz down the streets, their clustered headlights dotting the roadways like some sort of high-density meteor shower. Those putt-putting little wannabe motorcycles provide both the visual effects and the soundtrack for a typical evening of dining out in the southern Vietnamese city. The influx of foreign investment since the country's normalization

29

of relations with the West in the mid-1990s means there's no shortage of upscale eateries in Saigon and the country's other metropolises. And if that's your jam, go for it—though my pants would be burned to ashes if I were to tell you that's the best way to experience the city, and the country. Instead, find a street stand, pull up a small plastic dollar store–style chair, and have yourself a piping-hot bowl of pho, the world-famous Vietnamese beef noodle soup. And whatever that stand is selling in bottles, drink it. I guarantee that it'll seem like the best thing you've ever tasted, as cheap and watery as it may be.

I alluded to a similar experience in the epilogue of *The Year of Drinking Adventurously*, but even when I wrote it, I was too chronologically close to the moment to have fully grasped its significance. At the time, I was still in my "beer first" phase, other beverages be damned. I spent so much time seeking out the handful of craft breweries and brewpubs that were starting to pop up in Vietnam that I almost missed the forest for the trees. I was keen to regale the world with tales of the dunkel-style lager that I drank at the Saigon brewery Big Man Beer (and how horrified I was that Vietnamese millennials were dropping ice cubes in it, despite the fact that its temperature had been perfectly regulated), or the Czech-style pilsner I ordered at the local brewpub Gammer. I was too caught up in my own imbiber's biases to admit to myself that those were far from authentic Vietnamese experiences. I was cloistered in artificial environments that felt more like Central Europe than Southeast Asia, sequestered from the vibrant thoroughfares where the real action was taking place.

Sure, the regional mass-market lagers often sold at street stands, like Bia Saigon and 333, are based on a European brewing tradition, but they are far less removed from what is quintessentially Vietnamese than the new craft brewing upstarts. And nothing is more refreshing with that sweat-inducing bowl of pho than a no-nonsense macro-brew. Beer's also one of the few alcoholic drinks you're likely to find the Vietnamese consuming while they eat. In Vietnam, unlike other Asian countries like China or Japan, drinking usually isn't about pairing with food. It's its own event.

As dominant as beer is in the regular drinking repertoires of the Vietnamese populations, there are more indigenous experiences to be had. Like other countries on the continent, Vietnam boasts its own version of rice wine—though there are a few different types and not all of them are actually wine.

The first is ruou can, which is the most innocuous of the lot. It's the favorite drink in some rural areas for weddings and other big celebrations like Tet (the lunar New Year). The makers pour dark sticky brown or black rice into a ceramic vessel with local herbs, tree bark, and whatever else is not nailed down. It ferments in that jar for about two weeks. On the day of the celebration, they add liquid—coconut water or even beer—to the fermented mixture, let it steep for a couple of hours, and then serve it to eager partygoers. Guests drink the sweet, spicy, herbal, floral concoction through long bamboo straws. Everyone's got their own secret ruou can recipe, so it's rare that any two ever taste the same.

Now, here's where things start to get stronger—and, to be honest, a bit dicier. Ruou goa (or ruou de in the southern part of the country) is actually distilled rice wine—a very harsh spirit very often made in the home and, therefore, not always the safest thing to drink. All the usual risks associated with moonshine apply (methanol poisoning, blindness, you name it), especially if you don't know the maker personally.

There are some commercial varieties, which, as you'd expect, are much safer to drink (in moderation, of course), and there are a few being exported to the U.S., most notably the brand Sontinh.

And don't get me started on ruou thuoc, aka "medicine wine." File this one under "old wives' tale booze," as there are numerous recipes of ruou thuoc designed to remedy whatever malady may afflict a drinker. The more "conventional" ones—if we can call

31

them that—infuse the distillate (again, not really a wine) with herbal ingredients believed to provide some medicinal benefits (or at least the perception of medicinal benefits, which, in a placebo kind of way, is enough for a lot of people). A little indigenous nonpoisonous flora never really bothered anyone.

But spirits makers aren't content to use only flora. Fauna has a tendency to show up in these strong liquids as well. Snakes, lizards, and even bear parts have found their way into ruou thouc recipes. (And, as usual, the presence of such macabre oddities has something vaguely to do with male, um, performance.) I was in a village near the Mekhong delta when vendors tried to sell me a bottle with a cobra carcass in it. A striking visual, to be sure, but I suspected the seller was just trying to mystify us gullible Western tourists. (I did eventually drink a Japanese liquor with a pit viper floating in it when I was in Tokyo, but more on that later.)

Speaking of tourist attractants, you can't walk ten feet through Ho Chi Minh City's Tan Son Nhat International Airport without stumbling upon a coconut shell bottle filled with a wine fermented from said tropical fruit. Rice is the preferred fermentable throughout most of Vietnam, but in Ben Tre in the Mekhong delta region, it's all about coconuts. (The moment you step on a boat there, your guide hands you a whole coconut with a straw in it for you to sip the unfermented, nonalcoholic coconut water.) Gradually, consumption moved out of the region as producers commercialized production and sales (tourists are big business, after all). What's in the lacquered coconut shell bottle is likely to be around 29 percent ABV—remarkably high as far as "wines" are concerned. It'll also be fairly sweet, in an otherworldly kind of way. Here's a pro tip if you want to bring this beverage home for personal consumption or as a souvenir for a friend or family member: Plan to actually drink it. A cork closure seals the package, but it's far from airtight. If you let it sit on the shelf for, say, a year, it will likely evaporate completely, leaving not so much as a faint scent behind.

⋈ Di Nhau

One phrase a person is likely to hear on the streets of Saigon, Hanoi, or any other city in Vietnam is "di nhau." And when it's uttered, eyes light up, as it loosely translates to "going drinking" or "having a drinking session." Most of the time the voices will be male, as men still do most of the drinking in the country. Things are evolving, however, as it becomes more socially acceptable in the new Vietnam for women to drink.

CAMBODIA

"Tragic" would be a massive understatement when describing Cambodia's all-too-recent history involving the genocidal Khmer Rouge (Khmer being the dominant ethnic group in Cambodia; Rouge referring to the French-educated "red" Communists). And as great a movie as *The Killing Fields* is, it provides but a tiny snapshot of the horrors for which the Khmer Rouge was responsible in the mid- to late 1970s. In its grossly misguided and sinister attempt to create a Communist agrarian utopia, the regime slaughtered some two million Cambodians whom they deemed inconsistent with such a society (intellectuals, academics, medical professionals—you name it), while those who lived were forced to farm the land. Thankfully, the Khmer Rouge collapsed, but it took decades for the country's people to recover and emerge from the darkness. Outsiders have just begun to experience a culture that has managed to endure in the face of unspeakable atrocities.

As for drinking in the country, it's most definitely not for the faint of heart. For one thing, Cambodian imbibing habits are among the most robust in all of Southeast Asia. Part of the reason is that booze is incredibly cheap there. That, and the fact that longtime Cambodian prime minister Hun Sen has openly encouraged the populace to drink more beer because the tax revenue it

33

generates ultimately pays the salaries of teachers, doctors, and civil servants. (But, please, drink responsibly!)

The beer most Khmers and international travelers are drinking is the big national brand, Angkor, named for the famous Angkor temples near Siem Reap. And when they're not drinking beer . . . well, let's just say things get a little interesting—and muscular. Two beverages in particular, Special Muscle Wine and Golden Muscle Liquor, are both popular among Cambodian men. Special Muscle Wine has an acidic, saline flavor reminiscent of soy sauce and an alcohol content of about 35 percent. Golden Muscle Liquor is the stronger of the two, with an ABV of around 40 percent. Their real strength, however, is not in the volume of alcohol concentrated in every bottle, but in their shared signature ingredient: deer antler.

As outlandish as that may seem, if you're a high-impact sports nut (participant or spectator), you're probably already quite familiar with the substance as a performance enhancer, sometimes called deer-antler velvet. Users believe that the fuzzy outer layers of the beasts' bony branches help repair damaged cartilage and tendons more quickly than they'd heal on their own. The stuff is also supposed to enhance strength and endurance. It's one of those "makes you strong" propositions that's often code for "increases virility and boosts sexual performance," which is why Cambodian menfolk embrace Special Muscle Wine and Golden Muscle Liquor. The labels are unabashedly masculine, each bearing an image of an extremely buff bodybuilder.

Chapter 3

EAST ASIA

We're now going to backtrack ever so slightly as we head into the more economically developed nations of the Asian continent. For the sake of organization, I've defined East Asia as the area stretching from Japan through North and South Korea and China to Mongolia, though I'm sure plenty would dispute that definition—China extends well into what would be considered Central Asia and, in some cases, Southeast Asia, while the drinking customs of Mongolia, despite its easterly location, have much in common with those of Central Asia. But it makes for an easy way to divide up this enormous continent.

JAPAN

We begin with the least continental member of the region, geographically speaking. Drinking in Japan, especially in major cities like Tokyo and Osaka, is practically a contact sport—and I mean that in the best possible way. Entire traditions and industries have emerged because every hardworking salaryman and -woman is likely to miss the last train out of the city center at some point in their lives. You know those Space-Age capsule "hotels" that are like morgues with windows? They mainly exist because folks need a place to crash after a night of imbibing and before getting up a few hours later to get to work on time. Late-night karaoke? There are worse things to do than sing the night away if you failed to make it to the station in time for that 12:57 A.M. train (the next one's not until 5). If neither of those is an option, the last resort is finding a cozy spot in the station to slumber for a couple of hours. The image that forever will be etched into my brain is that of a thirtyish man passed out on his back on the Shinagawa Station floor about two feet from his smartphone (given how safe Tokyo generally is, I'd bet that the phone was still there when he woke up).

Walk into any convenience store (7-Eleven is ubiquitous throughout major Japanese cities, as is the competing chain, Lawson), and one of the first things you'll spy across from the register is a large rack with tiny bottles of tonics claiming to do everything from preventing hangovers to shielding your liver from the ravages of alcohol.

Despite such a visibly chaotic backdrop, there's a great deal of order embedded in Japanese drinking habits. Japan is known for producing fine spirits—its whisky is some of the best in the world, and shochu is gaining in popularity outside its home country—but these liquors are rarely the way locals begin the evening. The first sip of the night is usually of the malt and hops variety. Yes, it turns out that the imbibing mantra we all adopted in college—"Beer before liquor, never sicker; liquor before beer, never fear"—is total nonsense. The common expression for the sudsy start to the evening is "toriaizu nama" or "a draft beer in the mean time."

One of the first times I was out drinking with a group of locals in Kumamoto, there was much giggling and whispering when I attempted to order a shochu on the rocks to begin the evening. The Japanese way makes sense, I suppose. It's a gradual ramp-up in strength throughout the drinking session, culminating in some rather questionable choices before the night is through. (More on one of my own ill-advised decisions in a bit.)

And, I must admit, you can rarely go wrong drinking Japanese beer. Much as in the States, a craft brewing revolution has swept the country, and some of the best beer in the world is coming from the artisanal breweries of Japan. (The Japanese have a knack for improving on—perfecting, even—the beverage traditions of other nations. Try a Japanese whisky or soda pop in a Tokyo coffee shop and you'll see what I mean.) Every major city has its share of breweries and beer bars that more than hold their own among the beer-geekiest establishments in the world. And you don't need to travel through the entire country to try most of the artisanal products. I've spent more than a few hours on a barstool at Tokyo's Popeye—the country's most famous beer bar—and I can more than vouch for the fact that the Japanese have nailed this whole craft thing. One of my favorite producers is Yo-Ho, based in the city of Saku in Nagano Prefecture. Yo-Ho has made a name for itself with brews like Yona Yona, an American-style pale ale, and Tokyo Black, a porter. I'm also partial to the brewer Coedo, which has mastered a range of global styles, as well as one that's unmistakably Japanese: Beniaka, a sweet potato–based beer. Sweet potatoes are hugely popular in Japan (they were brought to the country in the sixteenth century by Portuguese explorers), although they're a bit different from the ones we're used to. The flesh of the Japanese varieties—grown in great abundance in Kagoshima Prefecture on the southern island of Kyushu—tends to be a very pale yellow, versus the deep orange ones we're accustomed to. There are purple varieties as well.

One last brewer shout-out: Osaka-based Minoh. Osaka is like the Chicago of Japan—it's surely no coincidence the two are sister cities—and is home to a couple of bars that go by the name of Beer Belly. These are essentially the downtown tasting rooms for the Minoh brand. Minoh produces an interpretation of just about every major international style.

Even if a so-called craft brew isn't available at a barstool near you, the country's macro-breweries are cranking out some pretty impressive beer these days. Suntory—better known for its fine whiskies, particularly the Yamazaki line—produces the ubiquitous Premium Malt's (the apostrophe always confounds me). This pilsner-style lager is as good as anything you'll find in Germany or the Czech Republic—and light-years ahead of what American macros produce for mass consumption. There are evenings I've skipped the spirits entirely and stuck to Premium Malt's. It's just that satisfying, and it pairs beautifully with virtually any dish, be it an izakaya-style small plate (say, Kurobuta pork belly), ramen, or sushi.

About those izakayas: Izakaya loosely translates to "place for drinking" (or, more directly, "stay sake shop"), but they're also places for eating. In Japan, people eat when they drink. Not to say Americans don't as well, but you're far less likely to find a watering hole anywhere in Japan that doesn't offer at least some rudimentary culinary attractions (even a couple of cherry tomatoes on a toothpick with a slice of cheese melted on top—that counts!). In the United States, you can't find anything to eat in pretty much every other bar on a given block.

Izakaya fare tends to be the Japanese version of what we'd call tapas—small, shareable plates of edible curiosities. It could be simple, like yakitori (grilled chicken skewers), or something that's a little less familiar to Western palates, like ei hire (stingray fin "jerky" served with Japanese mayonnaise). In a lot of ways, it's the Eastern equivalent of a gastropub, except you won't get the bum's rush after an hour. There's no pressure to turn tables as there is in the States. Japanese servers, like those in just about every country that's not America, get paid a living wage and don't work for tips. In fact, tipping is frowned upon in their country—I've even heard stories of a waitperson chasing a customer down an alley to give the money back. So hang out, nibble, and nurse a beverage or two all night. You can be there for a half hour or for four hours; no one will hover over you, passive-aggressively asking if you'd like anything else or dropping your bill and saying, "I'll take this whenever you're ready" (which, as we all know, means "Please pay me right now and leave").

Generally, the Japanese like to sit down while they imbibe, though there are exceptions. Tachinomi, or "standing bars," have become quite popular for a quick sip before dashing off. They're not unlike the bars you'll find in certain parts of Europe: In Italy you'll frequently pay a premium to sit at a table. If you want to stand at the bar, you just have to pay for the drink. But the Japanese equivalents usually consist entirely of standing spaces at counters and highboy tables. They used to be one-and-done, on-the-way-home-after-work kind of places, but they've recently been integrated into lengthier nights out, and often bookend a night's revelry.

The preference for sitting down to drink often throws Americans for a loop when they visit authentic izakaya-style bars in the States, let alone in Japanese cities. There's a certain demographic of Americans who are quite content to break every fire code imaginable to cram into overcrowded meat markets. At an izakaya, if there's not a free table, you simply won't get in.

Perhaps you'd prefer to drink beer all night; go right ahead! But if you've had your first beer and are ready to move on to something else, the options are vast and varied. I encourage you to give shochu a try, but keep in mind that you will need numerous

39

THE KAGOSHIMA
PREFECTURE IS FAMOUS FOR
ITS IMO (SWEET POTATO)
SHOCHU. BEFORE THE CROP
BECOMES A SPIRIT, THERE'S
A GREAT DEAL OF SLICING
INVOLVED.

evening drinking sessions to get acquainted with the spirit—and even then, you'll have barely scratched the surface. For one thing, there are some fifty-odd bases from which shochu may be distilled, and each imparts a unique flavor. Still, some base ingredients are more prominent than others, and you can get the best education by first trying one made from sweet potatoes (imo)— the most popular style—and then sampling a barley-based (mugi) variety, a rice (kome) selection, a buckwheat (soba), and a black sugar (kokuto). Once you're familiar enough with the nuances of those, you'll have enough of a frame of reference to experiment with some of the more outlandish offerings—carrot, shiso leaf, and even milk!

One of my most memorable experiences was joining a group of aficionados in a semiprivate upstairs room of the Tokyo bar Shochu Zanmai for a full-on shochu party. A good thirty or forty bottles covered the table, representing all the major styles, as well as a fair number of the less traditional creations.

Just when I think I've gotten a good handle on the popular ways to consume the drink, there's always some bar that manages to throw me a curve ball and, like Ygritte to Jon Snow in *Game of Thrones*, remind me that I know nothing. I've been fortunate to have two able-bodied sherpas on my shochu expeditions: Stephen Lyman, an American who's a self-described shochu otaku (loose translation: "geek") and very likely the foremost expert on the spirit in the Western Hemisphere, and Noriyuki Yamashita, a Japanese force of nature with a seemingly limitless energy reserve and an affinity for American slang terms ("dawg" and "maaaaaaan" are two of his favorite terms of endearment). Nori now runs his own shochu hot spot in Kumamoto City, Glocal Bar Imo Vibes.

Once, when I was out with both of them (as well as a cadre of other writers from New York, London, and Singapore) in Kagoshima, one of the many stops on our shochu crawl was a place called Gonbei. Nori and Stephen told us that we had to try one of the house specialties: shochu mixed with hot water with a dried, grilled flying fish steeped in it. The heated shochu softens the fish just enough to be eaten whole, bones, tail, and all. It was worth trying once (although you could twist my arm to try it again to initiate any unsuspecting traveling companions) and a truly eye-opening experience. It made me realize that there really are no bounds to Japanese drinking rituals. And that's a good thing: You wouldn't be reading about it now if it didn't leave a lasting impression.

{ YES, THAT'S A FISH IN THAT GLASS OF SHOCHU. }

41

Many Westerners' Japanese experience is limited to Tokyo, which is fine from a shochu standpoint. Those looking for a bit of a shochu adventure need search no farther than the Shibu-ya neighborhood, where Bar Gen offers one of the most extensive selections of the spirit in the world. Last time I was there, its list was approaching six thousand.

Despite the fact that shochu is Japan's unique offering to the spirits world, it's not as ubiquitous throughout the country as one might think, once you get off the southern main island of Kyushu, where about 90 percent of it is produced. It's easy enough to find at least one shochu selection in every second or third bar in Tokyo, but even more accessible is the distillate with which the whole world is familiar: whisky. Japanese whiskies have garnered quite a bit of attention in recent years and received plenty of accolades, like being named World Whisky of the Year in *Jim Murray's Whisky Bible*—the most recent honoree being Yamazaki Sherry

Wood 2013, from Beam Suntory, the entity formed in 2014 when Japan's Suntory Holdings acquired U.S.-based spirits maker Beam (owner of its namesake Jim Beam, as well as Maker's Mark and many brands).

Naturally, it's the finer whiskies that attract most of the world's attention, but those aren't necessarily the ones the average evening reveler is drinking. Like most multinational spirits marketers, Beam Suntory has virtually every whisky price tier covered. You can walk into a bar in any major city around the globe and pay US$150 for a glass of Yamazaki Sherry Wood 2013 (post–*Whisky Bible* price gouging didn't help). But that's the super-high-end stuff. In most bars in every sizable Japanese metro area, you're more likely to find the people's spirit: Suntory Kakubin, a low-cost blended whisky designed for no-nonsense drinking sessions. Kakubin means "square bottle," and that's exactly how it is packaged—the label does not even feature the word "Kakubin." It's a perfectly serviceable whisky to drink on the rocks or even neat, but a more popular method of consumption is as a highball—an English word that most Japanese know, even those with zero English fluency. It doesn't technically qualify as a cocktail, but it's almost criminal in its simplicity: Pour one part Kakubin and two parts sparkling over ice. Drink.

Suntory made it even simpler for entry-level drinkers in 2009, when it launched a canned version of the highball. It was a pretty smart move: On the shelf it looks like a beer, the beverage of choice for many in their early twenties (the legal drinking age in Japan is twenty). The ready-to-drink highball is a good introduction to whisky for those beer partisans.

I'll admit, I was resistant to the idea of the highball, as I usually don't like to dilute my whisky much—at most, I'll put it on the rocks or drink it in a very whisky-forward cocktail like an Old Fashioned. But I discovered that a properly prepared highball is surprisingly flavorful and refreshing, and I now drink highballs interchangeably with gin and tonics—as long as the right Japanese whisky is available. I'm not a fan of highballs made with Scotch or bourbon.

Naturally, not everyone's going to want to have a spirit at all, in any form, but they might still want something a bit stronger than beer. That's really the sweet spot for sake, one of the most tragically misunderstood beverages in Japan—and, quite possibly, the world. It's a brewed beverage, like beer, but uses rice rather than malted barley, and it's usually clear (only the unfiltered nigori type is cloudy). Sake's alcohol content is somewhere in the neighborhood of that of a dry or fortified wine—usually around 15 percent, though sometimes as high as 19 percent.

Though sake is widely available throughout Japan, its consumption is a mere fraction of what it used to be. Younger consumers have migrated to beer and wine and, in many cases, to whisky and shochu. Back in 2015, on a bar crawl in Kumamoto City, my wife and I ordered a carafe of sake. One of our millennial pals told us that she doesn't like to drink the fermented rice beverage because it's "too strong." She ordered shochu instead.

43

That's not necessarily a universal misconception among the younger generations, but it's far from uncommon. Sake has become such a small player in their drinking habits that they don't realize it's considerably lower in alcohol than its distilled counterpart, shochu. Brewers have started deploying twenty- and thirty-something brand ambassadors to help woo the younger legal drinkers.

{
SAKE
(NIHONSHU)
KEGS IN KOBE,
JAPAN
}

Sake is still a much-revered product in the country, and a huge part of Japan's heritage; it's just serving a smaller consumer base at home. The Japanese government has been looking to sake brewers to aid the country in its efforts to reverse years of economic stagnation. The government has provided, for instance, funding for tasting stations in international airports, in an effort to help give the rest of the world a taste for the product—and, it is hoped, boost exports.

If you find yourself in Japan, make sure that at least one of the drinks you consume in an evening's session is sake. You'll be doing the economy a huge favor. But keep in mind that "sake" is a generic term for Japanese alcohol. If you're in the epicenter of shochu country and you order sake, there's a good chance you'll get shochu—especially in Kagoshima, where sake production is virtually nonexistent. If you really want to score points, order nihonshu instead. Shu means "alcohol" and nihon means "Japanese"; "Japanese alcohol" has come to mean sake as Westerners know it.

⋇ Habushu

I'm convinced that half of Japanese booze culture is based on a dare—a desire to be entertained by the lengths drinking companions will go to get street cred. Case in point: habushu, which is essentially Okinawan awamori with some added herbal ingredients. Oh yeah, and a pit viper.

Awamori, Okinawa's proprietary spirit, is similar to shochu; it's made from Thai indica rice and is much revered among Japanese spirits connoisseurs. In the case of habushu, the botanical additives are there to make the snake's venom palatable. Often, the snake carcass is still floating in the bottle—either it enters the bottle live and drowns in the alcohol, or it's killed first and then added. (All horribly inhumane, I know.)

I'd heard vague stories about it but always assumed it was kind of an urban legend—or, at least, something that's available only in illicit *Fight Club*–esque venues. But I came across it, easily enough, in a tiny six-seat bar in Tokyo's Nonbei Yokocho ("Drunkard's Alley"), known for its pocket-size watering holes, able to accommodate only the smallest of groups.

Against my better judgment, I tried the stuff. There's definitely a pronounced floral, perfume-y quality that does its best to mask the pungent flavor of the snake and its venom. Other than bestowing major bragging rights on the daring imbiber, there's not much else that's noteworthy about it. It's a bucket-list sort of thing, but I recommend leaving it at that.

⚘ Japanese Rice Whisky

Japanese whisky is a direct descendant of the Scotch malted barley–based tradition. Much of the rest of Japan's alcohol heritage makes good use of Asia's staple grain, rice. And since whisky, in its simplest form, is a spirit distilled from grain, it's surprising that rice-based whisky isn't more popular in Japan. One brand, Kikori, hopes to change that.

Kikori Whiskey (which bucks Japanese tradition and spells the word with an "e") is distilled from 100 percent rice and aged for at least three years in American oak, French Limousin oak, and Spanish sherry casks. The wood is crucial to the maturation process, but make no mistake: Rice is the real star here. And it's not just any rice; it's from Kumamoto, the Kyushu prefecture best known for its rice-based shochu. Kumamoto's climate and water create optimal conditions for growing the grain.

The intention, says cofounder Ann Soh Woods, was to create a whisky with a crisp, light flavor profile and a delicate nose that would mix well in cocktails. Indeed, Kikori is already attracting the attention of the rest of the international spirits community. In 2016, it won a gold medal in one of the most prestigious contests, the San Francisco World Spirits Competition.

45

SHOCHU COCKTAILS

I'm a much bigger fan of sipping shochu on the rocks or neat and am usually ambivalent about having it in a cocktail. However, the world-class concoctions below will likely introduce droves of new drinkers to one of my favorite spirits in the world. And that's a very good thing. Thanks to Jesse Falowitz of Mizu Shochu for providing the following mixological wonders, which incorporate the smooth, barley-based Mizu.

☞ RINGO, I LOVE YOU

I love this one, not just because it's super tasty, but because I'm always a fan of clever puns—and I'm a big Beatles fan, even though this is more of an ode to a fruit than to a drummer. "Ringo" is Japanese for "apple," and its pronunciation is a bit closer to the name of a wild dog on the Australian outback than that of the lead vocalist on "Yellow Submarine." Falowitz himself developed this one.

46

➤ DIRECTIONS ◄

Put cinnamon stick in a cocktail shaker and break into several pieces with a muddler.

Add apple pieces and muddle, extracting all the juice from the apple.

Add shochu, lemon juice, and maple syrup and shake with ice.

Double-strain into a martini glass and serve up, or double-strain into a rocks glass over large ice cubes.

➤ INGREDIENTS ◄

1-inch piece cinnamon stick

½ cored red apple, chopped

75 ml (2½ ounces) Mizu Shochu

Juice of ½ lemon

7 ml (¼ ounce) maple syrup

☞ Harvest Swoon

Also created by Falowitz, Harvest Swoon combines shochu with another of my favorite Japanese beverages: mugi cha, or barley tea. Not surprisingly, the barley-based Mizu plays remarkably well with the mugi cha.

⇢⊶ DIRECTIONS ⊷⇠

The prep for the Harvest Swoon begins the day before you plan to drink or serve it.

Make extra-strong mugi cha by using two to three times the recommended number of tea bags per volume of water and steep overnight.

The next day, build the drink in a rocks glass, combining all ingredients with one large ice cube, and stir until chilled.

Garnish with a strip of orange peel, spritzing cocktail with the oils of the peel before you drop it in.

⇢⊶ INGREDIENTS ⊷⇠

60 ml (2 ounces) Mizu Shochu

60 ml (2 ounces) mugi cha (Japanese barley tea)

10 ml (⅓ ounce) hazelnut syrup

5 ml (1 teaspoon) Grand Marnier

Orange peel, for garnish

47

☞ Bloody Mugi

I love me a good Bloody, as well as the culinary wonders of Japan. Needless to say, the Bloody Mugi really speaks to me. Takeshi Uzuka created this one.

⇢⊶ DIRECTIONS ⊷⇠

Salt the rim of a Collins glass with a 50-50 mixture of pepper and salt.

Add ice and then remaining ingredients and gently stir.

⇢⊶ INGREDIENTS ⊷⇠

Shichimi pepper (regular black pepper is fine if you can't find shichimi)

Salt

60 ml (2 ounces) Mizu Shochu

90 ml (3 ounces) tomato juice

15 ml (½ ounce) fresh lemon juice

3 dashes soy sauce (genius!)

☞ FIVE FORTUNES

Joji Watanabe created this simple, classic delight, which brings Japanese flavors to a martini-like setting.

⇢⇥ DIRECTIONS ⇤⇠

Stir all ingredients with ice and strain into a martini glass.

Garnish with thin plum slice.

⇢⇥ INGREDIENTS ⇤⇠

60 ml (2 ounces) shochu

15 ml (½ ounce) Choya Umeshu (Japanese plum wine)

2 drops Shoots & Roots Japanese bitters (or other bitters brand that approximates the flavor profile)

Thin plum slice, for garnish

☞ SAGA 75

As you can probably guess from the name, this cocktail, created by Tazeki Uzuka, is a twist on the French 75, with shochu replacing the gin.

⇢⇥ DIRECTIONS ⇤⇠

Combine shochu, yuzu juice, and simple syrup in a shaker and shake with ice.

Strain into a Champagne flute and top with Champagne.

⇢⇥ INGREDIENTS ⇤⇠

30 ml (1 ounce) shochu

15 ml (½ ounce) yuzu juice

15 ml (½ ounce) simple syrup

90 ml (3 ounces) Champagne

☞ SHOCHU GIMLET

And, since we're on the topic of traditionally gin-based drinks, Falowitz recommends trying shochu in a classic gimlet.

⇢⇥ DIRECTIONS ⇤⇠

Fill a cocktail shaker with ice, pour in shochu, lime juice, and simple syrup, and stir.

Strain into a rocks glass filled with ice and garnish with lime twist or wheel.

⇢⇥ INGREDIENTS ⇤⇠

75 ml (2½ ounces) shochu

15 ml (½ ounce) fresh lime juice

15 ml (½ ounce) simple syrup

Lime twist or wheel, for garnish

KIKORI COCKTAILS

Rice-based Kikori Whiskey was made for mixing. See for yourself with these splendid imbibables.

☞ THREE STRANDS OF ROPE

Fans of the Manhattan may be drawn to Three Strands.

⇥ DIRECTIONS ⇤

Combine Kikori, vermouth, and bitters in a glass and add ice.

Stir and strain into a cocktail coupe, then garnish with lemon twist.

⇥ INGREDIENTS ⇤

60 ml (2 ounces) Kikori Whiskey

30 ml (1 ounce) Dolin Blanc vermouth

4 dashes orange bitters

Lemon twist, for garnish

☞ BATTLE OF KUMAMOTO

The addition of absinthe adds a vaguely Sazerac-esque element to this cocktail, named after the prefecture famous for its rice.

49

⇥ DIRECTIONS ⇤

Combine all ingredients in a glass and add one cube of ice.

Stir, then garnish with lemon twist.

⇥ INGREDIENTS ⇤

75 ml (2½ ounces) Kikori Whiskey

7 ml (¼ ounce) simple syrup

1 dash absinthe

2 dashes Peychaud's bitters

1 dash orange bitters

Lemon twist, for garnish

THE KOREAN PENINSULA

South Korea boasts a robust drinking culture, right up there with Japan's traditions. If the Kim regime ever falls and North and South unify, they'd be unstoppable.

In Korea, as in most countries throughout the world, beer (Koreans call it maekju) is the most consumed beverage. However, traditional alcohols continue to find their niche among the locals. Many of them are rice-based, which is a recurring theme across Asia because rice is just so abundant and ingrained—pun intended—in their shared cultures. But other Korean alcohols use ingredients more commonly associated with other large Asian countries—such as sorghum, the dominant grain that provides the foundation for China's baijiu, and sweet potatoes, which, as you recall, is the most popular base for Japan's shochu.

The Korean beverage in which those tubers frequently find themselves often gets confused with the Japanese spirit, primarily because their names are so similar. I speak, of course, of soju. If you happened to read my earlier book, *The Year of Drinking Adventurously*, you'd know that such confusion is a source of great frustration for Japanese distillers, because the Korean liquor differs radically from theirs. Like shochu, soju is often on the mild side, alcoholically speaking. It's common to find bottles that are between 20 and 25 percent alcohol by volume. But the similarities end there. The flavor of soju is much closer to neutral than that of shochu, which, when made well, retains much of the character of the base ingredient.

But Korea is not just about soju and beer. The locals enjoy plenty of other beverages that are still unfamiliar to most Westerners.

Makgeolli: Years ago, my wife and I were dining at a restaurant in New York City's Koreatown when a particular menu item intrigued us. Its proper name was makgeolli, but, for us Westerners, the English menu read "Korean rice wine." We had already been exploring Japanese sake and figured it would be similar. Boy, were we wrong! First of all, we were expecting it to arrive in a bottle, but it showed up at our table in a bowl with a ladle, accompanied by two smaller vessels from which to drink it (not dramatically different from sake cups). I've since learned that more traditional restaurants serve it in a metal bowl, while modern ones are likely to serve it from a wooden one. Makgeolli has a thicker consistency than most sake but, like nigori sake (the unfiltered variety), it has a milky, hazy hue.

Japanese nigori tends to be on the sweeter side of the sake spectrum, but makgeolli definitely registers even sweeter than that. It's also rather low in alcohol (usually around 6 or 7 percent ABV), so there's plenty of sugar that hasn't been fermented.

Makgeolli had traditionally been considered a farmer's drink and, specifically, a drink for the older generations. However, more and more millennials are gravitating toward it as a few tastemakers from the Korean entertainment industry—primarily some local hip-hop artists—have made it fashionable again. In that sense, it's kind of like the Pabst Blue Ribbon of traditional Korean beverages.

Not all soju are created equal; varieties packaged in green bottles tilt more toward the mass-produced side of the manufacturing equation and often use artificial sweeteners. White bottles are typically the package of choice for the ones that get their sweetness from the natural brewing process.

Dongdongju: Similar to makgeolli (and thus often confused with it), dongdongju frequently has some errant grains

51

of rice floating in it (they get strained out of makgeolli). This is intentional, as dong means "floating." And dong-dongju's alcohol content can be a couple of points higher than that of makgeolli, perhaps 8 or 10 percent.

Baekseju: Baekseju's alcohol content is much closer to that of the average sake—13 to 15 percent ABV—and it's made with rice, but the similarities end there. It's definitely on the sweet side, kind of like a cloying white wine, and is infused with about a dozen herbs, with ginseng usually being the star of the show. It's the herbs that give it the name; baekseju means "hundred years wine." The thinking is that if you drink enough of it, those herbs will help you reach at least the century mark before you shuffle off this mortal coil. (That could be why consumption often skews older.)

Bokbunja-ju: Often simply called bokbunja (ju means "wine," but people tend to default to the shorter moniker), this wine is made from black raspberries. It has a deep red color and a flavor that evokes sweeter fortified wines like port. Over the centuries, drinkers have claimed that it's good for the libido, but we won't go there (in other words, it's bunk). Its ABV is in a range similar to baekseju, usually no higher than 16 percent.

Maehwasu: Producers of this plum liqueur specifically target women because it's sweeter and lighter than soju—somewhat sexist, one might say. And the labels have lots of flowers on them, in case anyone had any doubt about this.

Sometimes, drinkers aren't content with consuming just one of these types of alcohol at a time. A desire for variety, coupled with an unquenchable thirst for experimentation, can produce some bizarre hybrid drinks that sound questionable on paper. But, as locals and American expats living in South Korea have told me, don't knock it till you've tried it.

The least bizarre of these hybrid drinks is somaek. Based on the extremely rudimentary primer in Korean booze lingo you've enjoyed in prior paragraphs, you might be able to deduce that this is a combination of soju and beer. It's really just the Korean version of a boilermaker; instead of whisky, it's got a shot of soju.

But take a look at the drink called Cojinganmaek, and things start to get a little weird. The very name contains clues as to what's in it. Maek, of course, is beer. Jin represents soju, as Jinro is the number-one brand of the spirit in Korea—and the world. Any thoughts on what "Co" might signify? Hint: It's the best-selling beverage of any kind in the world. That's right: Coca-Cola. So popular is this concoction that you can even find a glass with fill lines instructing you how much of each component to pour. (There's also a version that substitutes Sprite for Coke.)

But at the end of the day—as in 5 P.M.—it matters very little what you're drinking. A bigger concern is *how* you're drinking it. And in terms of drinking rules, Korea definitely rivals, if not exceeds, Japan.

In Korea, there are few terms that inspire as much joy and dread in equal measure as "hweh shik." This means, very loosely, "business dinner." Many of us can relate; we've all had to sit through work functions before. But the worst-case scenario for most of us born and raised in a country founded by Puritans and with an actual constitutional amendment on the books that (temporarily) banned alcohol is that such meals would be overlong and mind-numbingly boring. In South Korea, they're practically blood sport.

When American graphic designer Dominic Dinkins moved to Seoul in 2009, he wasn't fully aware of the culture shock that awaited him. But it didn't take him long to get the lay of the land.

"When work is done, all the workers get together and they drink," Dinkins tells me. "A lot of people feel that it's kind of stressful. The older men who are in charge, the bosses, the managers, they kind of force everyone to drink. A lot of Koreans really hate hweh shik." For that reason, the custom is dying out a little, Dinkins observes, "but it's still a very big part of the drinking culture here."

One of the more stress-inducing elements, especially for those new to Korean customs, doesn't relate to how much one drinks, but to whether one adheres to the rules. Dinkins and his significant other, HyoSun Kwon, run domandhyo.com, which features comics and infographics on life in Korea, including tips on proper drinking etiquette. Here are a few helpful survival tips they shared with me:

* Always pour and receive a drink with both hands.
* Never fill your own glass.
* If your glass is empty, it means you want to drink some more. If you don't want to drink a lot, drink very slowly so your glass doesn't empty often. Because as soon as it empties, it gets filled right back up.
* Koreans are very serious about age-related hierarchy. When a younger person is drinking with someone older, the younger person must look away while sipping. It's considered disrespectful to look directly at the older person.
* If someone offers you a glass, the last thing you want to do is refuse. "With a lot of the younger people," Dinkins says, "it's changing because they don't like being forced to drink. With the first round, it's kind of a given that you have to drink. After that, they kind of let it slide."

Whether or not you ever find yourself in South Korea, it doesn't hurt to practice. Try your drinking etiquette with some of these cocktails.

CHINA

Nearly a billion and a half people live in China, so trying to characterize Chinese drinking habits in a few broad strokes is a fool's errand.

Sure, there's the traditional stuff, like the spirit baijiu, made from sorghum and a few other cereals; most of these spirits sport a flavor that "intense" doesn't begin to describe. On the lower ABV side, there's huangjiu, the umbrella category for a host of rice-based fermented beverages (labeling something "huangjiu" is about as detailed as describing a Malbec as "wine"). Baijiu and huangjiu are widely consumed across the vast country (baijiu more so in the north, but available everywhere), but Chinese drinkers of late have adopted a few more Western beverage traditions, thanks to rapid globalization and the hyper-focus on China as a growth market.

Wine—the grape kind, not the rice kind—has been catching on in China. In fact, given its colossal population, China has emerged as the world's top consumer of the beverage. Wine is not new to China, per se. The first winery in China opened in the 1890s, but it took nearly a hundred years before foreign money started trickling into the industry. So, for all intents and purposes, wine wasn't really a "thing" in China until the 1990s.

There's an almost-even split between imported and Chinese-made wine, and the number of wineries in the country has grown dramatically. The grape wine market owes much of its expansion to the perception of the beverage as a status symbol. Drinking wine—particularly expensive wine—is an assertion of one's wealth and sophistication. Actually, I should rephrase that: *Having* wine is a display of wealth and sophistication. In many cases, people aren't even drinking it. And when they do actually drink it—usually with dinner, as imbibing without food is still a relatively new concept in China—well, let's just say it would make even the most stoic Frenchman cry.

55

Now, this is hardly what one would call a major trend; it's more anecdotal. But Chinese consumers, especially those on the freshly minted side of their adult years, have been known on more than a few occasions to mix red wine with anything from Coca-Cola to orange juice (and we're not just talking table wine here— sometimes it's vintages that cost four figures). There was even a point, in the not too distant past, when retailers would sell bottles of wine with containers of Sprite or Coke taped to them!

Others, meanwhile, have done shots of wine. And I guess this is somewhat understandable: When there are no real traditions associated with a particular beverage—and the Chinese are nothing if not traditional—there's no one in the older generations telling their progeny how or how not to drink it. So, if you're completely untethered to heritage, why not make up your own traditions?

Offbeat pairings aren't limited to wine—it's happening with Western spirits, too. Expat beer brewer Joe Finkenbinder, who had worked at Beijing's Great Leap Brewery before launching BionicBrew in the manufacturing hub that is Shenzhen (just outside Hong Kong), told me that he's been in more than a couple of nightclubs that serve whisky mixed with sports drinks! "They don't give a damn. They'll take a bottle of Chivas and whip out a bottle of the Chinese version of Gatorade and just mix them together in a big pitcher and serve them and drink them all night," Finkenbinder recalls. "When a lot of people have a lot of money and don't know what to do with it, it's weird the kind of things they'll invent." Well, there's something to be said for rehydration and electrolyte replenishment while one consumes alcohol, no?

Those make for some fun, silly stories, but for the most part Chinese wine and spirits consumption is starting to mimic that of the West. Consumers are increasingly educated and starting to appreciate the beverages on their own. Having said that, I'd hate to see the odd mixes disappear. They could be the trends of the future if people stick to their guns and give convention the old middle finger! I really don't believe there's any wrong way to drink anything, as long as you're enjoying it. Besides, in China, it's not really about what you drink; beverages are interchangeable and disposable. It's about being seen drinking it. It ties in with the Chinese concept of "face," taking pride in outward appearances.

"In China, you're not selling products, you're selling face," Finkenbinder notes. And "face," he points out, is packaging. "The package includes the retail establishment, it includes the glass, it includes the location," he says. "All of this stuff is kind of to show that this is ultra-premium and it's worth ten bucks a glass."

This idea of "selling face" is something that keeps Finkenbinder up at night, as he's been actively trying to stoke the craft brewing movement in China. He even started a beer festival in Shenzhen, showcasing the finest Chinese-made beers. But he worries that new brewers might be enticed to put a high price tag on subpar beer. "Some of the time, what's in the glass is very good and deserves a ten-dollar premium, but the price alone doesn't necessarily mean the beer is quality. I think we're going to see a flood of breweries that are going to be a lot of glitz and no substance and make shitty beer."

This face-centric orientation means that many consumers would rather spend the equivalent of ten bucks on a drink of questionable quality than spend six or seven bucks on a world-class option. "They assume it must be worse because it's cheaper," Finkenbinder points out. "It's tough—they don't want a good deal. They're only going to buy one pint anyway, take a photo of it, and send it out."

⚔ Anti-extravagance

If the Chinese government has anything to say about it, ostentatious displays of wealth could eventually become a thing of the past.

China, since 2012, has been on an anti-extravagance crackdown. The country outright banned high-end gift giving among

57

government officials and has led a campaign to end the practice in the corporate environment as well (the latter, for the most part, has been slow to catch on).

Diplomats had customarily given big-ticket wines and Cognacs, as well as up-market baijiu, to foreign dignitaries. When the state put an end to that, those categories took a bit of a hit financially. That's one of the reasons baijiu makers have been putting a great deal of money toward promoting the spirit in the United States, where it's largely unknown; they need to make up some of that lost volume.

⋈ Taiwan

Much as it does in the mainland People's Republic of China, sorghum figures quite prominently into the distilling activities in the island known as the Republic of China—the formal, political name of Taiwan. In Taiwan, however, the spirit is known mostly as kaoliang. There's not too discernible a difference; it wouldn't technically be incorrect to refer to kaoliang as a type of baijiu. The flavor is just as challenging and, strength-wise, it's in the same neighborhood—with an ABV in the high 50s usually (some can dip a bit lower and others jump a tad higher). The epicenter of kaoliang production lies in the tiny archipelagos of Kinmen and Matsu just off the coast of the main island. Internationally, Taiwan has been making a name for itself in the whisky world with its well-regarded brand, Kavalan. Taiwanese entrepreneur Tien-Tsai Lee and master blender Ian Chang enlisted the services of now-deceased whisky expert Dr. Jim Swan to launch the island's first single malt in 2005. Seven years later the distillery started exporting Kavalan and has since racked up a number of prestigious awards.

MONGOLIA

If you thought that people drank the milk of only cows and goats, you haven't spoken with a Mongolian. Horses are prevalent throughout Mongolia—and mares, therefore, are frequently milked. No one is drinking the milk of the mare raw, as lactose intolerance is pervasive across the country. However, fermenting the milk destroys much of the lactose and produces a beverage that many cultures in central Asia refer to as kumyss (also spelled koumis, kumis, or kumys, depending on which country we're talking about). The Mongolian version is the country's national drink, airag, and is very mildly alcoholic (around 2 percent ABV, so around what you'd get if you made your own kombucha), with a touch of subtle carbonation—a by-product of the fermentation process, of course. The drink is a little sour but full of all sorts of fortifying vitamins and minerals.

The ultra-traditional way to make airag is by first filtering the milk through a cloth and then pouring it into a large leather sack, which is suspended on the left side of the entrance to a yurt (in Mongolian culture, the left side is a symbol of masculinity). Yeast and lactobacillus are the microorganisms that do the bulk of the heavy lifting in the fermentation process. The sack hangs wide open, because the liquid must be stirred constantly over the course of about two days. Those entering and exiting the yurt typically give it a few stirs on their way in or out.

You're not going to find airag in large quantities at all times of year. Your best bet is during the summer, because June is the big month for producing airag. The beverage is a part of the annual Nadaam festival, the celebration that's best described as the Mongolian Olympics (with a touch of Burning Man thrown in). The main competitions, of course, involve lots of horses.

It's an age-old Mongolian tradition for hosts to offer a bowl of airag to each guest. It's preferable that visitors drink the whole bowl, but it's fine if they want to take just a few sips. What they don't want to do is turn down the offer. That would be the epitome of bad form.

And, as always, where there's fermenting, there's distilling. The traditional spirit in the country is called arkhi, sometimes referred to as milk vodka (if that's not enough to get your attention, I don't know what is). The milk in question this time is of the bovine variety—its distillable base is fermented cow's milk kefir, known locally as isgelen tarag.

Unlike airag, arkhi is typically clear (more like vodka, less like milk) and much harder to find as a commercial product. Like airag, it's mostly a homemade concoction; nomads traditionally produce it in their yurts with their own rudimentary stills—and are happy to share it with visitors. The production apparatus is closer to a small system of woks and bowls than it is to what we tend to think of as a still. Arkhi makers heat kefir in a wok on top of a stove. When the resulting vapor wafts to a second wok filled with cold water, it condenses back into liquid and is captured in a separate basin. The final spirit is a bit on the mild side, somewhere around 15 percent ABV, and therefore closer in potency to an average wine or sake than to vodka. The low alcohol content makes it easy enough to consume the traditional way: neat.

These days, the most consumed spirit in Mongolia is something that's a little more familiar to folks in the West: vodka. And for that, we can thank the Mongolian People's Republic, ruled by the socialist Mongolian People's Revolutionary Party, which had very strong ties with the Soviet Union for the nearly seventy years of its existence (1924–1992). When your country's that tight with the Russians, it's only natural that your people are going to start drinking plenty of vodka. Initially, most vodka was imported from the USSR, but Mongolia eventually developed its own vodka-producing industry. The biggest brand today is Chinggis Khan, named after the legendary Mongolian conqueror Genghis Khan. The brand is a product of the APU Company, whose origins date back to 1924, the very beginning of the Mongolian People's Republic era. Initially state-owned (as we're talking Marxism-Leninism here), APU is now publicly listed on the Mongolian Stock Exchange.

Chapter 4

SOUTH ASIA, CENTRAL ASIA, AND THE MIDDLE EAST

Westerners often view the drinking customs of India and other parts of South Asia (and much of the rest of the world) through the lens of colonialism. Play a quick game of word association with a beer drinker and the word "India" will likely generate an immediate response of "pale ale." I don't want to go too deep into the weeds of English (and now, mostly, American) brewing traditions, but India pale ale (more popularly called IPA), started out as a generously hopped and higher-in-alcohol version of traditional English pale ales. As the popular (and now factually questionable) story goes, brewers needed the extra hops because the flavor would inevitably weaken during the eighteen-thousand-mile journey from England to India before sailors enjoyed the luxury of canals. Hops also turned out to be a natural preservative—as is alcohol, hence the higher ABV—so the beer usually arrived in India in pretty good shape.

Another British beverage born out of colonialism: the gin and tonic. Brits in the eighteenth century were going gaga for their gin. However, those stationed in India weren't so gaga for the malaria with which they were frequently infected. British colonists in India, as well as in Africa and South America, discovered that quinine was quite effective against malaria. Read the label of your bottle of Fever-Tree or Seagram's tonic water and guess what ingredient you'll find in all those. Gin and tonic saves lives!

INDIA

Of course, the people of India also have drinks that are all their own, drinks that you'd likely have a hard time finding anywhere else in the world. One example is found in the Indian state of Goa on the southwestern coast of the country (its lengthy coastline makes it a popular tourist destination for Europeans and folks from other parts of the world). Locals there are quite proud of feni, the region's distilled spirit that's made from either the coconut palm or the cashew apple.

{ CASHEW FRUIT, SOMETIMES CALLED CASHEW APPLES

PHOTO: JULIANA GALLUCIO/DREAMSTIME }

The latter are not actually apples, but they bear a vague resemblance to those orchard fruits. The cashew apple is an outgrowth of the cashew nut itself. The nut grows first, but before it ripens, a fruit-like mass starts to emerge and ultimately balloons up until it is significantly larger than the nut. The nut-fruit-based variety of feni is usually the more revered of the two (though coconut feni lovers would beg to differ). Sixteenth-century Portuguese explorers get the credit for bringing cashews to India from South America, but it's the Goans who figured out how to turn the cashew's fruit—usually discarded when harvesting the nuts because it has very little culinary value—into feni.

Though other cultures—notably in Africa—produce liquor from the cashew fruit and palms, the only place the product can be called feni is within its home state. As of 2009, it enjoys regional protection as a "country liquor," native to Goa, so even if someone tried to make it a mile into bordering Maharashtra or Karnataka, they wouldn't be able to sell it as feni. The Goan authorities are trying to get it recognized as a heritage drink beyond their state's borders as well.

Goan drinkers often dilute it so it's about 50 percent feni and 50 percent water, but the truly fearless shoot it neat. In recent years, the spirit has attracted new attention as a cocktail ingredient.

A typical feni distillery is not a sprawling industrial plant, but rather a small makeshift operation that springs up near a cashew plantation between February and April, when the fruit is at its ripest. Distillers finish producing the liquor by the end of May and then ship it off to area stores and taverns, all within Goa.

The coconut palm variety, however, is produced year-round (which probably explains why Goans prize the cashew one over the palm; its availability is more fleeting). The truly brave drink the burning liquid straight, but it's acceptable to sip on the rocks as well. Others mix it with refreshers like Coke and lemonade.

Things start to get a little complicated when we get into other parts of India, as at least four of its states prohibit alcohol consumption altogether. And in many of the states that allow it, there's a considerable degree of ambivalence, as there's a "forbidden" air around drinking.

In fact, the farther you get outside a major cosmopolitan city like Mumbai, Bangalore, or New Delhi, the less liberal the attitudes toward alcohol consumption seem to get. In rural areas, drinkers—typically men, as imbibing is still a male-dominated pastime in India—often sit at tables in booths with adjustable curtains that can screen them off from the rest of the customers when they want to sip in private.

Despite all that, legal consumption has steadily increased, especially as the middle class grows and there's a bit more disposable income.

Even though antipathy toward the British colonial era is palpable in modern Indian society, the country has adopted a number of drinking habits from its former oppressors. For starters, Indians who consume alcohol are huge whisky fans—mostly of the Scotland-produced ilk. Johnnie Walker is ubiquitous; Johnnie Walker Blue, the blend of the venerable brand's rarest whiskies, is their Rolls Royce.

And they're not just drinking the imported stuff—India has a bit of a whisky-distilling industry all its own. Well, sort of. Much of what Indian producers call whisky is actually derived from sugarcane or molasses, as there's a lot of that growing on the subcontinent. By definition, that makes their "whisky" technically rum, but let them call it what they call it.

Keep in mind that whisky started out kind of arbitrarily, anyway. The Scots and the Irish had a lot of barley growing across their great lands—the grain loves cooler climates—but if they had been located considerably closer to the equator, you can bet they'd have been distilling sugarcane or even making palm wine for that matter. In fact, as you'll discover a bit later, Scotland was gaga over rum—imported from the islands, of course—before they even started distilling whisky in earnest. It was only later that the definitions of the spirits became standardized, thanks to the work of producers and the preferred grains with which they were distilling. And much of American whiskey is corn based—because corn is technically considered a grain, it gets to be called whiskey.

But there is an emerging grain-distilling industry in India, and much of what is coming out of the country is actually quite good, holding its own against some of the most established distilling traditions in the world. Many are producing single malts, too. The first Indian single malt to burst onto the scene was Amrut, whose distillery set up shop right after the end of British rule in the country. It took more than five decades of operation before it started making its single malts.

Another maker is John Distilleries, whose production facility is based in—where else?—Goa, though its corporate headquarters are in Bangalore, the country's tech industry capital. As with Amrut, John Distilleries' single-malt production is a relatively new development for the company. When the distillery started in 1992, it was making Original Choice Whisky, the flagship brand whose base was the classic Indian ingredient, molasses. The company launched the premium single malt Paul John brand in 2009, complete with Indian-made copper-pot stills. Now, I have never claimed to have the most sophisticated palate, but I've tasted a few whiskies in my day. If I were to do a blind tasting of Paul John alongside a Speyside single-malt Scotch or a glass of well-crafted Japanese whisky, I might not be able to pick out which one was made in India. And that is the highest of compliments.

65

"British imperialism left behind this rich taste, the sense that you've got to have the fine Scotch," says Ajay Bhoja, who is responsible for some of Paul John's export markets, including the United States. However, since consumption of the good stuff is still a new phenomenon at home, Bhoja acknowledges that there's a huge learning curve to overcome, especially when it comes to the "right" way to drink it (as subjective a concept as that is). While many are drinking it neat or on the rocks, others are still mixing it with Coca-Cola or orange juice. (Again, to each their own. And orange juice isn't that far off from the sour mix that goes into a whisky sour, is it?)

The home market is a tough nut to crack, and Indian distillers tend to have better luck in outside territories. (Amrut single malt, incidentally, first launched in Glasgow, Scotland.) The economy segment—that is, the rum-like molasses-based whiskies—will likely continue to dominate the Indian market. And producers are keeping costs down by using lighter, less costly packaging. These days, Original Choice shows up on retail shelves in Tetra Pak cartons. While great for the environment—lighter weight and easier to recycle—the containers have a more down-market feel when spirits are involved. (And while resealable Tetra Paks with cap enclosures are available, it's the non-resealable ones that tend to house Original Choice.)

The cocktail scene is beginning to take off in India, especially in Goa, which is essentially the country's party capital, but also in major metro areas like Mumbai, New Delhi, and Bangalore, as young professionals adopt more cosmopolitan lifestyles. With that, it's likely that the whisky culture will evolve as well. Cocktails are often a great introduction to any spirit, and it's likely that Indian drinkers will gravitate toward premium whiskies through mixed drinks.

Regardless, you're still more likely to find locals drinking Kingfisher, India's top beer brand, owned by flamboyant billionaire Vijay Mallya's United Breweries Group (that is, unless his partners, like Heineken, succeed in their efforts to edge him out of his ventures).

BHUTAN, NEPAL, AND TIBET

If you ever plan to climb Mount Everest (which likely applies to few, if any, of you, but indulge me), you're going to need some liquid fortification. And you're in luck, because Himalayan cultures have their own homegrown beer-like beverage that's a cult favorite among intrepid adventurers. It's called tongba, or chhaang, and it's usually millet-based but sometimes incorporates other grains like rice or barley. And since this is the snowy region where the yeti roam, it's usually served hot (except in the summer, when people drink it at room temperature). I'm only sort of kidding about the yeti. Local legends speak of the mythical abominable snowmen raiding villages and stealing chhaang. I guess sometimes their fur just isn't enough to keep them warm! Humans have also used the hot drink to fight colds and fevers while hiking through the frosty mountains.

Typically, chhaang makers pour hot water through the fermenting grain and then drink it from a pot with straws. The ones made predominantly from rice are more milky-white in color than the others. Tibetans distinguish between dre-chhaang (rice) and dru-chhaang (barley). The beverage is a huge part of Tibetan rituals, from the social to the religious. It's a key part of welcoming guests into one's home, as well as settling arguments. Chhaang also plays a role in courtship.

CENTRAL ASIA

It's easiest if we refer to this area as the "'Stans"—Uzbekistan, Kazakhstan, Tajikistan, Turkmenistan, and Kyrgyzstan. These countries lie to the west of China, and one of them, Kazakhstan, almost shares a border with Mongolia (there's a tiny sliver of south-central Russia in between them). That proximity creates a bit of overlap between Mongolia and the 'Stans, in terms of the resources to which they have access and how they transform those into beverages.

For starters, there's no shortage of horses galloping every which way, and that means that plenty of horses get milked. The equine-born beverage of choice throughout much of the area is the aforementioned kumyss, which, like Mongolian airag, has a relatively modest alcohol content. Kumyss is especially prevalent in Kyrgyzstan (or, as it's officially called, the Kyrgyz Republic) and is a staple at roadside stands. For the über-traditional version, you'd have to track down the horse herders' yurts out in the countryside and sample their personal stock. Its production process is not unlike that of its Mongolian cousin: It ferments in a pouch made from an animal skin dried over a flame. Kyrgyzstan is also where you're likely to find bozo—no clowning around here—a fermented millet (and sometimes corn) drink often called Kyrgyz beer.

Keep in mind, however, that those who do imbibe in many of these countries are in the minority. In much of the region, Islam is the dominant religion, which means that it's largely the non-Muslim population—which can be as low as 5 or 10 percent of the total population of certain countries—doing most of the partaking.

Having said that, these were at one time Soviet republics—and remained so for a good seven decades—so there's typically no shortage of vodka being poured. And because of that history, locals in many places like Uzbekistan and Kazakhstan are used to being around alcohol, regardless of whether they choose to indulge. It's not as much of a taboo as it is in many Middle Eastern countries.

In Kazakhstan, vodka is rivaled only by cognac—or, at least, what Kazakhs call cognac. If it's not made in Cognac, France, it can't legally be called Cognac. But, as you'll learn in a bit when we visit Armenia, many former Soviet states don't recognize French certification designations.

THE MIDDLE EAST

The Middle East, at least in its modern form, can be a bit of an enigma when it comes to alcoholic beverages. That is, of course, due to the fact that most of the countries in the region are predominantly Muslim, and devout Muslims abstain from alcohol. (The irony of the modern Islamic world's near abstinence is that, as historians generally agree, the first alcoholic beverages ever produced were born in the Middle East.) In the strictest Islamic nations, alcohol is completely banned. Others prohibit only the locals from partaking; many establishments are licensed to sell to foreigners. And then there are a handful of countries that are as wet as many Western nations.

Since it's hard enough to get alcohol in most predominantly Muslim countries, it rarely matters what a person is drinking. The act of drinking is an experience in and of itself. Having said that, there are many countries with renowned winemaking traditions within this region of teetotalers, as well as makers of their own local variations on the traditional Middle Eastern spirit, arak.

Arak (sometimes spelled arack, arrack, or, less frequently, araq) is one of those family secret–type creations, with traditional recipes passed down from generation to generation—in some cases, since the Middle Ages. Arak loosely translates from Arabic into "sweat" or "perspiration," which, admittedly, sounds pretty gross. But when you think about, that's essentially what a spirit is. In its crudest form, distillation involves boiling a fermented liquid and condensing the vapor back into a more concentrated alcohol; the vapor's essentially sweat, no? The word "arak," for that reason, has evolved into the generic term for "distillate."

Most commonly the distillate in question derives from grapes, so in its most basic form it's a brandy. However, its distinctive character, in both flavor and consistency, comes from its signature ingredient: anise.

Israel, Palestine, Syria, and Iraq

I'm always apprehensive when I have to write about the Israel/Palestine situation. Even though most—though far from all—Israelis and Palestinians living in the West Bank and Gaza Strip support (with varying levels of enthusiasm) a two-state solution, such an arrangement has yet to come to pass—and likely won't any time soon. Therefore, it's pretty difficult to pivot from a long-standing debate whose resolution—or lack thereof—has ramifications that extend well beyond the stability of its immediate region to something as frivolous as local boozing. But here goes.

One element on which few on either side of the argument can disagree is the region's place in early drinking history. Archaeologists and historians generally agree that the Sumerians, the ancient inhabitants of Mesopotamia—a region that encompasses parts of modern-day Iraq, Syria, and Kuwait—are likely the ones who invented what eventually would evolve into beer brewing. Since Israel and the Palestinian territories of Gaza and the West Bank are roughly adjacent to that massive swath of real estate, it's highly likely that some of the world's earliest brewing was happening there. And now some of its most modern activity is happening there as well, at least in the latter territory.

In 2015, in the West Bank city of Birzeit (which, coincidentally, kind of sounds like "beer time" in German), the Palestinian Sayej brothers produced their first batch of Shepherds Beer—a brand whose name is a nod to the herders who used to corral sheep on their hallowed land millennia ago. (Remember, in the story of the Nativity, a bunch of herders were present for Jesus's birth; that little town of Bethlehem is located in the West Bank.) To date, Birzeit Brewery has produced pilsner, stout, and Belgian-style amber beers under the Shepherds label.

"We wanted to introduce the market to beer culture and, at the same time, we want to tell the world that we had a beer culture before," says Alaa Sayej, CEO of Birzeit Brewery. "Beer was invented in the Middle East, and we're trying to bring it back to the Middle East."

One doesn't immediately think "booze culture" in conjunction with Palestinian territories, but in certain areas—especially those with dominant Christian populations, like Birzeit—strong adult drinks are very much part of the heritage. "The drinking habits are not controlled by religion; they're controlled by culture," Sayej points out. "So it's different between one city and another city."

Birzeit is part of the greater Ramallah area, which skews more Christian. There, you're likely to find many pubs and restaurants that serve alcohol. In Islamic cities, drinking is far less overt, and many travel to the Christian cities to buy their beverages. Sayej notes that members of all religious groups drink, some are just more open about it than others, and he estimates that about 70 percent of the population consumes some alcohol. "It's forbidden in the religious books," Sayej says, "but [the habits] are evolving."

In 2016, Birzeit Brewery hosted the first Shepherds Beer Festival, the response to which was music to Sayej's ears. More than six thousand people turned out, enjoying not only beer, but also local food and live Palestinian bands. It will likely be an annual event.

Beer has played a relatively minor role in local customs for much of the modern era. Wine and arak—largely homemade varieties—have been the elixirs of choice among Palestinians. Sayej recalls stories of his grandfathers and great-grandfathers fermenting wine and storing it in huge jars in their homes—a common practice among the older generations. Many also operated small distilleries at their residences to produce arak for personal consumption and to share with friends and family. There's a Palestinian wedding tradition, especially within Christian communities in Ramallah, where locals dance with the groom around the city, pouring out wine, arak, or beer while singing along to traditional songs.

"We're trying to keep our traditions alive through many things, even through alcohol," Sayej says. "Maybe it's banned or forbidden for certain religions, but at the end of the day, the country is not 100 percent Muslim and not 100 percent Christian. We have to live with each other, and everyone respects the opposite side."

In Israel, there's little religious apprehension about drinking. In fact, it's openly encouraged, even among the most observant in the Jewish community. Alcohol plays a crucial role during the Sabbath and Jewish holidays. It takes on an almost mystical function; it's as much a ritual as singing and dancing and uplifts the devout.

The weekend in Israel is Friday and Saturday, so Thursday's the big night to go out for most of the country. Friday is also popular for the secular population, but the most religious Jews drink at home during the Sabbath meal. The majority of what the Israeli population consumes mirrors European preferences—wine, vodka, and, especially, beer—with one notable, Middle Eastern–specific exception: arak.

71

In pubs, the pint or bottle in an Israeli's hand is likely to be either the light amber lager Goldstar or Maccabee, a pilsner, which are both produced by Netanya-based Tempo Beer Industries (the company acquired Goldstar in the mid-1980s). The country's compulsory military service means you're likely to rub elbows with many uniformed servicemen and -women blowing off steam after a long week or while on a brief furlough.

Anyone who's ever cracked open a Bible knows that Israel is historically wine country. But in modern times, much of the country's oenological output hasn't always had the best reputation. Part of the reason for that was due to one of the processes involved in achieving kosher certification. In order for a wine to be certified kosher, all grapes must be picked and all wine must be produced and packaged by Jewish people. When the beverage met those criteria, it usually ended up being pretty good. However, many vintners leaned on a cost-cutting workaround that satisfied all the kosher parameters while sacrificing quality: If you boil wine, it becomes kosher. So producers would often rely on low-cost labor from non-Jewish nomadic peoples—Bedouin and Druze, for instance—and then just heat the wine, boiling away its non-kosher-ness, as well as much of its flavor and character.

But the growing sophistication of worldwide wine consumers' palates spurred demand for higher-quality Israeli wine. It costs more because the winemakers aren't cutting any corners in the production process to achieve kosher status, but now people are willing to pay a little extra for the better stuff (which wasn't always the case). These days, Israeli wines are racking up all sorts of international awards, which hadn't been a regular occurrence just a couple of decades ago.

Some of the best Israeli wines come from the Golan region in the north—which is fascinating in its own right, as there's an ongoing dispute over whether it should even be considered part of Israel. Israel annexed the Syrian territory and imposed Israeli law on it, though much of the world does not recognize

Israel's authority over Golan. To complicate things further, Syria is embroiled in a seemingly endless civil war. The country won't be settling any disputes with Israel in the forseeable future. And when you've got extremist, ISIL-influenced groups trying to erase any part of Syria's history and culture that's not consistent with hard-line religious law, nothing related to alcohol will fare well. There's some irony in that: Not only is Syria part of the region where civilization began, it's also within the geographic area where alcohol began. That region includes modern-day Iraq, a country about which I'm hesitant to provide much detail, as the information will probably be obsolete by the time you read this. The country's lawmakers keep going back and forth between tolerance and complete Prohibition. Just a few years after the United States invaded Iraq, al Qaeda militants wanted no part of a secular society, so they violently trashed shops that were selling alcohol in Baghdad. A fragile order returned to the city in 2008, and the beverages started flowing once again.

But the pendulum is swinging back: In the fall of 2016, the Iraqi parliament passed a law banning the import, production, and sale of alcohol. This enraged members of the country's Christian community, whose economy relies on alcohol. At the time, Shia Islamist parties dominated the governing body.

As always, stay tuned . . .

Jordan

For a predominantly Muslim country, Jordan's alcohol laws are relatively liberal. That's a good thing for a country that's in the heart of a region known for its terroir. Jordan's namesake river is responsible for much of the agricultural irrigation in the region.

Jordanian winemaking dates back to antiquity. Some history scholars even suggest that the wine Jesus and his apostles drank during the Last Supper may have come from Jordan. However, commercial winemaking was more or less nonexistent in the

73

country until the twentieth century. That doesn't necessarily mean that the Muslim population suddenly decided to take up drinking. A tiny fraction of locals actually consume the wine produced within Jordan's borders, and it's mostly the Christian minority making it.

When Bulos Zumot founded Zumot Winery in 1954, he was among the first in Jordan to produce the beverage commercially in the modern era. The company has since gained international attention for its wines, mostly within familiar varietals like Shiraz, Merlot, Pinot Noir, Chardonnay, and Gewürztraminer, marketed under the Saint George label. Zumot continues to thrive under the leadership of the next generation, with Omar Zumot at the helm.

In 1987, Zumot Group opened Zumot Distilleries, initially concentrating on bottling internationally produced spirits under license from their respective producers. The group soon started distilling its own proprietary brands as well. Since Jordan is one of a small handful of Middle Eastern countries where a person can try the traditional distilled spirit of the region, arak, close to its place of birth, Zumot began producing Arak Al-Zumot, packaged in a sapphire-hued bottle with a gold label.

Though Bulos Zumot was a pioneer in the wine industry, he wasn't the first to start producing alcoholic beverages commercially in Jordan. Among those who predated his business was Mudieb Mousa Haddad. Haddad founded Eagle Distilleries Company, which today continues to produce an extensive portfolio of arak expressions under the names Arak Golden Eagle and Arak Haddad.

Lebanon

When it comes to attitudes toward alcohol, Jordan has a bit of kindred spirit in Lebanon. In fact, many travelers to the capital, Beirut, find it downright Western. The Lebanese love European tourists, and much of their embrace of strong liquids is due to a desire to attract tourists from the Continent. Billboards and television ads tout the country's fun-loving culture, usually featuring alcohol.

If this seems permissive compared to other Middle Eastern countries, it's because the non-Muslim population is considerably larger in Lebanon than it is in many other countries in the region. While more than 90 percent of Jordanians practice Islam—with around 6 percent identifying as Christian, and smaller minorities made up of religions like Druze—only 54 percent of Lebanon's 4.5 million people are Muslim. Various sects of Christianity—Catholic, Greek Orthodox, and others—account for around 40 percent of the country's religious composition. And as in Jordan, the non-Muslims are the ones responsible for the alcohol being produced, sold, and consumed.

Arak is, of course, a popular distilled beverage in Lebanon, and there are a number of competing brands to which locals and tourists swear their allegiance. But in recent years, the big star of the Lebanese beverage world has been its wine industry, which has gained international acclaim. And as was the case in Jordan, the industry was thousands of years in the making. Ancient peoples and conquerors stretching back about five millennia, from the Phoenicians to the Romans, have all had some hand in the development of viticulture in the country.

From around 4000 BCE until the seventh century AD, Lebanon reigned as one of the prime winemaking regions in the world. Wine production and consumption began to decline with the rise of Islam in the country, but the caliphate was okay with the Christian population making it and drinking it for religious purposes. However, there wasn't an industry to speak of for a good twelve hundred years or so—that is, until France started taking an interest in the country.

The French are the ones mostly responsible for bringing commercial wine back to Lebanon in the mid-nineteenth century. Jesuit monks brought grape vines—specifically of the North

African Cinsault varietal—to the country circa 1857. At that time, Lebanon was still part of the Ottoman Empire. After World War I, however, the League of Nations decreed that the provinces that today make up the Lebanese state be placed under France's direct control. You can guess the impact that such a mandate had on the local wine industry. Lebanon achieved its independence before the end of World War II, while the Germans still occupied France.

Much of Lebanon's wine renaissance can be credited to Chateau Musar, whose legacy dates back to 1930, when Gaston Hochar founded the company; it remains family owned to this day. There are currently some forty wineries in Lebanon, producing roughly eight million bottles; half slake the thirst of the local population (the Lebanese drink another four million imported bottles) and the other half gets exported to nearly seventy countries around the world.

Lebanon benefits from about three hundred sunny days a year, even more than California's average. That translates to an attractively long grape-growing season. You're likely to find the usual European varietals, as well as more iconoclastic wines made from indigenous grapes. Two varietals that are unique to Lebanon find their way into the country's wines: Obaideh, which bears a slight resemblance to Chardonnay, and Merwah, whose closest relative is the gold-skinned Sémillon, known for sweeter wines like Sauternes. Chateau Musar uses both Obaideh and Merwah in its signature white and rosé blends.

With any suboptimal grapes, the Hochar family produces arak (though they use the spelling arack), and they claim that their distillation method bucks tradition. Most araks are distilled three times, with anise seeds added in the third distillation. However, Chateau Musar distills the spirit four times, with the seeds added in the fourth go-round. Arak long had been the traditional drink of choice during meals among the imbibing Lebanese population. While that is still the case, modern citizens increasingly have followed the lead of much of the rest of the world and integrated

ARAK-TAIL

Cocktails haven't traditionally been the preferred delivery method for the anise-y goodness that is arak, but more and more international bartenders are discovering—and working wonders with—this ancient spirit of the Middle East.

☞ ADELAIDE

You could say that this drink comes from Lebanon by way of Charleston, South Carolina. It's the creation of Bethany Kocak at McCrady's Tavern in the charming Southern city.

⇒ DIRECTIONS ⇐

Shake arak, vermouth, elderflower syrup or liqueur, lime juice, and strawberry syrup with ice and strain over ice into a rocks glass.

Top off with club soda and garnish with lime twist.

⇒ INGREDIENTS ⇐

30 ml (1 ounce) Chateau Musar Arack

15 ml (½ ounce) Dolin dry vermouth

7 ml (¼ ounce) elderflower syrup or elderflower liqueur

25 ml (¾ ounce) fresh lime juice

15 ml (½ ounce) strawberry syrup

Club soda

Lime twist, for garnish

77

wine into their regular meals (it's a lot milder, after all, and pairs better with most types of food).

Conventional wisdom suggests that it's the large Christian population—nearly half of all Lebanese—doing all the drinking, while Muslims abstain. However, industry observers suggest that many Muslims must be partaking as well, since they say Lebanese wine consumption drops dramatically during the holy month of Ramadan. As noble as Lebanese Christians may be, it's not likely that they're abstaining out of deference for their Muslim brethren.

But you didn't hear that from me.

⋈ Temple of Bacchus

In ancient Rome, there was a deity for everything and, considering the fact that the Romans really liked a good glass of fermented grape juice, it's only logical that Bacchus, the god of wine, existed in the upper echelons of god-dom. When gods are particularly revered, they get their own extra-special temples. There were quite a few such structures of worship dedicated to Bacchus, but the most famous is the one the Romans erected sometime between the second and third centuries AD in Ba'albek, in what is now Lebanon. Nearly two millennia later, the United Nations Educational, Scientific and Cultural Organization (UNESCO) designated it a World Heritage Site. The fact that Rome chose Ba'albek speaks to the importance of Lebanon as a central wine-producing region of the ancient world—and it's now finally starting to make its comeback.

United Arab Emirates

When most Westerners think of the United Arab Emirates—or, more specifically, its two most famous cities, Dubai and Abu Dhabi—images of decadent displays of wealth and a garish Las Vegas–like artifice come to mind. But make no mistake: Whatever happens in Vegas may stay in Vegas, but if you apply that credo to a holiday in Dubai, the only thing staying in Dubai will likely be you—in a jail cell. Non-Muslim locals and expats must apply for a license to drink at home, and it's valid only in the individual emirate that issued the permit. As far as drinking in bars and restaurants is concerned, non-Muslim residents must obtain a special license to do that as well. Muslims shouldn't even bother applying, because it's against the law.

Non-Muslim locals who choose to drink at a bar or nightclub had better learn a thing or two about moderation. It's a criminal offense to be under the influence of alcohol in public; even simple possession of said beverage in public is a prosecutable offense.

What if you're just visiting? Technically, the law requires a license for tourists drinking in public, but it's not as if there will be spot checks for visitors drinking in licensed hotels and other establishments. However, if you find yourself in the middle of any sort of disturbing-the-peace-type scenario or other shenanigans that require police assistance at these venues, you can bet that the cops are going to charge you with drinking without a license.

Sounds like a blast, doesn't it? Makes you not want to drink, doesn't it? Relax, there's plenty to enjoy in Dubai and Abu Dhabi. Just be sensible about it.

You're not likely to find what one would consider an "authentic" UAE drinking experience. Most of the alcohol-licensed establishments sell beers, wines, and spirits imported from other cultures. And the cocktails are likely to be derivative of non–Middle Eastern traditions as well. For instance, the popular London tiki lounge Mahiki opened a Dubai location in 2011.

Saudi Arabia

It's no surprise that the country that's home to the sacred city of Mecca would have extremely strict alcohol laws. It's impossible to buy alcohol legally in Saudi Arabia. And it certainly wouldn't be a pleasant experience to get caught with it, especially if it's the Islamic religious police, known as the Mutaween, who catch you. (Expect to do a little time.)

Saudis generally follow the law—publicly, anyway—but that's not to say alcohol is completely absent from the country. Expats living there, as well as many native Saudis, can get their hands on booze in a number of ways. The more connected and well-to-do of the bunch often find access to major international brands on the black market. Those who don't have such resources or don't want to risk getting ratted out by anyone in that illicit supply chain are more likely to make their own alcohol—kind of a crude form of home brewing, akin to the DIY stuff many mild-mannered scofflaws were churning out during U.S. Prohibition for their own consumption. Those who don't want to bother going through that process, but know people who do, just buy the contraband off of those individuals.

There seems to be the least risk involved with making it yourself, mainly because there's no transportation involved. You never know when you might encounter a roadblock—a fairly frequent occurrence—and if it's the Mutaween running the checkpoint, things are not going to end well for you. Much of the time, drinking is limited to residential compounds that primarily house expats and visiting foreign workers. Sometimes there are full-on parties within those residences.

It's easy enough to buy the necessary ingredients legally—usually just fruit and/or sugar that will be fermented and then distilled. Friends who've lived in Muslim countries have told me there's a sort of "wink-wink" attitude with the sale of not only the ingredients, but also vessels that will clearly be used for fermentation: "I have no idea what you're going to use this for, but everything you need is right over there."

The classic homemade (and, remember, unlawful) tipple in Saudi Arabia is a concoction called siddique. It's essentially fermented sugar water that's then distilled to increase its strength—think of it as simple syrup that's turned into alcohol. The final distillate often clocks in at about 90 percent alcohol by volume. The drinker typically dilutes it to make it palatable and to stretch out the supply, turning one bottle of the stuff into three.

Those who buy siddique from other producers need to be extremely careful. Like moonshine during Prohibition, less reputable (or simply less competent) producers can end up peddling poison. You know that term "blind drunk"? It may be hyperbole to us today, but its origins are very real. Ethanol, remember, is the alcohol we can drink. Methanol is the one that can cause blindness and/or death, so if there's even the remotest chance that it is present in what you purchased, you have to ask yourself, "How badly do I want this drink?"

Sometimes it's important to hear a real-world cautionary tale: Consider the plight of a seventy-four-year-old Brit by the name of Karl Andree, who had been living in Saudi Arabia for twenty-five years. The BBC reported that Andree got caught with homemade wine in 2014 and ultimately ended up serving more than fourteen months in prison. The news agency also cited reports that Andree was sentenced to some pretty severe corporal punishment—360 lashes!—but the government decided to forgo such a beating because of Andree's advanced age.

The only truly legal drinking option for those who live in Saudi Arabia is to head to nearby countries with more liberal alcohol laws. However, even that's getting a bit harder to do, as you'll learn in the next section. . . .

Bahrain

The Kingdom of Bahrain, a relatively small island situated off the eastern coast of Saudi Arabia in the Persian Gulf, is accessible from the Arabian Peninsula via the sixteen-mile-long King Fahd Causeway. The causeway has been dubbed Johnnie Walker Bridge by many because about a hundred thousand passengers traverse the roadway each week, many of whom are seeking a legal drink on the island.

It's no free-for-all, however. The government restricts alcohol sales to non-Muslims, who may purchase it only in hotels and a limited number of off-license shops. In recent years, Bahrain's Culture Ministry has intensified these restrictions. In 2009, it banned alcohol sales in one- and two-star hotels; five years later, it did the same for three-star hotels. The measures were implemented incredibly swiftly, putting a financial burden on hoteliers. (Those who operate four-star establishments are probably getting pretty nervous right about now.) The ministry's stated rationale is that they want to encourage family tourism.

In the places where strong drinks haven't been prohibited, you're likely to find plenty of the aforementioned Johnnie Walker, as well as other iconic global brands. There's even some world-class mixology happening in those higher-end hospitality venues. In fact, in 2015, Sofitel Bahrain hosted its first-ever Mixology Week. But for a taste of something more traditional, there's always the old standby, arak.

Qatar

To the east and south of Bahrain, jutting into the Persian Gulf, lies the peninsula that is Qatar, an oil-rich, developed country whose attitudes toward alcohol somewhat resemble those of the nearby island nation—or at least they resemble what Bahrain's could be if that country continues the trend of gradually tightening restrictions. Like many other now-independent states in the region, Qatar spent a great deal of time as part of the Ottoman Empire, until becoming a British protectorate after World War I. It finally gained its independence in 1971.

Similar to the situation in Bahrain, five-star hotels are essentially the only places a person can get a drink in Qatar—and that person must be a non-Muslim expatriate and a long-term resident.

It wasn't too long ago that non-Muslims could also buy a drink on a manmade island near the capital city of Doha. However, the government rendered that illegal in 2011.

Those who wish to drink at home have only one option: Qatar Distribution Company (QDC), the sole business licensed to sell alcohol. It's also where the hotels buy their booze. Getting to it, for many, involves a trek. There are some additional headaches associated with that trip: transporting alcohol within the country is, technically, verboten, except to take it straight home from QDC's warehouse on the day of purchase.

Those wishing to purchase alcohol must possess not only a residence permit (usually available to those contracted to work for a lengthy period of time) but a permit to buy liquor as well. A person can't even set foot in the store without both. It goes without saying that those seeking the permit must swear an oath that they are not Muslim. If they're found to be lying, the consequences can be quite severe—from fines to imprisonment to possible corporal punishment, or any combination of the three.

In addition, QDC requires a letter from the applicant's employer; the letter must include specific information, such as the applicant's exact job title, salary, and marital status. Each applicant has to pay a deposit of 1,000 Qatar riyals (about US$275) and submit a copy of a valid passport and a copy of their residence permit. If everything checks out, the applicant gets access to a not-half-bad selection of international wine, spirits, and beer.

But that doesn't mean folks can expect to go on a shopping spree. There's a strict quota on how much booze an individual can buy. Total alcohol purchases at any one visit cannot exceed 10 percent of the person's monthly salary. Reasonable enough—if you're spending more than 10 percent of your income on booze, it might be time to rethink your priorities.

QDC is also the only company in Qatar that sells pork, but no additional permit is required; the alcohol license enables a shopper to buy the flesh of the pig, too. However, keep in mind

83

that Qatar has in the past completely banned pork and placed even tighter restrictions on alcohol purchases. It's really up to the whims of the ruling regime.

Qatar was probably not even on the average Westerner's radar until the Fédération Internationale de Football Association (better known throughout the world as FIFA) announced that it would be the host country for the 2022 World Cup. (Qatar had also made failed bids to host the Olympic games in 2016, 2020, and 2024.) Aside from being the biggest soccer event in the world, the World Cup is also quite the party. But without alcohol? Not necessarily. The Qatari government has indicated that it is open to designating special "fan zones" where alcohol may be sold. After all, the FIFA event is big business for anyone who makes a beverage, from soft drinks to beer, and it's also a huge sponsorship opportunity for the marketers of said products. In the end, commerce always prevails!

⚔ The Arak Ritual

The traditional arak consumption method isn't radically different from that of another anise-flavored spirit: absinthe. As with absinthe, the arak ritual calls for water—one part arak to two parts water. The water clouds the spirit—known in absinthe circles as louching—giving it a semi-translucent, milky color. The resulting concoction owes its appearance to the presence of anethole, a naturally occurring oil in anise, that dissolves in alcohol but not in water. Ice can cause the anethole to crystallize, so many won't include frozen water in the arak ritual (however, it tastes damned good over ice—trust me!).

⚔ Arak and Roll

Personal anecdote alert! Arak is one of the newest spirits in my life; I was already over forty the first time I tried it. But I'm always going to remember that moment probably better than my inaugural sip of any other spirit, because of the context. I was in Oakland, California, for a conference and was heading back east on a redeye that didn't leave until 11:53 P.M. I reached out to my friend Dean in San Francisco and he invited me to join him for his usual Friday night ritual: sipping arak while thumbing through new arrivals at Rooky Ricardo's Records in Lower Haight. Dean, who's half Syrian, developed an affinity for it when some Syrian friends in New York insisted he drink it alongside shankleesh, the only mold-ripened cheese of the Middle East. The night he introduced me to it ranks as one of my top-ten drinking moments—sipping a glass of water-clouded arak surrounded by a sea of vinyl while the crackle of vintage soul music piped through the speakers.

+≡ *Chapter 5* ≡+

AFRICA

Africa is huge. It's the second largest continent on earth (behind Asia) and the one with the most officially recognized countries (fifty-three at last count), made up of thousands of different ethnic groups and thousands of different languages or dialects within languages. So it's no surprise that there's a staggering diversity of customs—including those on the beverage side of things. But there are some recurring themes across many of the countries, and some customs and traditions that are regional in nature, with variations here and there.

Aside from the European-born beverage styles that invading colonial powers brought with them to Africa over the centuries, there's a host of traditional drinks that make the most of the local agriculture, from fruits and nuts to the ubiquitous cereal, sorghum. Even as more and more Africans gravitate toward mass-market beer and spirits, there still are pockets of the populace who—for economic reasons, largely—regularly consume the indigenous beverages.

NORTH AFRICA

The more "ancient" ancient history becomes, the more debate there is among its most educated scholars about who did what, what started where, and when exactly we'll find the answers to those questions. There rarely has been much dispute, however, about North Africa's role in creating some of the earliest alcoholic beverages.

But today, most of the region's sovereign states—like many of those in western Asia—are Muslim-dominated countries. At one extreme, alcohol is completely banned; at the other, there's a certain permissiveness regarding such beverages, at least as far as the non-Muslim minorities are concerned. And somewhere therein exists a nebulous gray area where beer, wine, and spirits are banned but their consumption is a bit of an open secret across the populace.

Libya

88

Take Libya, for example. Ninety-seven percent of Libya's population is Muslim, so it's safe to say that the country's relationship with alcohol is uneasy at best. The sale and consumption of alcohol are prohibited in the country, but those who want a name-brand international whisky, for instance, can get it if they want it. They just have to pay through the nose for it because it's contraband. The cheaper option is the local hooch called bokha, distilled from fermented regional fruits like dates, figs, and grapes. It's easy enough for an ordinary person to make the stuff: Just throw some yeast in a bowl of fruit, let it ferment for a couple of days, boil it in a makeshift still—usually a modified pressure cooker—and voilà! Booze! But of course, not everyone wants to make their own, so they resort to purchasing it from any number of unsavory suppliers. And that isn't always the best idea. In 2013, Libya had a massive health calamity on its hands when dozens—various reports say sixty, others as many as eighty—of Tripoli residents died from methanol-tainted black-market bokha. Another fifteen hundred or so got severely ill.

The crisis reopened the debate over whether Libya's alcohol ban should be lifted. (The ban, by the way, is a holdover from the Muammar Gaddafi days. He's long gone, but the prohibition still stands.) Legalizing alcohol would enable the government to control its production and distribution and, in theory, eliminate or dramatically hinder the market for the underground version. The move wouldn't be unlike what happened in Kenya, when that country decided to lift the ban on the local moonshine known as chang'aa in an effort to put black marketeers out of business and ensure that the available product was safe and completely on the up-and-up.

Tunisia

Bokha is actually a moonshine-y corruption of boukha, a legal, fig-based brandy created in Tunisia nearly a century and a half ago. (Boukha translates to "alcohol vapor," which can apply to anything that's distilled, for that matter.) As with many a European eau-de-vie, drinkers typically consume it chilled, in a small glass, after dinner. Commercial brands have an ABV in the high 30s to 40 percent.

Among the best-known brands is Boukha Bokobsa, which traces its origin to 1880. It's not widely known that around that time there were some thirty thousand Jews living in relative harmony with the Muslim population under the rule of Ahmad I, head of the Husainid Dynasty, which reigned from 1705 to 1957. The monarch famously attempted to Westernize his country and break away from the Ottoman Empire, an ultimately failed effort. He also abolished slavery (nearly twenty years before the United States, I might add) and generally improved conditions for the Jewish population, which had for centuries endured waves of hardship and persecution. When Ahmad I died in 1855, his cousin Muhammad succeeded him and enacted a constitution that guaranteed religious freedom for all (though it was more the result of pressure from Europe than altruism). The constitution proved short-lived, thanks to a revolution in 1864, but Jews generally continued to enjoy fair treatment, mainly because the government feared reprisals from Europe.

It was against this backdrop that Abraham Bokobsa, a Jew, was able to launch Boukha Bokobsa. Born in 1857, Bokobsa lived on his family's land outside of Tunis, where he grew some citrus fruits, figs, and dates. Kosher beverages for sipping on the Sabbath were difficult to come by in those parts, so Bokobsa set out to make a brandy for just that purpose. He attempted to distill dates, but the result was less than stellar. He tried figs next, and Bouhka Bokobsa was born. Shortly after he started making the brandy in 1880, he obtained the permission of Tunisia's chief rabbi to sell it to others in the Jewish community.

A year later, Tunisia became a French protectorate, which was a promising development for Tunisian Jews, as France was among the first countries to recognize the equal rights of Jews in that century. The protectorate years exposed Tunisian Jews to European culture and granted them greater access to education. Bokobsa's son, Jacques (Yaacov), studied modern winemaking and brandy distillation in France, then brought back this knowledge to the family business. His education seemed to have paid off, as the father-son team won a silver medal in the Brussels International Exposition in 1897 (it helped that Belgian King Leopold II tasted Bouhka Bokobsa and reportedly was enamored of it).

As the new century began, boukha's popularity expanded beyond the Tunisian Jewish community and soon became the national drink of Tunisia. Within the Jewish community, it was as popular as ever—so much so that it became a part of the bris ritual: It was customary at the time to put a drop of boukha on the baby boy's lips immediately prior to circumcision.

BOUKHA COCKTAILS

The Bokobsa family recommends these drinks as a good intro to the fig-based eau-de-vie that their great-great-great-grandfather created.

☞ CARTHAGO

Here's something to jazz up even the dullest of sparkling wines.

⇢▷ DIRECTIONS ◁	⇢▷ INGREDIENTS ◁
Pour boukha into a Champagne or wine glass.	30 ml (1 ounce) freezer-chilled Boukha Bokobsa
Fill with sparkling wine and garnish with a strip of lemon peel.	120 ml (4 ounces) Pearl white sparkling wine or Bartenura Moscato
	Lemon peel, for garnish

☞ SALAMBO

Think of it as a bit of a Tunisian spin on a Greyhound.

⇢▷ DIRECTIONS ◁	⇢▷ INGREDIENTS ◁
Pour boukha and pink grapefruit juice over ice in a small tumbler and stir.	30 ml (1 ounce) freezer-chilled Boukha Bokobsa
	90 ml (3 ounces) fresh pink grapefruit juice

The good times wouldn't last long, however. North Africa, of course, was a major theater of battle during World War II and, despite the fact that it was not part of the European continent, it was not spared during the Holocaust. By the time the Nazis got to Tunisia in 1942, the number of Jews living there had risen to one hundred thousand. Germany imposed the same anti-Semitic policies in Tunisia as it had in its occupied European territories. The ruler at that time, Moncef, tried to free Tunis from French rule and establish an independent state, and also attempted to resist imposing the Nazis' hateful policies, but was unsuccessful. More than five thousand Tunisian Jews were sent to concentration camps in Europe; that number could have been much larger had the Allies not expelled the Nazis in May 1943.

Lionel Bokobsa, part of the sixth generation of the Bokobsa spirits-making family, now runs the company with his cousins Clarisse and Rebecca Bokobsa. He explains that boukha was able to transcend the Jewish community and establish itself as a truly national product because of the relatively rare harmony among the religious and ethnic groups in North Africa during the nineteenth and early twentieth century. "Jews and Arabs in Tunisia, they were like this," Bokobsa explains, putting two fingers together. "Even in Morocco and in Algeria, Jews were living in peace with Arabs, no problem."

Moroccan King Mohammed V is particularly notable for his protection of North African Jews during World War II. By many accounts, when a German officer told Mohammed V that he wanted all the Jews in Morocco to wear yellow stars, the king reportedly told the Nazi that he'd have to order eight million stars because he'd require every citizen to wear them in solidarity.

After the war, there were multiple waves of Jewish emigration from Tunisia, first to the newly created state of Israel in 1948 and then to France after Tunisia achieved independence in 1956. The 1960s saw a rise in anti-Semitism and the nationalization of land (including that of the Bokobsa family), which prompted more Jews to leave the country. Today, there are fewer than two thousand Jews living in Tunisia, a mere 2 percent of the country's peak Jewish population.

"My grandfather decided that for the next generation, the future was not in Tunisia anymore," says Lionel Bokobsa. But Jewish emigration from Tunisia was not the end of Boukha Bokobsa. In 1966, brothers Albert and Leon Bokobsa—the latter was Lionel's granddad—launched a new wine- and boukha-making company, SIEVA, in Paris. The family still owns a distillery in Tunisia, but it's managed locally, and all its output is for the domestic market. So chances are, if you visit Tunisia, the boukha you're drinking is still a 100 percent local product.

Today, boukha has a reputation for pairing remarkably well with salty dishes. In the Jewish community, families traditionally gather in the living room before the Sabbath dinner and sip boukha while eating crackers topped with boutargue, salty dried fish roe (known more commonly by its Italian name, bottarga). Lionel Bokobsa recommends letting the bottle of boukha get good and frosty in the freezer before pouring it. It works as an aperitif, during the meal, and even as a digestif after the meal. Bartenders are starting to have a bit of fun mixing boukha in cocktails as well.

⋈ Egyptian Influence

Tunisia, Morocco, and the rest of North Africa—and most of the world, for that matter—owe a huge debt of gratitude to Egypt for the fact that anyone's drinking alcohol at all.

The ancient Egyptians were among the world's oldest brewers (the Sumerians, in what's now Iraq, are widely considered to be the first). Nothing in those days happened without some sort of divine intervention—the perception of such a force, that is— and the god Osiris gets the credit for teaching the ancient North African people how to brew. Well, make that *half* of the people, since women were the first brewers—remember that the next time you read an article about the "novelty" of the growing number of female brewers! But Osiris is not the *official* brewing deity; that honor belongs to the ancient goddess Tjenenet.

Bread was the earliest beer base. The brewers would break it into smaller pieces, pour water on it, and strain it through a sieve. Hops weren't used that far back, so they'd flavor the beer with dates or other fruits and then let it sit in a fermentation vessel until the supernatural forces—what we now call yeast—had their way with it. It likely tasted radically different from what we consider beer today. It also probably had a very thick, porridge-like consistency. Indeed, it was a form of sustenance that was often used as a method of payment for workers.

Today, beer plays a far smaller role in the everyday life of those living in the predominantly Muslim society. It is legally produced and available (officially to only the non-Muslim segments of the country but unofficially to, well, everyone), but the outlets in which it is for sale are relatively limited. The biggest retail chain for alcohol in the country is Drinkies, a subsidiary of the company that also controls most of the beverages' production and distribution, Al Ahram. Alcohol is also available in many pubs and hotels throughout the country.

WEST AFRICA

When a region is as close to the equator as much of Africa is, you can expect there to be a lot of palm trees. It should come as no surprise, then, that palms are a popular base for the traditional beverages produced in many of the countries in the northwestern chunk of the continent. Their drinks may go by different names in the various local languages and dialects, but they're all essentially palm wine.

In many West African countries, particularly Senegal, Gambia, and Guinea-Bissau, a sweet, mildly alcoholic palm wine (usually no more than 7 percent ABV) called bounok is quite pervasive. When it's good, expect it to taste like a tropical fruit juice with a slight kick of alcohol.

"It tastes better than it smells," concedes British-born Simon Fenton, a travel writer and author of the West Africa–based books *Squirting Milk at Chameleons: An Accidental African* and *Chasing Hornbills: Up to My Neck in Africa.* "Sometimes you can get a bit of a drain-like whiff that could put people off. If you were able to take the smell away, it would taste sweet." Fenton, who runs a guesthouse in Senegal with his Senegalese wife, has grown quite fond of bounok, though he cautions that it is a bit of an acquired taste.

Typically, tappers climb up the palm, pierce the tree, and funnel the coconut water–like sap through a palm leaf into a bucket. The producers let it ferment for a day or so, and then it's ready to drink. In fact, it's best not to let it ferment longer than two or three days, because after that, the flavor becomes unpleasantly pungent—which is a diplomatic way of saying "rancid."

"I like it when it's not too far gone," says Fenton. In May 2017, several months after I interviewed Fenton, he died tragically in a road accident. I offer my heartfelt condolences to his family and friends.

After the tappers return to town with their buckets full of bounok, they pour it into whatever bottles are available to them— empties that once held Coca-Cola or water, for instance—and sell it. (Be wary of bounok in plastic bottles; if the lid's too tight, it will likely explode within about twelve hours of bottling, since it continues to actively ferment once in the container.) Those who live in more rural bush villages are usually producing bounok for personal consumption or bartering purposes.

Producers of commercially available versions—which are more common in Gambia and Guinea-Bissau than in Senegal—halt the fermentation process through pasteurization or similar methods.

Senegal is a predominantly Muslim country, so most of bounok's consumption occurs within the Christian and other non-Islamic communities. There's also a considerable animist influence in the country, and the beverage often appears in ceremonies related to animism.

95

The typical bounok drinker these days is likely to be an older male, as they're the ones who grew up with it. Younger drinkers gravitate a bit more toward beer and other more widely known beverages. But bounok's low cost relative to more commercially available drinks makes it a favorite in rural areas.

The consumption of bounok is a communal event. Drinkers gather around a central bowl, often a large calabash (a hollowed-out dried gourd), and scoop up the bounok with a ladle made from a hollowed-out coconut shell with a stick attached (these days it's just as common to find people cobbling together a ladle out of a stick and an empty mayonnaise jar). One person sips from the ladle, then passes it on to the next person.

{ A COMMUNAL BOWL OF SENEGALESE BOUNOK
Photo: Simon Fenton }

In some West African countries, particularly Ghana, there's a homegrown spirit known as akpeteshie that's primarily made from distilling the wine of the palm nut (sometimes producers distill it from palm sap or, less frequently, from sugarcane juice, not unlike the process for rum). It's known to be incredibly potent; it comes off crude pot stills anywhere from 40 to 70 percent ABV—or even higher. It's advisable to mix it with water, but most in the region drink it completely uncut. And, as you might suspect with such a potent, rough-around-the-edges spirit, it's got a reputation for being akin to drinking fire. You're not going to find any national brands in flashy packaging. Most of it is home-distilled and poured into used, unlabeled bottles.

The word "akpeteshie" signifies its illicit history—it's actually a relatively modern term for the locally produced alcohol.

Distilling was widespread in the region prior to British colonization in the mid-nineteenth century (when Britain christened the
country "the Gold Coast"). By the '30s, the colonial government
had banned such distillation, forcing it underground. Akpeteshie
means, roughly, "to hide" or "hidden." The government said it was
for safety, but the more cynical (and probably correct) view is that
the colonials wanted to control the local alcohol trade and not be
undercut by this cheap liquor.

A side effect was that akpeteshie ultimately became a symbol
of the anti-colonial movement. Ghana gained its independence
in 1957, and the new republic's government legalized the spirit
five years later. Even when legalized, though, akpeteshie still had
a reputation as a poor person's beverage. The presence of various
impurities and fusel oils made it somewhat unpleasant to drink—
though a bit of a rite of passage nonetheless. It was dirt cheap
versus the other, imported alcohols available—in some cases just
north of a dime a shot.

In those early days, it was a social drink, no doubt about that.
But, it's also kind of an antisocial one as well. In other words, it's
legal, but not entirely socially accepted. This was not an uncommon phenomenon in many parts of Africa. The highly religious
would go to church all week and then consume considerable
quantities of akpeteshie in the privacy of their own homes, away
from the prying eyes and judgment of their neighbors (who were
probably doing the same thing!).

Perceptions, however, can change—especially if the entrepre-
neurially minded have anything to say about it. Some five decades
later, akpeteshie is enjoying something of a resurgence among the
young trendy set. Fashionable bartenders in Ghana's biggest cities
are using it to great effect as a base in their craft cocktails. Among
those leading the revolution is Tapatheo Amu Nyamekye, the bar
manager at the cocktail-enhanced eatery Burger & Relish in Ghana's capital, Accra. He's also the acting president of the burgeoning
Ghana Bartenders Guild. Akpeteshie and other locally sourced

beverages are also the specialty at another Accra bar, the Republic, run by brothers Raja and Kofi Owusu-Ansah.

Similar beverages take on different names in nearby West African countries, but they're more or less the same concept. In Nigeria, the distilled-palm-sap-wine beverage is called ogogoro, which is among the locally produced hooches across the continent that have gained unwanted notoriety. In 2015, news agencies reported that scores of people died after drinking batches of ogogoro that contained unsafe levels of methanol. The Nigerian federal government subsequently banned ogogoro consumption.

But in a number of countries, production of palm wines and spirits derived from those wines is on the up-and-up. In Benin, the spirit distilled from palm wine goes by the name of sodabi—more or less their own regional variation of akpeteshie—and is mostly a homemade beverage produced in small villages and sold unbranded in reused bottles at roadside stands or in tiny boutiques. (When the Spanish and French began colonizing the region—and engaging in the slave trade—they brought with them distilling technology and skills, which the locals learned.) While there's a certain moonshine-esque element to its production and distribution, sodabi is, for the most part, legal (or at least in a legal gray area). There's a much different economic situation there than in much of the Western world, as informal businesses account for a significant portion of people's incomes.

The region is considered the birthplace of voodoo (voudou in French, and often spelled vodun). It arrived in New Orleans and the Caribbean via the slave trade, with some modifications along the way—and sodabi plays a prominent role in many West African voodoo rituals. (A sizeable chunk of the population still practices the religion, while others have infused major faiths like Christianity with voodoo's iconography and customs.)

Alcohol is a big part of what voodoo practitioners offer up to the spirits during rituals. "Sometimes when they wanted to get in a trance mode, they would drink a lot, because they believe the beverage helps facilitate that and helps them communicate with the spirits," says Beninese expat Leila Abdoulaye, who runs a food and beverage marketing company called Palatable Marketing in New York.

Sodabi also makes an appearance in more mainstream events like baptisms, marriages, and funerals. Usually, participants drink it in the form of shots, because much of the DIY stuff can be a bit rough. Producers customarily steep herbs, spices, and other botanicals in it to soften some of those hard edges. It's not uncommon for locals to buy the clear base spirit, sans botanicals, and infuse it with their own recipes back home. As Abdoulaye says, "You grew up knowing sodabi."

The Beninese government has started to regulate the sodabi production process to make the drink a bit safer to consume—there had been some accidental methanol poisonings in the past—and it's starting to appear in more conventional retail settings. There are even some full-fledged commercial brands available. One of those is Tambour Original, which is expanding beyond West Africa (with the help of a crowdfunding campaign) and is now available in Europe and North America. It's distilled twice and then finished in small batches, and flavored with American oak, hibiscus, dates, honey, and assorted local tropical fruits and spices (fourteen spices and botanicals in all), which steep in the spirit for a period of three months. It's bottled at 45 percent alcohol by volume (90 proof).

Tambour Original is the product of a collaboration between a pair of American entrepreneurs and Beninese farmers; one of the former had served in Benin in the Peace Corps and became enamored of sodabi. He shared it with a friend, and the two ultimately decided to start a business in Benin's largest city, Cotonou. The cocktail culture is extremely new in Benin and other parts of West Africa, but bartenders are already developing drinks with Tambour Original. It goes especially well with fresh fruit juices and coconut milk.

WEST AFRICAN COCKTAILS

The makers of Tambour Original sodabi entice drinkers to try the distilled palm-sap spirit in a number of approachable cocktails.

☞ AFRICAN SUNRISE

Tequila Sunrise fans should recognize this Benin-inspired twist.

⇢⇒ DIRECTIONS ⇐⇠	⇢⇒ INGREDIENTS ⇐⇠
Combine sodabi and pineapple juice in a shaker with ice.	60 ml (2 ounces) Tambour Original sodabi
Pour into a rocks glass filled with ice and add club soda.	60 ml (2 ounces) fresh pineapple juice
	30 ml (1 ounce) club soda

☞ AFRICAN QUEEN

Dig up an old DVD of the Bogart-Hepburn classic and sip this one as you marvel at their vintage Hollywood chemistry. (Full disclosure: the drink has nothing to do with the movie.)

⇢⇒ DIRECTIONS ⇐⇠	⇢⇒ INGREDIENTS ⇐⇠
Muddle diced cucumber, mint, and sugar in a bowl.	¼ cup diced cucumber, plus 1 cucumber slice for garnish
Add sodabi and lime juice and stir until sugar is dissolved.	1 large mint sprig
Pour into a tumbler or rocks glass, add ice, and garnish with cucumber slice.	2 tablespoons brown sugar
	90 ml (3 ounces) Tambour Original sodabi
	60 ml (2 ounces) fresh lime juice

☞ HIDDEN PASSION

This is a bit like the African Queen's passionate, cucumber-less cousin.

⇢ DIRECTIONS ⇠	⇢ INGREDIENTS ⇠
Pour sodabi, juices, and sugar into a tumbler or rocks glass and stir until sugar dissolves. Add ice and garnish with a lemon wedge.	60 ml (2 ounces) Tambour Original sodabi 180 ml (6 ounces) fresh passion fruit juice (from about 3 passion fruit) Juice of 1 whole lemon, plus 1 lemon wedge for garnish ½ teaspoon brown sugar

☞ KO-KO-KO

This drink wouldn't be terribly out of place at a tiki bar, considering that you'll be drinking it out of an actual coconut.

⇢ DIRECTIONS ⇠	⇢ INGREDIENTS ⇠
Combine sodabi and pineapple juice in a cocktail shaker. Extract the juice from the coconut and add it to shaker, along with ice. Grate nutmeg and add shavings to shaker (or sprinkle it in if already grated). Shake until cold and serve in a hollowed coconut.	120 ml (4 ounces) Tambour Original sodabi 120 ml (4 ounces) fresh pineapple juice 1 ripe coconut ½ whole nutmeg (or ½ teaspoon grated nutmeg)

101

☞ THE CURSE

Despite this drink's name, it's an absolute blessing that it's so simple to mix from so few ingredients. It's more a flavored shot than a full-on cocktail.

⇢ DIRECTIONS ⇠	⇢ INGREDIENTS ⇠
Mix all ingredients and pour into a shot glass.	30 ml (1 ounce) Tambour Original sodabi 30 ml (1 ounce) fresh lemon juice 15 ml (½ ounce) honey

☞ BANANA HARMATTAN

Hope you saved room for dessert! Skip the crème brûlée, because this drink is all you need after dinner.

→⊷ DIRECTIONS ⊶←

Combine sodabi, bananas, and ice in a blender and puree until the mixture reaches a creamy consistency.

Drizzle the inside of a glass with chocolate syrup and pour in the puree.

Top with whipped cream and chocolate flakes, then garnish with slice of banana.

→⊷ INGREDIENTS ⊶←

90 ml (3 ounces) Tambour Original sodabi

2 bananas, sliced (1 slice reserved for garnish)

½ cup cubed or crushed ice

Chocolate syrup

Whipped cream

Chocolate flakes

AKPETESHIE COCKTAILS

Tapatheo (Theo) Nyamekye has been a pioneer among West African mixologists, having turned Ghana's native spirit, akpeteshie, into world-class cocktails. Here are a few of his genius concoctions.

☞ NATIVE

Think of this as a floral, citrusy, minty, boozy smoothie.

→⊷ DIRECTIONS ⊶←

Combine all ingredients in a blender, add ice, and blend until very smooth.

Pour into a pint glass and garnish with lime wedge and mint sprig.

→⊷ INGREDIENTS ⊶←

50 ml (1⅔ ounces) akpeteshie

50 ml (1⅔ ounces) simple syrup

50 ml (1⅔ ounces) hibiscus juice (sobolo)

25 ml (¾ ounce) fresh lemon juice

Lime wedge, for garnish

Mint sprig, for garnish

☞ Salamanda
How do you like these apples?

⇥ DIRECTIONS ⇤	⇥ INGREDIENTS ⇤
In a shaker, muddle apple chunks with cinnamon-sugar and simple syrup.	Four or five fresh apple chunks, plus 1 apple fan for garnish
Add akpeteshie and lemon juice, shake vigorously, and strain over ice in a rocks glass.	1 teaspoon cinnamon-sugar
	20 ml (⅔ ounce) simple syrup
Garnish with apple fan.	50 ml (1⅔ ounces) akpeteshie
	15 ml (½ ounce) fresh lemon juice

☞ Garden of Eden
Plan a couple of days ahead on this one; you'll need to infuse the akpeteshie with lemongrass by letting it steep in a jar of the spirit for a day or two.

⇥ DIRECTIONS ⇤	⇥ INGREDIENTS ⇤
In a shaker, muddle pineapple with simple syrup.	1 fresh pineapple ring
	20 ml (⅔ ounce) simple syrup
Add akpeteshie, elderflower liqueur, and lemon juice and shake vigorously.	50 ml (1⅔ ounces) lemongrass-infused akpeteshie (1 lemongrass spear reserved for garnish)
Double-strain into a chilled coupe glass and garnish with lemongrass spear.	20 ml (⅔ ounce) elderflower liqueur
	25 ml (¾ ounce) fresh lemon juice

☞ Green Coat
If lemongrass isn't your thing but you still like infusions, try Theo's basil-infused creation. For the infusion, grab a small handful of fresh basil leaves and let them steep in the spirit for a day or two.

⇥ DIRECTIONS ⇤	⇥ INGREDIENTS ⇤
Combine akpeteshie, lemon juice, simple syrup, and basil in a shaker and shake vigorously.	50 ml (1⅔ ounces) basil-infused akpeteshie
	25 ml (¾ ounce) fresh lemon juice
Pour into a glass filled with ice and top with tonic.	25 ml (¾ ounce) simple syrup
	Handful fresh basil leaves
	Tonic water

Benin is known for a few other traditional, non-palm alcoholic beverages, such as tchapalo, fermented from corn. It's produced in a wooden vessel with lemongrass, giving it a distinct woody, floral flavor. Its alcohol content is on the low side, and it's quite refreshing, especially when served cold. A much stronger version is called tchoukoutouou (or, simply, tchouk), which sometimes adds sorghum to its grain bill. Both drinks are frequently served in calabash bowls.

EAST AFRICA

East African Highland bananas are an abundant staple crop throughout the region of East Africa. In fact, Uganda boasts the highest-per-capita banana consumption in the world, at more than a pound and a half per day (no potassium deficiencies there!). And whatever bananas the locals aren't eating (or, in some cases, exporting), they're drinking.

Bananas form the base for popular beer-like fermented beverages in Uganda, Rwanda, Burundi, and Tanzania, as well as deeper into the interior in the Democratic Republic of Congo. In Tanzania and Kenya, banana beer is known as urwaga; in Burundi and Rwanda, it's the similar-sounding urwagwa; the Ugandans call it lubisi or tonto, depending on the region.

Different regions may have different names for banana beer, but they all follow a similar production process, with slight variations here and there. Villagers harvest the bananas, let them ripen, then dump into a long, narrow tank (sometimes just a pit dug in the ground), along with some local grasses. The brewers then commence to knead and press the tank's contents with their hands and sometimes feet. That continues for quite some time, until everything is completely crushed into what looks like baby food. Once they've achieved that consistency, the artisans add water, continue to mix it, and then spread a porridge of malted millet or sorghum (or sometimes corn flour) and water on top of it. The malted cereals possess the necessary enzymes to kick-start and sustain the fermentation process—much as they do in traditional barley-based beer (the bananas lack those enzymes). The brewers then cover the tank with banana leaves and store it in a warm area to let the yeast and lactobacilli do their thing for three days, give or take. After that, the banana beer is filtered, and it's ready to drink.

Some brewers add honey to the pre-fermentation banana juice (which makes it a kind of banana beer-mead hybrid, since mead is fermented honey). That changes the beverage's name to inkangaza.

Banana beer, in its various forms and under its various monikers, can range anywhere from a mild 3 percent ABV (or possibly lower) to nearly 15 percent, depending on who's making it and how much they dilute the banana juice. Whatever the strength and whatever the locals call it, the fermented banana concoction has traditionally been a staple of events both celebratory and mournful—from weddings, births, and holidays to funerals. The Banyankole people of southwestern Uganda speak fondly of gatherings called, in the native tongue, entereko. During such events, mirth-makers often gather around a giant clay pot or calabash and take turns drinking from a straw—a truly communal experience.

The banana-based home brew has largely fallen out of fashion in recent years, as tends to happen to drinks closely associated with one's grandparents. Younger Ugandan consumers have gravitated toward packaged traditional beers and other beverages. Among those "others" is the spirit waragi, which can be distilled from tonto or any number of indigenous fermentable fruits and grains.

There's legally made waragi and then there's the moonshine version, which, as is all too often the case with illicit spirits, has been known to kill people. The one that's produced on the up-and-up is a gin that's packaged in a plastic bag (bottles can be so cumbersome!). It's drinkable and won't make you sick (when consumed in moderation, of course), but it won't be winning any international gin competitions.

But there have been significant efforts to revive the tonto tradition with packaged versions of the age-old banana concoction. One such brand is Mutaka Tonto, whose dual-contoured bottle emulates the shape of the traditional calabash vessel. I'm a huge fan of preserving indigenous beverages as local customs get overshadowed by global drinking traditions. If products like Mutaka Tonto are what it takes, then I'm all for them.

Kenya

Kenya has one of the more developed commercial alcoholic beverage markets in Africa, and its most consumed beer brand, Tusker, is recognizable across much of the continent. In the United States and other Western countries, you can easily spot a person who's recently returned from an African business trip or safari or who is close with someone who has; they're often wearing a Tusker T-shirt, most likely procured at Jomo Kenyatta International Airport in Nairobi. The lager brand has been on the market since 1922 and is today owned by the holding company East African Breweries Limited—of which the British-based spirits and beer giant Diageo is a majority owner.

But just about every populated country in the world has some national lager brand (usually owned by a larger foreign holding company), and this would get boring really fast if that's all I talked about. When it comes to Kenya, I'm more interested in something called chang'aa—made from the usual indigenous ingredients of sorghum, corn, or millet, or any combination of those—which until 2010 was completely illegal. The Kenyan government repealed the Chang'aa Prohibition Act to combat the growing problem of adulterated versions harming or, in some cases, killing people, particularly in Nairobi's Korogocho slum (about 120,000 people are crammed near a city landfill into a space about a third of a square mile in area).

There was more evidence in Kenya than in the illicit home-made hooch industries of other African countries that people were actually being poisoned; the BBC reported that around a hundred people had died from chemically tainted chang'aa, usually purchased for the equivalent of about a quarter per glass. Some versions were rumored to have included jet fuel, while others were spiked with embalming fluid (and you could have failed grade-school science and still know that it's probably not a good idea to ingest either of those in any quantity). Interestingly, a lot of similar claims had been made during U.S. Prohibition about some of the bootlegged beverages hitting the streets.

Oh, and I should probably mention at this point that chang'aa means "kill me quick" in Swahili.

Legalization was part of an effort to take business away from the handful of bad actors who were poisoning their customers. The new law stipulates that chang'aa must be bottled, sealed, and affixed with a warning label. If regulatory agencies find any traces of methanol or other harmful ingredients (stuff that belongs in a dead body or pumped into the tank of an aircraft, for instance), the producer faces a stiff penalty.

Unfortunately, legalization hasn't entirely eliminated shady activity surrounding chang'aa sales. In many areas, the local equivalent of the mob controls much of the distribution. The upside, however, has been that Nairobi's chang'aa drinkers have been able to come out of the shadows and consume the beverage in public without fear of arrest. Chang'aa will likely never be counted among the world's most celebrated and prestigious spirits, but at least fewer of its drinkers will be counted among the deceased.

Madagascar

The French controlled Madagascar, an island country off the southeastern coast of Africa (whose closest continental neighbor

107

is Mozambique), for most of the last two decades of the nine-teenth century and the first half of the twentieth (and in the twenty-first it became a household name in the West thanks to a certain DreamWorks Animation franchise). Knowing that, few will be surprised that Madagascar has a fairly robust winemaking tradition. This tradition actually predates French colonial rule, going back to the early 1800s, when Jesuit missionaries culti-vated the first vines there, though that was mostly experimental, and there was not much wine volume to speak of. It wasn't until about the 1920s that production reached a level of significance.

And it remains so today, six decades after France officially ceded its authority. (The French language remains, too; French and native Malagasy are the country's two official languages.) Still, Madagascar hasn't made much of an impact on the world stage. The international wine industry and enthusiasts don't consider its wine to be bad—just not particularly noteworthy. Generally, Madagascar's reds, whites, and rosés have the reputation as ser-viceable table wines.

The wine industry is certainly not strong enough to lift most of the country out of poverty; and Madagascar is one of the world's poorest countries. Farmers rely on exportable agricultural prod-ucts, such as vanilla. Madagascar also has an abundance of lychee fruit, mostly grown by small family farms dotted along the country's east coast. The fruit accounts for nearly a third of Malagasy farmers' income. But there's another popular use for the fruit, beyond exports: litchel, an aperitif that's made with lychee and has become one of the most popular (and flavorful) drinks in Madagascar.

A more recognizable spirit, as far as the rest of the world is concerned, also plays a key role in Madagascar's beverage produc-tion industry: rum—or perhaps we should spell it "rhum," since that's the French spelling and Madagascar is a former French col-ony. Better yet, let's call it what the locals call it: toaka gasy. The leading producer on the island is Groupe Vidzar, known for the Dzama Rhum line.

Mozambique

Within the Indian Ocean (in which Madagascar lies) is a relatively compact section of the sea known as the Mozambique Channel. And about 250 miles from Madagascar, across the narrowest point of that small body of water, is the country after which the channel is named. Like much of the rest of Africa, Mozambique fell under colonial rule; in this case it was Portugal that controlled the country in one form or another for about 475 years, from the first trading outposts circa 1500 through the Mozambican War of Independence, which ultimately resulted in a free Mozambique in 1975. Well, "free" is a relative term. A one-party Marxist government replaced colonial rule; civil war dominated the next decade and a half, killing about a million Mozambicans in the process. The country finally held free elections in 1994 and the democratic republic remains in place.

As in many African countries in the region (and in much of the rest of the world, for that matter), the beer market is more or less a monopoly. The dominant brewer is Cervejas de Moçambique (more commonly known by its acronym, CDM), a subsidiary of South African Breweries, which in 2002 acquired Miller Brewing Company to form SABMiller. Now, following the 2016 acquisition of SABMiller by Anheuser-Busch InBev, it's just one piece of the gargantuan global portfolio of the world's largest brewer.

But that's not the only beer Mozambicans drink. As with many of its neighbors, there's a considerable DIY brewing tradition in the country. The home brew in Mozambique is mostly derived from millet bran, sorghum, and/or corn, and goes by the name phombe. Most people in the rest of the world had never heard the term until early 2015, when it appeared in international news stories for a very tragic reason. Seventy-five people died and nearly two hundred others were hospitalized after attending a funeral in a village in the western part of the country. All had consumed phombe from the same drink stand, the owner of which

109

was among the fatalities. It turned out that the corn flour used in the brew's production had been contaminated with the toxic bacterium *Burkholderia gladioli* during recent floods.

It's unfortunate that drinking in Mozambique has to be linked with such a tragic event. Phombe was generally considered a safe beverage, and now it's likely to just be one big red flag.

However, there are other local alcohol-making traditions that don't have any high-profile fatalities associated with them. One of those is the beverage known as cashu; as you can probably guess by reading that word, it's derived from the nut with the similar-sounding name. As is the case with feni, the favorite beverage of Goa, India, cashu is made not from cashew nuts themselves but from cashew apples, those pseudo-fruits with which the nuts grow in tandem. Mozambicans, as well as Indians, can thank Portuguese traders for introducing the cashew to both countries—it's indigenous to Brazil.

CENTRAL AFRICA

The drinking traditions of Central Africa draw from all sorts of surrounding influences, such as the banana-based beverages of the eastern part of the continent and the palm-based drinks of the West. In places like Equatorial Guinea and the Central African Republic, for instance, you're likely to find a fair amount of homemade palm wine. In the former, there's also a traditional brew called malamba, made from fermented sugarcane and infused with local herbs and spices—anything from typical baking ingredients like cinnamon and cloves to indigenous fruits, depending on what's available. Many consider malamba to be Equatorial Guinea's national drink, but in more populous areas you're likely to find locals drinking that familiar standby, beer. (Indeed, you'll find this to be the case throughout most of Africa, especially as the beer business continues to globalize, and the multinational mega-brewers acquire regional operations and set up shop throughout the continent.)

The tipple of choice throughout many parts of the Democratic Republic of Congo is a distilled spirit called lotoko, whose alcohol content (not to mention flavor and quality) can vary wildly—it's essentially Congolese moonshine and, as such, not exactly legal. The typical base for the product is cassava, but corn and plantains are also frequently fermented and distilled into the final beverage. Some maintain that the corn version is less safe than the cassava and plantain versions, as corn-based lotoko has been known to include unhealthy levels of methanol. Best to go with the ones made from the more exotic ingredients anyway, since there's no shortage of corn-based spirits in the United States.

HORN OF AFRICA

Archaeologists and anthropologists believe that the first upright-walking proto-humans originated in the peninsular region on the central eastern coast of the African continent, from where they ultimately headed north and spread out across the world. So that's probably the best reason to raise a glass to the Horn of Africa!

My first foray into African cuisine of any kind—and I'm sure this holds true for a large percentage of Americans—was at an Ethiopian restaurant. What's not to like? An assortment of tasty, often spicy, stewed meats and vegetables are arranged atop a base of the spongy, flat, sour bread known as injera on a large circular tray for all to share. Diners are given no utensils; instead, you rip off pieces of the injera and use it to scoop the delicious food off the tray and into your mouth.

It's one of my favorite cuisines in the world, so I've always found it depressing that most Americans and Europeans identify a country with such a vibrant culinary tradition as that place with all the famines in the 1980s. (Band Aid's "Do They Know It's Christmas?," USA for Africa's "We Are the World," and the original Live Aid concert all raised money for Ethiopian famine relief.) The

111

saddest part about it is the fact that long before the Communist military dictatorship assumed control of the country in 1974 and subsequently starved much of its population, Ethiopia served as a beacon of freedom for much of the continent. It was the only African country to successfully resist European invasion and colonization during the big imperialist push across the continent during the late nineteenth and early twentieth centuries.

The oppressive military regime fell in 1991 after the breakup of the Soviet Union; today, foreign commercial interests are investing more and more in Ethiopia. And that includes beverage producers, many of which had previously been state-owned. In 1998, France's Castel Group, for instance, purchased Ethiopia's Kombolcha Brewery, known for the country's oldest beer, St. George. And the Harar Brewery, maker of its namesake pale lager brand, as well Hakim Stout, caught the eye of Heineken, which acquired the Ethiopian producer in 2011. A year later, Diageo, the British company behind Guinness but better known for its spirits portfolio, bought the country's Meta Abo Brewery.

Any one of those brews will pop up from time to time on menus at Ethiopian eateries in the States and, though they're not much to write home about in the grand scheme of the beer world, they do hit the spot when paired with the spicier elements on the table. But what really caught my eye when I started frequenting such establishments in the mid-1990s was a certain item on the wine list: t'ej. Though it's usually listed as a honey-based wine, t'ej (often written as "tej," without the apostrophe) is technically mead, given its fermentable base. It also shares a bit in common with beer, as its recipe calls for gesho, a hops-like bittering botanical that's a species of buckthorn, whose earthy bitterness plays well off the country's signature dishes. Some modern versions include hops themselves.

Since t'ej is the word for "wine" in Amharic, Ethiopia's dominant tongue, you might think you need to specify "honey t'ej" when ordering it in the country. But when Ethiopians say wine,

DIY T'EJ

☞ T'EJ AU NATUREL (WITHOUT YEAST)

For the really adventurous, we'll first explore making t'ej without the addition of yeast, allowing ambient microbes to ferment the honey. (The recipe that includes yeast follows.) Batch sizes will vary, depending on how big a vessel you have (a gallon jar or large homebrew carboy, for instance), but the ratios can be scaled up or down for any volume. Harry Kloman, who runs the blog T'ej: The Ethiopian Honey Wine (ethiopiantej.wordpress.com) and wrote the book Mesob across America: Ethiopian Food in the USA, provided this recipe and recommends using a container no smaller than a gallon. He also strongly advises that you use gesho inchet (the woodier kind) rather than gesho kitel (the crumbly leafy kind).

⤝ DIRECTIONS ⤜

Combine honey and water in a wide-mouthed gallon jar (or other vessel).

Keep in mind that you'll be buying the honey by weight but mixing it by volume.

The best way to achieve the appropriate ratio is to dump the honey into the gallon jar and then fill the empty honey container three times with water and pour that into the jar.

Blend the mixture very well with a spoon, but don't shake it.

Keep stirring until the honey has dissolved completely into the water, creating a smooth liquid with a consistent amber color.

Add the gesho inchet—3 ounces is a rough guideline; it wouldn't hurt to add a little bit less, but try not to add too much more, as it will make the t'ej a bit more pungent that you might like.

Trial and error over multiple batches will get you to the sweet—er, bitter—spot, so it's best not to overdo it on the first go-round.

⤝ INGREDIENTS ⤜

1 part honey (about 3 pounds for a 1-gallon batch)

3 parts water

3 ounces gesho inchet (for a 1-gallon batch)

Put the lid on the jar, but not too tightly—maybe just one turn, or even just place it gently on top without twisting.

If it's not a screw-top lid, put a piece of wax paper over the mouth of the jar and place the lid on top of it to keep bugs and dust out.

Make sure the environment in which the t'ej will be fermenting is warm enough—at least 70 degrees Fahrenheit, but try not to go over 80.

Don't touch the jar for a week. After the first two or three days, fuzzy mold will start to form on the gesho.

This happens only in the yeast-less method and is no cause for concern.

A couple of days later, tiny bubbles will rise from the bottom of the jar, giving the liquid a very foamy head.

When the first week is up, lift the lid, stir the mixture, close it again, and don't touch it for another week.

When the second week ends, open the jar again and remove the gesho inchet with tongs (if you use gesho kitel, you'll have to strain the liquid because the pieces are tiny).

But you're not done yet. You've got another month before the t'ej is ready.

Open and stir weekly for the next four weeks.

At the end of the fourth week after the removal of the gesho, it's time to strain the t'ej.

By all means begin tasting the t'ej after about three weeks; the drier it gets, the more sugar is consumed and, therefore, the higher in alcohol.

If it's not strong enough, it wouldn't hurt to let it go even to five weeks.

Line a wire mesh strainer with cheesecloth and place the strainer over a large pitcher.

Pour the t'ej through the cheesecloth and strainer to get rid of any residual gesho parts.

Refrigerate the pitcher of t'ej for a few days before bottling.

Sediment will form at the bottom of the pitcher during this time.

At the end of that period, pour the t'ej through a funnel into bottles (wine bottles work well, as do beer bottles; so save the empties once you finish that Cabernet or case of IPA), leaving the sediment behind.

The t'ej should keep for quite a while, without any appreciable flavor loss, as long as it's stored in the fridge.

☞ T'EJ WITH YEAST

With the natural method—the traditional way it's made in Ethiopia—
you're really at the mercy of whatever microbes may or may not be
lingering in your neighborhood and home. If you do not get the desired
result with that method, head to a home-brew shop and pick up some
trusty Saccharomyces cerevisiae—the fancy scientific name for beer
yeast—and use that in your next batch for a more consistent result.
Aside from the yeast addition, the ingredients list is the same as for the
natural version.

Begin the process the same way, mixing the same proportions of
water and honey noted above. When you've completed that step, add
the yeast. A little yeast goes a long way, so Kloman recommends a
pinch no bigger than your thumbnail—half a teaspoon, max. Cover
the jar and set it in a warm place. After thirty-six to forty-eight hours,
you should start to see a layer of white bubbles on top of the liquid (the
magic of fermentation!). A day or two after that, it will be a thick,
white foam. After a full week, stir in the gesho. Remove the gesho after
ten days and cover the jar again. After about three weeks, taste the
t'ej. If it's too sweet, give it another week or two. Filter and bottle as
described above.

they mean honey wine. It's only when a person is looking for something like a Cabernet or Merlot that they'd have to specify "grape t'ej." T'ej, or some version of honey wine, has been produced in the Horn for more than two thousand years. At least, that's about as far back as written records go—it very likely existed for a considerable amount of time before that.

"T'ej is sort of the brand name of honey wine, because it comes from Ethiopia; and Ethiopian cuisine, among all African cuisines, is so widely known in America, far more than any other cuisine in Africa," explains Harry Kloman, a professor at the University of Pittsburgh who writes about t'ej and Ethiopian cuisine and culture—and makes t'ej in his home. "Many cultures use honey to make wine, but t'ej is the sort of foundational honey wine."

Despite the hop-ish balance, t'ej is usually quite sweet, often more so than popular dessert wines. Alcohol-wise, it's usually in the same neighborhood as those, between 7 and 10 percent ABV (considerably lower than traditional mead, which can be stronger than grape wine), but producers trying to appeal to non-Ethiopian wine drinkers often ferment their t'ej to 12 or 13 percent, the same general range as grape wine. T'ej making has evolved to include a number of different varieties, with added flavors such as ginger, orange, coffee, and banana.

Commercially produced t'ej is usually exported in conventional wine bottles. But since about the nineteenth century, or perhaps even a bit earlier, t'ej has been served in Ethiopia in a brele (pronounced like "umbrella" without the "um"), a clear glass container with a bulbous bowl at its base and a narrow neck, resembling a sort of translucent genie's bottle. The brele became the preferred vessel mostly out of necessity. "The reason they exist is because when you drink a sweet wine in an African country where there are insects everywhere, the insects go after your wine," says Kloman. "But if you're drinking out of a flask with a narrow mouth on that flask, you simply put your thumb over it when you're not drinking it and that keeps the insects from getting in."

Today, there are two primary venues in which Ethiopians produce t'ej: at home and in bars known as t'ej bet (bet is derived from the Amharic word for "house"). Think of the t'ej bet as a brewpub for t'ej. The usually tiny establishments are great places for the locals to socialize over a brele or two while the proprietors make the next batches in the back. Sometimes small snack items are involved, but Ethiopians go mainly for the t'ej. Some finer restaurants also make t'ej in their kitchens, but most buy it from other producers.

One regional beverage that's a bit closer to beer without actually being beer is the home brew called t'alla. Its grain base is a combination of barley flour, whole-wheat kernels, and gesho leaves—the same bitter flora found in t'ej.

Another drink you're likely to find only if you travel to the Horn of Africa is katikala, a grain spirit that, at various times, has been called Ethiopian vodka or Ethiopian moonshine. And that of course means it's going to be a heck of a lot stronger than t'ej— expect it to be somewhere between 40 and 50 percent alcohol, depending on who's making it (there are commercial versions that are closer to the vodka-esque 40 percent/80 proof mark; the homemade stuff is anyone's guess).

SOUTHERN AFRICA

Let's jump down to the bottom of the continent, which offers an eclectic mix of beverages—everything from fine wine to moonshine.

South Africa

South Africa has had a rather . . . complicated history, to put it euphemistically. Its darkest period in modern times, of course, was the apartheid era between 1948 and 1994. However, that was just the officially implemented policy based on colonial racial segregation dating back to the seventeenth-century Dutch. When the British came, they didn't exactly improve the situation. After World War II, apartheid became the structured political system that dominated the second half of the twentieth century.

As with any part of the world that was subject to colonial rule, beverage traditions in South Africa today are an amalgam of drinks imported by the oppressors and those of the native populations. Let's address the former first.

In the seventeenth century, the Dutch East India Company—sometimes thought of as the world's first multinational mega-conglomerate—set up a supply station at the Cape of Good Hope on the Atlantic coast of South Africa's Cape Peninsula. The Dutch had recognized that it was a strategic point for ships on their way to and from Asia to stock up on fresh fruits and vegetables, as well as water (not to mention drop off any of the crew who'd fallen ill).

Johan Anthoniszoon "Jan" van Riebeeck, who had been tasked with establishing a ship-refreshment post at the Cape, discovered that wine had been somewhat effective in preventing scurvy. Since the Cape climate was hospitable to grapes, he imported some European vines, planted them, and was pressing gapes by 1659. Fast-forward twenty-six years, when a Cape governor by the name of Simon van der Stel established what would become the world-famous Constantia wine estate, known today for the well-regarded dessert wine of the same name. The South African wine industry thrived under Dutch rule, and when the Brits came on the scene in the late eighteenth century, it opened up a highly profitable export market back in Great Britain.

The local industry suffered the same devastation that Europe endured during the phylloxera epidemic of the 1860s—those nasty little aphids obliterated a huge fraction of all existing grape vines—but eventually grape growers replanted. In fact, the new vines' yields were particularly robust, which led to a glut in the early twentieth century.

For most of the twentieth century, South African wine producers weren't big players on the world stage, and things got worse
for them when the country's apartheid policies forced much of the
rest of the civilized world to boycott South African products. It
wasn't until the regime change in the 1990s that many modern
wine lovers got their first tastes of South African wines, which
quickly catapulted the country to the upper echelons of New
World winemakers.

But wine is the beverage of colonials. Native South Africans were
there first, and naturally they have their own traditional beverage customs. One of the most popular is a type of beer called umquombothi
(in the native Xhosa language), brewed from corn and sorghum
malt. Flavors vary from region to region; it's one of those "family recipe passed down from generation to generation" things.

Umquombothi is typically unfiltered, so it's usually an opaque
amber or tan color with quite a bit of sediment. It's got a sour
taste to it, making it very distinct from most common beer styles.
But it's also pretty light on the alcohol—the ABV hovers around
3 percent, so it's in the range of, say, a Berliner Weisse. And, like
a Berliner Weisse, there often are some detectable fruity esters,
courtesy of the yeast. Traditional preparation methods are rather
rustic, with the beer brewed outdoors over a fire and cooled naturally. Back in the day, it was only men who were consuming it, even
though the women were the ones making it. Drinking umquombothi was part of the Xhosa ritual of abakwetha—the initiation
into manhood, which also involves circumcision. There are also
commercially produced versions, the leading brand of which is
Chibuku, whose country of origin we'll get to in a moment.

⋇ Witblits

South Africa wouldn't be a key wine-producing country if it didn't
have some sort of brandy to call its own. That would be witblits,
which, as you can probably surmise, is a word of Dutch-derived

Afrikaans origin. It translates to "white lightning," a label commonly applied to American moonshine. Witblits is pretty much that, just a high proof (anywhere from 43 to 70 percent alcohol), and rather intense on the palate. It's not unlike Italian grappa in that it's made from the leftovers of the winemaking process. Despite its association with moonshine, it's actually quite an artisanal product. Farm distillers have refined their own recipes over many years of trial and error and continue to pass those family secrets down through the generations.

⋊ Amarula

African safaris tend to be once-in-a-lifetime, bucket-list-type trips, and I was lucky enough to participate in one through Zimbabwe and Botswana in the summer of 2014. My favorite parts of the trip (aside from coming within spitting distance of a vicious hyena and nearly face-to-face with a lion) were the mid-morning coffee breaks and the "sundowner," a sort of happy hour out in the wilds of Africa. The guides would pull over their jeeps, set up makeshift bars, and serve all sorts of beverages—mostly stuff familiar to Westerners, like beer, wine, and maybe a gin and tonic or two. It was hard to get anything truly local, beyond whatever national beer brands the guides had in their coolers—typically something from South Africa.

What I looked forward to the most, however, was the shot of Amarula Cream that I took in my tea. Most of the party enhanced their coffee with it, but I've never been much of a coffee drinker. Tea's been my preferred caffeine delivery system since my early twenties. (I've only recently recovered from a taste aversion I developed pulling all-nighters at the college newspaper office (my home for about eighteen hours of any given weekday) drinking pot after pot of bargain-basement coffee as I crammed for exams back in the early '90s.) I apparently invented a new taste sensation on the safari, as I got weird looks when I asked for Amarula in my teacup. But it really worked with tea, and I hope more folks discover this perfect marriage.

Amarula Cream is a sweet, flavorful liqueur made from a combination of the fruit that grows on marula trees indigenous to the region and, of course, cream. The fruit's a favorite snack of elephants; the pachyderms travel miles to the trees when the fruit's reached peak ripeness. That's when harvesters know it's time to gather the greenish-yellow pods. So important are elephants to the process that the bottle bears one on its label, and the liqueur producer set up the Amarula Trust to support conservation of their natural habitats.

Distillers ferment the flesh (after removing the stones), producing a sort of wine that's then distilled and combined with cream. Southern Liqueur Company of South Africa first launched it as a spirit in 1983 before releasing the cream-based cordial six years later. In 2014, the company, now a subsidiary of the international marketing corporation Distell Group Limited, launched its first cream-less version in more than thirty years, Amarula Gold. It gets its golden tint from the two years it spends in oak barrels and sports an ABV of 30 percent, versus Amarula Cream's modest 17 percent.

Amarula may be the most widely available commercial spirit to use the fruit, but its roots are steeped in an older distilling tradition in which farmers would ferment and distill whatever fruit they could get their hands on. Witblits was the typical grape brandy. But those who used marula fruit flesh in the process produced a different form of "white lightning" called maroela mampoer (using the Dutch-derived Afrikaans spelling).

Amarula, in its cream and neat varieties, may have only a few decades under its belt, but it's the closest thing you'll get to tasting the terroir of southern Africa. Sure, the wines and grape-based witblits are made with a local crop, but remember, those vines originated in Europe. The same can't be said for marula. And it's probably the only beverage that lets you commune with elephants!

121

SOUTH AFRICAN SIPS

☞ AMARULA SPICED DRAM

This is for the whisky lovers out there who want to add a little African twist to their favorite spirit. It comes courtesy of the marketers of Amarula.

→⊷ DIRECTIONS ⊶←

Stir the Amarula and whisky in a glass beaker until chilled.

Fine-strain into a chilled Champagne glass.

→⊷ INGREDIENTS ⊶←

35 ml (1 ounce + 1 teaspoon) Amarula Cream

20 ml (⅔ ounce) spice-infused whisky*

* There are spiced whiskies on the market, but it's more fun to make your own. It takes a little time, but it's not active time, just a lot of waiting. So plan accordingly. Pour 2 cups of whisky into a large mason jar. Bourbon's a good option; the spiciness of rye whisky may compete too much with the spices, so I'd avoid using that one. Add 1 cinnamon stick, 3 or 4 whole cloves, 1 or 2 pieces of star anise, 1 tablespoon juniper berries, and 1 tablespoon cardamom seeds. Cover and let the whisky sit for about 2 weeks. Voilà! Spice-infused whisky!

☞ AMARULA CITRUS CRÈME

This recipe's a little less complicated, as it doesn't involve infusing and waiting. I like this drink because it's vaguely reminiscent of one of my all-time favorite desserts (and milkshake flavors)—the orange dreamsicle.

→⊷ DIRECTIONS ⊶←

Combine Amarula and orange liqueur in a shaker and shake vigorously.

Pour into a glass over ice and garnish with strip of orange zest.

→⊷ INGREDIENTS ⊶←

50 ml (1⅔ ounces) Amarula Cream

20 ml (⅔ ounce) orange liqueur

Orange zest, for garnish

☞ AMARULA STORM IN A CUP

Here's something that's like cookies and cream in a glass—if the cookies were gingerbread and the cream had the flavor of a fruit grown on African trees.

⇢ DIRECTIONS ⇠

Combine the Amarula, whiskey, gingerbread syrup, and half-and-half in a shaker and shake well.

Fine-strain over ice in a short glass. Garnish with the crushed candy bar.

⇢ INGREDIENTS ⇠

37.5 ml (1¼ ounces) Amarula Cream

15 ml (½ ounce) Irish whiskey (Or live a little and make it a full ounce. Nobody puts Irish whiskey in the corner.)

10 ml (⅓ ounce) gingerbread syrup

50 ml (1⅔ ounces) half-and-half

Crunchie bar, crushed, for garnish*

* The original recipe calls for a garnish of a crushed Cadbury Crunchie bar. Crunchie is a milk chocolate–covered honeycomb bar available all over the UK and in countries once affiliated with Britain or members of the commonwealth. It's available in the States but kind of hard to find, but you can order it from Amazon. In a pinch, though, a chocolate-covered toffee confection like a Heath bar or even a Butterfinger (whatever the heck is in that) will also do.

123

Zambia

South Africa can't claim credit for the Chibuku brand of umquombothi; that honor belongs to Zambia. There's quite a vibrant home-brewing tradition among many of the ethnic groups that make up Zambia, a country that's divided into ten distinct provinces. In the northern provinces, particularly Luapula, the traditional fermented drink there is a beer-like concoction known as katubi. The primary fermentable in this case is millet—which, like sorghum, grows in abundance in many parts of Africa. Artisans brew it in a large earthenware pot and then let it ferment for one or several days, depending on how much sugar there is for the yeast to gobble up. It's usually heated and served warm and drunk through long straws (often hollow reeds) out of a large, hollowed-out gourd. The straw is necessary to get to the liquid below the thick layer of sediment that usually floats to the top.

On the more potent end of the spectrum, Zambians, especially in rural areas, frequently consume a distilled beverage known as kachasu. I've seen many articles refer to kachasu as a beer, but it's technically not. The fermented product that results in its first stage of production absolutely can be called a beer, but because it then goes through a distillation process, however rudimentary, it is not a true beer. Corn (or, as most people outside the United States call it, maize) is the preferred base. Artisans customarily take half-germinated maize, dry it, and then pound it until fine. (Sometimes the maize is combined with other sugar sources like banana peels.) The makers then use a sieve or winnowing basket to filter out any refuse from that process and put the mixture in cold water to ferment for several days. As with many brewed beverages, fermentation can take longer when it's colder out, because heat tends to make the yeast work faster to convert sugar to alcohol (not extreme heat, of course, which will kill the yeast; 70 to 80 or so degrees Fahrenheit is typically the ceiling for fermentation).

At the end of the fermentation period, the producer extracts the liquid and puts it into a crude still that consists of a large bowl or drum, an attached pipe, and a smaller receptacle. The maker heats the drum until the liquid boils, then the steam passes through the pipe and is cooled and recaptured in the smaller vessel. It's essentially Distilling 101.

Now, here's the thing: This is totally illegal. I guess that makes kachasu the Zambian version of moonshine. (When it's mostly corn, it is in fact a kind of rustic, rotgut version of unaged corn whiskey; put it in some charred new American oak barrels, let it sit there for at least two years, and you've essentially got a very primitive form of bourbon. But you couldn't call it bourbon unless this process happened in the States, so never mind.) It's technically not illegal for at-home consumption; it's just illegal to sell it. But that's how a lot of poor rural dwellers make ends meet.

And, as with anything intoxicating and illicit, there's plenty of fearmongering (some of it from the government) surrounding the beverage to get folks not to drink it. Some have asserted that kachasu, on occasion, can contain battery acid to enhance its kick. There hasn't been a lot of evidence to support such a claim. And anyway, kachasu distillers trying to eke out a living selling the stuff would lose a lot of potential return customers if most of them died; in rural areas, they're hard to come by in the first place. The most constructive course of action would be for the government to legalize it through some licensing process (for a nominal fee) to ensure some level of quality.

Botswana and Zimbabwe

When I visited Botswana and Zimbabwe in 2014, I was desperate to have the guides and safari camp staff tell me all they could about any of the traditional beverages their friends and families liked to drink, beyond the bottled, mass-produced beers and imported spirits that the camp bars stocked. Indigenous beverages were pretty hard to come by; it was the sort of scenario in which you had to know someone who knew someone who could procure some.

125

Similar to the customs in neighboring African countries, villagers in Botswana ferment whatever they can forage, be it sorghum, millet, corn, or any other cereals native to the region. Villagers have many names for those creations, depending on the fermentable base. If it's made with sorghum, it's known as mokuru. If it's corn-based, the most common term is laela mmago (which loosely translates to "say good-bye to your mom").

When locals want something with a bit more of a kick, they may turn to a drink called tho-tho-tho, a distilled spirit with a sorghum base. It's usually not advisable to drink it, since its alcohol content often exceeds 80 percent.

The peoples of southern Africa also have numerous fresh fruits at their disposal, and they employ them to great alcoholic effect in a variety of beverages. Among those is the fruit of the marula tree—the same source used for South Africa's Amarula Cream liqueur—which locals transform into marula beer. Villagers also turn the exotic fruit of the *Grewia flava* (commonly known as raisin bush) into fermented drinks such as mbamba and khadi. And then there's a fruit with which we Westerners are much more familiar: watermelon. The large pods that have become a staple of American cookouts in the summer are indigenous to Africa, and Botswana boasts an abundance of the fruit. Beyond the fact that they make for a sweet and refreshing snack, they're also the base for a Botswana-born beverage known as chetopoti.

To make chetopoti, the local producers hand-crush the sweet watermelon flesh by hand and then ferment it in plastic tubs or earthenware pots. The fruit ferments in the open air for three or four days. After that, the foamy liquid that forms is served in a calabash at weddings and other celebrations. It's a major source of income for families in rural areas, as watermelons are quite easy to come by and chetopoti is relatively simple to make.

Many believe that, among chetopoti's supposed health benefits, it relieves constipation. Anyone who's devoured too much watermelon in a single sitting can certainly attest to that.

Chapter 6

EASTERN AND CENTRAL
EUROPE AND THE BALKANS

Up until this point, we've witnessed the influence that major European nations have had on Australia, Asia, and Africa. Our itinerary now brings us to that Western continent to take a look at what they've got going on at home. Before many of the intercontinental empires were intercontinental empires, they were conquering their own continent and spreading the libational goodness to all their conquests. For instance, the fact that we call European viticultural regions "Old World" wine producers is thanks to the Roman Empire's grape-stained escapades. And if a country's climate wasn't friendly to the vines, its people likely were growing grain and brewing beer. Later, they were distilling those fermented grapes and grains into brandy, vodka, or any number of national and regional derivatives of such spirits.

Our entry points into Europe are the eastern and southeastern sections of the continent, as well as the central region that bridges the customs of east and west. We'll start with Russia, which, like Turkey, divides its geographic area between Europe and Asia.

RUSSIA AND
OTHER FORMER SOVIET REPUBLICS

Mention "Russia" and "drinking" to anyone and the first response you'll get is "vodka." And that response would be right. There's this stereotypical image of hard-drinking Russians tossing back shot after shot of the clear, neutral spirit and living to tell the tale quite lucidly. Anthony Bourdain, in his book *A Cook's Tour*, details one particular imbibing session in Moscow when the rounds numbered somewhere around seventeen.

But Russia's relationship with alcohol has been, at least in the past couple of decades, a bit more complicated. Yes, drinking is deeply ingrained in Russian culture. But that doesn't mean everyone necessarily likes it—least of all the government. Around 2010, the powers that be in Russia decided it was time to seriously crack down on binge-drinking in the country. This started under President Dmitry Medvedev—although many say it was really Vladimir Putin, who preceded Medvedev and was still pulling the strings as prime minister before he returned to the presidency in 2012.

The government began enacting anti-alcohol policies in earnest, crafted to curtail what it considered problem drinking. And it wasn't just high-ABV beverages like vodka. The initiatives also targeted beer, which for generations hadn't even been viewed as an alcoholic beverage (when 40ish percent ABV vodka is such a visible component of everyday life, 5 percent ABV beer barely registers). Prior to the measures, street kiosks peddling beer were pervasive. They were also unregulated and sold the beverage for less than a song. Once temperance laws were put in place, such venues' numbers diminished greatly. Soon after, the government banned alcohol advertising, imposed significant taxes on beer, and mandated minimum pricing for the beverage.

Has this helped quell immoderate consumption? Possibly. But it's also made it harder for more responsible members of

Russian society to get a good drink. And it worsened Russia's already-tenuous economic situation: Multinational adult beverage purveyors that had put a lot of stock in the Russian market—most notably Danish brewer Carlsberg—took a big hit.

It may have been an unwelcome development for lawful producers, but it's likely created more . . . shall we say . . . hobbyists who wanted to reconnect with another facet of their heritage: samogon ("self-made" or "self-distilled"). Samogon is Russia's answer to moonshine, available in one form or another for around seven hundred years. It actually predates vodka. During the mid-sixteenth century, Ivan the Terrible had a statewide wine monopoly. People wanted their booze and they wanted it cheap, so they took matters into their own hands and distilled whatever ingredients they could get their hands on and created a little home hooch. And the spirits they were making were far stronger than any wine that was on the medieval market, not to mention the yet-to-be commercialized vodka. There were also logistical motives for samogon production: Good wine couldn't always reach folks in rural parts of the country if you've ever seen *Doctor Zhivago*, you know how treacherous the icy terrain can be.

So, in modern Russia, what's a person to do when the government enacts stringent measures on commercial alcohol products that make them too costly for lower-income citizens? Turn back to illicitly produced home spirits, whose safety and quality are questionable at best. People aren't using professional-grade stills, after all. A lot of times they're tinkering with appliances, car parts, and home heating devices. Sound familiar?

You know what else samogon has in common with American moonshine? An artisanal revival. Around the same time that unaged corn whiskey packaged in mason jars and dubbed "moonshine" became a category unto itself in the United States, some Russian distillers began appealing to the same sense of romance and nostalgia that's fueled the Appalachian white whiskey renaissance.

129

NA ZDOROVIE!

The best way to enjoy vodka is to dirty it up with all sorts of infusible herbs, spices, or fruits. Here are a few of my own personal favorites. It's best to use high-end Russian vodka, rather than the standard stuff, for these recipes.

CUCUMBER AND DILL VODKA INFUSION

If you're a pickle fiend like me, this is probably up your alley.

→☞ DIRECTIONS ☜←

Put dill and cucumber in a mason jar, pour in vodka, and seal the jar.

Set aside for 3 days—or 4 for a dillier flavor.

Serve chilled in 2-ounce glasses or over ice in a rocks glass.

It's also a great base for a Bloody Mary, so be sure to save some for brunch!

Have a couple of gherkins or cornichons on hand—they make a nice garnish as well as post-sip chaser.

It's fine to let the dill and cucumber remain in the jar until the vodka is gone. It'll make for a more intense flavor.

→☞ INGREDIENTS ☜←

½ cup fresh dill fronds, thick stems removed

1 large cucumber, cut into ¼-inch-thick slices

2 cups vodka

☞ ONION-INFUSED VODKA

I love onions. They can rescue just about any dish from Bland City. But there's no denying that this next recipe is sure to make you cry. (Once it's ready, though, you'll be shedding tears of joy.)

⤞ DIRECTIONS ⬾	⤞ INGREDIENTS ⬾
Put onion in a mason jar, pour in vodka, and seal jar.	1 medium onion, cut into six wedges
	2 cups vodka
Set aside for 3 to 5 days.	
This is another one to enjoy neat, in those 2-ounce glasses, or on ice in a rocks glass.	
It's also a Bloody Mary's best friend, should you choose to go that route.	

☞ BLACKBERRY-INFUSED VODKA

This one's on the sweeter side.

131

⤞ DIRECTIONS ⬾	⤞ INGREDIENTS ⬾
Put blackberries in a mason jar, pour in vodka, and seal jar.	½ cup fresh blackberries
	2 cups vodka
Set aside for 3 to 5 days.	
Served chilled in 2-ounce glasses, over ice in a rocks glass, or in fruit-forward cocktails. (It adds a nice blackberry twist to a classic Cosmo.)	

◁ Russian Imperial Stout

When American craft brewers venture into "extreme beer" territory—those aggressive in alcohol content and flavor—a popular canvas on which they like to paint is the imperial stout, often called Russian imperial stout. So, what exactly does it have to do with Russia? As the story goes (and as with any marketing-enhanced quasi-history, take it with a grain of salt), eighteenth-century Russian Empress Catherine II (better known as Catherine the Great) became quite enamored of English stout when she visited Britain, so British brewers created a much boozier version (ABV was usually upwards of 9 percent) to survive the voyage to Russia mostly intact and please the taste buds of the thirsty monarch.

Ukraine

Ukraine can be a lonely place for teetotalers. If you're invited for a night out or at someone's house, imbibing is assumed. And more often than not, that will involve vodka. Nearly as often, Cognac will be part of the consumption equation, as will beer. Sometimes, as is the case in nearby countries like Belarus, Estonia, and Latvia, folks might be drinking a curious amber-hued concoction known as kvass, but very few are likely to even consider it an alcoholic beverage. It's made from steeping and fermenting dark bread, usually rye, which tints the liquid to resemble, in many cases, green tea. And its ABV is almost negligibly low, sometimes only around a percent or two. Therefore, most Ukrainians consider it a soft drink; it's usually available from street vendors, who sometimes add berries, fruits, and herbs to it for flavor diversity.

Though Ukrainian drinking habits increasingly resemble those of western Europe—Ukrainians have a real taste for Scotch—vodka remains the default, as it's the cheapest and most accessible. A bottle of middle-of-the-road Scotch might set a person back the equivalent of US$40. The same volume of a national vodka brand would cost around US$5.

Neat vodka shots are the most common accompaniment for a night's meal, which can be a bit of a sprawling affair. Salads, varenyky (essentially pierogies), borscht, stuffed cabbages, sausages, and assorted pickled vegetables are among the components of a traditional spread. Consuming three shots throughout the course of the evening is practically teetotaling (drink-nursing skills come in handy, especially if you want to avoid falling over during the course of the evening).

Many restaurants and bars offer some house-made vodka infusions—pickles, horseradish, and honey are quite common. Don't expect a vast selection in the more traditional places. If there's an extensive list of fruit- and savory-ingredient-infused vodkas, chances are you're in a more tourist-friendly establishment. In other words, inauthentic.

Toasting is as much an expected part of the meal as using eating utensils. Everyone will give a toast at some point over the course of the evening. The easiest and most common is "bud'mo," the equivalent of "to your health." The Russian salutation "na zodorovie" also makes more than a few appearances, just as it does throughout most former Eastern Bloc nations.

It's also traditional to drink at funerals and may even be considered rude to decline the offer of alcohol. But don't worry. The object here is not to get hammered. It's one of the few occasions when two glasses of vodka suffice. But no matter where you are and what the occasion, there's really no such thing as "one and done" as far as vodka shots are concerned in Ukraine.

Georgia

Georgia is well-known throughout Eastern Europe for its wine industry. In fact, it's among the oldest in the world—if not *the* oldest, as many (even outside the Georgian wine industry) claim. In the South Caucasus valley, archaeologists have found residue on kvevri (ancient earthenware vessels used for fermentation) that's six or perhaps even eight thousand years old, suggesting that grape cultivation has been going on in the region for at least that long.

Even Georgia's unique alphabet is allegedly modeled after curly grape vines. What's more, the Georgian word "ghvino" may be the basis for "wine" in Latin ("vinum") and thus many other languages, such as "vin" in French and "vino" in Italian and Spanish.

Today, Georgia and Moldova are the two biggest wine producers among the former Soviet states. We often think of the erstwhile members of the USSR as depressingly frigid and bleak, but, as is typical with gargantuan masses of land, there's a vast spectrum of climatological conditions. Georgia is pretty far south as far as former Soviet republics go; it's just north of Turkey, and its western coast is on the Black Sea. The winters are relatively mild and the summers are warm, but not sweltering. Perfect for growing grapes, in other words.

The country grows more than five hundred different varietals, including the famed Rkatsiteli ("red horn") grape, one of the oldest known varietals in the world. It's one of the easiest grapes to spot, thanks to its characteristic red stem and amber skin with little pinkish-lavender blotches.

I must say, I've never experienced a more life-changing wine moment than the first time I tried a flight of Rkatsiteli-based whites. Full disclosure: I generally hate white wine, save for the bubbly kind. I almost exclusively drink reds. But these quintessentially Georgian bottlings were unlike anything I'd tasted before. Some were pleasantly sour and mildly reminiscent of sherry and Basque ciders, with a cheese-like funk and faint salinity. Even the color varied wildly. Some had a practically water-like clarity, while others resided in deep amber territory. I wouldn't say they're for everyone, but they're definitely for those who think they'll never be white drinkers.

As far as reds go, the most common grape one is likely to encounter is the Saperavi, as it grows across most of Georgia's main wine regions. It's the heart of Georgia's semisweet red Akhasheni. The appellation derives from the name of a village in the country's most prominent wine-growing area, Kakheti, in eastern Georgia. The other principal grape regions include Kartli, also in the east, and the more westerly Imereti, Racha-Lechkumi, and the Black Sea coast.

Beyond commercial production, there's also a strong home winemaking tradition across the country. It's inseparable from family gatherings, Orthodox Christian rituals, and holidays.

The breakup of the Soviet Union certainly came as good news for Georgians, as well as nationals in all the other former member states. But the post-Soviet era hasn't been without its major bumps in the road, especially where the wine business is concerned. In 2006, Georgia lost a huge export market when Russia imposed an embargo on Georgian wine, claiming that a significant number of counterfeit bottlings were making their way across the border. Most suspected that this claim was unfounded and was simply Russia's way of punishing Georgia. Indeed, the United States was soon also on the receiving end of such an action. In 2014, Russia's consumer safety agency reported that it had found a chemical component of insect repellent in bottles of Jack Daniel's Tennessee Honey whiskey. Russian regulators also asserted that bottles of Jack and rival Jim Beam were improperly labeled, even though Russia had been importing both products for years without making a peep. It was no coincidence that this happened immediately after the United States and European Union imposed sanctions on Russia when it annexed Crimea from Ukraine.

Still, Georgia has been able to hold its own in its home market, as well as in other parts of Europe and the world as international oenophiles discover the country's award-winning wines.

It's become quite predictable by this point in the book that where there's wine, there's brandy. Chacha is the moniker of the

Georgian variety, which is more in the grappa camp as a pomace-based brandy. (Pomace is the unpressed skins, seeds, stems, and other leftovers from winemaking; though some versions of chacha start with whole, albeit unripe, grapes.) It's available in mainstream commercial versions that typically hover around 80 proof, as well as homemade versions. Some may call chacha "grape vodka" or "vine vodka," but the distillate has little in common with vodka beyond its lack of color and odor. The flavor is quite strong, but that doesn't stop Georgians from pairing it with all sorts of traditional foods, especially the national dish, khinkali, which consists of dough dumplings stuffed with meat (typically lamb) and spices.

⋈ Varsity-Level Toasting

Most cultures around the world have their signature toasting traditions. But they're bush league compared with Georgian rituals. Attendees of a supra—a formal dinner—know that the star of the show is the tamada, the toastmaster. The tamada will toast anything and everything throughout the meal. When the tamada toasts an honored guest, that guest must rise and thank the tamada once the toast is finished—but the guest shouldn't drink until the other diners have added their own toasts. "Alaverdi" is usually the signal for another person to build on the tamada's remarks. When that person is finished, he or she downs the contents of a glass in a single gulp, and the next person offers a toast, and so on. The ritual continues with the next guest to be toasted. The cardinal sin for a dinner guest would be to speak while others are toasting.

{
A TRADITIONAL

GEORGIAN

KHANTSI

PHOTO: ISTOCK BY
GETTY IMAGES
}

Sometimes the tamada brings out a goat, ram, or ox horn called a khantsi, a custom with roots stretching back several millennia when the peoples of the region worshipped Bacchus, the god of wine. That's when things get hardcore. It's up to the guest of honor to drink every last drop of wine in the khantsi. (Those concerned about animal welfare needn't fret. It's more likely these days that the khantsi will be constructed from clay or glass.)

You'll know it's finally time to drink when you hear "Gagvimarjos!"—loosely, "To victory!"

Armenia

You might start to notice a pattern among the former Soviet republics: Their populations share an affinity for strong drink—and a remarkable ability to hold their liquor and not exhibit any outward evidence of inebriation.

Armenians like their local fruit brandies, known collectively as oghi. They might as well be calling them eaux-de-vie, though, because they've appropriated French culture in a rather blatant way: Their finer, aged brandies are marketed around Armenia, and other former Soviet states, as "cognac." But "cognac" is a protected appellation, and only brandies produced by a certain method in the Cognac region of France may wear that label. Armenians have a thirst for the stuff, though, and since there's no real enforcement of French and EU standards within Armenia, the people will be drinking "cognac." (I'll spell it with a small "c" and use quotation marks out of deference for true Cognac.) And, to be fair, Armenian producer Yerevan Brandy Company—founded in 1887 and acquired in 1898 by Russian vodka magnate Nikolay Shustov—so wowed French judges during a 1900 Paris blind tasting that its product actually earned the Cognac moniker. However, in the decades after the dissolution of the USSR, a number of former Soviet states opted to adhere to France's appellation system and just call the liquid brandy.

137

Yerevan's most famous product, Ararat, is really what put the local industry on the map. Pernod Ricard, the second-largest spirits conglomerate in the world, now owns Ararat—and given the fact that Pernod Ricard is a Paris-based company, the brand has to tread very lightly when throwing around the term "cognac." Ararat is available in three-, five-, six-, seven-, and ten-year-old expressions that still hold up pretty well against some of the biggest Cognacs—the actual French ones—on the market today.

Back in the Soviet years, many Armenians started using the terms "oghi" and "vodka" interchangeably, though "crude brandy" likely would be a better descriptor of oghi. To complicate things even further, locals often called it aragh, which is the colloquial Armenian term for vodka. And what does "aragh" sound like? That's right, the classic Middle Eastern anise-flavored spirit arak (even though there's nary an anise-flavored drink throughout Armenia).

Oghi producers use any number of fruits as the base, but one of the most popular sweet, fermentable ingredients is mulberry, known locally as tuti oghi. Other fruit bases include a red berry known as hon, apricots, pears, grapes, plums, blackberries, figs, and apples. And Moonshiners often use raisins to produce their illicit oghis.

THE BALTIC STATES

The drinking habits of citizens of countries that once made up the Soviet Union may have been overshadowed by the hegemony of vodka, but that doesn't mean local tipples weren't able to shine through in some regions. One of the best examples is a certain liqueur of Latvian origin that has gained a small cult following even beyond its borders.

In 1752 Abraham Kunze, a pharmacist in the capital city, Riga, concocted an herbal blend (which, as you'll discover throughout these pages, eighteenth- and nineteenth-century apothecaries everywhere were wont to do) consisting of twenty-four natural ingredients. Today that bitter liqueur, Riga Black Balsam, is a source of great pride among natives, representing centuries of Latvian artisanship. The recipe now features a blend of seventeen herbs, roots, and grasses infused in a neutral spirit and then blended with natural juices, honey, and a host of other secret ingredients that give the drink its character. Its pitch-black color—hence, its name—comes from burnt caramel, which the producers char in-house.

Back in the day, the locals gravitated toward this liqueur to enhance their well-being, enjoying it nearly daily with their coffee or tea or on its own, especially when they detected the early signs of a cold or other illness (every bug was serious in the 1700s, so no one was taking any chances). In the late 1800s, its consumption shifted toward the recreational, though many continued to drink it as a health remedy. "Nowadays, we're not claiming that this is a medicine, because, first of all, we're not allowed," says Riga Black Balsam's global brand director, Maris Kalnins. "But also, we really want to change that pattern of consumption and the perception of this brand. We are going with the trends in the world spirit market, so we are trying to establish this brand as an excellent accompaniment for different kinds of drinks."

Still, old habits die hard, and plenty of Latvians seek out the liqueur as a cure for whatever ails them. Usually, they'll sip a little when they feel like they're getting a sore throat or when they're traveling to exotic places to help settle their stomachs as they adjust to the journey and the regional cuisine. It's especially popular during Latvia's wintry deep freezes—for many, there's nothing better than a few sips of Riga Black after coming home from work when the temperature's in the single digits or subzero Fahrenheit.

So, what does it taste like? Hard to say, as comparisons are difficult. The closest relative would be Italy's Fernet Branca, but even that is a loose association. Kalnins agrees that the flavor is tricky to define: "It's not really sour, it's not really sweet, it's not really bitter—it's somewhere between all of those tastes."

The maker has since expanded the product line to include Riga Black Balsam Currant (the original recipe blended with black currant juice), Riga Black Balsam Element (with added rum), and Riga Black Balsam Cream (a mild, 17 percent ABV cream liqueur with notes of vanilla and caramel).

The spirit is so much a part of the zeitgeist in Latvia that it's even a popular flavor in confections. "We have ice cream with Riga Black, we have different cakes produced here with Riga Black, and we have different kinds of candies with Riga Black," Kalnins explains. The company has even been working with food marketing partners to develop a Riga Black barbecue sauce (sign me up!).

For a sweeter counterpoint to Latvia's famous tipple, look no further than nearby Lithuania, whose own traditional liqueurs are an institution unto themselves. Krupnikas is a bona fide Lithuanian institution, an often homemade honey liqueur for which family recipes have been passed down through the generations. Versions also exist in Poland and Belarus, where it's more commonly called krupnik.

Commercial brands tend to be on the milder side alcoholically, as producers usually start with vodka, which hovers around 80 to 90 proof. But all bets are off when you're drinking the stuff made in someone's home kitchen. The base is far more likely to be grain alcohol—at least double the proof of vodka—and, therefore, infinitely more potent. Honey's the main ingredient, giving it its signature sweetness. However, expect to find some forty or fifty different herbs and spices joining the party.

⋆ Latvian Legends

Because Riga Black is a strong beverage tied to hundreds of years of history, there are innumerable legends associated with the Latvian elixir, likely with varying levels of truth to them. The modern producers are more than happy to tout some of these tales in their marketing efforts—and who can blame them? There's some

RIGA BLACK BALSAM COCKTAILS

The Latvian makers of Riga Black Balsam have a few tricks up their sleeves, incorporating the original bitter liqueur as well as its line extensions.

☞ BLACK BALSAM SHOOTER

The two-tone shot looks like a layer cake when poured properly—a dark chocolate–colored layer floating atop a deeper layer of yellowish vanilla. The flavor of course is something else entirely.

⇒ DIRECTIONS ⇐	⇒ INGREDIENTS ⇐
Pour the peach juice into a shot glass and slowly add the Riga Black by pouring it over the back of a spoon.	15 ml (½ ounce) peach juice 15 ml (½ ounce) Riga Black Balsam Classic

141

☞ BLACK CHERRY COLA

You won't find this in the soda aisle!

⇒ DIRECTIONS ⇐	⇒ INGREDIENTS ⇐
Fill an Old Fashioned glass with ice. Add Riga Black, cherry juice, and cola and stir.	40 ml (1⅓ ounces) Riga Black Balsam Classic 80 ml (2⅔ ounces) cherry juice 80 ml (2⅔ ounces) cola

☞ George Washington's Lie

I was sold when I read the name of this cocktail. Our kindergarten teachers all perpetuated the myth involving the boy who would become America's first president and a certain cherry tree. Cherry juice makes another appearance in this hot toddy, along with some aromatic baking spices.

→≡◉ DIRECTIONS ◉≡←	→≡◉ INGREDIENTS ◉≡←
Combine the Riga Black, cherry juice, and cloves in a heat-resistant glass.	40 ml (1⅓ ounces) Riga Black Balsam Classic
Heat to about 170 degrees Fahrenheit (75 degrees Celsius)—don't let it get to a boil.	120 ml (4 ounces) cherry juice
	3 to 5 whole cloves
Add the slice of lemon.	1 lemon slice

☞ Clavis Riga

Up until this point, I've been fairly easy on you with the Riga Black recipes. Now we're going to kick things up a notch with a more intricate concoction.

→≡◉ DIRECTIONS ◉≡←	→≡◉ INGREDIENTS ◉≡←
Pour everything into a chilled mixing glass with ice and stir well.	20 ml (⅔ ounce) Riga Black Balsam Classic
Strain into a chilled cocktail glass without ice.	10 ml (⅓ ounce) rhubarb liqueur
	60 ml (2 ounces) apple juice
Squeeze the oil from a strip of orange peel into the cocktail and garnish with the peel.	5 ml (1 teaspoon) pomegranate syrup
	5 ml (1 teaspoon) white chocolate syrup
	Orange peel, for garnish

☞ STAIRWAY TO HEAVEN

When a spirits producer hosts the lead singer of one of the biggest rock bands of all time, of course the company has to come up with a drink named after that group's greatest hit. This cocktail uses the currant variety of Riga Black.

⟶ DIRECTIONS ⟵	⟶ INGREDIENTS ⟵
Muddle ginger in the bottom of a rocks glass and add ice.	4 thin slices ginger
	100 ml (3⅓ ounces) tonic
Add tonic and Riga Black Balsam Currant. Stir.	50 ml (1⅔ ounces) Riga Black Balsam Currant

☞ RIGA FASHIONED

Most non-whisky spirits brands like to promote some version of the Old Fashioned, substituting their product for the rye or bourbon. However, the ingredients in the Riga Fashioned are so eclectic it's hard to put it in the same category with those. Riga Black Balsam Element is the star attraction here, but the Classic version also makes a cameo appearance.

143

⟶ DIRECTIONS ⟵	⟶ INGREDIENTS ⟵
Squeeze the oil from a strip of grapefruit peel into a chilled mixing glass.	Grapefruit peel
	50 ml (1⅔ ounces) Riga Black Balsam Element
Fill with remaining ingredients, add ice, and mix well.	5 ml (1 teaspoon) Riga Black Balsam Classic
Strain into a chilled coupe glass and garnish with the peel.	10 ml (⅓ ounce) Amaretto
	10 ml (⅓ ounce) fig syrup

serious historical name-dropping going on here. For instance, it is alleged that when Russian Empress Catherine the Great fell ill in 1764, it was Riga Black Balsam that saved her life.

The spirit was (again, allegedly) a favorite indulgence of the likes of twentieth-century VIPs such as the Soviet leader Leonid Brezhnev and iconic French president Charles de Gaulle. It's also built a fan base among famous musicians, old and new. German composer Richard Wagner was known to partake on occasion (perhaps he hallucinated about Valkyries in his drunken revelry), and Led Zeppelin front man Robert Plant and Queen's Brian May have visited Riga Black Balsam's cellars. Led Zeppelin's most famous song also inspired a cocktail, which I've included.

THE BALKAN REGION

The Balkan Peninsula throughout history hasn't exactly been the picture of stability. By the end of the sixteenth century, the Ottoman Empire controlled much of the region; the rival Austro-Hungarian Empire held the rest. The early twentieth century ushered in a period of seemingly endless conflict. The first among those was the First Balkan War in 1912–1913, principally involving Bulgaria, Greece, Montenegro, and Serbia joining forces and rising up against the Ottomans. And since every good war deserves a sequel, the Second Balkan War closely followed. This time, the instigator was Bulgaria alone. The Bulgarians weren't happy with their share of the settlement from the First Balkan War, so they launched an offensive against Serbia and Greece (how quickly alliances go south!).

Bulgaria's opponents proved formidable; Greece and Serbia beat back their attack and initiated a counteroffensive. Then Romania—a frequent rival to Bulgaria—got involved. Things got worse when the Ottoman Empire, still smarting from the outcome of the First Balkan War, decided that it was an opportune time to try to get its hands on some of the territories it had lost in the previous conflict. The war soon ended, with Bulgaria worse off than when it started (Romania was not a country to be trifled with). And the entirety of the Second Balkan War played out over the course of about a month.

Then, about a year and a half later, there was a little scuffle known as the War to End All Wars (later rebranded as World War I). In fact, Serbian radical Gavrilo Princip fired what was essentially the opening shot to that four-year-long global conflict when he gunned down Archduke Franz Ferdinand of Austria and his wife, Sophie, Duchess of Hohenberg. (It's a testament to the patriarchal lens through which we're conditioned to view history that the archduke's name has become a household term—there's even a band named after him, for crying out loud—especially in the context of the chain reaction his assassination set up, leading to the Great War. Rarely has the duchess's name come up as a victim in that attack; her luck was bad enough having married such a doomed member of the royal family.) The Balkans represented a significant front during the war. The end of the war resulted in many of the Balkan nations becoming part of the newly formed state of Yugoslavia.

Then came World War II, and along with it the totalitarian Communist-backed dictator Tito, and things got even more out of hand. The end of the twentieth century saw about a decade of ethnic conflicts and atrocities that ultimately led to the formation of the independent states that exist today.

A number of the Balkan nations that weren't part of the former Yugoslavia still had to deal with Soviet-backed dictators, though. When I was in high school, we learned about Nicolae Ceaușescu, Romania's Stalinist dictator, who was deposed and then executed along with his wife on December 25, 1989 (Merry Christmas!). The Romanian firing squad's bullets were among the last nails in the coffin of Eastern Bloc Communism as the Soviet Union crumbled. The end of the Ceaușescu regime followed closely on the heels of the end of the Communist party's political monopoly

145

in Bulgaria and the forced resignation of Bulgarian Communist party head Todor Zhivkov (mere hours after the Berlin Wall fell).

The Balkans have had a rough run of things. Beyond the unspeakable human toll, a collateral casualty in many of the countries in the region was the beverage market. The region's proximity to the Mediterranean Sea means that the microclimates of Slovenia, Croatia, and other Balkan countries sit firmly within the wine belt of Europe. But Communism, dictatorships, and bloody conflicts kept much of the rest of the modern world from experiencing the wonderful liquid bounty of the region. Fortunately, that has changed—in a big way.

As is the case in most great winemaking regions from the Mediterranean to South America, there's equally vibrant grape distilling activity. Any spirit made from a grape or other fruit technically falls under the heading of "brandy" or "eau de vie." But the Balkan region boasts a unique contribution to global brandies and thus it gets its own name: rakia. Rakia is common across Croatia, Bosnia-Herzegovina, Serbia (where it's considered the national drink), and Montenegro, but Bulgaria is perhaps the most famous for it. It's also the place where some archaeologists believe this genre of Eastern European fruit brandies originated. In 2011 researchers found a fragment of a thousand-year-old distillation vessel believed to have been used to produced the earliest iterations of rakia.

Distillers may use any fermentable fruit base to produce the stuff, but the two most popular bases are grapes (naturally) and plums. The plum versions usually fall under the more specific category heading of slivovitz (sometimes spelled slivovice, depending on which country you're in), derived from sljivovica, the Serbian word for "plum." Serbians also consider the plum to be their national fruit, and it plays a role in many of the country's customs, both religious and secular. Slivovitz is usually distilled with the plum pits and all—many aficionados say the pit contributes to the spirit's character—though there are pitless versions. The resulting liquor can be quite high in alcohol, with a proof ranging from 80 to a whopping 140.

Many of the countries in the region—and in other parts of eastern and central Europe, like Poland and the Czech Republic—have their own noteworthy slivovitz varieties. Bulgaria's most famous slivovitz is Troyanska Slivova, which Troyan monks first produced as far back as the fourteenth century. It's available in four-year-old and seven-year-old versions. Wood aging gives it some vanilla nuances.

In Romania, most of the fruit brandies are also based on plums, but the name for the drink in that country is tuica. There's a very active moonshining culture in Romania, which means that tuica can cover ABVs from around 30 percent to about 60 percent. A key factor that distinguishes tuica from slivovitz is that tuica usually doesn't include any sort of pomace in the fermentable base. Romanians call any spirit made from fruit other than plums rachiu (very similar to the word "rakia").

The 80-proof Maraska Star Sljivovica is the brand that most people encounter in Croatia (the producer also makes popular cherry brandies), but these days the country is better known around the world for its wine—though it's hardly new.

Winemaking in Croatia dates back to some time in the last millennium BCE, when the ancient Illyrians started fermenting grapes in the narrow strip of territory on the country's southwestern Adriatic coast that is now known as Dalmatia. Since then, Croatia has grown to become one of the great viticultural nations in the world. It's technically an Old World producer—three or four centuries BCE certainly qualifies it as such—but its profile on the global stage is relatively new. Well, *r*enewed, anyway. Croatian wines were quite well regarded for centuries on the continent, but all those aforementioned sociopolitical calamities curtailed the country's winemaking activities. Mother Nature gets some of the blame as well; Croatia was not immune to the phylloxera epidemic of the mid-nineteenth century, during which a mass

147

infestation of the aphid-like scourges obliterated most vineyards across Europe.

The Croatian War of Independence took its own toll on the country's vineyards in the 1990s, but in the next decade its wine producing activities emerged stronger, drawing a rapidly increasing number of wine tourists each year.

Four key regions within Croatia are responsible for the country's output of more than sixty grape varietals, resulting in about 60 percent white wines and 40 percent reds. Let's take a quick tour of the four regions.

> **Dalmatia:** Here's where it all started, nearly twenty-five hundred years ago. Dalmatia encompasses its own archipelago in the Adriatic Sea, as well as a lengthy sliver attached to the continent, which is home to the picturesque city of Dubrovnik (a shooting location for *Star Wars: Episode VIII—The Last Jedi*). The region's warm climate, hilly terrain, and ample sunshine make it especially friendly to growing grapes, so it's no surprise that you'll find more than sixty wineries here. Among the grape varietals common in Dalmatia is Plavac Mali, known to be very rich in dark cherry and blueberry notes, as well as having some peppery spice. It's a popular grape for reds in the coastal region. Many people may not have heard of Plavac Mali, but most likely they have heard of Zinfandel. Dalmatia is the birthplace of that grape.

> **Istria and Kvarner:** To the northwest of Dalmatia, in the Kvarner Bay, Istria and Kvarner boasts its own collection of islands, in addition to a sizeable peninsula dangling into the Adriatic—that's Istria proper. (Italy and Slovenia also occupy small slices of the Istria peninsula.) The grapes responsible for many of the finest wines of this region are the Teran and the Malvazija—not surprisingly, they're found in some Italian and Slovenian wines as well.

Uplands: The Uplands region is inland, to the east and northeast of Istria and Kvarner. It's home to the Croatian capital, Zagreb. In the southwestern corner of the Uplands is Plešivica, home to the Plešivica Wine Road, first opened in 2001. Forty-odd wineries occupy the area, producing wines from proprietary local varietals like Portugieser, Sipelj, and sweet Zelenac, as well as some of the better-known continental favorites like Pinot Noir, Chardonnay, and Riesling. The climate here is typically cooler than in the coastal regions; as in Alsace and other cooler regions of France, the whites dominate and the reds are of a lighter hue.

Slavonia and Danube: This region occupies the easternmost chunk of Croatia and is also the most inland portion of the country. Popular grape varietals include Grasevina, known to produce fruity and floral whites.

Slovenia

To most of the world, Slovenia is well-known as a winemaking country—and rightly so. In fact, Slovenia has a little something on many other countries throughout Europe. Whereas much of the continent's wine-producing activities began with the Romans, Slovenia's predates that mighty empire, dating back to about 400 BCE, when the Celts and Illyrian tribes occupied the region. Then, of course, Rome came a-conquering around the first century CE and brought its own legendary grape-growing and -fermenting skills to Slovenia—not to mention its commercial prowess—and expanded the wine production considerably. Such activities waned about a half millennium later when the Slavs took over (they weren't too attached to the beverage during that period), but then went back on the upswing during the Middle Ages (say, around the ninth century or so) when the Catholic

149

Church Christianized the region. The clergy needed their wine, after all, and the monks controlled most of the medieval industry. That also meant that it was the holy men who hoarded most of the winemaking know-how.

The industry modernized by the eighteenth century and developed significantly in the nineteenth century. Toward the end of the following century, the Yugoslav wars sent the industry into brief decline, but it managed to bounce back fairly quickly. Today, some twenty-eight thousand (!) Slovenian wineries are responsible for about a million hectoliters of wine each year, or a little less than 0.05 percent of the global total.

Slovenian soil boasts a multitude of grape varietals growing throughout its major winemaking regions that result in fifty-two different types of wine (thirty-seven whites and fifteen reds). The most popular among those is Laški Rizling (known to German speakers as Welschriesling, but no relation to the much more pervasive Rhine Riesling). Other well-regarded whites include Malvazija, Rebula (better known by its Italian name, Ribolla), and Šipon (popular in Hungary, where it's known as Furmint). As far as reds are concerned, the dark-skinned Refošk (also more recognizable in Italian, as Refosco) is the go-to varietal, producing deep ruby–colored beverages.

Many different varietals go into making what is a quintessentially Slovenian wine style: Cvicek. It's a mad scientist's blend of red and white varietals, producing a beverage with a light ruby-red hue, slightly brighter than, say, a Pinot Noir. It's characterized by a mix of intense dryness and a pronounced sourness and has been a protected denomination in the European Union since 2001. Many wines from Slovenia are reminiscent of other popular continental products, but Cvicek really is its own animal and the one to try if you visit. Slovenes frequently consume it with traditional regional dishes like goat, suckling pig, the local blood sausages called krvavice, and the rolled dumplings known as struklji.

The country boasts three distinct wine-producing regions, each with between two and four sub-regions:

Podravska: Slovenia's largest wine region by far, Podravska is best known for sparkling and sweeter dessert wines. Nearly all the wine produced there—save a mere 3 percent of its output—is white. Located on the east-central side of the country, Podravska borders Hungary and Croatia. Within Podravska are two sub-regions, Prekmurje and Stajerska Slovenija.

Posavska: Located just south of Podravska, Posavska has three distinct sub-regions: Bizeljsko Sremic, Dolenjska, and Bela Krajina. Dolenjska is the best known of those, being the epicenter of Cvicek production.

Primorska: This region lies in the southwestern corner of Slovenia and shares a border with a tiny sliver of northeastern Italy. The influence of its boot-shaped neighbor manifests itself a bit in the cuisine, the culture, and, of course, the viticulture of the region. Its winemakers are relatively prolific, producing some 250,000 hectoliters a year. Primorska includes four sub-regions: Goriska Brda (sometimes known as Slovenia's Tuscany), Kras (internationally known as Karst), Vipaska Dolina, and Slovenska Istra (one of the few areas within Slovenia where red wines are more prevalent than whites).

151

You'd think that in a country with such robust wine activity, the corresponding indigenous spirit would be a grape brandy. However, Slovenia's most distinct distilled tipple shares a bit more in common, flavor-wise, with gin—at least as far as one prominent ingredient is concerned. Brinjevec (or brinovec), as it's known, is distilled from juniper (often referred to as the juniper "berry," but, as I'll explain in a bit more detail later, it's not actually a berry).

In fact, many people incorrectly refer to brinjevec as "Karst gin" because it contains juniper, but it's definitely not gin. Note that I wrote "distilled from." The spirit base of gin usually derives from grain, which tends to be distilled to neutrality. The juniper comes in later, as its primary source of flavor. But with brinjevec, juniper is actually the source of its spirit base.

Brinjevec production is most prevalent in two regions: Karst, a plateau that extends from southwestern Slovenia to northeastern Italy, and nearby Brkini. It's on the moderately strong side of the spirits spectrum, usually in the 40 to 50 percent ABV range. Kraški brinjevec (the variety produced in Karst) gained regional protection from the Slovenian parliament in 2003 and the European Union in 2008.

Greece and Turkey

Scholars trace Greek winemaking back some six and a half millennia, so it's pretty safe to assume that the ancient Greeks were all guzzling wine when they came up with the concept of democracy. If there's ever been a good reason to kick back every now and again with a drink, that's it—and don't forget, colonial leaders planned most of the American Revolution from inside taverns. Take *that*, Prohibitionists!

Greece has a wealth of idiosyncratic grape varietals, including the ever-popular (and oppressively difficult to pronounce) Agiorgitiko. This red grape, which plays well with Cabernet and also works just fine on its own, is the most-planted varietal in the country, followed closely by the Xinomavro varietal. Common white varietals include Assyrtiko, Athiri, and Robola, and then there's the White Muscat, with which most are familiar for its legendary presence in dessert wines.

As far as styles go, the one that's gotten Greece the most attention, for better or worse, has been a little curiosity called Retsina. The prevailing flavor in this white can be found not-so-hidden within its name: resin. Retsina is famous for its piney, resinous flavor. And that's by design: Modern winemakers achieve that characteristic by adding pine resin during fermentation.

Greeks have many origin stories for the style, and no one's quite sure of the truth. Many swear that the winemakers of some two thousand years ago—when Retsina first appeared on the scene—would seal wine vessels with pine resin to prevent oxidation (this was long before anyone knew what oxidation was, of course, but they had figured out that when it comes to winemaking, air is bad). Others maintain that ancient wine producers likely stored their beverages in pine barrels, which imparted those resinous notes. Another theory suggests that the makers would put a little pine resin in their products as a preservative. The stuff did have to travel long distances, after all.

I say, who cares, really? Retsina exists, and it's a quintessentially Greek product. It reached its peak in popularity by the 1980s, so it's now drunk mostly by older Greeks—because, as we see all over the world, members of the younger demographics just hate to drink what their parents drink. That, and the fact that the flavor is something of an acquired taste. Regardless, it's a taste that drinkers can't associate with any place other than Greece. And sense of place is everything!

The good news is that Retsina may be enjoying a tiny resurgence among certain segments of the younger adult population. Millennials have been seeking out traditional, authentic products to get more in touch with their roots. Retsina fits that profile perfectly. But I wouldn't call it a full-on renaissance.

On the distilled side of things, the drink most think of when they hear the words "Greek spirit" is ouzo, which is fairly pedestrian when compared with some of the other distilled beverages the country has been responsible for over the years. Ouzo begins its life as a brandy, distilled from the grape leftovers of the winemaking process, similar to how Italian grappa makers use pomace to make their product. But ouzo goes a step further: The

153

distillers add anise to the mix, and often other aromatic botanicals in a similar licorice-y vein.

Anyone who's been to nearby Turkey is probably yelling at this page right now, saying, "I had that when I was in Istanbul, but they didn't call it ouzo!" And that's because Turkey has its own anise-centric tipple: raki. It's no accident that raki sounds a lot like rakia, the brandy of the Balkan region; it's pretty much the same stuff, though Turkish versions usually, but not always, incorporate aniseed into the distillation process.

The addition of the licorice-like botanical to both ouzo and raki, of course, makes the Greek and Turkish spirits just about identical to Middle Eastern and North African arak. Like arak, these spirits also cloud (or "louche") as they come into contact with ice or water, thanks to our old friend anethole, that oil found in anise. But please don't add ice to your ouzo or raki; neat is the preferred method for imbibing. Sometimes a little water is okay to reduce the strength, but ice causes crystals to form in the liquid, which looks unappetizing and also makes the oils separate, giving the drink an uneven flavor.

Quality can vary wildly among ouzo and raki brands. Many producers refuse to use anything but the anise distillate from their copper pot stills, which they consider the authentic production method. However, others use only 20 to 30 percent of their own distillate and then add neutral ethanol to make up the difference (it's less expensive that way). In Greece in particular, some distillers incorporate flavor additives to get their products to taste more like ouzo. There's nothing wrong with that, legally—the Greek government allows it.

It's hard to walk through most Greek cities without stumbling on the dedicated watering holes known as ouzeries. Their Turkish counterparts might be a bit harder to find—not because fewer exist, but because in 2013, the majority-Muslim country banned advertising and promotion for alcoholic beverages, including at the establishments that sell them. Regardless, once inside, the scene isn't all that dissimilar from a Greek ouzerie: five or six people hanging out around a table and sipping their spirits as they work through a table full of food. The customary culinary companions for ouzo and raki are small, tapas-like plates called mezethes (the plural form of meze). This can include anything from cheese to cold fish.

There was a time not too long ago—as recently as the early '80s—when there wasn't much else besides ouzo to drink in Greece, as far as spirits were concerned (there was wine, of course, and some beer). That changed when Greece became a part of the EU, and vodka, Scotch, and Cognac became more widely available. Until then, entire generations knew only ouzo. And they'd grown accustomed to drinking the spirit with just about any type of food put before them or as a digestif at the conclusion of dinner.

Your enjoyment of ouzo or raki depends on your tolerance for the anise flavor. You either love it or hate it; there is no middle ground (I'll keep my own anise allegiances close to the vest). If you fall into the "hate" camp, you're in luck, as there are a number of other curious flavor experiences in the region.

On the island of Chios, there grows a tree known as the mastiha, a regionally specific member of the mastic family unique to Chios—it even enjoys protected-designation-of-origin status. The mastiha grows to about six feet high, so it's more of a tall shrub, and its sticky sap falls to the ground in July and August and hardens to a rock-like consistency. Harvesters collect those crystallized sap-stones, which by then will have picked up all sorts of particles, leaves, and other detritus that need to be scrubbed off. Greeks have discovered multiple medicinal uses for mastiha sap; they believe it to be a particularly effective remedy for ulcers and other stomach ailments. The hardened sap can be ground into a powder, which many people bake into their breads and desserts.

Mastiha oil derived from this sap is its most prized component and can be quite expensive. But because the oil is ultra-concentrated, distillers don't need much of it to achieve their desired

155

GREEK COCKTAILS

Stoupakis Distillery on the island of Chios provided these tastes of Greece.

☞ FRESH BREEZE

Mint liqueur brings the breeze to this ouzo-based cocktail.

⇥ DIRECTIONS ⇤	⇥ INGREDIENTS ⇤
Combine all ingredients in a tall highball or Collins glass.	25 ml (¾ ounce) Kazanisto Stoupakis ouzo (or comparable brand)
	5 ml (1 teaspoon) crème de menthe
	140 ml (a little more than 4½ ounces) fresh lemon juice

☞ HOLIDAYS IN CHIOS

This is quite the fruit-forward concoction, with special guest star Homeric Mastiha liqueur.

⇥ DIRECTIONS ⇤	⇥ INGREDIENTS ⇤
Stir all ingredients together in a tall glass with ice.	20 ml (⅔ ounce) Homeric Mastiha
Garnish with lime wedge.	40 ml (1⅓ ounces) vodka
	35 ml (1 ounce + 1 teaspoon) lime sweet and sour mix
	50 ml (1⅔ ounces) fresh peach juice
	20 ml (⅔ ounce) pear puree
	15 ml (½ ounce) orange syrup
	Lime wedge, for garnish

☞ SPICY HOMERIC

Botanical fans will love this tart, earthy concoction, as the mastiha liqueur harmonizes nicely with the gin.

⇥ DIRECTIONS ⇤	⇥ INGREDIENTS ⇤
Combine mastiha liqueur, gin, and sweet and sour mix in a martini glass. Drop in a slice of ginger.	20 ml (⅔ ounce) Homeric Mastiha 40 ml (1⅓ ounces) gin 40 ml (1⅓ ounces) lime sweet and sour mix 1 slice ginger

☞ CAIPIRINHA LA GRECA

Brazilians may have mixed feelings about replacing their national spirit, cachaça, with mastiha liqueur in their most famous cocktail, but this Greek twist on the caipirinha really is its own thing.

⇥ DIRECTIONS ⇤	⇥ INGREDIENTS ⇤
Pour mastiha liqueur into a rocks glass. Squeeze in lime juice and add brown sugar. Stir and add ice. Drop in spent lime wedges (optional).	50 ml (1⅔ ounces) Homeric Mastiha ½ lime, cut into wedges 1 teaspoon brown sugar

157

☞ PASSION LOVE

Finally, we've got something that's a best-of-both-worlds scenario, combining ouzo and mastiha liqueur.

⇥ DIRECTIONS ⇤	⇥ INGREDIENTS ⇤
Combine all ingredients in a tall, Collins, or highball glass. Garnish with fresh strawberries.	25 ml (¾ ounce) Homeric Mastiha 25 ml (¾ ounce) Kazanisto Stoupakis ouzo (or comparable brand) 40 ml (1⅓ ounces) lemon sweet and sour mix 3 or 4 fresh strawberries, for garnish

results. Chios-based Stoupakis Distillery produces Homericon Liqueur Mastiha, named, as you can guess, after the famed poet of Ancient Greece. Homer, many historians believe, was born on the island and returned to it late in life. (Stoupakis also produces Ouzo Kazanisto, which translates to "boiled" or "distilled" ouzo.)

There seems to be a bit of magic to the island. Mastiha trees in other parts of Greece have no problem growing to their normal height, and the sap leaks out just as it does from mastiha trees at the southern end of Chios. However, the resin never transforms into that signature rock-solid state. I'm sure there are scientists out there who can explain the reason behind that, but it remains a mystery to the average Greek and, more importantly, the average Greek distiller.

"It only grows on our island and only on the south part of our island," says Manolis Haviaris, co-owner of Stoupakis Distillery. "If I take a tree to the north part of the island or to any part of Greece, it will grow up and the juice will come out from the trunk, but when it falls to the ground, it will stay liquid. It's impossible for anyone to process. It's a mystery why only our island has the mastiha. We know people who have tried to cultivate the trees in different areas of the world and they've failed to do it—it's as simple as that."

Drinking Homeric Mastiha is a Homeric journey in itself. Okay, maybe I'm overselling it, but it definitely tastes the way you'd expect a drink made from tree resin to taste, even if you're not familiar with Retsina. Though I must say, I've found the aroma to be less like trees and more like a vague collection of raw vegetables. My first thought when I opened the bottle was, "It smells like a farmers' market." Sometimes I get a bit of carrot, other times turnip, and a few other times a hint of celery. It's sweetened with sugar and is a moderate 28 percent alcohol, so it's quite an easy-drinking concoction and worth trying if you find yourself on Chios, or in any other part of Greece. (If you don't want to make the trip, it is available in well-stocked liquor stores in some major U.S. cities.)

It was only a matter of time before bartenders got their hands on this stuff; it's become one of the top-trending ingredients in Greece's burgeoning cocktail culture—though mostly as a secondary spirit, since it's considerably lower in alcohol than gin or vodka.

❧ Flavored Flora

The flavor of mastiha harmonizes well with a number of other botanicals, which is why Stoupakis Distillery offers several flavor blends that aren't all about trees—think of them as Ocean Spray's "cran-" combos, but with mastiha instead of cranberries. And, well, alcohol. The portfolio includes Homeric Mint, Homeric Strawberry, and Homeric Rose (the latter infused with rose petals). For those looking for a break from the trees altogether, there's OneDrop Mandarin, which bottles another native item from Chios. Nicknamed the myrovolos orange (meaning "the fragrantly sweet one"), the Chios mandarin is a variety unto itself and even received protected status from the European Union. OneDrop is a distillate made from 100 percent Chios mandarins, sans mastiha.

159

POLAND

If you're Russian, you might want to skip the next couple of sentences. If you choose not to, I beg you not to kill the messenger. Okay, here goes: In all likelihood, vodka was born in Poland. Yes, Russia and vodka are pretty much joined at the hip, but many experts suggest that Polish vodka predates the Russian version. That's not 100 percent definitive, and I'm sure you can easily find a scholar who will dispute that claim. But many Poles claim to have a bit of documented history on their side. The first recorded mention of vodka in Poland, they point out, dates back to the fourteenth century. The word did not appear in Russian writings until about five hundred years later. That doesn't, of course, mean that it didn't exist in Russia prior to the eighteenth century; perhaps it's just the case that no one was writing about it.

Frankly, I don't really care which country had it first. The fact is, it's so embedded in both of their histories and cultures that one doesn't have more of a claim than the other. However, personally speaking, Poland gets a bit of an edge, as it's the first place I ever truly drank vodka. Not literally my first taste of vodka, mind you. My memory's a bit fuzzy about my very first sip of the neutral spirit, but it was during college. (I won't say which year, as I do not want to retroactively incriminate myself.) No, Poland is the place, where, at a fairly advanced age, I fully appreciated vodka for the first time.

I've made no secret about my complicated relationship with the spirit. In my first book, *The Year of Drinking Adventurously*, I even went so far as to call it "a bit of a scam" because of its supposed flavor and aroma neutrality—the fact that it serves no other purpose than that of an alcohol delivery system. I was making a case for natural vodka infusions (of which I'm still a huge fan— see the recipes in the section on Russia in this very book), insinuating that the spirit comes alive only when you add stuff to it. Turns out I was only half right, and a series of bar crawls through Warsaw and Gdansk in 2016 completely set me straight. (In hindsight, I should have taken my own "consumption within context" advice—the central thesis of that first book's epilogue.)

Enter: the shot bar, a staple of the modern Polish drinking scene. Most are fairly no-frills joints where a person can stop for a beer (or a piwo in the local tongue) or, naturally, a shot or four of vodka at the beginning or end of a night on the town—or both, bookending the evening. Some establishments are a tad fancier, with extensive vodka lists from world-class distilleries. A number of them have a curious affinity for Communist-era décor—old newspapers, propaganda posters, and even mannequins sporting military uniforms and gas masks. No, the proprietors don't miss the bad old days; it's just a healthy helping of playful irony. (If there's any doubt, just ask some of the locals who are old enough to remember or who have parents who lived through the era. It's not uncommon for them to speak of stores with nothing on the shelves but vinegar; when fresh vegetables were in season—the kind that would be perfect for pickling for future consumption—those same stores would be out of vinegar.)

The country has been doing quite well in the years since the end of Communism in the country. The economy is strong, and Polish cities, especially Warsaw, are among the most cosmopolitan across the continent. I first visited Warsaw back in 1999—barely a decade after the end of Communism—and it was already quite a vibrant city then. But I had a sense that it was still finding itself. There were still traces of the Iron Curtain aesthetics and infrastructure. (Returning seventeen years later, I discerned a much more pronounced Paris- or Milan-like vibe—but, at the same time, it was entirely Polish.)

As was the case with most former Eastern Bloc countries that were getting their first tastes of Western capitalism some five decades after World War II, Poland experienced a rapid influx of international investment and products—not to mention an accelerated sense of worldliness. Many residents soon acquired a taste for whisky, Cognac, and other non-Polish spirits and began to regard vodka as passé. That attitude persisted from the mid-'90s until the early aughts. It was around then that drinkers started rediscovering their roots. The shot bars offered the perfect arena for that—and usually quite cheaply to boot. A shot would run you at most four or five zloty (about a buck, buck and a quarter) or even as little as two zloty (fifty cents). Granted, it wasn't the ultra-premium stuff, but at the end of the day, who really cares?

And I'll tell you, I never in a million years would have thought of straight vodka as a food-pairing beverage, but I became a believer. Now I'll take a couple of ounces of straight Zubrowka with a plate of sour Polish pickle slices—they just call them cucumbers—over a Cabernet and cheese any day!

It finally dawned on me that vodka is like the tofu of spirits—in the sense that it's a culinary chameleon, taking on the flavor of what's around without ever losing itself. There's really no other way to explain it, so you'll just have to trust me on that.

Now, the unadulterated shot with a few Polish-style tapas may be one of the most traditional ways to enjoy the spirit, but that doesn't mean it's the only way the Polish population sips the stuff. For one thing, shot bars usually have an entire menu of flavored shots—including anything from raspberry syrup to Coca-Cola—which are more like mini-cocktails. And then there are bottled oddities like Zubrowka Bison Grass vodka, a spirit with a single strand of bison grass immersed in the liquid. That lone blade imparts a strangely apple-cinnamon aroma.

Although I seem to be spending a great deal of time extolling the virtues of Polish vodka and the culture that surrounds it, I don't want you to get the impression that it's the most consumed alcoholic beverage in the country—far from it. As in most countries, beer is the runaway favorite. Poland's most famous national brands are Zywiec, Okocim, and Tyskie, and they're fairly ubiquitous throughout the country. Grupa Zywiec, of which Dutch brewer Heineken owns a majority stake, produces its namesake brand. Danish brewer Carlsberg, one of Heineken's closest competitors, is Okocim's parent, while Anheuser-Busch InBev owns Tyskie. AB InBev picked it up in the big SABMiller deal of 2016.

There was a time not too long ago that those three brands were pretty much the only games in town (domestically speaking, of course). But now you can add Poland to the rapidly growing number of countries worldwide that have been bitten by the craft beer bug. One of the best places to witness that revolution unfold is PiwPaw Beer Heaven in central Warsaw. The bar offers ninety-odd different brews—a large percentage of which are from Polish producers (All Ryed Lager from the Pinta brewery is one of my new favorites). Best thing about PiwPaw? The tens of thousands of beer bottle caps that adorn the walls—and parts

POLISH COCKTAIL

☞ VISTA LITE

Arek Stan, a Warsaw-based photographer and bartender (he previously worked at the city's modern craft cocktail bar Lazy Dog) developed this recipe with orange-infused Polish vodka. He named it after the legendary drum kit, which has the same color and transparency.

⇢⊫◎ DIRECTIONS ◎⊨⇠

Pour all ingredients into an ice-filled coupette glass and stir.

Garnish with pickled pearl onions on a skewer—arrange to resemble drumsticks.

⇢⊫◎ INGREDIENTS ◎⊨⇠

40 ml (about 1½ ounces) orange-infused vodka* (if you don't want to take the time to infuse the vodka yourself, Stan recommends J. A. Baczewski orange vodka)

20 ml (⅔ ounce) extra dry vermouth

15 ml (½ ounce) Aperol

2 dashes Regan's bitters

Pickled pearl onions, for garnish

163

*For the orange infusion: Pour a full bottle of vodka into a jar or other container with 70 grams (2½ ounces) of orange peel with the white part removed. Store in a warm place (75 or so degrees Fahrenheit) for forty-eight hours.

of the ceiling—throughout the space. That's more than enough eye candy for a lazy afternoon. Second-best thing? The bar is open twenty-four hours! Finally, a place that operates on *my* schedule!

Circling back to spirits, another global phenomenon that's well entrenched in Poland is the craft cocktail movement. Cocktails hadn't traditionally been a part of everyday drinking in the country, but now there are neighborhoods of the major cities that you could easily mistake for Brooklyn.

⍺ Starchy Starters

There's a common misconception that what distinguishes Polish vodka from Russia's version of the spirit is that the former is made from potatoes and the latter from grain. The reality is that grain-based vodkas are more common in Poland than potato ones— but potato-based vodkas did originate there. (The Russians have unsuccessfully tried to get the international definition of vodka to apply only to grain-based spirits.)

Truth is, "What exactly is vodka made from?" isn't much of a topic of conversation within the general populations of most countries. The folks behind Belvedere vodka—a Polish brand owned by international marketer Louis Vuitton–Moët Hennessy— have sought to change that conversation by playing up the role that the base grain, rye, plays in the spirit. They even flew out a bunch of journalists in July 2016—myself included, the shameless shill that I am—to stroll through rye fields and tour distilleries to drive the point home. It was really the first visible example, in my experience, of a major, super-premium vodka company putting the fermentable base of its flagship brand front and center in its marketing.

The spirits world had just come off a decade and a half of luxury-centric advertising and promotion where marketers prioritized "bling" and flashy imagery over authenticity. Showcasing the vodka's rye base was a pretty pragmatic move on Belvedere's part, considering that the super-premium vodka price tier in its largest export market, the States, was down double digits in the prior year. Drinkers were gravitating toward other spirits categories, namely whiskey, tequila, and Cognac, for their super-premium experiences. And the brand stories for those were more rooted in ingredient and process authenticity. (It certainly doesn't hurt that rye whisky and even rye beers have been surging; there was really no downside to shining a spotlight on this popular grain.)

{ A HARVESTER MOWS THROUGH A POLISH RYE FIELD. THE GRAIN WILL EVENTUALLY BECOME BELVEDERE VODKA. }

165

Another upscale Polish brand, Chopin, offers a range of single-ingredient vodkas, but those single ingredients alternate among rye, potato, and wheat. Chopin also markets a couple of niche bottlings—Single Potato, Single Wheat, and Single Rye—each distilled only once. There's also a Single Young Potato label, made with potatoes harvested early. Now, you can't really call these "vodkas" because they're distilled only once and retain the character of their base ingredients. Single Potato and Single Young Potato actually taste like liquid potato. Single Rye tastes like a new-make rye whisky, and Single Wheat has a flavor that is difficult to classify, but it's a flavor nonetheless. Vodka's supposed to be flavorless and odorless, and these are far from being either. But they're good spirits in their own right and, like Belvedere's "Why Rye?" campaign, could get drinkers focusing more attention where they ought to: on what's in the bottle, not what's on the bottle.

⋈ Goldwasser

No, it's not the German name of a former presidential candidate. It's a liqueur that is sort of the unofficial spirit of the Polish city of Gdansk. Danziger Goldwasser (Danzig is the German name for Gdansk), much like the similar German-produced spirit Goldschlager, contains small flakes of gold suspended in the liquid.

As the story goes, Gdansk was such a wealthy port city during the Renaissance that its inhabitants drank gold. The brand is no longer produced in Gdansk; the city was leveled during World War II and all production was eventually moved to Germany. Today, it's regarded as neither a Polish drink nor a German one—but simply a Gdansk spirit.

⋈ Polish Vodka Tours

I'm not big on tours when I travel; you usually don't get an authentic, local experience. Often it's just a guide holding up an umbrella in front of throngs of tourists clad in Tommy Bahama sweatpants and mom jeans, all carrying maps and generally looking lost as their leader explains to them the significance of a fountain.

But I was intrigued when I came across Eat Polska, a group that organizes foodie and boozy tours for travelers looking to discover a bit about the culinary culture in Poland's major cities. The vodka tour in Gdansk promised a nearly four-hour excursion through the spirit's past and present, with some tasty snacking along the way. I wasn't disappointed.

For one thing, it was a small group. On that particular day there were only four of us: three Scots and me. And our guide, Daniel Hucik, was incredibly knowledgeable and passionate about vodka. He was very eager to separate the facts from the myths. Of the latter, there's one that he was especially adamant about disavowing: "No, we do not have vodka for breakfast."

Daniel told us about the rigorous research that went into choosing the right places to visit in order to tell the vodka story and avoid inauthentic tourist traps (a few of which he was more than happy to point out along the way). He also introduced us to what he likes to call Polish Nutella—which bears absolutely no resemblance to the Italian hazelnut confection, beyond its spreadability. The savory paste is glorious in its simplicity: lard, onions, and spices. It's great on bread and pairs impeccably with vodka.

He also shared a popular theory on why God gave us hands with five fingers: The thumb and the index finger hold the vodka shot glass, a pickle goes between the index finger and the middle finger, a slice of bread between the middle and the ring finger, and a sausage between the ring finger and pinky. It's a joke, of course, so don't try this at home. (Though if you do, I want to hear how you managed to maneuver that arrangement!)

HUNGARY

167

"You've got to try lots of wine" was always the unsolicited advice I received from people when I told them I'd be spending a few days in the Hungarian capital, Budapest. And as much as I hate having people tell me what to do, these voluntary advisors were absolutely spot-on about Hungarian wine.

But first: Calling it "Hungarian wine" is doing the whole country and its traditions a huge disservice. Hungary's winemaking activities are spread across six major regions: Balaton, North Transdanubia, Pannon, Danube, Upper Hungary, and Tokaj. Within these regions are a total of some twenty-two sub-regions, each with its own terroir and grape specialty, and each demanding the drinker's attention.

The most distinctive Hungarian white wines come from the Somló and Badacsony sub-regions of Balaton and from Tokaj, with each known for a grape varietal rich in minerals. In Somló, it's the Juhfark grape; in Badacsony, it's Kéknelyű; and in Tokaj, it's

Furmint. Furmint grapes are grown throughout Hungary, but the ones in Tokaj have a higher level of minerality. If you were to taste these and other Hungarian whites alongside whites from other parts of Europe, you'd easily pick out the Hungarian ones because of that dense mineral content. Sometimes, it's so pronounced that the minerality is immediately apparent on the nose. Much of that character comes from the volcanic soil concentrated in many of the wine-production centers. You don't immediately think "volcano" when you think Hungary, but the peaks in the hillier parts of the country were once active ash-spewers.

Hungary's reds, on the other hand, are comparable to other continental styles. The most significant red wine makers are based in Eger (in Upper Hungary) and Szekszárd (in Pannon). You might detect a bit more minerality in the reds in Eger than those in Szekszárd, but it's far less apparent than in the whites. For the sake of comparison, Eger's grapes aren't too far removed from the Pinot Noirs of Burgundy. Szekszárd's, however, share a kinship with some Bordeaux rouges. The reds from these two Hungarian regions are well known internationally as bull's blood (or bikavér on its home turf). They're based on the dark blue–skinned Kékfrankos grape, which goes by the German name Blaufränkisch in other parts of the world.

Hungarian soil has been home to wine-producing activities for a good thousand years. But Hungary's industry came dangerously close to disappearing behind the Iron Curtain. After World War II, Hungary's winemakers were forced to serve the needs of the Soviet Union. As a Warsaw Pact nation, Hungary had to sacrifice quality in favor of mass production to satisfy Soviet demand. People planted grapes on any available land, even where the climate and soil were not conducive to growing high-quality fruit. Naturally, the wine suffered. When Russian domination ended in 1990, Hungary was finally able to regain control of its winemaking destiny, but the damage had been done. The country faced a steep climb back up the quality pyramid, but since the late 1990s and early 2000s, it's been able to reestablish a stellar reputation.

EASTERN *and* CENTRAL EUROPE *and the* BALKANS

That's Hungarian wine in a (very small) nutshell, but that's enough to map one's way through its vast wine-growing territories. Now on to something even more notably Hungarian: its national spirit. Hungary's signature eau-de-vie, pálinka, orbits the slivovitz realm, especially when it's made from plum (plum is "szilva" in Hungarian, so you can see the linguistic connection). Other popular fruit bases include, but are not limited to, apple ("almák" in the native tongue) and apricot ("sárgabarack" or simply "barack"—no relation to the former U.S. president).

The word pálinka derives from the root palit, meaning "to burn"—a term that recurs in many languages throughout the world. The name of the Nordic spirit brennivín means "burned wine"; the same is true of the Dutch brandewijn, which in English became "brandy wine" and then simply "brandy."

Records indicate that the earliest form of pálinka appeared in the country in the fourteenth century in its initial medicinal form, which likely had more herbal additives—rosemary, for instance. In the seven hundred years since, it's evolved, like all good liquors, into an everyday recreational beverage, weaving itself into the very fabric of Hungarian life. The Hungarian government ultimately standardized its production, and no beverage with an alcohol content below 37.5 percent may bear the name pálinka. Its base must be fresh native Hungarian fruit; dried fruits and concentrates are prohibited. The European Union has, since 2004, recognized pálinka as a Hungarian specialty spirit. There's also a subcategory called törkölypálinka that is pálinka made from, you guessed it, törköly, or pomace.

Much like Hungary's wine output, pálinka has enjoyed a bit of a quality renaissance as well. Since about 2011, there's been a marked improvement in pálinka production, thanks to better distilling technology and a better-educated consumer base seeking finer products.

When city folk travel to the country to visit family or friends, the hosts will likely greet them with pálinka, usually in shot form. It's also drunk as both an aperitif and a digestif surrounding the meals on major holidays like Christmas and Easter. And of course pálinka plays a central role in Hungarian cultural festivals, particularly the spring Pálinka Festival and the fall Pálinka and Sausage Festival, both in Budapest. I'd be remiss if I didn't mention another quintessentially Hungarian beverage: Unicum. The brownish-amber liqueur is a spiritual (pun intended) cousin of Italian amari (more on those in a bit) and Hungarians traditionally enjoy it as an aperitif or digestif. Dr. József Zwack, royal physician to the imperial court of the holy Roman Empire, created the bittersweet and floral liqueur in 1790, and the company remains in the Zwack family today.

When you're toasting with wine, Unicum, or palinka, the preferred salutation is "Egészégedre!" Sustained eye contact during the toast is mandatory. However, if you're drinking beer in Hungary, be extremely careful. No, the brews won't poison you (they're actually quite good). The critical moment is the one mere seconds before the beverage touches your lips. When you're toasting your drinking companions, be sure that your glasses never touch. Hungarians consider it incredibly bad form and downright disrespectful. Their attitude is based on a legend stemming from the 1848–1849 Hungarian Revolution. The Austrian Habsburgs defeated Hungary in the latter's relatively brief war for independence. Afterward, in the city of Arad, the Austrians executed a group of Hungarian generals, who became known as the Thirteen Martyrs of Arad.

According to the tall tale, Austrian generals clinked their beer-filled drinking vessels to celebrate the execution. Hungarians then vowed to never clink their glasses for 150 years. That period, of course, ended in 1999, but many Hungarians continue the tradition. However, many younger drinkers have abandoned it, arguing that it's time to move on. Wherever you may drink in Budapest or beyond, there's always likely to be a mix of anti-clinking loyalists and the less traditional bunch, so it would be prudent to not clink. Consider yourself warned.

THE CZECH REPUBLIC AND SLOVAKIA

My favorite development related to the former Czechoslovakia is that beer drinkers are finally giving it its due as the creator of the most successful beer style in history. I'm speaking, of course, of pilsner, so named for its birthplace, the city of Plzen (spelled Pilsen on most English-language maps), in Bohemia, a region within the country today known as the Czech Republic.

Most across the globe had credited Germany with the style, which nations on just about every continent have adopted and adapted, so that it has become the dominant, albeit commoditized, style internationally. Crediting the Germans is understandable, because the beer quickly spread across Germany, supplanting many local styles as the go-to brew. And the man who, in 1842, created the crisp, golden, refreshing beer with a bitter bite, Josef Groll, was actually born in Bavaria.

The pilsner prototype still exists today as Pilsner Urquell—a German word, thanks to the Habsburg Empire's dominion over nineteenth century Bohemia but the Bohemians called it Plzensky Prasdoj (decidedly un-German). Despite the fact that the macro-brewers had thinned out much of pilsners' flavor, it's finally become exciting to drink them again. In fact, some of the tastiest offerings coming out of American craft breweries these days aren't just pilsners, they're Czech-style pilsners.

During my first visit to Prague in 2005, my impression was that the locals were a bit blasé about their national style. To be sure, they drank a hell of a lot of it; per capita beer consumption among Czech drinkers is among the highest in the world. But it was so ubiquitous and so damned cheap—a 33-centiliter bottle (slightly less than an American 12-ounce bottle) cost the equivalent of seventy-five cents at corner kiosks, and dance clubs were literally giving away unlimited amounts of the stuff for free when you paid a very modest cover charge (I think the conversion rate put it at about two bucks). The brew is poured into those unsightly

171

7-ounce plastic cups that quick-service restaurants in the States give you when you want to pour your own complimentary water and not spring for a bottle of Dasani.

But even though these were the Czech equivalents of macro brands, they were still exponentially more flavorful than the "premium" domestics to which Americans had grown accustomed—and they have existed since before the concept of craft beer made its way to the Czech Republic. (When it finally did, consumers of mass-marketed brands were floored to see a glass or bottle of beer selling for—gasp!—the equivalent of US$4.) And though the whole craft thing is catching on, especially among millennial Czech drinkers, when I'm in the country, I have no interest in American-style pale ales or IPAs. I want the national style. I don't care that most of the available options are owned by some of the biggest multinational brewing conglomerates in the world. The reason I love Czech pilsners so much? The secret's in the Saaz—the floral, spicy hop variety that gives the style its signature aroma and flavor.

So famous is the Czech Republic for its beer that most forget that the country does produce other forms of alcohol. One of the best known is an herbal liqueur, Becherovka, produced in the town of Karlovy Vary since 1807. Two years prior to that, local merchant Josef Vitus Becher hosted in his home Count Maximilian Friedrich von Plettenberg-Wittem-Mietengen (whew, now there's a name), who brought with him his personal physician, a Brit by the name of Dr. Christian Frobrig. During his stay, the good doctor explored the healing power of herbs, an interest he shared with Becher. At the end of Frobrig's stay, he left a parting gift for Becher, the recipe for what would become Becherovka. Becher dubbed it "English Bitter" and began to sell it in his shop; eventually his son, Johann (Jan) Becher, ramped up production and expanded its commercial distribution.

In the two centuries since its creation, Becherovka has emerged as something of a Czech national icon. Most Czechs have a bottle somewhere in their houses, and when they travel abroad they often bring the bittersweet spirit with them as a gift to foreign friends, family, and colleagues as a symbol of their Czech pride. It's also a popular souvenir for visitors to the Czech Republic to bring back home.

Becherovka, like Unicum, is similar to an Italian amaro, with a combination of thirty-odd herbs—the exact recipe, like so many others of its ilk, is a closely guarded secret, but the prevailing botanicals are cinnamon and anise (think kinder, gentler absinthe). Chilled and neat as an aperitif or digestif is the preferred consumption method for the 76-proof clear spirit (on the high side, alcohol-content-wise, for a liqueur). Some are fond of drinking it with a beer, combining the country's two big beverage traditions. Czechs are also known to mix it with tonic, as their own sort of homegrown riff on a classic G&T (see below).

⋈ What about Slovakia?

173

When it comes to the two main components of the country formerly known as Czechoslovakia, the Czech Republic has undoubtedly gotten a lopsided amount of the attention (we've probably got Prague to thank for that). But Slovakia has contributed quite a few of its own spirited traditions to the local, European, and global communities.

For one, there's the country's own answer to Becherovka, Demänovka. Demänovka is also an herbal liqueur (with fourteen herbs and spices, as well as honey) and is frequently drunk as an aperitif or digestif. It's available in three different versions: Horká (bitter; 38 percent ABV), Sladká (sweet; 33 percent ABV), and Brusnica (cranberry; 30 percent ABV). The company that produces Demänovka, St. Nicolaus, has some very specific suggestions for how to best enjoy those products. For Horká and Sladká: straight up at room temperature or chilled to 6 degrees Celsius

BECHEROVKA COCKTAILS

Pernod Ricard, which now owns the Becherovka brand, offered up a few classic mixed drinks.

BeTon

A Czech alternative to the gin and tonic, this recipe dates back to 1967. It's about as no-nonsense as you get in mixed drinks and just as satisfying as the fancier, more complex stuff.

→⊷ DIRECTIONS ⊷←	→⊷ INGREDIENTS ⊷←
Fill a glass with ice.	40 ml (1⅓ ounces) Becherovka
Add Becherovka.	Tonic water
Top off with tonic.	2 or 3 lemon slices
Add lemon slices and enjoy.	

Apple Sling

Here's a refreshing sipper for those who prefer something a bit more fruit-forward.

→⊷ DIRECTIONS ⊷←	→⊷ INGREDIENTS ⊷←
Fill a tall glass with ice.	45 ml (1½ ounces) Becherovka
Pour in Becherovka and apple juice and top with tonic.	45 ml (1½ ounces) unfiltered apple juice
	45 ml (1½ ounces) tonic water
Stir well and garnish with fresh apple slices.	Fresh apple slices

☞ B-Celebration

Fancy a little ginger with that apple?

⇒ DIRECTIONS ⇐

Fill a tumbler with ice.

Pour in Becherovka and apple liqueur and top with ginger ale.

Garnish with lime wedge and mint sprig.

⇒ INGREDIENTS ⇐

30 ml (1 ounce) Becherovka

10 ml (⅓ ounce) sour apple liqueur

Ginger ale

Lime wedge, for garnish

Mint sprig, for garnish

☞ Avalanche

Those Czech winters are known to be quite nippy, so here's a hot toddy to warm your bones until spring. You can use any red wine, but the creators recommend one with a lighter body, especially since you're not going to want to draw too much attention away from the Becherovka. Also, feel free to add whatever other winter spices you have lying around; they'll harmonize very well with Becherovka's ingredients.

175

⇒ DIRECTIONS ⇐

Heat all ingredients in a small saucepan and pour into a coffee mug.

Garnish with cinnamon stick.

⇒ INGREDIENTS ⇐

45 ml (1½ ounces) Becherovka

120 ml (4 ounces) red wine

20 ml (⅔ ounce) honey

10 ml (⅓ ounce) fresh lime juice

Cinnamon stick, for garnish

(about 43 degrees Fahrenheit, to us metric-averse folk). For Brus
nica: chilled with ice.

And remember brinjevec, that Slovenian juniper spirit that
was sort of a cousin to gin? Slovakia has a similar juniper-based
tipple called borovicka. And, just as brinjevec is the Slovene term
for juniper, the same is true for borovicka in Slovak. It's another
spirit in St Nicolaus's wheelhouse; the company markets a brand
called Borovicka BOREC, double-distilled from red juniper berries
and clocking in at 38 percent ABV.

Chapter 7

NORTHERN AND
WESTERN EUROPE

When most of us sip a cocktail or neat spirit, a glass of wine or a nice, frothy beer, eight or nine times out of ten that drink has some connection to northern and western Europe. For such a relatively small mass of land—you could fly from one edge to another in around three hours—the region has had a massive impact on what much of the world drinks. The imperialistic habits of many of the major countries within the region had more than a little to do with that.

THE NORDIC COUNTRIES

The frostier areas of northern Europe are famous for one type of spirit in particular: aquavit. Sweden, Norway, and Denmark all produce some version of the tipple, each with its own nuances. These countries adhere to the European Union guideline that the spirit should be at least 37.5 percent ABV and have a prevailing flavor of caraway, but the other herbs and spices the makers put in can vary wildly, giving each a distinct character.

Danish and Swedish versions are usually clear or at least very, very light in color, while many Norwegian offerings can have an amber-ish tint from barrel aging—especially the latter's most famous brand, Linie, which matures in wooden casks on ships as it crosses the equator.

Aquavit is a big part of holidays, especially Christmas, and is usually drunk as a shot—or snap—with the traditional fare of the region, pickled herring. It's a key component of the Swedish smorgasbord, which is a buffet featuring all kinds of hot and cold delicacies, including the aforementioned fish—the herbs work wonders in helping revelers digest some of the fattier elements of the gastronomic adventure.

{
SNAPS OF
INFUSED
AQUAVIT
}

Sweden

As ubiquitous as aquavit may be in the region, other spirits sometimes capture the drinking public's attention, especially in Sweden. For instance, there's besk—sometimes spelled "bask"—a liquor whose dominant herbal ingredient is wormwood. That botanical is better known for its role in absinthe, but the two spirits taste nothing alike. Besk is much more bitter and lacks the licorice-like components (mostly from the presence of anise) in absinthe.

Another age-old Swedish sipper is a liqueur called punsch. Though it's not quite the same thing as the category of refreshing mixed drinks we call punch, its origins are somewhat related. They also have similar etymology. Both words are derived from an ancient Sanskrit word for "five," referring to the number of ingredients in them.

Punsch has ancestral roots in Indonesia. The Swedish East India Company started importing various commodities from Java in the 1730s, among them the Indonesian spirit Batavia arrack. "Initially, it basically was just to bring something back and keep the boys happy on board," says Henrik Facile, who, in 1993, launched Facile Punsch, improving on the old traditions for a new generation.

The spirit also served as a preservative for all the meats and other perishable products the Swedes were carrying back to Scandinavia. Less pleasant cargo that the shippers needed to keep from spoiling included dead animals that were traveling back not to become food but to be displayed in museums. "The story goes," Facile notes, "that even if there was a dead monkey in [the arrack], they still tried it and drank it."

English sailors, who mixed a variety of ingredients to make rum punch, inspired their Swedish counterparts to try the same with Batavia arrack. Typical combinations included the spirit plus water, sugar, lemon juice, spices, and tea. Not only was it a tasty recipe, it also had some health benefits: The citrus helped prevent scurvy, which claimed a lot of seafarers' teeth during that era.

Initially, people mixed their own herbs and spices into the Batavia arrack, but about a century after the spirit came to the region, recipes involving multiple ingredients started going commercial. Most drank it warm back in those days, as a matter of both preference and necessity. It was cold on the ships, and the sailors wanted something warm and alcoholic to heat up their shivering bones. Also, it was harder to dissolve the sugar without heating it up, especially in the chilly temperatures.

Back on land, punsch became a drink of the wealthy, as it was pretty pricey. Well-to-do Swedes served it in large bowls (perhaps a precursor to our own punch bowls) crafted from fancy porcelain imported from China.

Later in the eighteenth century, Swedish drinkers began to appreciate punsch's role with regard to food. The most traditional pairing partner was Swedish pea soup, known to be quite fatty thanks to its hefty pork content. The punsch was an effective digestive for the richness of the soup.

By the 1820s, producers had begun bottling the beverage; around the same time, people started drinking it cold. "So then we had two ways of drinking it, either warm, with the pea soup, or room-temperature or cold with, for instance, cigars, which was a very, very popular way to consume it," Facile says.

Punsch reached its heyday in the early 1900s, when producers were selling five million liters a year to a population of about five million people, and the number of punsch brands climbed into the fifties. That would change over the next few years as, little by little, the state gained a monopoly on producing, distributing, selling, and importing alcohol. The government bought a couple of the larger brands, and soon there were only a handful left. The spirit entered a period of creative stagnation that lasted until the early 1990s, when Facile launched his brand.

"The thing I noticed when I started, having worked in the wine and spirits business for many years, was that there had been no development whatsoever in the quality of punsch," Facile explains. "If you're in Cognac or any other alcohol, there's always development toward better, cleaner, more adapted to the tastes of the period. But the Swedish punsch was basically untouched, same recipe, same quality of Batavia arrack , because there are a lot of different qualities of those from absolutely undrinkable to fairly good."

Punsch had been widely considered a "man's drink"—especially since much of its consumption was within the military. It was also popular at college parties, primarily because the

FEELING PUNSCH-Y?

Cocktails with punsch are more popular in export markets, but Sweden is starting to develop a scene of its own.

☞ PUNSCH AND BOURBON

Here's an easy one, though it doesn't really qualify as a cocktail, since it's only two ingredients. It adds a fruit-forward dimension to a glass of whiskey.

⇢ DIRECTIONS ⇠	⇢ INGREDIENTS ⇠
Pour ingredients into a rocks glass and mix well.	45 ml (1½ ounces) bourbon 30 ml (1 ounce) punsch

☞ ALEX'S SWEDISH PUNSCH

If you're feeling really adventurous and want to attempt to make your own punsch. This one comes from Washington, D.C.'s Alex Luboff, who co-hosts the home bartending podcast, Speaking Easy, with fellow cocktail enthusiast Jordan Wicker. (I must also give a shoutout to producer "Silent Tyler" Lloyd.)

181

⇢ DIRECTIONS ⇠	⇢ INGREDIENTS ⇠
Combine the sliced lemons, rum, and arrack in a large glass container that can hold at least 5 cups.	2 cups (roughly ½ liter) aged rum
	1½ cups (roughly ⅓ liter) Batavia Arrack
Cover and steep for 6 hours. Make your tea with double strength (twice as much as you'd use for making tea alone) and add in the sugar to dissolve and the cardamom pods to flavor.	2 cups (roughly ½ liter) spiced tea, double-strength brewed (Luboff recommends something exotic like Pu erh or the smoky Lapsang Souchong. But chai works in a pinch)
Be sure to do this with plenty of time to cool, including if you need to throw it in the fridge.	8 crushed cardamom pods (throw these in with the tea)
After 6 hours, pour the liquor from the lemon-rum-arrack container (straining out the lemon) into a larger container of at least 7 cups (1⅔ liters).	2 cups (roughly ½ liter) Muscovado sugar
Add the tea from the fridge to the large container with the rum-arrack.	3–4 lemons sliced thinly (peels and flesh)
Filter if you'd like. Let it set and mellow for at least 24 hours.	

corner-cutting in production made it a much cheaper indulgence than it was in its earlier years. Facile and some other punsch revivalists have been able to slowly change its perception and its consumer base. Consumption still tilts more toward men, but women have increasingly been drinking it and closing the gap.

How it's drunk, especially among older drinkers, hasn't changed all that much, though. Swedish pea soup isn't nearly as popular as it once was, but plenty of Swedes still enjoy a warm glass of punsch with the traditional dish. Others drink it straight up and cold, often with a cup of coffee. If you're having dessert with that coffee, try a slice of warm apple pie or rich chocolate cake. Punsch is a great partner for those confections.

Denmark

It is a bitter thread that binds much of Europe together, and that is no less the case in Scandinavia, especially Denmark. When we think bitter liqueurs, we usually think Italy (and the boot is the undisputed champ, don't get me wrong), but don't count out the Danish, at least until you've tried Gammel Dansk.

The top brass at Danish Distillers, best known for the Aalborg brand of aquavit (named for the town in which the company is headquartered), directed its team to develop a Danish bitters brand. In 1964, master of engineering J. K. Asmund devised the recipe for Gammel Dansk Bitter Dram. Among the twenty-nine ingredients in the 38 percent ABV spirit are gentian root, coriander, wormwood, angelica, China bark, clove, and a host of other leaves, roots, flowers, spices, and herbs, all harmonizing to form the "bitter, but not too sharp" flavor profile Danish Distillers sought. The complex flavor hints at the spicier elements, with cardamom and cinnamon up front and notes of sweet red berries and almonds hanging in the background.

In less than a decade after its launch, Gammel Dansk usurped Germany's Jägermeister as the best-selling bitters in Denmark.

The brand has gained a massive following, both cult and mainstream. During the bitter liqueur's heyday, Danes discovered that it fostered a relaxed, cozy atmosphere—what the native speakers call hygge—whenever and wherever it was poured. And that included the workplace. Office workers from the 1970s through the 1990s were toasting with it on colleagues' birthdays and when business deals were completed. But it was Gammel Dansk and only Gammel Dansk. If people drank whisky or vodka in the office during those years, they'd be considered alcoholics. (In the ensuing decades, global attitudes toward alcohol shifted, and even Gammel Dansk pretty much disappeared from places of employment.)

The chill Danish vibe benefits from—or, perhaps, contributes to—the fact that Denmark is the only one of the Nordic countries where the state doesn't have a monopoly on the spirits business. The country also never endured a period of Prohibition, unlike many of its neighbors.

Gammel Dansk has inspired the formation of clubs dedicated to the spirit, even outside of its home turf. Swedish and Norwegian drinkers from diverse sectors of their respective populations—everyone from entertainers to society folk—regularly gather in restaurants, sip Gammel Dansk, and engage in spirited (no pun intended) discussions on the affairs of the world.

The spirit has become such a symbol of Danish-ness that it's the key ingredient in a dessert, Gammel Dansk ice cream, at the country's most famous restaurant, Noma. The renowned Copenhagen eatery often cracks the top five on leading "Best Restaurants in the World" lists (and frequently snags number one).

But despite the spirit's Danish roots, its production moved to Norway in 2014. At around the same time, the company launched a chili-and-licorice-flavored line extension, Gammel Dansk Shot. Its name speaks to its recommended method of consumption.

183

Finland

The first thing that comes to mind when someone mentions "Finland" and "drinking" is, for obvious reasons, Finlandia vodka. And if you were to find yourself among the Finnish population, you'd have no trouble finding the spirit. And neither would all the other tourists gravitating toward it, because it's the one brand they all know. Granted, vodka as a category still leads all others in the hearts and minds of Finnish drinkers (the country was once an autonomous duchy of the Russian Empire), though the population has been gradually moving on to other beverages. If you're in Finland, by all means drink plenty of vodka, as you're likely to find some really good stuff. But make sure you save some room for lakka.

Not exactly a household name outside its native country, lakka is the Finnish word for cloudberry, and also for the liqueur whose primary flavor comes from the cloudberry. The Nordic countries—Finland in particular—provide an especially hospitable environment for the fruit, which grows in thick, untouched forests and swampy areas in cool to arctic climates. Summers up there are short but extremely bright, thanks to the northerly latitude. Finland is one place that is often called the land of the midnight sun, and that's not hyperbole. Especially in the northern parts of the country, the sun doesn't set for a good two months (and in the south, it barely even gets dark; it's more like dusk during the wee hours). The virtually nonstop sunlight during the (albeit) brief summer enhances cloudberries' flavor and aroma.

They're rather pricey berries, thanks to the laborious harvesting process—remember, they grow in areas largely devoid of human contact. They're also pretty striking to look at. The berry is a yellow-orange cluster of bumps that almost look like oblong corn kernels at the end of a cob.

As is common with liqueurs, lakka usually falls in the low 20s on the ABV spectrum. The most popular brand, Lapponia, takes its name from the Latin word for Lapland, which refers to northerly countries like Finland and its neighbors. It's a 21 percent ABV spirit with an amber-yellow hue that comes from the berry extract, which steeps in a neutral spirit for about a month or a month and a half. It's then matured for about two months before sugar is added.

Berries and the Finnish people are very much intertwined culturally. That's because in Finland, the forests belong to all people. It's been that way for centuries. Foraging for wild berries and mushrooms is a kind of natural right the Finns enjoy—and one that visitors to the country are allowed to participate in as well.

Lapponia traces its origin story to 1867, when Russian Czar Alexander II granted the company's founder, Anders Nordfors, permission to produce alcohol. Since then, it's become a popular digestif after a big meal, usually consumed in tandem with coffee—when the Finnish people aren't drinking Cognac, that is. Finland has one of the highest per capita Cognac consumption rates in the world.

But Finnish drinking habits are beginning to more closely resemble those throughout the rest of continental Europe. They've really developed an affection for wine, particularly of the sparkling variety. And like most of the rest of the world, they've been thirsting for craft beer, mostly the same sorts of styles drinkers have fallen in love with across the Continent and in the United States. These days, spirits consumption is declining in Finland, according to market research company Euromonitor, and that trend is likely to hold as the population continues to discover the world's other great drinking traditions.

❉ Sahti

Finland is arguably better known for its spirits, but it also has a centuries-old beer brewing tradition all its own: sahti. Most people outside the Nordic region probably never heard of sahti until an American brewer, Dogfish Head, released a product called Sahtea

LAKKA LIBATIONS

Pernod Ricard Finland, marketers of Lapponia lakka, provided a few recipes using the cloudberry-based liqueur.

☞ MORNING MIST

Ginger has become a hugely popular ingredient all over the world, especially with the revival of the Moscow Mule. That popularity extends to Finland, as the root plays a key role in the Morning Mist.

➤➤ DIRECTIONS ➤➤	➤➤ INGREDIENTS ➤➤
Muddle ginger at the bottom of a shaker glass.	1 small piece fresh ginger
	40 ml (1⅓ ounces) Lapponia lakka
Add Lapponia lakka, apple juice, and lime juice.	40 ml (1⅓ ounces) apple juice
	Juice of ½ lime
Shake with ice until cocktail is cold.	Mint sprig, for garnish
Double-strain into a martini glass and garnish with sprig of mint.	

☞ NORTHERN LIGHT

The key word here is "tart." This drink features a guest appearance by Scandinavia's most popular spirits brand, Absolut (a sister brand to Lapponia, as Pernod Ricard is their shared parent company).

➤➤ DIRECTIONS ➤➤	➤➤ INGREDIENTS ➤➤
Pour Lapponia lakka, Absolut Rasperri, and lemon juice into a tall Collins or highball glass.	20 ml (⅔ ounce) Lapponia lakka
	20 ml (⅔ ounce) Absolut Raspberri
	20 ml (⅔ ounce) fresh lemon juice
Fill glass with ice and top off with an even split of cranberry juice and Schweppes Russchian. Garnish with lemon slices.	Cranberry juice
	Schweppes Russchian*
	Thin lemon slices, for garnish

* Schweppes Russchian is available only in Europe. You can order it online, but a good substitute is Starbucks Very Berry Hibiscus, from its Refreshers line.

☞ SPARKLING CLOUDBERRY

Here's a nice Nordic twist on a classic spritz. This one has "outdoor brunch on a summer day" written all over it.

➺► DIRECTIONS ◄

Pour Lapponia lakka into narrow wine glass or Champagne flute.

Top off with sparkling wine and garnish with orange twist.

➺► INGREDIENTS ◄

40 ml (1⅓ ounces) Lapponia lakka

Dry sparkling wine

Orange twist, for garnish

187

that's based on the ancient Finnish brew. Historians theorize that it's of Viking origin, possibly dating as far back as the ninth century (casks of sahti were reportedly found aboard a sunken vessel piloted by the mighty conquerors). Back in the day, white-hot stones heated the mash, which caramelized some of the sweet liquid, imparting some fairly distinct flavors.

As with most beer, malted barley was the primary fermentable base, but it really depended on availability. Other cereals like rye, wheat, and oats would often find their way into the grain bill. And, since sahti originated in the pre-hops era (hops didn't start to become prevalent in beer until around the thirteenth or fourteenth century), Finnish brewers flavored the beverage with whatever they could get their hands on. And gin fans will be happy to learn that what the sahti brewers could get their hands on was generous helpings of juniper. And not just juniper "berries"— the whole plant was thrown into the mix, branches and all (the branches served as filters). Sometimes the juniper even provided additional fermentable sugars to supplement the grain.

The beverage has evolved over the centuries, and there are even some commercial brands available (though it's a really minuscule niche market). Those brands are likely to be around 8 percent ABV and sport an opaque, Coca-Cola-like hue. There are often some fruity banana-and-clove notes, not unlike the flavor elements present in a German Weissbier.

Iceland

Iceland is one of the strangest places on earth. No, it's not because its moss-covered volcanic countryside makes it appear unearthly, but because of its rocky relationship with alcohol. Here's a brief twentieth-century timeline:

1908: Iceland holds a referendum on the question of Prohibition; 60 percent of Icelandic voters elect to ban alcohol.

1915: On New Year's Day, the law voted on in the 1908 referendum goes into effect. Iceland's alcohol ban serves as a model for U.S. Prohibition, which is enacted five years later.

1921: Spanish importers, who had been buying fish from Iceland, refuse to continue to do so unless Iceland starts purchasing Spain's number one export. Hint: It's made from fermented grapes. Wine, therefore, becomes the only legal alcoholic beverage in Iceland for the next fourteen years.

1933: In another referendum, not long after American Prohibition is repealed, Icelanders vote to legalize spirits. But, oddly, beer with an alcohol content above 2.25 percent—which pretty much means all of it—remains illegal.

1989: An increasingly cosmopolitan Icelandic population comes into more frequent contact with beer abroad. Eventually something has to give and, on March 1, the beverage flows once again on the Nordic island.

189

Before modern Icelanders developed a relationship with beer, they'd grown acquainted with a little domestic tipple known as brennivín. (The word loosely translates to "burned wine," a term that, you'll recall, recurs in many languages when referring to a particular country's indigenous alcohol.) It's technically a schnaps; indeed, you're more likely to get a shot of it at a bar if you just ask for schnaps, rather than calling it by its true name.

I like to think of brennivín as the "reluctant spirit." Well, at least the government, which had a monopoly on alcohol production and distribution after the 1933 semi-repeal of Icelandic Prohibition, seemed reluctant to allow the populace to experience any joy in life. The state monopoly tried to make the product—its presentation, at least—as unappealing as possible. "They really believed that they could just hold back consumption by making a black label that, pretty much, was just missing the skull and crossbones and the word 'poison,'" explains Óli Rúnar Jonsson, export

BRENNIVÍN COCKTAILS

Reykjavik's cocktail scene is exploding, which has been great news for brennivín. The spirit, traditionally served neat and chilled, is being introduced to a whole new generation. Here are three libations developed by Kári Sigurðsson of Reykjavik's Apotek bar.

SKALLAGRÍMS SOUR

Sours provide an ideal way for brennivín newbies to ease into enjoying the spirit.

⇢ DIRECTIONS ⇠

Dry-shake brennivín, lemon juice, simple syrup, and egg white.

Add ice, shake again, and double-strain into a glass.

Garnish with horseradish shavings and a drop of bitters.

⇢ INGREDIENTS ⇠

60 ml (2 ounces) chilled brennivín

30 ml (1 ounce) fresh lemon juice

30 ml (1 ounce) simple syrup

1 egg white

Fresh horseradish shavings, for garnish

1 drop Bitter End Memphis Bitters

☞ VINDÁS

This carrot-forward drink won the 2015 Best Brennivín Cocktail contest.

⇢ DIRECTIONS ⇠

Combine all ingredients in a shaker and shake.

Strain into a glass and garnish with strip of lemon peel and pickled carrot.

⇢ INGREDIENTS ⇠

60 ml (2 ounces) chilled brennivín

30 ml (1 ounce) carrot syrup

30 ml (1 ounce) fresh lime juice

3 drops yuzu juice

Lemon peel, for garnish

Pickled carrot, for garnish

☞ PINEAPPLE PICKUP

Sigurðsson's final offering brings a little fizz to brennivín.

⇢▪ DIRECTIONS ▪◄⇠

Combine brennivín, syrup, lemon juice, and bitters in a shaker and shake. Strain into a glass and top with a splash of club soda.

Garnish with pineapple chunks and sprig of rosemary.

⇢▪ INGREDIENTS ▪◄⇠

55 ml (1¾ ounces) chilled brennivín

30 ml (1 ounce) pineapple and rosemary syrup*

25 ml (¾ ounce) fresh lemon juice

2 dashes rhubarb bitters

Club soda

Pineapple chunks, for garnish

Rosemary sprig, for garnish

* To make the pineapple and rosemary syrup, combine 1 part water, 1 part sugar, ¼ part fresh rosemary leaves (stems removed), and two handfuls of fresh pineapple chunks in a blender. Puree, then strain through cheesecloth.

☞ GHOST RIDER

191

American bartenders have been experimenting with the Icelandic spirit as well. Here's one from Mark MacMinn, based at La Moule in Portland, Oregon.

⇢▪ DIRECTIONS ▪◄⇠

Combine brennivín, Campari, grapefruit juice, lime juice, simple syrup, and bitters in a shaker and shake.

Add soda water and pour into a bucket glass on the rocks.

Garnish with lime wheel.

⇢▪ INGREDIENTS ▪◄⇠

45 ml (1½ ounces) brennivín

7 ml (¼ ounce) Campari

30 ml (1 ounce) fresh grapefruit juice

15 ml (½ ounce) fresh lime juice

15 ml (½ ounce) simple syrup

9 drops Scrappy's Grapefruit Bitters

30 ml (1 ounce) soda water

Lime wheel, for garnish

manager at Icelandic drinks supplier Ölgerdin Egill Skallagrims-son. "And of course they dramatically failed, and it became a hot drink right away." Brennivín quickly became a symbol of Icelandic drinking culture. When beer finally became legal again, a beer and a shot of brennivín emerged as the standard pairing.

Brennivín's most visible brand comes in a green bottle, which understandably leads many a tourist to think the spirit inside bears such an emerald hue. Visitors often load up on the stuff at Reykja-vik airport's duty-free shop to distribute among their nearest and dearest—who, more often than not, are crestfallen to discover that, when poured into a shot glass, brennivín looks no differ-ent from vodka. However, it tastes nothing like vodka—which is to say it tastes nothing like *nothing*, since vodka, by definition, is supposed to be flavorless. But flavor brennivín does have, and plenty of it. The original idea was to create something that loosely mimicked the aquavits of mainland Scandinavia. As in aquavit, the principal flavor of brennivín is caraway, though it's not as pro-nounced as it is in aquavit. There's a bit of a floral, herbal thing going on in brennivín.

The spirit is the traditional accompaniment for Iceland's most pungent dishes, devoured during Þorrablót, the annual winter festival that begins in mid-January and continues until mid-February—the month of Þorri on the old Icelandic calen-dar (blót being "festival"). The observance also honors the god Þor, who's most closely associated with the turbulent climatic period. Þor may seem unfamiliar at first glance, but that's just the Old Norse way to express the name of a god with whom I'm sure you're much better acquainted: Thor. Thunder gods (and Mar-vel heroes) aside, Þorrablót is more affectionately known as the Ugly Food Festival. That's when the locals keep their gag reflexes at bay and chow down on mouthwatering temptations like boiled sheep's head (svið), pickled ram's testicles (hrútspnugar), and, the most famous, rotten (aka fermented) shark (hákarl). When I said "accompaniment," I really meant "chaser." At the very least, brennivín should help erase the pungent (to put it very mildly) ammonia-forward flavor of rotted *Jaws* flesh.

Even if you never partake of a bowl of fermented Bruce the Great White, that shouldn't deter you from enjoying brennivín as a shot (its most traditional form) or in a cocktail. Brennivín has begun to play a larger role in Iceland's mixology scene since about 2010. Before that, bartenders designed drinks that were overly sweet or sour to mask the taste of the alcohol in the glass. At that time, it was all about how "clean" a vodka was so a drinker could barely detect that it was there. Brennivín really didn't figure much in that scene.

But, as the street food and craft cocktail revolution swept through Reykjavik, Icelanders were keen to taste things again. They started to appreciate brennivín's flavor complexity and are now more likely to sip it slowly. It's helping them get in touch with their inner Icelander.

⚔ Krona Coffee

193

Brennivín may be playing a larger role in Iceland's budding craft cocktail scene, but mixing with the spirit is nothing new. There are traditional concoctions whose charm more than compensates for their crudeness. A classic is krona coffee, whose recipe has just three components: coffee, brennivín, and a krona—Iceland's monetary unit. The drinker drops a coin into a partially filled cup of joe and then pours in the brennivín until the krona is visible. You haven't added enough brennivín until the clear spirit has diluted the opaque coffee enough to make it semi-translucent.

Greenland

An independent Danish territory, Greenland has the distinction of being the world's largest island. (Apparently Australia doesn't count because it sits on something called a continental lithosphere.) It also has some of the strangest alcohol laws in the world, thanks to a history of rampant abuse. (There's something about arctic Scandinavian islands and their uneasy relationship with alcohol. The cold remoteness of such places seems to facilitate abuse of strong beverages.)

Greenland has had an on-again, off-again affair with Prohibition. After centuries of settlement by various Nordic peoples, as well as the arrival of migrant Thules from Alaska (the ancestors of modern Greenlanders) in the fourteenth century, the Danish began colonizing the island in the 1720s. In 1882, Denmark barred the sale or distribution of alcohol to Greenlanders. (There was no such ban for the Danes; double standard much? The ban was widely viewed as a means of subjugating the Inuit population.)

As history has taught us, convenient loopholes often accompany any sort of Prohibition. For instance, native Greenlander employees of the Royal Greenland Trade Department could get their hands on beverages here and there. And if they didn't work for the government, they still could procure alcohol as a reward for other types of skills and labor not directly in the employ of the powers that be.

In 1929, the Danish government imposed an alcohol rationing system upon Greenland, which remained in place until 1954, the year after Greenlanders gained equal rights with the Danes in the form of their constitution designating the colossal island as an integral province of Denmark. With the enactment of the constitution, the rationing system as it existed was deemed discriminatory and repealed.

However, that was far from the last time Greenlanders would be subjected to rationing. In 1979, the island imposed a similar system to curb excessive drinking. At the time, Greenlanders reportedly had the highest per capita alcohol consumption in the world, three times that of the United States. This version of the rationing system really was the lesser of two evils. Under the new system, alcoholic beverages were assigned points. Adults of legal drinking age (eighteen) were allowed to consume up to seventy-two points' worth of alcoholic beverages per month. A typical bottle of beer— 33 centiliters in metric terms, which is slightly less than the familiar American 12-ounce bottle or can—was worth one point. So, that's roughly two and a half beers a day, which isn't exactly in the realm of teetotaling (though considering the extraordinarily high consumption among islanders, it probably seemed a bit punitive). And that rule covered "strong" beers, which, at the time, would have been between 5.5 and 6 percent alcohol.

A bottle of wine was worth six points and a quart of a distilled spirit was twenty-four points. That translated to approximately two typical glasses of wine a day and around 3 ounces of liquor. Fairly sensible amounts, to be sure, and certainly preferable to complete Prohibition. But the fact that the system didn't work is a testament to the internationally prevalent notion that people just don't like to be told what and how much to drink. The government reported a 40 to 45 percent drop in alcohol consumption, which it considered a win. However, those numbers covered only legally produced and distributed beverages. Moonshine-making and bootlegging started to boom. There also was an underground market for ration points trading (just imagine how out of hand that would have gotten had there been an internet in those days!).

Long story short: Greenland replaced rationing with higher taxes on spirits in 1982.

Alcoholism remains a problem in Greenland, as it does in many cultures whose indigenous populations had no connection to strong beverages before European colonists arrived. At most, such peoples may have been producing lightly alcoholic—3 percent ABV or so—fermented beverages from local cereals and sugar sources, but spirits were completely foreign. During periods of rationing and outright bans, the main source of alcohol in Greenland was the home brew, immiaq. And that, not so coincidentally, is the name of one of the (slowly) growing number of craft breweries on the island.

When you're a country as chilly and remote as Greenland, you have to make the most of what you've got. And one thing Greenland has a healthy stock of is ice—some of the purest, most untouched ice in the world. There may not be much going on in the way of distilling in Greenland, but some producers go out of their way to get their hands on that ultra-pristine water for their vodka. Siku Glacier Ice Vodka's branding is all about the remoteness and unspoiled beauty of it source: Greenland's Qalerallit Sermia glacier, purported to be around sixty thousand years old. Siku employs a pretty complicated process to get the soul of that glacier into its bottles. The harvesters crush the ice, pack it up, and then ship it off to Denmark. But the journey doesn't end there. Refrigerated transport then carts the ice off to a distillery in the Netherlands. But the branding is all Greenland, in whose native tongue siku means "ice." And I guess the large, glacial island has earned it, given the convoluted logistics around the spirit's creation.

GERMANY, AUSTRIA, AND SWITZERLAND

I'm going to state the obvious here. Germany, like the Czech Republic, is beer country—and perhaps even more so when you take into account general global perception rather than just per capita consumption. It's the place that most people associate with the beverage without even thinking about it. Every city in Germany has its own style of beer, though pilsner has become the de facto national style (despite the fact that it was created in Bohemia, part of what's now the Czech Republic).

Some of my most cherished beer-related memories are from Germany. From standing at a narrow shelf in a vestibule, sipping Bambergator Doppelbock at Brauerei Fässla in Bamberg to enjoying a private tasting with the world's top beer sommelier at a trade fair in Munich, there are plenty of German experiences that I credit with making me a better drinker. I must admit, however, that I arrived a bit late to the German beer appreciation party. For a while, I was all about the Belgians, and I felt German styles were a bit too constrained. But I was silly and naïve. After multiple return trips to Germany, I finally started to get it. Where Belgium was all about hitting you over the head, Germany was more about nuance.

Cologne's famous local style, Kölsch (which means "of Cologne," Köln being the German name for the city), took years to truly woo me. I was much more a fan of the copper-hued Altbier, the rival style from nearby Düsseldorf (Altbier translates to "old beer"—old because it's an ale, which all beers used to be before lagers came along in the nineteenth century). It was hard to believe that two cities barely thirty-five miles from each other could have such disparate brewing traditions, but such is Germany!

I must admit, the 20-centiliter cylindrical glasses in which Kölsch is traditionally served in its home city certainly charmed me during my first visit there. But it took another half a decade or so before I was ready to rank the pale, straw-colored, semi-fruity, top-fermented (making it, like Altbier, an ale) brew among my top five beer styles.

The same can be said of Berliner Weisse. I originally steered clear of wheat-based beers for one of the stupidest reasons possible: Their ABVs were on the low side, and I was a drinker of big, boozy Belgian brews, dammit! Fortunately, I grew up and began to appreciate beers at all levels of intensity. I was drawn to Berliner Weisse, the style born in Berlin (though now rarely seen within the capital city's limits), for its moderate and refreshing tartness.

As a fan of darker, maltier beers, dunkels were my initial refuge, no matter where I was in Germany. The roasty, chocolaty elements always proved an ideal match for a heaping bowl of käsespaetzel, those tiny dumplings smothered in cheese—essentially the Bavarian equivalent of mac and cheese. But I was ignoring the paler brews for which different regions in Germany were famous because I thought they seemed too "global." Thankfully, I came to my senses and fell in love with the subtle nuances of pale, malty lagers like Munich Helles (I now actively scan beer menus for my personal fave, Hacker-Pschorr Münchner Gold).

197

Not surprisingly, you can find quite a bit of beer flowing through the streets of Vienna and Salzburg in neighboring Austria, too. Austrians are fiercely proud of the beers produced within their borders, and the top brands are widely available in the United States. The most recognizable of those is Stiegl, whose Salzburg brewery claims roots dating all the way back to 1492 (yet another reason why that year is famous!).

Both Austria and Germany also boast thriving wine businesses, though it's usually not the first beverage to be mentioned in conversations about drinking in either country. When the topic does turn to wine, the first German grape varietal that comes to most people's minds—and rightly so—is Riesling. The general perception is that Rieslings are quite sweet, but there are some astonishingly dry versions out there if you look hard enough. Whites outnumber reds in both Germany and Austria, somewhere in the neighborhood of two to one, but red varietals are beginning to assert themselves more in both countries.

But enough about beer and wine; there'd be a bit too much stating the obvious with either. I'd rather focus on the distilled beverage traditions that are also a part of the fabric of daily life in German-speaking Europe.

There are few boozy terms that are as complicated as the word "schnaps." You're likely most familiar with concept when it's spelled "schnapps," but I've left the second "p" off for a reason. The single-p spelling is traditional in German-speaking countries, while the double-p version is popular in many other parts of the world, particularly English-speaking countries.

But it's more than just a matter of spelling. When American drinkers hear the word "schnapps," we immediately think of cloyingly syrupy-sweet liqueurs that often are the entry-level alcohols we hide in our college dorm rooms. The peach version is the most popular American schnapps and one of the core ingredients of the Fuzzy Navel.

When German, Austrian, and German-speaking Swiss imbibers order schnaps, they're also expecting to get a spirit that involves
fruit, but not one that necessarily tastes like fruit—at least not a
sugar-sweetened, artificially flavored, confectioner's version of
fruit. Schnaps (one "p") is not a liqueur; it's distilled from fruit
and, therefore, a brandy/eau-de-vie.

In short, schnaps with one "p" is boozier, though these brandies are often marketed as "schnapps" to an English-speaking
audience.

Glad that's cleared up.

I was on a Lufthansa redeye to Frankfurt when the flight atten-
dant asked if I wanted some schnaps to help me on my way to
slumberland. The brand was Scheibel, and it was made from wild
raspberries (waldhimbeeren, as they say in Germany), which I
loathe, so I was a bit wary. But I tried it, and it was astonishing in
its complexity—and in the fact that it tasted nothing like the fruit
from which it was distilled. Maybe the essence of the berry was
there, sans its sweet-tartness, but it was a far more vegetal taste
sensation than a fruity one. Germans might slug me for saying
this, but schnaps is one area where Austrians have a slight edge.
(Aw, let them have *something!*)

Given that Switzerland's three main languages are German,
French, and Italian, you can bet that the drinking traditions in
that notoriously neutral country draw from the best of those
three. Naturally, there's a taste for wine there, all influenced
by the styles made famous by those Old World viticultural
countries. But German is the dominant tongue; it's the first language of about 65 percent of Swiss citizens. French is next, at
just under 20 percent, followed by Italian, at about 12 percent;
the rest speak Romansch and a few other rural dialects. So let's
focus on the more German of the country's beverage habits:
kirsch, or kirschwasser ("cherry water"), as it is more formally
known. The cherry-based schnaps isn't unique to Switzerland—
it likely originated in Germany's Black Forest—but it's become

199

more closely associated with Switzerland, thanks to its role with Swiss food. If you've ever made fondue—few dishes are as Swiss—you've probably had to run out to the liquor store to pick up a bottle of kirsch. It's frequently an ingredient in the pot of glorious cheesiness. It also finds its way into recipes for Zuger Kirschtorte—a Swiss meringue, sponge, and buttercream layer cake—as well as cherries jubilee, and is a popular filling for Swiss chocolates.

Kirsch also does just fine on its own, served cold and neat in a 1½-ounce tulip glass, before or after a meal. Like most other fruit brandies, don't expect kirsch to be sweet. There's no sugar added to it, as it's not a liqueur. As with the flavor profile of the Scheibel schnaps I had on that transatlantic flight, you're tasting the essence of the fruit and not its sugar.

The easiest places to find authentic schnaps are in shops like Spirituosen Sporer, a Salzburg, Austria, institution that not only sells schnaps, liqueurs, and wines, it also produces some spirits in-house. It's been a family-run business since 1903, situated on a narrow block in a charming fifteenth-century building. The more adventurous might consider exploring the Black Forest, home to thousands of tiny farm distilleries (as many as 14,000 by some accounts). Hikers and day-trippers have become well-acquainted with the tiny, self-serve (!) schnaps stations housed in rustic kiosks at the edge of pastoral fields and wooded trails. Most operate on a kind of honor system; grab a bottle, drop a few coins in a box.

⋈ Stroh

It's a bit counterintuitive that one of the biggest cult alcohol brands in Austria is not a beer, a wine, or a schnaps. It's a rum, as molasses is its base. It's also one of the oldest continuously existing products in the country. Its story began in 1832 when Sebastian Stroh distilled his first batch. By the end of that century, the spirit had swept through Austria and, at the beginning of the next, it stood poised to conquer the world. In 1900, it won the Grand Gold Medal at the World Exposition in Paris. Today, it's available in more than forty countries and is distinguishable by its rectangular-ish dark amber bottle and orange label. The Austrian Alps may be a world away from the Caribbean, but the region proves that it's every bit as capable of producing a world-class rum.

ITALY

The first image most folks have when someone mentions "Italy" and "alcohol" is a bulbous-bottomed bottle partially enclosed in a wicker basket dangling from the ceiling of a red-sauce restaurant. The familiar image was made popular in movies and TV shows in the '70s and early '80s. But what's not nearly as familiar is the name of that style of bottle: a fiasco. How something can mean both a wine receptacle and a complete failure is a mystery. But then again, there's very little associated with Italian drinking that doesn't make you scratch your head.

Okay, I'm not talking about wine here when I say Italian drinking is a puzzle. Italian wines are world-famous—Montepulciano d'Abruzzo, Chianti Classico, and Dolcetto d'Alba, to name but a fraction of them. I'm referring to some of the more, shall we say... challenging Italian alcohols. For one thing, what's the deal with all the bitterness? Italy has turned that flavor into a culinary art form, as anyone who's ever had a plate of broccoli rabe can attest. The Italians are so renowned for their attraction to bitterness that the category for such beverages uses the Italian word for bitter: amaro (amari in the plural form).

This orientation toward bitterness is a function of the terroir, more than anything else. Typically, amari get their flavor from various macerated roots and botanicals, so whatever happens to be growing in a particular region will likely find its way into a drink. Italian palates have adapted to their local flora over centuries, and

201

those things are often pretty bitter. Bitterness isn't always the defining component of an amaro, but it's usually present in some way.

Italy being one of the great winemaking countries, the base of most amari is grape brandy, usually distilled to neutrality. The list of other ingredients common in various types of amari are familiar to anyone who's thought seriously about a bottle of gin. For one thing, juniper, the defining botanical in gin, is sometimes present in an amaro, as are angelica, lemon verbena, and orange peels, all very common in the English-by-way-of-Dutch spirit. That's only a few of the rather extensive roster of herbal items that have shown up in amari from various parts of Italy.

Traditionally, Italians enjoy amari as a way to wrap up a rich meal—usually drunk neat or with ice. In a sense, amari—and other digestivos (when in Italy, why not use the Italian version of "digestif"?)—serve as a metaphor for the country's entire outlook on life, especially as it contrasts with American traditions. Italians are all about taking it easy and not rushing through experiences, especially dining.

A generous helping of culture shock accompanied at the first meal I ever had at a restaurant in Italy—in Milan, to be precise. Two hours in and we were still getting through the antipasto. The main dish wrapped up at around the three-hour mark, and we were sipping espresso at around four hours. And I wouldn't have had it any other way! It was a nice counterpoint to the bum's rush I'm used to getting stateside, where restaurant staffers are eager to turn the tables as quickly as possible to bring in the next group of big tippers.

You could easily argue that lengthy, lazy dinners out are typical in any country where food service workers get paid a living wage and don't rely on gratuities to survive. But in Italy, they're in a dimension of their own. Why else would the Italians have an oft-repeated phrase consistent with the taking-it-easy mindset: "dolce far niente," or "the sweetness of doing nothing"? Having an amari at the end of a meal is just such a stop-and-smell-the-flowers moment. You've enjoyed your coffee; now have a little nip of something to settle the stomach and give you a moment to ponder the next epic meal.

"We don't like fast food," says Luca Collia, who moved to the United States in 2015 to rep a number of liqueur brands for Gruppo Caffo, including Vecchio Amaro del Capo. "We like to take our time to sit, to eat, and then we have something to help digestion after the meal. That's why, in Italy, we invented amaro. And you, in America, invented fast food; you don't take your time to eat—it's a question of culture."

Ouch! But he's absolutely right.

Worldwide—especially in the United States—drinkers' first entrée into the amaro world is through cocktails, but Italians are still warming up to the concept of mixing amari with other alcohols. "European palates are more comfortable with the bitter taste," explains Matteo Boloni, the master herbalist and blender for Amaro Montenegro, a popular brand that's been produced in Bologna since 1885 (which, as the brand team likes to point out, makes it a year older than Coca-Cola). "We've consumed amaro especially as a digestif at the end of the day, but [Italians] are not very confident with the use of amaro in cocktails."

Amaro Montenegro boasts a sweeter profile than many amari, especially the one with which most Americans are familiar, Campari—the signature component of the Negroni cocktail. And from its origin, Montenegro has not diverged from its closely guarded late-nineteenth-century recipe—passed down through the generations and now known only to Boloni. (At the 2016 Tales of the Cocktail in New Orleans, he revealed some of the ingredients for the first time to the audience of bartenders and other industry folks, but there are certain components he's taking to his grave.) The brand was the creation of Stanislao Cobianchi, whose family intended for him to become a priest. But Cobianchi had more worldly pursuits in mind and traveled about collecting any exotic botanicals that came his way. Forty of those became the flavor agents for Amaro Montenegro, which he named after Princess Elena of Montenegro.

The favored tipple of bar and restaurant personnel, Fernet Branca, falls into the amaro category, though flavor-wise it tends to be more licorice- and mint-forward than bitter.

Another of the more visible amari on bar shelves is Cynar, which boasts thirteen botanicals, including its central ingredient, artichoke (the spirit's name derives from *Cynara scolymus,* the scientific name for the plant whose hearts we like to pickle; the producer credits a naturally occurring substance called cynarine for its flavor). However, despite its name and the presence of its signature vegetable on the label, don't expect it to taste much like artichokes. It's a relatively mild tipple, at 16.5 percent ABV, and has a bit of sweetness to balance out all the herbal bitterness. Cynar is the brainchild of Venetian entrepreneur Angelo Dalle Molle, who first launched the brand in 1952. Campari Group, the corporation behind the namesake liqueur—which pops up frequently in these pages—is Cynar's parent company.

Another amaro icon within the Campari portfolio is Averna, whose origins date much farther back than Cynar's. Salvatore Averna gets the credit for creating his liqueur in Caltanissetta, Sicily, back in 1868. Averna is considerably stronger than Cynar, about 29 percent ABV.

That's still lower than the punch packed by grappa, Italy's often hard-to-love spirit distilled from grape pomace. Grappa can range anywhere from a relatively moderate 35 percent ABV— five points below your average whisky or vodka—all the way up to about 60 percent ABV (typically the domain of absinthe and cask-strength whiskies). Although grappa and amari both begin with grapes, their flavors are quite different.

⌁ Aperitivo Time

I've talked a great deal about what Italians typically drink during and after dinner—but what about before? The Italian after-work, pre-dinner drinking occasion known as the aperitivo is pretty much happy hour on steroids. The leisurely attitude toward dinner in Italy also applies to the period before Italians are ready to eat. They may not be rushing through dinner, but they're also not rushing to get *to* dinner (those dining at 8:30 P.M. are early birds).

On any given weeknight in Rome, the bars start to get crowded between about 6:15 and 6:30 P.M. By 7 P.M., good luck finding a place to sit. Romans sip bubbly Prosecco, tall glasses of beer—be it the dominant macro brand Peroni or any of a growing number of fine Italian craft brews—or the traditional mixed drink: the Spritz. You don't need to speak or understand a word of Italian (as I don't, despite my last name) and the bartender doesn't need to speak or understand a word of English. Just say the word "Spritz," and your drink is on its way.

Usually that concoction is a combination of the mildly bitter orange liqueur Aperol, Prosecco, a squirt of soda water, and a slice of orange or other available citrus fruit, served over ice. Personally, I feel the soda water is unnecessary, as do more than a few bartenders who've served it to me seltzer-free. On the other extreme, I encountered one bartender who completely phoned it in and diluted the drink with soda water to the point where I detected no Prosecco at all.

The best Aperol Spritz I've had was at the drinking establishment Doppio Zeroo (the double-o spelling is intentional as Doppio Zero means "double zero"). The bartender also mixed a fairly badass Campari Spritz as well. I should mention, if you've got a high threshold for bitterness, opt for the Campari version. Some barkeeps will ask you if you prefer one liqueur over the other (Gruppo Campari owns them both, by the way), but most of the time, if you don't specify, they'll pour an Aperol Spritz.

Doppio Zeroo also hits it out of the park with its epic assortment of snacks. Small bites are a staple of aperitivo time and you get to nibble on them at no additional charge when you buy a drink. Edibles range from olive focaccia bread to charcuterie and mini-pizzas. But Doppio Zeroo's spread takes

205

AMARO COCKTAILS

Quick caveat: As I mentioned, mixing amari in cocktails hasn't traditionally been a "thing" in Italy (Spritzes notwithstanding). However, non-Italian cultures are discovering the bittersweet liqueurs through their own native cocktail scenes. The team behind Vecchio Amaro del Capo scoured the globe for the best recipes top bartenders have developed for the spirit. These first three are a result of that search.

23 + 6

This one comes to us from Munich, where bartender Michele Fiordoliva developed it for the city's Negroni Bar. It's got a faint spicy kick from the chili powder.

⇾ DIRECTIONS ⇽

Combine all ingredients in a shaker filled with ice, shake, and pour into a cocktail glass.

Top with a pinch of chili powder and garnish with a slice of dried apple (a good match for the calvados, which is essentially distilled apple juice).

⇾ INGREDIENTS ⇽

25 ml (¾ ounce) Vecchio Amaro del Capo (or equivalent)

30 ml (1 ounce) Calvados Château du Breuil 8-year-old (or comparable brand)

7 ml (¼ ounce) falernum

25 ml (¾ ounce) fresh lemon juice

1 pinch chili powder, for garnish

Dried apple, for garnish

☞ CALABRIAN BUCK

Another recipe from Michele Fiordoliva, this ginger-forward delight is sure to please fans of the Moscow Mule looking to step a bit outside the conventional. (Another name for the Moscow Mule is the Vodka Buck; the "Calabrian" part of this drink is a shout-out to Vecchio Amaro del Capo's home region.)

⇥ DIRECTIONS ⇤

Combine all ingredients in a highball glass filled with ice and garnish with cucumber slice.

⇥ INGREDIENTS ⇤

30 ml (1 ounce) Vecchio Amaro del Capo (or comparable brand)

30 ml (1 ounce) Cognac VSOP

25 ml (¾ ounce) fresh lemon juice

120 ml (4 ounces) ginger beer

Cucumber slice, for garnish

☞ TICKET TO LIMBADI

Appropriating the name of a town in Calabria, Mario La Pietra created this riff on the Season Ticket (which appeared in William Terrington's cocktail book, Cooling Cups and Dainty Drinks) for the Luggage Room cocktail bar in London. As you'll see by the ingredients list, it's got quite a bit going on.

207

⇥ DIRECTIONS ⇤

Shake all ingredients with ice.

Serve in a julep cup or Collins glass and garnish with a sprig of mint, a dusting of superfine sugar, and a strip of orange peel.

⇥ INGREDIENTS ⇤

85 ml (2¾ ounces) Aspall Premier Cru dry cider (or comparable brand)

55 ml (1¾ ounces) Vecchio Amaro del Capo (or comparable brand)

25 ml (¾ ounce) San Pellegrino Chinotto (bittersweet orange soda available in Italian specialty stores and at Amazon)

25 ml (¾ ounce) yellow grapefruit sorbet

15 ml (½ ounce) fresh lemon juice

2 drops orange flower extract

Mint sprig, for garnish

Superfine sugar, for garnish

Orange peel, for garnish

it well beyond the next level, with a buffet including all of those things as well as pesto fusilli, rigatoni with cherry tomatoes and oil, salads, and both red and white pizzas. And that's what you eat *before* dinner.

THE NETHERLANDS

As is the case in most modern European cultures, beer is the drink of choice among the Dutch. The second-largest brewer in the world is based there, after all (that would be Heineken, also known as Dennis Hopper's *Blue Velvet* character's least favorite beer). However, as is the case with most ale-and-lager-loving countries, there's a spirited side to the story. In fact, the Netherlands popularized one of the world's most celebrated distilled beverages in the world. Well, the beverage's ancestor anyway—the United Kingdom takes most of the credit for its derivative product: gin.

The Dutch drink is jenever (sometimes spelled genever) and, like the English tipple it spawned, its name and flavor derive from juniper. A rudimentary form of the beverage may have appeared as early as the thirteenth century. Philip Duff, a world-renowned gin and jenever historian, notes that the earliest recorded mention of a juniper-based medicinal tonic appeared in 1269 in the Dutch publication *Der Naturen Bloeme* by Jacob van Maerlant. The first known recipe for recreational consumption appeared considerably later, in a Dutch cookbook published in 1495.

Around that time, jenever was still most commonly found in Dutch pharmacies. Apothecaries sold a rather, shall we say, aggressive-tasting remedy made from distilled barley—the same base as Scotch whisky, but far less pleasing to the palate. To make up for its sensory shortcomings, those same apothecaries started combining the spirit with juniper and other herbs and spices. After all, the Dutch were leaders in the global spice trade at the time, so they had plenty of exotic botanicals lying around with which to experiment.

Though England's twist on jenever is by far the more recognizable spirit, jenever is still very much alive and well. And, as with gin, there are some very strict, EU-enforced guidelines for its production. For one thing, its provenance is protected. The EU mandates that it be made only in the Netherlands and Belgium and some parts of Germany and France.

There are three general categories of jenever: oude, jonge, and korenwijn. You can probably figure out what the first two words mean: Oude means "old" and jonge means "young." But we're not talking about maturation here—oude refers to the old style of making jenever, while jonge is the relatively new-fangled method.

The terms became popular in the first half of the twentieth century. A process called column distillation enabled producers to make larger quantities of alcohol more quickly; it also resulted in a more neutral base spirit, losing much of the grainy character of the malt wine. Even a hundred years ago, young consumers didn't want to drink what their parents drank, so they started to gravitate toward these more neutral jenevers, which were a lot closer to the profile of what we now know as gin. But even though that neutral spirit had become all the rage, many still preferred the old, malt-wine-forward style. So the oude designation was born in the 1920s to distinguish the original style from the less flavor-forward stuff that all the whippersnappers were drinking.

Then history intervened, which forced jonge jenever to the forefront. A grain shortage during World War II meant less malt wine and more distillates produced from other bases, like sugar beets.

By definition, oude must contain between 15 and 50 percent malt wine; neutral grain spirit composes the rest of it. When the malt content is on the high end of that continuum, it unsurprisingly tastes faintly like Scotch whisky. With jonge, on the other hand, 15 percent is the ceiling for malt wine content—though most brands tend to contain only 1 or 2 percent. The remaining 85 to 99 percent is neutral grain spirit and/or sugar-based alcohol. This flavor is much more vodka-like than Scotch-like, thanks to its

209

considerably enhanced neutrality. Distillers developed the style as vodka increasingly became the international tipple of choice. Most of the jenevers produced in the Netherlands today are of the jonge variety. As Duff noted at the 2017 Gin Summit in Washington, DC, some of the worst people to ask how to drink jenever are Dutch people, especially if they're under the age of eighty. They'll mostly be consuming the near-neutral stuff, which doesn't taste all that much like traditional jenever to begin with.

The third type, korenwijn (which translates to "grain wine" and is sometimes spelled koornwyn or corenwyn) is even more whisky-like in character than oude. In fact, malt-content-wise, it picks up right where oude leaves off: 51 percent is the bare minimum for its malt-wine composition; 70 percent is the absolute max. Scotch drinkers definitely can find a lot to love about it. There are some versions that contain no juniper and, therefore, must be labeled simply as "korenwijn" and not "korenwijn jenever."

Typically, Dutch jenever aficionados drink the spirit out of a small tulip glass that holds an ounce to an ounce and a half. In more traditional Dutch bars, you're likely to encounter older drinkers performing a ritual the locals like to call the "head butt." The bartender fills the glass to the absolute brim—to the point that it's practically overflowing. Drinkers then lean over, with both arms behind their backs, and slurp the head off the top before picking it up with their hands and drinking. Sometimes they'll do so alongside a beer, sort of a Dutch variation on the whisky-based boilermaker pairing.

{ THE TRADITIONAL JENEVER HEAD-BUTT SLURP

PHOTO COURTESY LUCAS BOLS }

JENEVER COCKTAILS

Many of today's classic gin cocktails very likely began as jenever cocktails in the late nineteenth century. Even those that weren't born that way can get an added level of grainy flavor complexity when you swap out the gin for jenever.

☞ MARTINEZ

It's easy to infer from the name which classic mixed drink evolved from this one: the martini. Some argue that jenever was likely the first base spirit for the Martinez, since the cocktail was born at the height of the Dutch spirit's popularity in the United States (the late nineteenth century). Old Tom gin (a sweeter style of gin) became the preferred base, though, so many dispute the jenever theory, asserting that Old Tom was always the core ingredient of the cocktail. Which one was first matters very little to me. The best Martinez I've ever had was jenever-based and as far as I'm concerned, there's no other way to drink it. Here's Rutte Distillery's recipe, using its Old Simon Genever.

211

⇥ DIRECTIONS ⇤

Combine all ingredients with ice and stir until cold and diluted.

Strain into a chilled cocktail glass and garnish with the orange zest.

⇥ INGREDIENTS ⇤

60 ml (2 ounces) Rutte Old Simon Genever (or comparable brand with significant malt wine content)

30 ml (1 ounce) sweet rosso vermouth

1 dash orange bitters

Orange zest, for garnish

☞ OLD SIMON NEGRONI

The Negroni makes a couple of appearances throughout these pages because it's such a popular canvas on which bartenders like to paint. Here's another one from Rutte.

⇢ DIRECTIONS ⇠	⇢ INGREDIENTS ⇠
Combine all ingredients with ice and stir until chilled and diluted.	30 ml (1 ounce) Rutte Old Simon Genever
Strain over ice into a rocks glass and garnish with a strip of lemon peel.	30 ml (1 ounce) Campari
	60 ml (2 ounces) bold rosso vermouth
	4 drops fleur de sel solution*
	Lemon peel, for garnish

*To make fleur de sel solution, combine ½ cup fleur de sel sea salt with ½ cup water in a small pot. Bring to a boil on the stove, stirring continuously for about two minutes after boil.

☞ MR. SIMON

212

The next Rutte recipe also has a bit of the bitter liqueur Campari in it, but far less.

⇢ DIRECTIONS ⇠	⇢ INGREDIENTS ⇠
Combine all ingredients with ice and stir until chilled and diluted.	60 ml (2 ounces) Rutte Old Simon Genever
Strain into a chilled cocktail glass and garnish with the orange zest.	15 ml (½ ounce) Mandarine Napoléon
	5 ml (1 teaspoon) Campari
	5 ml (1 teaspoon) agave syrup
	Orange zest, for garnish

☞ DUTCH COSMOPOLITAN

The team behind the Bols brand supplied this jenever-centric reinvention of the cosmo.

⇒ DIRECTIONS ⇐

Pour jenever, triple sec, and cranberry juice into a cocktail shaker, squeeze lime wedges into mixture, and toss in squeezed wedges.

Shake well with ice and double-strain into a chilled cocktail glass.

⇒ INGREDIENTS ⇐

30 ml (1 ounce) Bols Genever 21

30 ml (1 ounce) triple sec

30 ml (1 ounce) cranberry juice

2 lime wedges

☞ DUTCH ELEGANCE

Another Bols recipe, the Dutch Elegance takes herbal aromatics to a whole new level with the addition of Green Chartreuse.

⇒ DIRECTIONS ⇐

Pour jenever, Chartreuse, lemon juice, and simple syrup into a glass and stir.

Top with soda water.

⇒ INGREDIENTS ⇐

45 ml (1½ ounces) Bols Genever

20 ml (⅔ ounce) Green Chartreuse

20 ml (⅔ ounce) fresh lemon juice

10 ml (⅓ ounce) simple syrup

Soda water

☞ ELDERFLOWER COLLINS

This Bols concoction jazzes up a traditional Collins with some blossomy and grainy elements.

⇒ DIRECTIONS ⇐

Combine jenever, elderflower liqueur, lemon juice, and simple syrup in a shaker with ice and shake.

Strain into a tall Collins glass filled with ice.

Top with soda water and garnish with lemon wedge.

⇒ INGREDIENTS ⇐

30 ml (1 ounce) Bols Genever

30 ml (1 ounce) elderflower liqueur

30 ml (1 ounce) fresh lemon juice

10 ml (⅓ ounce) simple syrup

Soda water

Lemon wedge, for garnish

☞ DR G PEPPER

Bols offers a boozy interpretation of Dr Pepper with a Coke base. Confused? You won't be when you try it. And it's oh-so-simple to make.

⇝ DIRECTIONS ⇜	⇝ INGREDIENTS ⇜
Build in a Collins glass with ice.	30 ml (1 ounce) Bols Genever
Top off with the cola and garnish with the cherries.	15 ml (½ ounce) cherry brandy
	Coca-Cola*
	2 maraschino cherries, for garnish

* Or, for a more flavorful, artisanal twist, why not try a craftier soda like Boylan Cane Cola or Fentimans Curiosity Cola?

☞ ALAMAGOOZLUM

Legend has it that J. P. Morgan first concocted this one. Whether that's true or not, one thing's for sure: It's about as complex as the banking procedures at the financial institution that bears his name.

⇝ DIRECTIONS ⇜	⇝ INGREDIENTS ⇜
Shake all ingredients together and strain into a chilled coupe glass.	90 ml (3 ounces) Bols Genever
	45 ml (1½ ounces) Jamaican rum
	45 ml (1½ ounces) Green Chartreuse
	15 ml (½ ounce) Bols Dry Orange Curaçao or other orange curaçao
	90 ml (3 ounces) water
	45 ml (1½ ounces) simple syrup
	15 ml (½ ounce) Angostura bitters
	15 ml (½ ounce) egg white

☞ House Old Fashioned, Rosalia's Menagerie

Here's one that includes both Rutte and Bols products. As has been the case across other major European cities, the craft cocktail scene in Amsterdam has been booming. Among the modern mixological hot spots in the Dutch capital is Rosalia's Menagerie, which I was lucky enough to visit only a week after it opened in 2017. Back in the seventeenth century, Dutch pubs and inns used to collect animals (dead or alive), as well as other curiosities from around the globe. Sailors often would drink themselves into debt and use such exotic critters to settle their bar tabs. The establishments would display them and the public would pay to see those worldly wonders. The most famous of those "menageries" was Blauwe Jan, the inspiration for Rosalia's Menagerie. Shout out to the Menagerie's Wouter Bosch and Thomas Datema for letting me include their Dutch twist on the Old Fashioned, which exhibits some remarkably nutty flavor notes.

⇥ DIRECTIONS ⇤

Stir all ingredients and serve over ice. Garnish with an orange twist.

Rosalia's Menagerie batches the cocktail in glass bottles, so there's a tiny bit of bottle aging going on with it.

⇥ INGREDIENTS ⇤

30 ml (1 ounce) Rutte Old Simon

30 ml (1 ounce) Bols 6-year Corenwijn

5 ml (1 teaspoon) simple syrup

4 dashes Peychaud's bitters

1 dash Mozart chocolate bitters

215

"You cannot miss or spill a drop of the precious jenever," says Sandie van Doorne, creative and communications director for Lucas Bols, the Amsterdam company behind the most visible jenever brand, Bols. "The Dutch are very frugal—we like to get our money's worth." Hence, filling the tulip until it's impossible to squeeze another drop into it.

✸ Tasting History

I give a lot of credit to the Rutte Distillery for being one of the most devoted guardians of jenever's history and heritage. The producer, the self-declared smallest distillery in the Netherlands (though now a subsidiary of the much larger company DeKuyper Royal Distillers), boasts a history dating back to 1872, when founder Simon Rutte made use of some of the most exotic fruits and spices from the ships of the Dutch East India Company.

{ THE RUTTE
DISTILLERY IN
DORDRECHT, THE
NETHERLANDS }

Naturally, I could not pass up an opportunity to visit Rutte when I was traveling through the Netherlands in 2017. Situated on a pedestrian-friendly cobblestone street in the small, charming riverside city of Dordrecht in the western province of South Holland, the distillery could easily be mistaken for any run-of-the-mill retail shop. The red-awninged storefront invites visitors into a shop that retains a classic turn-of-the-twentieth-century look (including an ornamental antique cash register) stocked ceiling-to-floor with bottles of jenever, gin, and cocktail paraphernalia. But that quaint little shop also hides a working distillery, complete with copper still, aging barrels, and shelves full of jars loaded with an extensive range of aromatic herbs and spices that would make even the most accomplished botanist jealous. Master distiller Myriam Hendrickx took the time to show me around and guide me through a tasting of six of the spirits—including many not available in the States—running the gamut of oude, jonge, korenwijn, and oak-aged expressions.

Hendrickx has been presenting seminars on jenever history and culture at major lifestyle and drinks industry events like Tales of the Cocktail in New Orleans. One of the most fascinating tidbits Hendrickx shares with the audience is just how crazy about jenever the rest of the world was from the late nineteenth century up until World War II. She notes that at the spirit's peak, the Netherlands exported about 85 percent of its jenever supply. North America, West Africa, and other parts of Europe were major destinations for the traveling bottles. Wartime grain rationing severely limited jenever supply, however, and the Nazi occupying forces took most of what producers were making. Rutte's archives preserved a letter from a dissatisfied drinker who, in 1943, whined that due to the restricted inventory, he couldn't buy enough jenever relative to the volume he was able to get his hands on four years earlier (way to make it about you, dude!). The head of the company was having none of that; he pointed out in his reply that the customer had access to more than he should have between 1939 and 1943 and would get even less the following year.

217

BELGIUM

The funny thing about Belgium is there's really no such thing as a Belgian. Yes, there are some twelve million people living within its borders, and they all (well, most of them, at least) recognize the sovereignty of the state in which they live. But ethnically, the citizens are more likely to closely identify as either Flemish (natives of Dutch-speaking Flanders) or Walloon (of French-speaking Wallonia). There's a tiny sliver of German speakers as well, but they're a small minority. As far as countries go, Belgium is younger than the United States, having been officially declared a nation in 1830. Culturally, of course, it goes back many centuries.

But despite the fact that "Belgian" is really an incomplete description of the distinct cultural groups that occupy this Maryland-size slab of land the map calls Belgium, it has become synonymous with the most storied of brewing traditions. As a matter of fact, you wouldn't be reading the very book you hold in your hands right now if it weren't for Belgium. And that has nothing to do with the fact that I'm a quarter Belgian (Flemish, actually) on my mother's side. Mom's dad's family hailed from the country that, I admit, I knew or cared very little about when I was a child. (The other 75 percent of me is Italian, whose food was a lot more accessible and delicious to a young boy—I lived for Macaroni Night.)

No, for me, my better drinking life began with the beer. I had my first sip of a Belgian brew circa 2002, and the world changed forever for me. Belgian was the gateway beer for me. Eventually, I would declare my love for non-Belgian styles like porter, Kölsch, stout, Vienna lager, and some of the weirder stuff experimental brewers have concocted. And in the first couple of years of my malt-and-hops-enhanced odyssey, I refused to drink anything but beer (I was kind of insufferable that way). But without my realizing it at the time, beer itself was a gateway to better beverages of all sorts: from sake and shochu to gin and whisky.

But Belgium will always hold a special place in my heart for its contributions to world beer culture and, especially, to my place in it. And I was pleased to discover, in the handful of times I've visited the country, that the reality of the role beer plays in day-to-day Flemish and Walloon life matched the fantasy that had formed in my mind and the minds of millions of other American beer geeks. It's pretty much what they're drinking most of the time, whether right after work or at the tail end of an evening's imbibing adventure (not to give wine and spirits the shaft; I'll get to them soon enough).

But I'm getting way ahead of myself here. It's time to get medieval.

We have twelfth-century monks to thank for all that is good and holy in global beer. At that time, abbeys doubled as breweries, with the brotherhood producing the beverage to raise money for the monastery, as well as for use as sustenance during fasting periods (there was a liquid loophole).

Across the centuries, new regional traditions emerged, and laypeople got pretty adept at making good beer, too. Some co-opted the abbey traditions—as well as the monastic iconography—while others developed their own. And there were dramatic distinctions, depending on where in this relatively tiny country one traveled. The Walloons were largely responsible for putting saison on the map. Saisons are those earthy, floral, sometimes wild farmhouse-style ales that have since been adopted and adapted in countries far and wide. But most of those products owe fealty to what remains one of the most revered brands in the bunch, Saison Dupont, produced in the French-speaking town of Tourpes.

Flanders has made countless positive contributions to the world of beer, not least of which is the fact that it made sourness palatable. The flavor profile wouldn't be gaining so much traction had it not been for the Flemish originals.

But more than teaching the world *what* to drink, Belgium gets credit for teaching us *how* to drink. The romance and theater around enjoying a glass of beer is a fairly recent development for American drinkers. Stateside enthusiasts didn't really start talking about it in earnest until the turn of the millennium. But if you'd walked into a pub in Belgium decades prior to that, you'd be in for a treat that was as much a visual and tactile one as it was a gustatory and olfactory one.

Few travel to Belgium solely for the spirits, which is a shame because the country is responsible, but gets tragically little credit, for what we now call gin. Yes, I already noted that gin evolved from the Dutch beverage jenever, but remember, Belgium was officially part of the Netherlands until less than two hundred years ago. What we call the Benelux countries today—Belgium, the Netherlands, and Luxembourg—were once known as the Low Countries, as they were below sea level. Gin's origins can be traced to the Flemish cities of Antwerp and Brugge (or, in the more popular French spelling, Bruges; it's in Flanders, so I prefer to use the Flemish spelling). Belgians like to point out that the earliest documented references to the juniper-based spirit (known as peket to the locals) appeared in those cities (though the Dutch often dispute that claim). But, like so many traditional beverages tied to a specific place, peket consumption declined among the locals, to the point where it became mostly a niche product.

World War I certainly didn't help, as the military confiscated most of the country's copper supply for the war effort, which meant there was none left for the stills. Distilleries went bankrupt, and the few that were left suffered catastrophic damage from heavy artillery fire. In later decades, peket was there for those who wanted it, but it wasn't part of the everyday Belgian experience (that would be beer). Rather, it was a staple of festivals in places like Liege, in French-speaking Wallonia. Liege is also home to a pub called La Maison du Peket that has specialized in the spirit since 1993.

There's since been a marked effort to make the spirit more appealing to new generations of drinkers—a movement that has played to a mixed reception. François Monti is among those who haven't embraced the trend. Monti is a native Walloon cocktail writer whose books include *101 Cocktails to Die For* and *El Gran Libro del Vermut* (that's Spanish for vermouth; more on that one when we get to Spain). He moved to Madrid in the early 2000s but still gets home to Belgium a couple of times a year.

On a recent visit, he dropped in for a drink at La Maison du Peket and ordered the house's specialty spirit from its extensive list of high-quality offerings. When he ordered straight peket—"as it should be drunk," he points out—the servers were a bit per-plexed. "The waitress came back later and asked me to tell her my story, why I was so depressed," he remembers. You see, the bar had grown accustomed to serving peket as a shot mixed with fruit juice and a bit of sugar—hardly the "traditional" way. And this is a bar that specializes in the spirit! "So, that should give you an idea of where jenever is in the French-speaking part of the country," Monti laments.

As far as the Dutch-speaking Flemish part of Belgium is concerned, folks are at least marginally more in touch with the drink's traditional roots (after all, Flanders is supposedly where jenever/gin/peket—whatever you want to call it—was born). In a city like Antwerp, especially, there's been a moderate surge in enthusiasm for the spirit—consumed neat, of course. "For a while it was just a vestige of an old tradition, but there's definitely more interest now, and there are a lot of new brands on the mar-ket," Monti observes.

Authenticity-minded bartenders have been seeking out brands with throwback recipes. Even in Antwerp, though, beyond craft cocktail and jenever-centric bars, you're still more likely to find drinkers' glasses full of beer—and I'd bet the beer would be the local favorite, De Koninck.

FRANCE

Detailing French alcohol consumption is an incredibly difficult task. I know it sounds counterintuitive, given that "France" and "wine" are pretty much synonymous, but it's these very obvious drinking countries that are hardest to really pin down. And France is probably the most difficult.

I don't want to spend too much time on French wine, because entire libraries have been written about the subject and have still barely scratched the surface. In a nutshell, the country produces some 50 million hectoliters of the beverage, or around 1.3 billion gallons for us non-metric-minded folks. If you prefer to think in terms of cases (a case typically holds twelve 750-milliliter bottles), that's more than 550 million cases.

France is considered one of the primary Old World wine producers, which is kind of an understatement. Historical evidence suggests that French winemaking began two and a half millennia ago. The country was called Gaul at the time, and its ideal climate and soil attracted Greek settlers, who colonized the southern region (Marseille began its epic history as a Greek colony, for instance).

"French wine" itself is a bit of a meaningless term, since there are so many distinct winemaking regions throughout the country—each officially recognized and protected, and each with its own personality and terroir. If wine has an air of pretension around it, that's probably because of France, though it's not their fault. They just have so many world-renowned wine regions that it's incredibly intimidating for a novice to get a handle on the country's myriad varietals and viticultural traditions. So it's pretty easy to feel left out. Keeping that in mind, I've provided a cheat sheet of the most important French winemaking regions:

> **Alsace:** Located in the northeast of the country, Alsace shares a border with Germany as well as with Switzerland. It shares a great deal more with Germany, though, as control of Alsace has gone back and forth between France and Germany throughout history. For instance, one of the staple Alsatian dishes, choucroute garnie, has a very distinct German accent: it consists of a few encased and cured meats (think würsts) over a heap of sauerkraut. It's not uncommon to encounter someone with a French first name and a German surname (Françoise Müller, for instance), though they'll be speaking French. Alsace is known for its dry whites and its celebrated sparkling Crémant d'Alsace.

Beaujolais: Located in France's southeastern quadrant (just south of Burgundy, of which it's sometimes considered a sub-region), Beaujolais is known for its fruity reds based primarily on the Gamay grape varietal. Beaujolais-Villages and Beaujolais Nouveau are the two you're most likely to encounter in your local wine shop.

Bordeaux: If there's one word even those unfamiliar with wine have encountered nearly as frequently as Champagne, Bordeaux is very likely it. Located on the southeastern Atlantic coast of the country, Bordeaux isn't so much a single region as a collection of many sub-regions responsible for wines that are just overflowing with character. Among those are Médoc, Graves, Libournais, Bourg, and Blaye, and many further sub-regions therein, all with their own protected appellations. (See what I mean about how intimidating it is to keep up with all these?)

Burgundy: One of the big dogs of global wine regions, Burgundy, in the east central part of France, is equally known for its whites as its reds. Burgundy's Chardonnay and Pinot Noir are quite well regarded. If you've ever eaten in a French restaurant, chances are you've encountered some signature dishes from the region. Boeuf bourguignon and coq au vin are just two of those iconic edibles.

Champagne: This one's a freebie. Anyone not inhabiting the space below a rock has heard of this one. So familiar is it that most throw the word around a bit too much, using it as a generic term to describe any sparkling white. But only those produced within this stretch of land in the northeast of France get to wear that label.

Jura: Wedged between the vast Burgundy region and Switzerland, Jura is known for its Chardonnay and Pinot Noir output. But the real conversation piece for which it is responsible is a bit of an oddity called Vin Jaune, which translates literally to "yellow wine." It's made from the Savagnin varietal and, no surprise, has an intense yellow, almost golden hue. Like sherry, which is a fortified wine, it is matured under a film of yeast, but Vin Jaune is not itself fortified. It's a popular partner for the French cheese Comté, as well as many other regional dishes.

Languedoc-Roussillon: The southern portion of this area in southeastern France shares a border with Spain's northern Catalonia region to the south and the Mediterranean Sea to the east; it's like the frontier between two of the great Old World wine-producing cultures. Languedoc-Roussillon's principal grape varietals include Cabernet Sauvignon, Chardonnay, Merlot, and Sauvignon Blanc.

Loire Valley: A very long swath of land that extends from the Atlantic coast on the west to about halfway to the eastern edge of the country, the Loire Valley is a vast collection of sub-regions producing a host of well-known styles. Given the variable microclimates across its diverse terrain, those styles run the gamut from dry whites like Sauvignon Blanc to fruity reds like Pinot Noir.

Provence: The southeastern region is more or less a household name; you've probably cooked with herbes de Provence at one time or another. Viticulturally speaking, the region is famous for its rosés, though the majority of wines produced are reds (it's about a 65-30-5 red-rosé-white split).

South West: Regional names don't get much more direct than this. The area spans the Atlantic coast to about a third of the way across the southern section of the country to the city of Toulouse. It's a stone's throw from northeastern Spain. Among its best-known sub-regions is Bergerac, situated along the Dordogne River and frequently overshadowed by its much more famous neighbor to the west, Bordeaux. Given its proximity to the more prominent production area, Bergerac wineries produce many of the same red and white styles, like Cabernet Sauvignon and Sauvignon Blanc.

We have fortuitously (and alphabetically) concluded this brief exploration of French wine in the region that is home to one of the world's greatest spirits-making traditions. So let's talk about liquor.

Armagnac and Cognac are France's most famous region-specific brandies. The obvious difference between the two is that Armagnac is produced in Armagnac and Cognac is made in Cognac. And if a distiller produces a spirit elsewhere, it can't use either name. But naturally, there's a lot more to it than that. For starters, Armagnac is usually distilled once, while Cognac goes through a second distillation. (I should note that Armagnac makers have been allowed to distill their products twice since 1972, but most still opt for the traditional one-and-done method.) That's a pretty huge distinction, because single distillation translates to bigger, bolder flavors. The extra round that Cognac goes through refines and smooths it out a bit. That's not a bad thing—it just makes for a softer flavor profile, a desired characteristic of Cognac. And whereas most Cognacs clock in at 40 percent ABV, Armagnac frequently skews several percentage points higher.

The grape varietals used in Cognac and Armagnac can differ as well. The vast majority—about 98 percent—of Cognacs use the Ugni Blanc varietal. Armagnacs also use Ugni Blanc, but they use Baco, Colombard, and Folle Blanche, too. Both brandies are barrel-aged for extended periods of time, but the choice of wood imparts different flavor nuances to each. Most Cognac producers

225

use only Limousin oak (or, occasionally, Tronçais oak). Armagnac houses commonly use Limousin oak as well, but they also use the local Gascon oak.

All these distinctions result in flavor differences that are fairly pronounced. "Floral" and "citrus" tend to be recurring terms associated with Cognac; "leather," "jam," "quince," "candied fruit," and "spice" are the ones that usually describe Armagnac.

And the biggest distinction? Chances are at least 90 percent of you have at least heard of Cognac. I'll go out on a limb and suggest the number is considerably lower for Armagnac. Thing is, Cognac production far exceeds that of Armagnac—by nearly 3,000 percent! Cognac houses make about 160 million bottles a year. Armagnac producers are responsible for a much more modest 6 million bottles. A little more than two hundred thousand of those Armagnac bottles get poured into American glasses; the same is true of 47 million of the Cognac bottles. Armagnac is the underdog's underdog.

However, most of Armagnac's consumption—53 percent of it—happens within France's borders. That contrasts starkly with Cognac's French consumption: a paltry 3 percent. This has nothing to do with one being "better" than the other; it's mostly just a matter of history and geography. Armagnac had a two-century head start on Cognac, dating back to about the fourteenth century. It's the oldest eau-de-vie in France and, many suggest, possibly all of Europe. But Armagnac is concrete proof that it doesn't always necessarily pay to be first.

Cognac benefited on the world stage—which, at the time, pretty much just meant Europe—from its very strategic location on France's west coast. It also didn't hurt that it's just north of Bordeaux, whose wines were already among the most sought-after on the continent. Additionally, the region was a big part of the salt trade; as merchants came seeking fine wine and high-quality sodium chloride, they couldn't avoid the distilleries that dotted the area. So Cognac just became one more product to bring to the world. (And it attracted foreigners not only as distributors, but as producers as well. It's no accident that the top-selling Cognac in the world today has an Irish name. Irishman Richard Hennessy founded his eponymous distillery in the mid-eighteenth century.)

Armagnac, located to the southeast of Cognac, is a bit more inland. Back in the late Middle Ages, there were no roads or easy access points to Armagnac. The distilling tradition, for the most part, developed in isolation. Being produced in the middle of nowhere meant that the spirit developed as a truly local beverage. Eventually, though, merchants began pushing deeper into the interior and discovered Armagnac for themselves, long after Cognac had become all the rage outside of France. Today, Armagnac is the brandy that the French drink most—even those who live in Cognac.

Christine Cooney, who grew up in Cognac, now runs a successful Boston-based importation company known as Heavenly Spirits. While the company has a few Cognac brands in its portfolio (as well as quite a few French single malt whiskies see "Whisky for Francophiles" for more on that category), Heavenly Spirits has found a great deal of success preaching the gospel of Armagnac (as well as the apple-based French spirit Calvados) to American consumers. "The first spirit I tasted, aside from my grandfather's awful plum brandy, was an Armagnac," Cooney tells me. "And I always asked, why are you making me taste an Armagnac when we're in the Cognac region? 'Because in France, we drink Armagnac.'"

For the most part, the French continue to consume Armagnac in its most traditional context, as an after-dinner digestif. However, part of the mission of many of today's Armagnac evangelists is to broaden the spirit's drinking occasions. Producers and marketers are positioning young and, in some cases, unaged or "blanche" Armagnac as a versatile cocktail mixer. See for yourself.

ARMAGNAC COCKTAILS

Special thanks to Heavenly Spirits for providing these tantalizing treats.

☞ BLANCHE MOJITO

Who says rum is the only game in town for the mojito? How about a little French-Cuban fusion?

⇥ DIRECTIONS ⇤	⇥ INGREDIENTS ⇤
Muddle mint and one lime wedge in a glass to release oils and juices.	7 mint leaves
	½ lime, cut into thirds
Add sugar and another wedge of lime and muddle to release juice and combine.	2 teaspoons sugar
	60 ml (2 ounces) blanche Armagnac
Fill glass with ice and pour blanche Armagnac over the ice.	Soda water
	1 dash Angostura bitters
Then fill glass with sparkling water and stir.	
Add a dash of Angostura and garnish with remaining lime wedge.	

228

☞ BLANCHE SUNRISE

Keeping with the Franco-Latino theme, here's a Gallic twist on that old standby, the Tequila Sunrise.

⇥ DIRECTIONS ⇤	⇥ INGREDIENTS ⇤
Pour Armagnac over ice in a glass.	45 ml (1½ ounces) blanche Armagnac
Top off with orange juice and add a dash of grenadine.	150 ml (5 ounces) fresh orange juice
	1 dash grenadine

☞ BLUSH BLANCHE

This refresher adds a bit of flavor to a traditionally vodka-based cocktail. It's perfect to sip by the pool.

⟶ DIRECTIONS ⟵

Fill a glass with ice.

Add strawberry liqueur and Armagnac.

Top off with lemon juice.

If you feel like you need a little extra color, garnish with mint, but it's certainly not required.

⟶ INGREDIENTS ⟵

30 ml (1 ounce) strawberry liqueur

90 ml (3 ounces) blanche Armagnac

30 ml (1 ounce) fresh lemon juice

Mint sprig, for garnish (optional)

229

⋈ Whisky for Francophiles

You want to know what a significant number of French spirits enthusiasts are drinking these days? Single-malt whisky. Wait, do I mean Scotch? Well, yes, discerning French drinkers have a taste for the Scottish tipple, but their fellow countryfolk have been making some damned fine whisky of their own. It's a little-known fact that the French are among the biggest whisky consumers in the world—38 percent of the spirits they drink are whisky—so it was only a matter of time before their own industry developed. And though they're understandably overshadowed by the products of Scotland, Kentucky, Ireland, and Japan, many of the best French single malts are starting to attract quite a bit of attention.

Whisky is still a relatively new industry in France. The first such product of any significance was Armorik Breton from the Brittany-based Warenghem Distillery. Warenghem, founded in 1900, had gained fame for its botanical liqueur, Elixir d'Armorique. It wasn't until the mid-1980s, however, that the producer made the first French whisky, from 100 percent French-grown malted barley.

French whisky really started to pick up steam in the 2010s. Between about 2011 and 2016, the number of whisky distilleries went from four to more than forty. One relatively young brand that's been garnering all sorts of accolades—it won Best French single-cask single malt at the 2016 World Whiskies Awards—is something of a transatlantic collaboration. The brand is Brenne, the brainchild of American Allison Parc, who worked with a distiller in Cognac to craft the memorable spirit. It's double-distilled from malted barley grown in the region, aged in Limousin oak, then finished in Cognac casks.

THE UNITED KINGDOM

The beverage traditions of the United Kingdom are as diverse as the people who populate the confederation of cultures that make up Great Britain. It's impossible to paint the UK with broad strokes, and the same goes for the individual countries within it. Drinks-wise, the one thing they all have in common is a beer culture, but those brews barely resemble one another region to region, with each taking on the personality of its locality.

What many would argue is the style responsible for the American craft brewing revolution got its start in the English town of Burton-on-Trent. The town's water, courtesy of the River Trent, is the stuff of legends, with its high minerality. Because of that, brewers set up shop near the river and created what came to be known as Burton pale ale. It became the gold standard for the pale ale style, which inspired the pioneers of what was called microbrewing in the late 1970s and early 1980s to Americanize the concept.

And don't even get me started on India pale ale. Before IPA, as it's more commonly known, became the undisputed champ among most popular American craft beer styles, it was an English innovation. Brewers (allegedly) upped the hop and alcohol content of the classic pales to help it survive the lengthy, canal-less voyage to India. Today, English- and American-style IPAs bear only a passing resemblance to each other. That's all thanks to the stark differences between English and American hops; the latter tend to be more citrus-forward and robustly floral. (There are now some British craft brewers who have eschewed the English style entirely and brew only American-style IPAs.)

And though the most popular brand of stout—the dark, roasty, sometimes coffee-and-chocolate-like style—is brewed in Ireland (Guinness), that tradition was born in England. Stout's cousin, porter, was purportedly so named because the brew gained an affectionate following among porters working in early eighteenth-century London markets.

Thanks to the efforts of the Campaign for Real Ale (CAMRA), most of the classic English styles have survived in all their glorious, cask-conditioned splendor, even as the majority of drinkers

231

in the United Kingdom have gravitated toward macro lagers on draft and in bottles.

On the spirit side of things, the demarcation point between dark and light, as it turns out, is the line between North and South. Scotland, of course, is world-famous for its whisky (the Scots are adamant about spelling it without an "e"), whereas England's greatest distilled contribution to the world is its gin, usually devoid of any visible color.

As I mentioned, what English speakers call gin evolved from the Dutch beverage jenever (or genever), which existed for centuries before the Brits distilled their first batch. Like the Netherlands-born spirit, gin's primary flavoring agent (among many) is juniper. We can all thank one of the most devastatingly bloody conflicts in European history—not to mention one of the longest—for the birth of England's answer to the Dutch-born juniper-forward distilled beverage.

The Thirty Years' War, which kept most of Central Europe busy between 1618 and 1648, was essentially the prequel to the War to End All Wars (World War I) three centuries in the future. As has so often been a theme throughout history, combatants fired the first shots over religious disputes—in this case, between Catholics and Protestants—but ultimately, both sides forgot what they were fighting about and just continued to fight. Many historians characterize the war as a series of individual skirmishes and campaigns that overlapped to form one great conflict, which can in fact be used to describe any warfare situation that escalates and drags all sorts of peripheral players into it (think of the United States, in the twentieth century, earning a reputation for being fashionably late to such cataclysmic events).

Everyone who was anyone across Europe joined the fray, and that included the British. Brits stationed across the English Channel on the continent's coastal region, known as the Low Countries—what we know today as the Netherlands, Belgium, and Luxembourg—fortified themselves with the local Dutch liquor as they endured protracted stints in the notoriously damp environs. And thus was born a love affair for the ages. Surviving soldiers were eager to bring their new paramour, jenever, back with them to the British Isles.

Philip Duff suggests that Britons likely had been exposed to the juniper-based spirit even earlier than that conflict. In 1585, when Antwerp—now part of Belgium—fell to Spain, Protestant refugees fled the Low Countries, with thousands of them settling in England. They brought their distilling traditions with them.

Ultimately, what evolved to become the gin we know today is a completely different beverage. Distillers eventually weren't using malt wine at all and instead were infusing the spirit with botanicals to make it palatable. They knew juniper was involved, but not really how much and were rather heavy-handed with its inclusion—hence, the juniper-forward nature of the spirit today (the botanical is barely detectable in the Dutch forerunner). Despite all of the English distillers' efforts to mask the unpleasantness of the neutral base spirit they were using (their distilling knowhow lagged behind that of the Dutch), the early gins still didn't taste that great. So they started adding sugar to it to make it a tad more approachable. That concoction came to be known as Old Tom gin, sort of the bridge between jenever and what eventually would become the London Dry style most common today.

Four decades after the close of the Thirty Years' War, King William III assumed the throne of Britain and ushered in a veritable gold rush of distilling activity. William of Orange, as he is more commonly known, strongly supported spirits-making and eliminated any semblance of red tape that may have previously hindered such practices. It wasn't purely out of benevolence, of course—there were economic and political motivations for William's decree. And, wouldn't you know it, it was, once again, war-related. By that time, the Nine Years' War with Britain's then bitter rival, France, had begun. The British government levied a crippling import duty on foreign spirits as it removed the hurdles

233

for domestic producers. It was a one-two punch that boosted the local economy while flipping its continental enemy the bird.

The "licensing" process was now incredibly simple: Prospective distillers needed only to post a public notice, wait ten days, and then fire up the still. And, given the nearly nonexistent barriers to entry in the spirits-producing trade, the drink was dirt cheap to purchase—equivalent to about seventy-five US cents in today's currency. The English capital city's streets were practically awash in the stuff. By 1730, London distillers were producing around 10 million gallons of gin. For a little perspective on just how much that is, consider that annual British gin consumption today is about one-tenth of a gallon per capita. Historians estimate that eighteenth-century Londoners drank about 14 gallons of the liquor annually—or about 140 times as much as they do today. Yikes!

Of course, there is such a concept as too much of a good thing, and that pretty much summed up the climate in England during the first half of the eighteenth century. Soon the public and the powers that be began blaming gin for all society's ills—from general malaise to prostitution and violent crime. Something had to give, and give it did in 1736 with the passage of the Gin Act, which applied a 20-shilling-per-gallon tax to retail sales and an annual license fee of £50, equal to about US$11,000 in modern currency. Very few (by some historical accounts, only two) distillers ponied up for the license. Predictably, many law-abiding distillers who couldn't make a profit with the new taxes in place were forced to close up shop.

But a logical, if unforeseen, consequence was the exponential rise in illicit production and distribution of the spirit—bootlegging long before it became fashionable in the United States (which wasn't even its own country at that point). And much like some of the questionable product that hit the street during American Prohibition, much of this illegal hooch wasn't what a person would call safe. If you were looking for that unmistakable juniper flavor, you were likely to be disappointed. Cheap, often toxic chemical compounds (turpentine and sulfuric acid, for instance) were the "botanicals" of choice.

Needless to say, the Gin Act of 1736 wasn't very popular with the masses. The population rioted and, in 1743, Parliament repealed the law. However, everyone loves a sequel, and the 1736 legislation was not the last Britain would see of such consumption-curbing measures. Eight years after the first act's repeal, the government enacted the Gin Act of 1751, which proved a bit more sensible. Parliament lowered the license fee but stipulated that distillers must sell only to licensed, reputable retailers.

Unfortunately, six years later, economic and climatological factors intervened. A bad harvest in 1757 prompted Parliament to bar the production of distilled spirits entirely as an emergency measure to ensure that England had enough grain for food. Parliament lifted the ban in 1760, but the lawmaking body raised spirits duties significantly, which once again made drinking gin a cost-prohibitive pastime among the underclasses. The more affluent members of society still had a taste for it, though, and since they were willing and able to pay for it, the quality of ingredients and production methods (and thus the gin) improved.

The end of the original, mostly disreputable gin craze made way for a succession of individuals dubbed the "gentleman distillers." Alexander Gordon was among the earliest of those, creating Gordon's London Dry Gin in 1769. Six decades later, in 1830, Charles Tanqueray unveiled his own now-iconic product, while the 1840s saw the release of Boodles British Gin, named for the London-based gentlemen's club of the same name. Then in 1876, pharmacist James Burrough transitioned to commercial distilling and launched Beefeater Gin, drawing inspiration from the extravagantly clad guardians of the Tower of London.

There were quite a few gin distillers operating in the British capital into the twentieth century, but eventually it proved too expensive. Most left London by 1850—all but one, that is. Beefeater has remained a London Dry Gin in every sense of the term,

235

continuing to operate in the city proper. (That's not to say it carries on at its original site in the Chelsea district. It moved to Lambeth in 1908 and to its present site in Kennington in 1958.)

For nearly sixty years, Beefeater—now owned by French global spirits marketer Pernod Ricard—got to claim the distinction of being the only remaining London-based distillery. That is, until 2009, when old friends Sam Galsworthy, Fairfax Hall, and Jared Brown decided to quit their jobs, sell their flats, and put every penny they had into opening Sipsmith Distillery in West London—Chiswick, to be precise. Of course, before they could do that, they had to convince the city to grant them a license. Not an easy task, considering the government hadn't issued such a permit in nearly a century and a half. Just obtaining the license was a two-year ordeal.

It was an absolutely bonkers idea, to be sure. Don't forget, most of the top gin distillers—the ones that didn't go belly-up or get gobbled up by a bigger fish—had long since fled the city to save heaps of money on cheaper plots of land. And the relative property values of twenty-first-century London make mid-twentieth-century London look like a quaint community for retirees. (My London friends practically drown in their own tears every day as they lament their rent and mortgage payments.)

"Consumer taste wasn't changing then," Galsworthy points out as he pours me a gin and tonic at the distillery's tasting room. "Businesses were being bought out by bigger businesses and CFOs were going, 'We can take 30 percent out of our overhead and take [production] out of London.'"

But when Sipsmith opened its doors, the dynamic had changed considerably, and it turned out to be exactly the right time to bring distilling back to the city. The London—and pan-UK—gin renaissance was just beginning. "Now there's a consumer movement, not just in search of experimental or different flavors," Galsworthy says, "but there's this endless pursuit for transparency, for authenticity, and for a story to tell."

That's a common refrain among most people involved in the production and marketing of a craft or artisanal beverage of any kind. That's what's made craft beer the worldwide force that it is. And that's what thoughtful imbibers are after when they buy bottles of Sipsmith. "You get to tell a very rich story, and that's what people have been seeking. That's what they want today, but they didn't give a shit about it in the 1950s."

Virtually every corner of Sipsmith's distillery has a story to tell. Each of the company's three primary pot stills has its own personality. The original still, Prudence, is a nod to former prime minister Gordon Brown, who famously urged Britons to be prudent as the nation headed for fiscal disaster. Prudence is a bit of an ironic choice for a name, considering that the founders sold their homes and launched a business on the precipice of one of the biggest financial meltdowns of all time. Prudence is responsible for Sipsmith's specialty offering, VJOP—Very Junipery Over Proof. As the name suggests, it's quite juniper-forward and rather high in alcohol content—115.4 proof, or 57.7 percent ABV.

It takes a bit more time and a considerable degree of patience to concoct custom-made spirits. That's where Patience, the workhorse behind the distillery's bespoke gins, comes in. One such creation was Raffles 1915, crafted especially for Singapore's famed Raffles Hotel. As you'll recall, the colonial-era hotel gained fame in drinking circles as the birthplace of the Singapore Sling, which celebrated its one-hundredth anniversary in 2015—hence, the 1915. The partnership with Raffles was a personal one for Galsworthy. You see, "Sam" is short not for Samuel but for Stamford, as in Sir Thomas Stamford Raffles, namesake of the hotel and founder of the Singapore colony in the early nineteenth century. Raffles was Galsworthy's great-great-great-great-uncle.

The largest of the pot stills is Constance, with a 2,400-liter capacity to Prudence's and Patience's 500-liter capacities. Constance is charged with producing Sipsmith's flagship London Dry

237

Gin. Since London Dry accounts for the majority of the distillery's output, consistency—or constancy—batch after batch is critical.

"All of these words are virtues, reminders of how we must live," Galsworthy says of his pot stills.

The Chiswick facility houses one more small pot still, out of the main production area, which the founders have dubbed Cygnet, after a baby swan. Cygnet sits in the corner of a room reserved for recipe tinkering, across from shelves full of jars and bottles containing experimental ingredients. The space is a bit of a shrine to Sipsmith's "restless enthusiasm," as Galsworthy calls it, a place for pushing the boundaries on the gin category, free from the shackles of precision required for the higher-volume liquids. He admits, though, that most of the spirits born in Cygnet's quarters never see the light of day.

It didn't take long for the world to notice the magic that emanated from those Chiswick stills. In late 2016, international spirits giant Beam Suntory acquired Sipsmith—not only a significant testament to the small distillery's gin-making prowess, but a vote of confidence in the longevity of the British gin renaissance.

City of London Distillery (COLD), another of the new wave of gin producers in the capital—in the more central City of London, just off Fleet Street—offers more of a bar-forward experience. And by bar, I mean speakeasy: It's subterranean and moodily candlelit. Guests lounge in comfy chairs and sip from among COLD's selection of five gins, including an Old Tom and a sloe gin (the latter is a gin-based liqueur made from the sloe, or blackthorn, a tiny relative of the plum). Bartenders, as expected, are in *Boardwalk Empire*–era vests. What stands out against this ambience, though, are the twin pot stills visible through a window to the gin lab, where visitors can learn how to craft their own gin. It doesn't get any more interactive than that.

I always find it a bit weird to encounter a speakeasy-style bar in a country that's not the United States. Britain technically never had big-P Prohibition like we had in the States—their 1757 ban was just on production, not on distribution, sale, or consumption. The speakeasies that are all the rage these days are based on the romanticism of a period that is decidedly American. However, the UK does get a pass. After all, gin was among the more popular illicit liquids consumed by American scofflaws between 1920 and 1933. After all, much of what people produced, distributed, and drank was called bathtub gin, not bathtub vodka or bathtub rum. And many under-the-radar establishments of the day were called gin joints; even today, I know of two great bars—one in Washington, DC, and one in Charleston, South Carolina—that go by that name. So, the story of gin—an English spirit of Dutch ancestry—is very much intertwined with that of American Prohibition.

There's no greater representation of this dynamic than at Gin Festival, a series of—at last count—at least twenty annual events in cities throughout the United Kingdom celebrating the spirit the country made famous. I was surprised by how much the speakeasy spirit suffused the London edition of the event, held at what is quite possibly the capital city's most stunningly gorgeous event facility, Tobacco Dock. The sprawling two-story brick structure is a converted nineteenth-century tobacco warehouse that reopened in 2012 as a 170,000-square-foot all-purpose function space. Inside, 1920s-era suspenders-wearing bartenders sporting (mostly fake) twirly mustaches were joined by female counterparts donning couture straight out of a portrait of Art Deco New York (tattooed arms notwithstanding), tossing around silver cocktail shakers with athletic flair. And those were just the visuals; bluegrass was the prevailing style among live entertainers—nothing evokes illicit moonshine more than the homegrown music of Appalachia.

Gin Fest London 2016, I must admit, was the backdrop for a significant moment of personal growth for me. My previous book, *The Year of Drinking Adventurously*, carries the subtitle *52 Ways to Get Out of Your Comfort Zone*, and I titled the gin chapter "Gin Up (and Toss the Tonic)." The point I was trying to make was that gin—like many of the other wonderful beverages

239

profiled in the other chapters—should be appreciated on its own. And I still believe that. However, I've come to embrace the gin and tonic—mainly because I finally had my first really good G&T at Gin Fest. I got to have my cake and eat it, too: Distillery reps offered samples of their wares naked (the gin, not the reps) in one room, while the aforementioned mixologists poured the G&Ts (and other, more complex cocktails) in another. I learned that not only have most bars been using the wrong gin, they've been using the wrong tonic as well. The real star of Gin Fest was Fever-Tree, which has emerged as the official tonic of the British Gin Renaissance. And I would say it's an equal partner in a proper gin-and-tonic experience.

The next night, I texted my wife from COLD (she had gone shopping with a friend while I drank my way through the city) to say, "I've had more gin and tonics in the past three days than I have had in the past eighteen years." And that was no exaggeration.

{
HOGARTH'S BEER
STREET (T) AND
GIN LANE (B)

IMAGE CREDIT: ISTOCK
BY GETTY IMAGES
}

GIN COCKTAILS

You'll find no shortage of gin-based drinks in other parts of this book, but these are the only ones that come from a London-based producer of the spirit, Sipsmith.

☞ PERFECT GIN & TONIC

Sure, it's as simple as mixed drinks get—and technically not a "cocktail"—but not including a G&T recipe from one of the UK's best gin distilleries would be a crime.

⇢ DIRECTIONS ⇠	⇢ INGREDIENTS ⇠
Fill a thin-rimmed highball glass to the top with ice cubes.	50 ml (1⅔ ounces) Sipsmith London Dry gin
Pour in gin.	Fever-Tree Tonic (Accept no substitutes!)
Top off with tonic.	
Rub lemon twist (make sure all the pith is removed) or lime wedge along the rim of the glass before garnishing.	Lemon twist or lime wedge, for garnish (I'm partial to the former.)

☞ NAVY ROSE

Would a cocktail by any other name taste as sweet? Probably, but without Sipsmith's VJOP (Very Junipery Over Proof) gin, it wouldn't taste nearly as juniper-y.

⇢ DIRECTIONS ⇠	⇢ INGREDIENTS ⇠
Combine all ingredients in a cocktail shaker and dry-shake.	40 ml (1⅓ ounces) Sipsmith VJOP gin
	20 ml (⅔ ounce) rose tea
Fill shaker with ice and shake again, then double-strain into a chilled glass.	20 ml (⅔ ounce) fresh lemon juice
	15 ml (½ ounce) simple syrup
Garnish with dried rosebuds.	3 raspberries
	1 egg white
	Dried rosebuds, for garnish

☞ LEMON DRIZZLE SOUR

This last one from Sipsmith is a sour that uses the distillery's Lemon Drizzle Gin, which amps up the citrus with layers of sun-dried lemon peels, lemon verbena, and vapor-infused fresh lemons.

→▣ DIRECTIONS ▣←

Combine all ingredients in a cocktail shaker and dry-shake.

Add crushed ice and shake again.

Double-strain into a chilled glass and garnish with lemon twist.

→▣ INGREDIENTS ▣←

40 ml (1⅓ ounces) Sipsmith Lemon Drizzle Gin

30 ml (1 ounce) fresh lemon juice

20 ml (⅔ ounce) simple syrup

1 egg white

Lemon twist, for garnish

☞ BLOOD-RED SNAPPER

The first time I had this one was at London Gin Festival in February 2016. A year later, I returned and the same festival bartender (one of many), Peter Barrett, recognized me from 2016 and told me he'd since updated the recipe to include beetroot juice. (No, I didn't make that much of an impression on him. I happened to Instagram a shot of him mixing the drink and he started following my account.). I didn't think it was possible to improve on an already stellar gin-based Bloody Mary variation, but the 2017 iteration was even better.

⟞ DIRECTIONS ⟝

Stir all ingredients with ice.

Strain into a partially ice-filled glass (not too much—you don't want to water it down).

Garnish with lemon wheel, celery stick, and a couple of grinds of pepper on top.

⟞ INGREDIENTS ⟝

50 ml (1⅔ ounces) gin

6–8 dashes Henderson's Relish (an English brand that you'll have to do some legwork to find, but it's well worth it; Worcestershire sauce can be used in its place)

2 dashes Bitter Truth celery bitters

1 pinch celery salt

2 grinds salt

2 grinds pepper, plus one more for garnish

Juice from 1 lemon wedge

Tabasco to taste (If you're like me and enjoy a lot of heat, shake the hell out of the bottle.)

100 ml (3⅓ ounces) tomato juice

35 ml (1 ounce + 1 teaspoon) beetroot juice

Celery stick, for garnish

Lemon wheel (in addition to squeezed wedge), for garnish

243

◁ Gin Lane vs. Beer Street

In 1751, the same year as the second Gin Act, William Hogarth created a rather famous engraving called *Gin Lane*, depicting a decidedly apocalyptic vision of eighteenth-century London, rife with the type of morally bankrupt debauchery the crude gin of the time promoted. The star of the piece is a woman of ill repute (with both breasts exposed), lounging drunkenly on the front stairs of a gin shop, digging in to a can of snuff. Her look is one of oblivious, inebriated contentment—I say oblivious because she fails to notice that her baby is tumbling to certain death over the railing. Meanwhile, barely a few steps away from her, another mother is pouring a cone-shaped cup of gin down her own infant's throat (to quell the crying, of course!). Other characters in the black-and-white drawing include a seemingly dead pamphlet seller a few steps down from the soon-to-be-childless prostitute. The pamphlet he was trying to hawk extolled the evils of gin—which, naturally, no one was buying, so he starved to death. In the background, there's a rather loopy-looking fellow holding a bellows to his head in one hand and an impaled baby in the other. Other folks of varying levels of derangement populate the rest of the picture.

This is a popular image among modern gin distillers of all sizes. A print hangs in the museum at the Beefeater distillery—where visitors await their guided tour—as well as at the entrance to the much newer establishment City of London Distillery (COLD), which opened in 2012.

The illustration was obviously gross hyperbole, but there was no denying that things had gotten a little out of hand at the time, and some sort of effective regulation was necessary to keep cheaply made, borderline poisonous product off the streets. Hogarth had some overt biases, beverage-wise. The companion illustration to *Gin Lane* was a veritable love letter to Britain's drink of moderation. *Beer Street* presents a much happier, cleaner version of London. Folks are going about their daily business—fishmongers deliver the day's catch, an artist paints a scene, and all sorts of tradesman take a break from their hard work to hoist a few tankards of ale. There's even a background cameo by King George II, to whose birthday the locals toast. In other words: Gin bad, beer good.

SCOTLAND

Yes, technically Scotland is part of the United Kingdom. But despite its pesky little connection to the British crown, it is, for all intents and purposes, its own country. (And it may regain its sovereignty soon enough. At the time of this book's publication, the Brexit vote had prompted the Scottish to consider a sequel to their 2014 independence referendum, in which the majority voted no to the question of whether Scotland should become an independent country. The results of that referendum affirmed their desire to remain a part of the UK, primarily because of its membership in the European Union. Post-Brexit, all bets are off. Another referendum is tentatively scheduled for 2019.)

Scotch whisky, naturally, is the first thing to come to mind when talking about Scottish beverages. I know I'm far from alone in the opinion that it is one of the greatest contributions any ethnic group has ever made to the modern drinking world. Enough books have been written on Scotch and other types of whisky that were influenced by Scotch that you could probably fill a mid-size city's library with them. I'm not going to attempt to cover any new ground here, though I will say that the best way to educate yourself is to go out and drink the stuff. And do so in Scotland, if you can. It's one of the few places in the world—if not the only place— where you can pay the equivalent of US$3 or $4 and enjoy a dram of 12 Year Old Macallan or Glenfarclas in a townie "old man" dive bar with no trace of hipster irony. (You'd pay about $12 for it in a tavern in a major American city.) The best such bars are in small villages in the middle of nowhere, especially those within a few

245

miles of a relatively dense concentration of distillers (especially in the valley near the River Spey, known as Speyside, in the northern section of the Highlands). The selections will likely be limited to a handful of single malts and blends, but they'll be well curated.

But if you're looking for a broad-based palate education and want to try as many as possible, there are a number of specialty whisky bars that would probably keep you busy for about six months—and you still wouldn't have tried everything. I'm a fan of the Pot Still in Glasgow for such purposes. The pub boasts around six hundred different whiskies (including some non-Scotch options, but those are a fraction of the overall menu). The best part about drinking at the Pot Still—and any traditional Scottish pub with a decent list—is that there's a complete absence of pretension. And that's a one-eighty from the way American bars and restaurants present Scotch.

At the Pot Still, I once saw someone eating a slab of deep-fried haggis (from an outside chip shop; the bar doesn't serve food) while sipping a dram of cask-strength Edradour whisky—not something you're likely to see stateside. To be fair, you're not likely to find haggis in many places in the United States, so think of it as someone eating a corn dog on a stick while nosing an eighteen-year-old single malt.

Oddly enough, though, it's not the Scots who are keeping the country's distillers in business. Most have drinkers in the States, the rest of Europe (especially France), Australia, and Asia to thank for their success. Domestic Scotch consumption has been on the decline in recent years, and producers have become dependent on the export business. While distillers in America, Ireland, and Japan have been the greatest beneficiaries of the global whisky boom, the Scots were a bit late to catch up. That's mostly due to the fact that an outsized proportion of their output has been in blended whiskies, which have been in sharp decline, as single malts have been on the upswing. Scotch whisky makers have been racing to keep up with the trend.

Meanwhile, the newbie distilleries on the block have been racing to keep up with another trend: gin. Scots have been bitten by the gin bug at least as severely as their neighbors to the south, and distilleries producing that spirit have been popping up just as fast in Scotland as in England. The fact that the juniper-forward liquor has set much of Europe aflame (figuratively, of course) has provided a logistical advantage for startup Scottish distillers. There's no way they'd be able to compete with established whisky brands with decades-worth of barreled stock, so they probably shouldn't even try. And if they do make whisky, it's got to sit in oak casks for at least three years before it can even be called whisky. There's no such waiting period for gin, so the distillers' output can start generating a profit right away.

⋇ The Taster's Tool

I'm not going to tell you which Scotch whisky to drink—pick up *Tasting Whiskey* by Lew Bryson and give yourself an education. But I am going to recommend my favorite method of tasting and exploring it: with a Glencairn glass. The small tulip-like vessel with a protruding, stemless base has become virtually ubiquitous at Scotch distillery tasting counters since its introduction in 2001. Designer Raymond Davidson worked with a team of master distillers from top producers to create the Glencairn. The sensory advantages of the glass are in its shape: It tapers at the mouth,

{ THE GLENCAIRN

GLASS

PHOTO COURTESY
GLENCAIRN CRYSTAL }

247

which concentrates the aromas while facilitating ease of sipping. The bowl of the glass is wide, which optimizes visual presentation and fully accentuates the spirit's color. The base is designed for easy grabbing; you wouldn't want to hold it by the bowl because your body heat would affect the liquid inside.

Scotch whisky may be Scotland's greatest contribution to the drinking world, but its beer is a very close second (and let's not forget that whisky, in its most basic form, is distilled beer). "Scotch ale" has become a catchall term, especially among non-Scottish brewers looking to replicate the quintessential Scottish beer-drinking experience. Their focus is more heavily on the malt side of the brewing equation than the hops, though hops are most definitely still a significant part of the recipes. Even before hops became a primary ingredient in beers produced across Europe, the Scots were flavoring their brews with indigenous botanicals, primarily heather.

More often than not, when we hear the term "Scotch ale," it refers to the stronger "wee heavy" within a full spectrum of Scottish-born styles. A wee heavy, characterized by intense caramel notes and hints of dark fruit, as well as a nearly opaque deep copper hue, represents an evolution of the original "shilling system" of ale designations, based on typical prices on invoices. A 60-shilling was the lighter, easier-drinking brews of the group, followed by 70-, 80-, and 90-shilling descriptors. The wee heavies were usually the stronger, 90-shilling variety.

Even though the British shilling is a defunct monetary unit, its name lives on for many Scottish breweries (as well as American ones that probably never came within a thousand miles of an actual shilling; one of my favorite domestic craft beers is 90 Shilling Ale from Odell Brewing Company, based in Fort Collins, Colorado). Walk into any pub in Scotland, and the hand pumps will usually feature brand plates marked "80/"—the symbol for shilling.

And, as in most other European countries experiencing a craft beer renaissance, Scottish producers have been incorporating styles popularized by American craft brewers. However, perhaps more so than their English counterparts, they're fiercely asserting their native heritage; even among the most globally minded of the new band of artisanal beer makers you're likely to find at least one or two traditional Scotch styles.

Once, while I was touring a major Scotch whisky distillery, one of the operations managers told me he had launched his own craft brewery, which he runs on the side (only in Scotland would a startup brewer identify "distillery manager" as a day job). I asked if he was producing the usual international suspects: IPAs, pale ales, wheat beers, and the like. He was adamant that Scotch styles would be his flagships, as that's what his culture is all about. And I absolutely love that. Though, I must admit, I'm a bit biased: I much prefer brews that emphasize malt characteristics than the IPAs of the world that are all about hops. That puts me in the minority among American beer geeks, but I feel right at home in the Highlands.

IRELAND

249

Whether or not you've been to Ireland, there's a pretty good chance you've been to an Irish pub. Or at least you think you have. One of the ever-expanding roster of declarations that have earned me the label of "curmudgeon" among those in my social circle is that I refuse to go to "fake Irish pubs."

How does one divine an authentic Irish pub from a fake one? It's simple.

Step 1: Walk into a pub.

Step 2: Ask yourself, "Am I in Ireland?"

If the answer is no, then you are in a fake Irish pub.

Okay, that's neither fair nor true. There are plenty of authentic Irish pubs throughout the United States. They're usually owned by Irish immigrants or second- or third-generation descendants of said immigrants, and a sizeable percentage of their clientele have some ties to the Old Country. And it's likely they've been fixtures in their neighborhoods for at least four or five decades.

The others? They usually call themselves things like the Dub-
liner, O'Grady's, or McMahon's, and they've got wall-to-wall
Guinness signage and wall-to-wall frat boys. Their decor looks dis-
tressed and weathered, but that's a very calculated design element.
Fact is, the place probably opened three weeks ago.

I'm exaggerating a little, but the point is this: The Emerald Isle
motif is among the most popular branding in bars, primarily due
to the fact that Ireland has a legendary drinking culture. However,
it's also one of the least understood drinking cultures. "Drinking
culture" here is far too often equated with "perpetual inebriation."
One need only attend a St. Patrick's Day parade in a major U.S.
city to witness that misconception in action.

Drunkenness does, of course, exist in Ireland, as it does in
every country with alcohol. But when I think of an Irish pub, I
think of Michael Flannerys in downtown Limerick—or at least
part of it. (Flannerys has got a bit of a split personality.) The main
entrance has a traditional façade, with red trim and a hand-painted
"Michael Flannerys" sign.

A pair of repurposed Bushmills whiskey barrels stand guard on
either side of the doorway (interestingly enough, Bushmills is produced in Northern Ireland). Walk inside and it's a low-lit (candles
galore!) wonderland composed of two cozy rooms, branded whiskey placards, and vintage beer bottles. Then you go through a con-
necting door that leads to simply "Flannerys Bar," a more modern
space with a bit of a sports bar feel, where you can get breakfast and
lunch from 10 A.M. to 3 P.M. on most days. There's also an upstairs
terrace bar that's equally rooted in the twenty-first century.

I, of course, prefer the first area that I described. The music's
low, as are the voices of the sparsely scattered regulars enjoying
their pints or their glasses of Redbreast 12 and Green Spot. The
pub has one of the most extensive whiskey selections in all of Ireland and, for my money, there's probably no better environment in
which to sip them. The pub even offers private, one-on-one whiskey tastings, in which you get a flight of three high-end spirits—a

trio of some of the rarer offerings bearing the Jameson trademark or single pot still selections, including the aforementioned Redbreast and Green Spot, as well as the Powers John's Lane brand, all owned by Pernod Ricard. (I spend a lot of time maligning large multinational companies, but Pernod Ricard is among the select few that get a pass from me. In 1966, when whiskey-making across Ireland was in rapid decline, rivals John Jameson & Son, Cork Distilleries Company, and John Powers & Son merged to form Irish Distillers. Twenty-two years later, Paris-based Pernod Ricard acquired Irish Distillers, opened up markets worldwide, and sowed the seeds for today's Irish whiskey renaissance.)

A remarkably knowledgeable staffer guides you through the tasting—you just have to call ahead and reserve; Flannerys needs to make sure there's someone else staffing the bar while you're sitting off in the corner with one of the pub's resident experts. You could easily burn away an entire afternoon if you and your guide end up chatting about religion, politics, or whatever else is of interest. My own tasting occurred on the day of the national Irish election and in the midst of the decidedly ugly 2016 U.S. presidential primary season.

251

$\{$ THE MIDLETON DISTILLERY, WHICH PRODUCES SUCH BRANDS AS JAMESON, GREEN SPOT, YELLOW SPOT, AND REDBREAST $\}$

There's an almost church-like quality to the space—a place for quiet reflection and appreciation, be it of a local craft brew, a fine whiskey, or a reliable pint of Guinness. That's what comes to mind when someone says "Irish drinking culture" to me. Not cramming, sardine-style, into the Delta House that's trying to pretend it's an authentic Gaelic pub.

We can blame the existence of such wretched places on Ireland's legacy of getting the shaft. That's pretty much what defined the nineteenth and twentieth centuries for the country. The eighteenth century was the heyday for Irish distilling. Distillers were getting wildly rich off the stuff because, frankly, they were so damned good at making great whiskey. One thing that they weren't, however, was invincible. The mid-nineteenth century brought the potato famine. There was unprecedented emigration to the United States, which meant a mass exodus of a large chunk of the whiskey-drinking market. Those who remained in Ireland and didn't starve to death had to prioritize food production over whiskey making; the people needed to eat most of the grain growing on the island, rather than distill it.

The whiskey industry managed to survive the famine and was able to thrive once again, gaining a reputation around the world as the best there was. Distillers were exporting to markets across Europe, as well as far-afield destinations like Singapore, New Zealand, and Egypt. Irish whiskey was synonymous with quality. And then in the twentieth century, Ireland encountered the greatest threats to the reputation of its most cherished beverage. The resulting damage was nearly irreparable.

The 1920s brought a double whammy. In 1921, the Irish War of Independence ended in a treaty, affirming Ireland's independence from Britain. About a decade after the end of the physical conflict, the economic one began. The Anglo-Irish Trade War spanned a considerable chunk of the 1930s, which meant there was no economic relationship between Ireland and Great Britain. Cross the United Kingdom off the list of export markets. While you're at it, cross off Australia, New Zealand, Canada, and any other country within the British Commonwealth.

That's okay, there's always America! Oh wait, never mind. In 1920, this little thing called Prohibition went into effect, erasing another major export market and further devastating an already crippled industry. Hold on, you say. I watched *Boardwalk Empire,* and I know Americans were drinking illicit Irish whiskey—Nucky Thompson was an Irish-American, after all! While it's true that some of the Old Country's spirit found its way to these shores during the (not-so) Noble Experiment, most of what was labeled "Irish whiskey" was actually hastily produced barely drinkable liquor made in an American bootlegger's distillery. They knew that in cities with large Irish-American populations—Boston, Chicago, and New York come to mind—there was a market for those who missed their homeland. Problem was, what they were getting was a poor facsimile of the spirit that made Ireland famous, and eventually Americans began to believe that Irish whiskey was unpalatable. That perception stuck for the rest of the century.

⚜ Poitin on the Ritz

It seems that any country with a distilling tradition (read: pretty much all of them) has a storied history with illegal production. In other words, moonshine is universal. And that includes Ireland, so renowned for its whiskey industry.

253

Throughout history, most legitimate whiskey distilleries in Ireland operated in densely populated areas—they were big industry and they required a lot of staff. The people living in the sticks, however, made do with their own small-batch stuff. The fruit of their labors came to be known as poitin (pronounced "puh-tcheen," not very far off from the pronunciation of poutine, the Canadian fries, gravy, and cheese curd concoction). The name derives from pota, meaning "pot," referring to the fact that producers traditionally crafted their spirit in a small pot still.

The British, who controlled Ireland, found that they couldn't control these small stills, especially the ones in remote rural regions. And that was a big problem for the Crown because, as those of us living in their former colonies well know, the British really liked taxing whatever they possibly could. And anything they couldn't? Make it illegal! Thus, in 1661, Britain banned poitin.

POITIN COCKTAILS

As intense a flavor as poitin can have, it does know how to play well with others. Two of Ireland's modern purveyors of (legal) poitin were gracious enough to share a few cocktails for your mixing pleasure. The first ones come from Mad March Hare, a brand produced under contract at West Cork Distillery.

☞ MIDNIGHT MADNESS

Coffee liqueur and espresso bring the darkness—and a bit of a peppy kick!

⇢⊨◉ DIRECTIONS ◉⊨⇠	⇢⊨◉ INGREDIENTS ◉⊨⇠
Shake all ingredients with ice and strain into a chilled glass.	40 ml (1⅓ ounces) Mad March Hare poitin (or comparable brand)
Garnish with coffee beans.	10 ml (⅓ ounce) Kahlúa
	10 ml (⅓ ounce) Frangelico
	30 ml (1 ounce) espresso
	Coffee beans, for garnish

☞ THE MAD FASHIONED

The classic Old Fashioned is a favorite blank canvas among many skilled bartenders. Mad March Hare's contribution is one of the more massive departures I've encountered.

⇢⊨◉ DIRECTIONS ◉⊨⇠	⇢⊨◉ INGREDIENTS ◉⊨⇠
Build cocktail over ice and stir for 30 seconds.	40 ml (1⅓ ounces) Mad March Hare poitin (or comparable brand)
Garnish with cherry.	10 ml (⅓ ounce) tawny port
	5 ml (1 teaspoon) Mozart dark chocolate liqueur
	5 ml (1 teaspoon) maraschino cherry syrup
	Maraschino cherry, for garnish

☞ MOONEY'S MULE

Riffs on the Moscow Mule (part of the "buck" family of ginger-based drinks) are just as popular as riffs on the Old Fashioned, if not more so. Naturally, this one speaks with an Irish accent.

⇒ DIRECTIONS ⇐	⇒ INGREDIENTS ⇐
Build cocktail over ice and stir for 30 seconds.	40 ml (1⅓ ounces) Mad March Hare poitín (or comparable brand)
Garnish with lime wedges and mint.	20 ml (⅔ ounce) Giffard Manzana Verde green apple liqueur
	30 ml (1 ounce) ginger beer
	10 ml (⅓ ounce) fresh lime juice
	Lime wedges and mint sprig for garnish

☞ BLOODY MOONEY

As I've said before, I'm a sucker for a good Bloody Mary—and an even bigger sucker for one that throws convention to the wind and uses a nontraditional spirit in place of the vodka. The intensely vegetal flavor of the poitín adds a little extra oomph to this savory favorite.

255

⇒ DIRECTIONS ⇐	⇒ INGREDIENTS ⇐
Build cocktail over ice and stir for 10 seconds.	50 ml (1⅔ ounces) Mad March Hare poitín (or comparable brand)
Garnish with celery, lemon wedge, and a few grinds of black pepper.	150 ml (5 ounces) pressed tomato juice
	2 dashes Worcestershire sauce
	1 dash Tabasco sauce
	15 ml (½ ounce) celery liqueur
	Celery stick, for garnish
	Lemon wedge, for garnish
	Pinch of cracked black pepper, for garnish

☞ BOOTLEGGER NEGRONI

The Sidecar Bar at Dublin's Westbury Hotel features this rethinking of the legendary bitter cocktail, the Negroni. Don't worry—the Campari is still there; poitin replaces the gin. This cocktail and the next two come to us from Teeling Whiskey.

⇢► DIRECTIONS ◄⇠

Stir all ingredients together in an Old Fashioned glass with ice.

Garnish with orange twist.

⇢► INGREDIENTS ◄⇠

30 ml (1 ounce) Spirit of Dublin poitin (or comparable brand)

30 ml (1 ounce) Campari

30 ml (1 ounce) sweet vermouth

Orange twist, for garnish

☞ THE CHAPTER'S END

You'd think it was Christmas with all of the green and red ingredients in here!

⇢► DIRECTIONS ◄⇠

Shake all ingredients and serve straight up in a small coupe glass.

Garnish with lime wheel.

⇢► INGREDIENTS ◄⇠

30 ml (1 ounce) Spirit of Dublin poitin (or comparable brand)

20 ml (⅔ ounce) Green Chartreuse

20 ml (⅔ ounce) maraschino liqueur

20 ml (⅔ ounce) fresh lime juice

Lime wheel, for garnish

☞ THE FULL REGALIA

This last one from Teeling incorporates a decidedly floral element: hibiscus syrup. You can find dried hibiscus leaves for the garnish and the syrup at Whole Foods Markets and most health food stores, as well as Caribbean groceries.

⇢ DIRECTIONS ⇠

Dry-shake all ingredients and pour into a small coupe glass.

Serve straight up, with dried hibiscus leaves as garnish.

⇢ INGREDIENTS ⇠

30 ml (1 ounce) Spirit of Dublin poitin (or comparable brand)

20 ml (⅔ ounce) apricot brandy

30 ml (1 ounce) fresh lemon juice

20 ml (⅔ ounce) hibiscus syrup (recipe below)

15 ml (½ ounce) egg white

3 dashes rhubarb bitters

Dried hibiscus leaves, for garnish

HIBISCUS SYRUP

257

⇢ DIRECTIONS ⇠

Combine all ingredients in a medium saucepan.

Bring to a boil over high heat, then drop heat to low and simmer, uncovered, for 10 minutes.

Remove saucepan from heat, cover, and let steep for 5 minutes.

Place a fine-mesh sieve over a large measuring cup or bowl with a pour spout and pour syrup through.

Let it drain completely, then discard solids.

Pour syrup into a clean, dry, 32-ounce jar, cover it with the lid, and let cool.

You can store the syrup in the fridge for up to 1 month.

⇢ INGREDIENTS ⇠

¾ cup dried hibiscus leaves

4 cups water

1 cup sugar

½ cup dark brown sugar

1-inch piece fresh ginger, crushed

2 whole star anise

Peel from 1 lemon, removed in strips using a sharp peeler or paring knife

1 pinch salt

Naturally, that stopped no one. All it did was force poitin production into the shadows. In some cases, the poitin being produced on the sly was superior to the legal stuff, since many of the law-abiding distillers were forced to cut corners on quality in order to afford the draconian taxes.

Over the course of the next three-hundred-plus years, poitin became a fabled beverage, woven into the very fabric of everyday Irish life. Families passed down recipes and distilling techniques through generations. "If you were a rich farmer, you would've used barley; if you were a poor farmer, you would use potatoes," says Jack Teeling, founder of Teeling Whiskey Distillery. "If you were someone who didn't even have potatoes, you would've used fruit or whatever was available at the time."

Eventually poitin became legal again, but not until 1997. Many new and existing distilleries found the spirit to be a great way to get product on the market quickly while they were waiting a few years for their just-distilled whiskey to mature in oak barrels. The strategy is similar to that of the legal American "moonshine" producers; market it as new-make whiskey while having a little fun with your region's forbidden past.

Teeling, who has distilling in his blood (his father founded Cooley Distillery a generation before, and the Teelings have traced their ancestral whiskey-making history back to the eighteenth century), markets his own poitin brand, called Spirit of Dublin. Teeling's was the very first poitin I tasted; I saw it behind the bar at a pub called Nancy Blake's in Limerick, and I just couldn't resist.

Flavor-wise . . . let's just say it's a little rougher around the edges than the famously smooth, complex whiskeys coming from the big distillers. The initial words that come to mind when describing the flavor are "cumbersome" and "chaotic." There's a pronounced vegetal quality—not a grassy, peppery one, mind you, but something more akin to a salad that's been sitting out for a few too many days. There's a vaguely tomato-like note, but not of the heirloom or San Marzano variety. This reminds me more of the tomatoes steeping in a bowl of Sichuan dough-drop-and-mixed-vegetable soup.

Poitín has a reputation for being ludicrously strong; over the years, it wasn't uncommon for a distiller to bottle a 160 proof (80 percent ABV) spirit. But, since there was no real definition or regulation during its centuries underground, there was a vast range of ABVs, from the approachable to the mind-numbing. The first iteration of Teeling's legal barley-based interpretation was a hefty 61.5 percent, but the distillery has since dialed it back to a less flammable 52.5 percent. I've tried a few other brands that are meant to appeal to mainstream whiskey drinkers, with ABVs in the low 40 percent range. Even at that more moderate alcohol content, it still doesn't taste anything like what we traditionally think of as whiskey.

I will never forget the moment I had my first poitín on that damp February evening in Limerick. Not just because the flavor is rather unforgettable, but because I also had a pretty stellar soundtrack for my drinking session. As I was sipping my way to the bottom of the glass, the sound system blasted—almost as if on cue—U2's "Sunday, Bloody Sunday." I reckon that's about as Irish as experiences get.

SPAIN

Before we move westward, we're going to head southbound to the Iberian Peninsula, a treasure trove of world-class wines, ciders, beers, and spirits. It's hard to even know where to start, especially when talking about the largest of the two Iberian countries, Spain.

The obvious place would be wine. The dominant wine-producing region in Spain is Rioja, whose viticultural heritage dates back to ancient times. The first recorded references to significant winemaking activities can be traced to around the ninth century, or smack-dab in the middle of the Middle Ages. And, as was the case with most alcoholic beverages across the continent in that era, it was mostly monks doing the producing.

259

Rioja, located in the north of the country, is less than a hundred miles from the French border. It's just about equidistant from the Atlantic Ocean and the Mediterranean Sea; being located hundreds of miles from either coast gives the landlocked region a continental climate. Rioja wines, as one would expect, are a protected appellation. The region is best known for its reds, though it produces great whites and rosés as well. Visit any restaurant during lunch—Spain's biggest meal, which precedes the country's famous two-hour-plus siesta—and you'll likely behold a sea of red glasses on tables across the dining room.

But wine is only a small part of the Spanish drinking story. Beer has been a big part of the culture in the country, with ubiquitous macro brands like Alhambra, owned by Madrid-based Mahou San Miguel, and Estrella Damm, a product of Barcelona-based S. A. Damm. There's also a burgeoning craft beer movement happening in the country, mimicking America's brewing revolution, though on a much smaller scale than in the States and in other parts of Europe.

One element of Spain's diverse beverage traditions that's all its own is its cider. Yes, cider consumption is fairly pervasive in the UK and Ireland and has really started to catch on recently in the United States, but Spain's centuries of apple-fermenting heritage have resulted in regional ciders that are unlike those produced in other apple-rich regions. Two regions in particular have gained quite a bit of attention throughout Spain and internationally: Asturias and Basque Country. Which region produces the better cider is, naturally, a source of much heated debate.

Asturias is a small, autonomously governed region in northwestern Spain bordering the Bay of Biscay (the large gulf that washes up on the shores of two-thirds of northern Spain and just about all of western France). Cider production developed there thanks not only to the twenty-two native Asturian apple varieties, but also to the fact that the tart, mildly alcoholic apple drinks pair well with regional stews, seafood, and sausages.

But nearby Basque Country is starting to grab much of the spotlight from its neighbor. Located just to the east of Asturias and with equal access to the Bay of Biscay, Basque Country produces ciders known to be even drier and every bit as wild and funky as many of those made in Asturias, but they are often a bit less carbonated.

However, if you're looking to find cider in bars and on the tables in restaurants in Madrid or Barcelona, you might be looking for a while. Asturias and Basque Country are really the only parts of Spain with any sort of pronounced cider culture, save for restaurants in major cities that specialize in Asturian and Basque cuisine.

There is one emerging drinking custom that the country cannot claim is uniquely Spanish. The go-to spirit-based beverage of choice among today's modern Spanish drinkers is . . . wait for it . . . gin and tonic. Yes, the English invention designed to fight malaria in India is now a huge part of the fabric of Spanish nightlife.

When Belgian-born cocktail writer François Monti relocated to Madrid in the early 2000s, the Spanish gin-based cocktail trend was in its embryonic stages. Specialty gin bars started to sprout up in big cities like Madrid and Barcelona around 2006. "When those bars started popping up, they were very proud because they had ten to fifteen gins," Monti recalls. A few years later interest in the spirit exploded. "Now, basically, you have to have fifty, sixty, seventy, eighty gins to be able to claim that you're a gin and tonic bar," he says.

The Spanish G&T bonanza is a case study in how to revive a drink by making it seem classier. Prior to the surge, the cocktail did exist across Spain, but most considered it a passé tipple for an older generation. The rum and Coke had a similar distinction. It was something to drink at sundown, but by no means a concoction that even approached "fancy."

Some bartenders in northern Spain theorized that the first step toward jazzing it up was nixing the vessel in which it typically had been served. Back then, the most common way to consume a

261

gin and tonic was from a tall, thin container, even narrower than a highball or Collins glass. The problem was, Spanish bartenders like using large ice cubes, but could shoehorn only one or two in such vessels. So they experimented with all types of glassware. Some started serving the drink in the traditional Spanish cider vessels— sort of like shaker pint glasses, but shorter, wider, and more cylindrical. Those glasses had plenty of room to fit those colossal cubes.

Many others in the bar industry, however, didn't think that those glasses were fancy enough, so they started playing around with stemmed beer goblets. That practice ultimately evolved into using wide-mouthed stemmed glassware with spacious bowls in which a server easily could fit more than half a liter of liquid (without ice, that is; it was a more sensibly sized pour when it included ice). It made for a very striking presentation and quickly became the standard vessel, which helped escalate G&T mania.

Any Barcelona or Madrid hipster will likely tell you that the wind is already out of the G&T's sails, but for the general population, that is hardly the case. Monti likes to think his own modest suburban neighborhood in greater Madrid is a pretty reliable bellwether for the hottest trends sweeping the country. A sign of the gin and tonic's mainstream staying power was when, in 2016, his local no-frills supermarket started stocking upscale-skewing gin brands like Scotland's Hendrick's and France's G'Vine. "Those gins just arrived there," Monti says. "Although we don't see the same growth and although it's not in the lifestyle magazines as much as it used to be, the gin and tonic is still very important in Spain and it's going to remain with us."

Just as Spain was reaching peak G&T consumption, the country's drinkers were also beginning to rediscover a more traditional component of their imbibing heritage: vermouth. Now, before you stab this page with your pen: Yes, vermouth is often more closely associated with Italy and has been part of that country's culture for at least a century longer. But Spain, too, has a vermouth-making history, one that dates back to the nineteenth

century. The epicenter of Spanish vermouth production is Catalonia, the autonomous region in the northeastern corner of the
country, near southwestern France.

Vermouth had always been easy to find throughout Spain; it's
not uncommon to see it on tap in many pubs. However, for many
decades leading up to about 2014, most viewed it as a stodgy, conservative drink that you would choose only if you're a senior citizen or a cash-strapped university student (it's quite cheap).

As is so often the case when an old-timey beverage becomes
cool again, hipsters deserve some of the credit for Spanish vermouth's newfound popularity. But that's only part of the story;
another part is pure economics, since vermouth's resurgence
roughly correlated with a financial downturn in Spain. Drinkers
may have been scrapping more expensive tipples and incorporating vermouth into their imbibing rotations out of necessity.
A well-made mixed drink, even something as simple as a gin and
tonic made with high-quality ingredients, is going to set a person
back 12 or 13 euros at the bar. The price tag on a pour of vermouth
is chump change compared with that, barely 3 euros.

And the shift has been palpable. Now vermouth specialty
bars, called vermuterias, are sprouting up all over Spain, and new
brands are coming on the market (though only a small number of
operations actually make vermouth; many new brands are contracting out to existing producers).

Spanish vermouth is quite distinct from Italian vermouth,
primarily because production in Italy became more or less standardized, and there hasn't been a great deal of variation among the
leading brands—Martini being the best known of those. But in
Spain, production has been fragmented, especially since it never
exploded to the macro level that it did in Italy.

"You'll find some very odd stuff when you travel around
Spain—stuff that usually didn't go out of the village where it was
produced," reveals Monti. "But now, with growing interest, they're
starting to be marketed outside."

263

VERMOUTH COCKTAILS

François Monti—cocktail writer, vermouth expert, and Belgian expat living in Madrid—tipped me off about these drinks that showcase the aromatized wine.

☞ MITIA COMBINACIÓN

The Mitia Combinación is a modern twist on the Media Combinación, which is traditionally two parts vermouth, one part gin, a touch of Curaçao, and sometimes a few dashes of bitters. This version comes to us from the Barcelona bar Boca Chica, whose bartenders age the first three ingredients together in oak for three months before mixing them in the drink. That can be fairly impractical for the home bartender, but it's perfectly fine unaged. (However, might I recommend oak aging sticks? You can drop one in a jar of a spirit for just twenty-four hours and still get much of the barrel effect.)

➻ DIRECTIONS ⤞	➻ INGREDIENTS ⤞
Build cocktail over ice in a rocks glass and top with cava.	50 ml (1⅔ ounces) Vermouth Dos Deus Reserva (or comparable brand)
Garnish with orange twist and olives.	15 ml (½ ounce) Cointreau
	15 ml (½ ounce) Tanqueray No. Ten Gin (or comparable brand)
	Cava
	Orange twist, for garnish
	Olives, for garnish

☞ AVERY

Diego Cabrera, bartender at Madrid gastropub Salmon Guru, created this vermouth-and-tequila recipe. His drink calls for Martini Bianco, which is probably the easiest vermouth to find anywhere in the world. However, since Martini is Italian and we're talking about Spain here, why not try it with a Spanish vermouth? If you can get your hands on one with a flavor profile that's in Martini's neighborhood, that is. I don't want to tamper too much with Cabrera's vision.

⇢ DIRECTIONS ↩

Stir and serve up in a cocktail glass, and garnish with a strip of grapefruit peel and a celery stick.

⇢ INGREDIENTS ↩

50 ml (1⅔ ounces) Martini Bianco vermouth (or comparable brand)

30 ml (½ ounce) tequila blanco

1 dash celery bitters

1 dash grapefruit bitters

Grapefruit peel, for garnish

Celery stick, for garnish

265

☞ PERICOLATE

Juan Valls hangs his hat at Niño Perdido in the northwestern Spanish town of Valladolid, where he developed this complex sensory adventure.

⇢ DIRECTIONS ↩

Crush cacao beans in a cocktail shaker, then add remaining ingredients.

Shake and fine-strain into a cocktail glass.

Garnish with an orange twist.

⇢ INGREDIENTS ↩

2 cacao beans

60 ml (2 ounces) gin

25 ml (¾ ounce) Yzaguirre Rojo red vermouth (or comparable brand)

5 ml (1 teaspoon) bitter orange marmalade

1 dash Jerry Thomas Decanter bitters (or comparable brand)

Orange twist, for garnish

Even sherry producers in Jerez are starting to make and market their own vermouth. And they've definitely had practice: Sherry-based vermouth existed as far back as the late nineteenth century. It gradually faded away, as it wasn't a significant source of revenue for sherry houses, especially as vermouth consumption declined. But sherry-based vermouth may actually get the Spanish population interested in drinking sherry again. Spain is the only country whose fortified wine can be called sherry, but most of the people who consume the beverage live everywhere but Spain. It's a similar dynamic to Cognac in France, where only about 3 percent of its drinkers live in its home country.

⋈ Vermouth Revisited

People sometimes refer to vermouth as a fortified wine, but the more accurate label is "aromatized wine." In addition to a little extra alcohol to enhance flavor, vermouth includes various botanicals as flavoring and aroma agents. Chief among those is wormwood—yes, the same signature ingredient in absinthe. The word "vermouth" actually derives from the German word for wormwood, "wermut."

PORTUGAL

Everyone loves a good coastline—who doesn't go gaga over beachfront property?—but it can be a double-edged sword. Sure, easy access to oceans means access to the rest of the world. Why else were the French, British, Dutch, Spanish, and Portuguese among the largest global imperialists that spread their cultures, for better or worse, across the planet? But on the flipside, lots of seaside real estate means that traders and explorers from the rest of the world can pretty much come and go as they please. And sometimes you just want to be left alone!

That scenario does have a bit more upside, though, as those not living within your borders often take an interest in what you're making and selling and take it back home. And that's more money in your pocket! Still, as wealthy as it makes your nation, it does foster many misconceptions. Misconceptions such as these: The Spanish love their sherry, the French love their Cognac, and the Portuguese love their port. By this point, you know that the first two statements aren't true and you can probably figure out where I'm going with the third one. Yes, the only country in which a producer can make a fortified wine and call it port is Portugal—and only within the very specific Douro Valley region in the north. But most of its consumption happens everywhere but in its home country.

Port gained a particularly rabid following in England in the early eighteenth century, when Britain was embroiled in one of its many violent scuffles with France and stopped importing French wines. Today, many port labels bear English names thanks to the fact that British companies continue to be responsible for most of the beverage's international trade.

Interestingly, one could argue that Portugal is more famous for the influence it has exerted on international imbibing cultures than on its own. The Portuguese brought sweet potatoes to Japan, and now the Japanese can't get enough of them; it's the most popular shochu base. Portugal moved sugar production from the Madeira archipelago (known for the Portuguese-created fortified wine of the same name) to Brazil, and the Brazilians eventually turned the pure sugarcane juice into its national spirit, cachaça. The Portuguese also brought the stills that made cachaça-making possible. Additionally, the Iberian colonizers moved cashew plants from South America to Africa and India, both of which were able to develop their own spirits distilled from the cashew apple.

This all, of course, prompts the question: What drinkable legacy have the Portuguese left for Portugal?

267

For one, there's ginjinha (commonly known by the diminutive "ginja"), a sour cherry liqueur that's quite popular in the northern part of the country, especially when drunk at room temperature after dinner. There's some dispute over its origins, but the prevailing story is that monks started making it in their monasteries three to four hundred years ago. It's quite common to serve ginja with a cherry at the bottom. Sometimes the pit of that cherry remains in the drinker's mouth for hours after they've nibbled the flesh off it. And they'll just keep talking to their friends with a pit lodged somewhere in their cheek. In the early 2000s, one brand, Ginja de Óbidos Oppidum, popularized the practice of drinking it out of little edible chocolate cups, creating a kind of chocolate-covered-cherry drinking experience at dessert time.

Proving that the locals love their liqueurs, Licor Beirão is another go-to tipple in Portugal. Its recipe, like that of many European liqueurs (I'm looking at you, Italian amaro), is a take-it-to-the-grave scenario among its makers, but it also reflects centuries of global trade and exploration. Herbs, roots, and other botanicals from far-flung regions of the world (South America and Southeast Asia, for starters) are among Licor Beirão's known ingredients.

Licor Beirão was born at the end of the nineteenth century and, like many a (marketing-enhanced) brand origin story, there's a bit of romance surrounding its creation. A port wine salesman was passing through the central Portuguese town of Lousã when he fell in love with the daughter of a local pharmacist, whom he subsequently married. You can probably guess where this is going: Dear old dad had been concocting all sorts of secret alcohol-based remedies but, unfortunately, the government then decreed that anything boozy didn't qualify as medicine. The apothecary's enterprising new son-in-law saw opportunity in that reality and began producing the tasty, herbal delights in a small factory instead of the pharmacy. It didn't take too long for the main product to catch on. In 1929, new owner J. Carranca Redondo christened the concoction Licor Beirão, so named for the Beira region of central

Portugal (a "Beirão" is a person from Beira). Today, the third generation of the founding family runs the company and hand-selects
the thirteen herbs and spices that constitute its recipe.

As with so many of the world's finest spirits, consumption flattened in the latter part of the twentieth century, but Licor Beirão's
management team has been successful in appealing to a new generation of Portuguese drinkers seeking an authentic connection
to their roots (the brand has been making inroads abroad as well).
The company sells about three million bottles of the stuff a year,
with a presence in more than 95 percent of alcohol retail outlets in
Portugal, as well as forty-three sovereign states outside its homeland. Most cafés and restaurants in Portugal have a bottle of it,
whether or not they sell a lot. "They have a bottle displayed as a
sign of 'Portugality,'" notes Nuno Rocha, export director for the
brand. Indeed, the official tagline for the beverage is "the liquor
of Portugal."

The key to courting modern Portuguese consumers has been
reaching them in their natural habitats. In Portugal's case, that
means outdoor events and concerts. The country's moderate
climate and ample daylight hours make open-air celebrations a
regular facet of Portuguese life. Sponsoring and sampling at such
events has brought many hip, young, legal-drinking-age adults
into the Licor Beirão fold. The common thread among all Licor
Beirão consumption occasions is sociability. "Everyone drinks it,
especially when they're hanging around with friends," explains
Rocha. "It's not a drink to be drunk like a whisky, not at home
on the rocks just by yourself." The interactive aspect of the tipple
is the inspiration for its secondary, unofficial tagline: "the sharing spirit." The drink makes regular appearances during dinners,
reunions, group nights out, and romantic encounters.

The combination of its sweet flavor profile—caramel is a discernible note among all the other complex tastes and aromas—
and its herbal components firmly plants it in the post-main-course
portion of the meal. It often accompanies a cup of coffee and pairs

with sweeter desserts. The brand marketers have been promoting it as a dessert ingredient as well, especially in confectionery crêpes.

Now, for a bit of a caveat: Yes, the Portuguese drink a goodly amount of Licor Beirão and ginja, but to call their homeland a country of spirits drinkers would be misleading at best. Wine is still the big beverage of Spain's next-door neighbor (as it is, for the most part, in Spain), though those of the fortified variety are mostly an outsider's indulgence. But the spirits culture is palpable and earns its place among the diverse drinking habits of the Iberian people.

LICOR BEIRÃO COCKTAILS

The marketers of Portugal's Licor Beirão invite you to try these concoctions, ranging from sweet to tart to bitter and everything in between.

☞ BEIRÃO TONIC

It's all there in the name and couldn't get any easier. The Beirão folks recommend an attractive stemmed glass, like the ones that have become popular for the Iberian gin and tonic.

→▣ DIRECTIONS ◉←	→▣ INGREDIENTS ◉←
Fill a glass with ice cubes.	Cinnamon stick
Using a bar spoon, frost glass with circular movements through ice.	Star anise
Strain out excess water.	60 ml (2 ounces) Licor Beirão
Rub rim of glass with cinnamon and star anise.	125 ml (a little more than 4 ounces) premium tonic water
Pour in Beirão and mix with bar spoon.	Orange twist, for garnish
Top off with tonic, and garnish with orange twist.	

271

☞ GINGER BEIRÃO

Next, we buck things up with this easy ginger-forward drink.

→▣ DIRECTIONS ◉←	→▣ INGREDIENTS ◉←
Muddle ginger in the bottom of a large glass.	3 slices ginger
Fill glass with ice cubes and add Licor Beirão and ginger beer.	60 ml (2 ounces) Licor Beirão
	200 ml (6⅔ ounces) premium ginger beer
Stir with a long bar spoon and add lime juice.	5 drops fresh lime juice
Rub another ginger slice around rim of glass for some added spicy flavor and aroma.	

☞ BEIRÃO FIZZ

If you're up for a truly botanical bonanza, this fizz is just the thing, as it combines Beirão with gin, lemon, rosemary, and mint.

⟶ DIRECTIONS ⟵

Fill a cocktail shaker halfway with ice.

Add Beirão, gin, lemon juice, and syrup.

Shake for 8 seconds, then pour into a Champagne flute.

Top off with soda and garnish with rosemary and mint sprigs.

⟶ INGREDIENTS ⟵

50 ml (1⅔ ounces) Licor Beirão

20 ml (⅔ ounce) gin

30 ml (1 ounce) fresh lemon juice

20 ml (⅔ ounce) simple syrup

120 ml (4 ounces) soda water

Rosemary sprig, for garnish

Mint sprig, for garnish

☞ SUNBEAM

Let's keep things in the juniper family, this time making it a bit of a Dutch treat with jenever. It'll come as no surprise that the Sunbeam was developed in Amsterdam—by Filipe Braz, bartender at Pulitzer's bar. If you're into frothy cocktails, then this golden concoction (whose foamy head, courtesy of the egg white, makes it look like a beer) is your jam.

272

⟶ DIRECTIONS ⟵

Combine all ingredients in a shaker and shake vigorously for 8 to 10 seconds.

Strain into a glass, pour back into the shaker, and then dry-shake for about 5 seconds.

Strain into a rocks glass filled with ice.

Garnish with a strip of grapefruit peel and dehydrated lime slice.

⟶ INGREDIENTS ⟵

50 ml (1⅔ ounces) Licor Beirão

10 ml (⅓ ounce) jonge jenever

20 ml (⅔ ounce) fresh lime juice

20 ml (⅔ ounce) grape juice

1 egg white

1 dash Angostura bitters

Grapefruit peel, for garnish

Dehydrated lime slice, for garnish

☞ CAIPIRÃO

Portugal and Brazil already share a language, and here's one more thing to bridge the Iberian and South American countries. But whereas the famous Brazilian cocktail, the caipirinha, uses that country's national spirit (cachaça), this version uses Portugal's de facto national spirit for its base.

⇝ DIRECTIONS ⇜

Smash lime wedges very thoroughly in a shaker.

Add Beirão and lemon juice with crushed ice.

Shake for about 8 seconds, pour into a glass, and garnish with lime slice.

⇝ INGREDIENTS ⇜

½ lime, cut into quarters

60 ml (2 ounces) Licor Beirão

40 ml (1⅓ ounces) fresh lemon juice

Lime slice, for garnish

273

CENTRAL AND
SOUTH AMERICA

At long last, it's time to cross the Atlantic. We'll head south first.
The story of Latin American alcohol production and drinking traditions is really a legacy of conquest and the gradual merging of the customs of conqueror and conquered. It all started long before the advent of distillation, in the time of the Incas and the Aztecs, when "the gods" turned any indigenous sugary substance into a mildly intoxicating elixir. Around the sixteenth century, Spanish conquistadors brought distilling technology to the New World, and over time each region in Central and South America developed a proprietary spirit. Some were sugarcane-based and fell under the rum umbrella; others grew out of local winemaking industries and are most closely associated with brandy.

SOUTH AMERICA

Trying to encapsulate the South American drinking experience results in a curious paradox. It's both a simple task and a fool's errand that's as difficult to surmount as the Andes Mountains themselves. The borders between one country's imbibing cultures are at once clearly defined and blurred. Call it Schrödinger's continent.

Across many countries you'll find brandies that all start with a grape and share many characteristics but are worlds apart. You'll also encounter chicha, the fermented corn beverage that's an early forerunner of beer, an indigenous drink often closely associated with Peru but with a presence that recurs well beyond that limited region. But first let's talk about the aguardientes.

Colombia and Ecuador

Whenever someone mentions drinking in Latin America, it's likely that the term "aguardiente" will come up once or twice. It doesn't refer to any specific beverage; it's a generic term (loosely translating to "fiery water") for any number of spirits, from relatively mild liqueurs (48ish proof) to potent, burning hooches (120 proof or so). Technically, Brazil's cachaça could be considered an aguardiente, but certain other countries don't have an alternative name for their national spirits and simply call them all aguardientes. That doesn't necessarily mean they're interchangeable, though. For instance, Colombia's aguardiente shares a bit in common with Mediterranean beverages like ouzo and arak, in that the prevailing flavor is anise. It's usually around 60 proof and notably sweet, thanks to the fact that sugar is often added. Colombia may share a border with Ecuador, but one thing they don't share is an affinity for anise, at least as far as aguardiente is concerned. Ecuadorians use the terms "aguardiente" and "punta" ("tip" or "peak") pretty much interchangeably and, depending on the region or city, punta may also be called puro ("pure") or caña ("cane").

Aguardiente forms the backbone of a traditional Ecuadorian cocktail called the Canelazo, usually made by boiling water with sugar and cinnamon sticks and then combining that with punta. It emerged from the Ecuadorian highlands, where it's known to get quite chilly at night.

Peru and Chile

It's not too hard to figure out what the national drink of Peru is. (Hint: The country and the spirit both begin with the letter "p.") Yes, it's pisco, a brandy derived from the distilled juice of any of eight Peruvian grape varietals.

Pisco consumption is pretty widespread across the country, but just because most Peruvian imbibers are drinking it doesn't mean they're all drinking it in the same way. In large urban areas, especially the cosmopolitan capital, Lima, a typical evening out begins with the spirit's most famous cocktail, the pisco sour, whose origins, incidentally, owe as much to North America as they do to South. In 1916, an American bartender named Victor Vaughen Morris opened a watering hole in Lima and tweaked a classic whisky sour recipe, replacing the whisky with Peru's native spirit. The recipe evolved over the next decade or so to settle on what most cocktail enthusiasts today recognize as the pisco sour: pisco, lime juice, egg whites, bitters, and ice. (The original whisky sour contained egg whites, which have long since been abandoned, but they are retained in the pisco version of the drink.)

Though they're typically mixed by hand at bars, at home parties hosts usually combine the ingredients in a blender. Melanie and Lizzie Asher, the sisters behind the Macchu Pisco brand, tell me that guests always know it's a good party when they hear a blender buzzing in the kitchen. Partygoers often hover outside the kitchen, eagerly awaiting the first pour.

Recently, there's been a surge in the number of Peruvians taking a shine to the Chilcano, another pisco-based cocktail that's a little less complicated to mix (those egg whites aren't always the easiest ingredients to work with). The Chilcano is simply pisco, ginger ale, a few dashes of bitters, and a squeeze of lime. The Ashers point to a rise in Peru's middle class for Chilcano's current popularity: People are increasingly able to afford leisure time at the beach, and they prefer an easy-to-mix, everyday drink for such occasions, versus the relative labor intensity of the sour—which tends to appear more at celebratory events.

Bartenders in major urban centers have gotten rather creative with the local spirit, introducing indigenous Amazonian herbs and fruits to their pisco cocktails. Bars are also experimenting more with infusions; don't be surprised to see large jars of pisco with coconuts, cinnamon, lemongrass, or even coca leaves steeping in them.

Bar Capitán Melendez in Lima has one of the more creative pisco cocktail menus I've seen. Peruvian bartending icon Roberto Melendez is world-famous for his pisco sours and Chilcanos and is keen to incorporate as many local traditions and ingredients as possible. Among those variations is the Camu Camu Sour, made with the juice of the Amazonian camu camu fruit, known to be very high in vitamin C and antioxidants. Another, the Chicha Morada Sour, gets its flavor from the sweet purple corn-based chicha morada (versus the alcoholic yellowish version, chicha de jora—more on that in a moment). Another, Achilcanado de Maracuyá, is a Chilcano enhanced with the juice of the maracuyá, the South American passionfruit.

In non-urban areas, you're likely to encounter more traditional drinking rituals. A common scene is a group of eight to ten friends sharing a bottle of pisco and a glass. The person who opens the bottle pours a glass, takes a drink, and then passes the bottle and glass to the next person, and so on, until it comes back to the one who started it (assuming there's anything left at that point).

Back in coastal Lima, or anywhere else near the ocean, at mealtimes you can expect the pisco to be flowing as an accompaniment to the national dish, ceviche, as well as arroz con mariscos (rice and shellfish, kind of a Peruvian paella). Pisco also helps wash down an emerging type of fusion cuisine, nikkei, which merges Peruvian traditions with Japanese influences (there's a significant Japanese population in Lima). Sushi rolls with a Latin influence are fairly prevalent.

Chileans also claim pisco as their national drink, and there's a bit of a dispute between the two countries over who had it first. (I believe it's likely the country I wrote about first.) Though they share a name, the two drinks don't taste exactly alike. Some of the difference comes from the grape varietals (Peruvians can choose from eight varietals; Chileans only three), but most of it derives from the number of distillations the spirits go through. Peruvian pisco makers distill once; in Chile, the sky's the limit. So if you're into vodka, you'll probably prefer Chilean pisco. But if you want flavor complexity, you'll be drawn to the Peruvian variety. (If you're interested, I go into greater detail on the distinctions between Peruvian and Chilean piscos in my first book, *The Year of Drinking Adventurously.*)

279

Of course, a drinker cannot live on spirits alone, so fortunately Chile and Peru are also smack in the middle of prime chicha country. The fermented corn beverage predates the Spanish conquest, as the ancient Incas were the first to consume it in the Andean region. Despite the fact that their countries border each other and share a mountain range, the contrast between what Peruvians and Chileans call chicha couldn't be more stark.

Let's start with the quintessential Peruvian variety, which is relatively easy to produce. Germinate the corn, extract the sugars, boil the liquid (chicha's version of what, in beer-making, is called wort), and then let it sit and ferment for about a week. The über-traditional way to produce it also involves human spit (yes, you read that correctly). Ptyalin, an enzyme required to help convert the starches to fermentable sugars, is found in great abundance in human saliva. Chewing on the corn and then expectorating into a vessel jump-starts the process.

Chicha is fairly hard to come by these days, as Peruvians are more likely to drink beer as their preferred low-alcohol drink. However, when you head to the south of the country, around Cusco, you're more likely to encounter numerous chicherias— small shops selling the beverage by the pitcher (the venues are often called picanterias because, along with the chicha, they sell small plates of spicy food). Sometimes, season permitting, vendors add strawberries to the chicha; that version's called frutillada. If you do come across Peruvian chicha, be sure to ask whether it's chicha morada or chicha de jora. The former is unfermented and alcohol free. The latter has a kick—though a low, beer-ish ABV.

Chicherias are not the easiest places to find, especially if you don't have a good command of Spanish or the indigenous language, Quechua (many Peruvian colloquialisms mix the two). I was on a specific mission in Cusco to find one of the truly authentic watering holes (there are a couple of places near Plaza de Armas, the city's main square, that serve it, but they cater to tourists). I knew I wasn't going to find any on Google Maps, or even the city guides that helpful concierges provide at local hotels. I had to keep my eyes peeled for a "chicha flag:" a red plastic bag tied around the end of a dowel or broomstick, vaguely resembling a long-stemmed rose. When one of those dangles from an outside wall, it means there's chicha de jora inside. Don't expect to see a flag at all hours of the day. Your best bet is between about 1:30 and 4:00 P.M. And once the chicheria runs out of the sweet, cloudy yellow beverage (which sometimes looks like a cross between grapefruit and pineapple juice), the flag goes down.

After much hunting through the midday heat, I finally spied the glorious banner. I've retained some (i.e., not nearly enough) of my high school Spanish and was able to convey what I was looking for (I just said "chicha de jora" with an interrogative lilt). The proprietor ushered me inside the tiny, rather run-down dining and drinking area with dusty yellow walls and dirt floor. While I was waiting for my glass of chicha, I noticed, out of the corner

PISCO COCKTAILS

☞ PISCO PUNCH

And oldie but a goodie, pisco punch is a great party drink, as you can make a huge batch and let people have at it all night. Here's the preferred recipe from the people behind the Pisco Portón brand.

➤ DIRECTIONS ❦	➤ INGREDIENTS ❦
Mix all ingredients in a large punch bowl or beverage dispenser.	1 (750 ml) bottle Pisco Portón (or comparable brand)
Serve in glasses filled with ice.	375 ml (12½ ounces) simple syrup
Garnish with mint sprigs and pineapple chunks.	250 ml (8⅓ ounces) fresh pineapple juice
	250 ml (8⅓ ounces) fresh lime juice
	Mint sprigs, for garnish
	Pineapple chunks, for garnish

☞ PORTÓNERO

We switch from classic to contemporary with this Pisco Portón creation.

➤ DIRECTIONS ❦	➤ INGREDIENTS ❦
Pour pisco, lime juice, and bitters over ice in a tall glass.	60 ml (2 ounces) Pisco Portón
	30 ml (1 ounce) fresh lime juice
Top with ginger ale and gently stir.	2 dashes Angostura bitters
Garnish with lime slice.	Ginger ale or ginger beer
	Lime slice, for garnish

of my eye, a small, black critter scurrying across the kitchen floor. My initial thought: "Oh, a rat." (I've experienced far worse). But then I saw a little girl chasing after it and, when I got a closer look, realized it was a guinea pig. I should mention that fried or roasted guinea pig is a delicacy in Cusco—it's actually one of the big local dishes (on the menu as "cuy"). (I guess it's not uncommon for a child to get attached to these furry creatures, much like a farmer's kid might have some affection for a pre-slaughter pig.) And honestly, it's not as off-putting as it sounds. Once you get past the thick, rubbery outer layer of skin, you find a rather boney beast whose cooked flesh tastes, yes, like chicken.

On that particular occasion, though, I was only there to drink. When I went to settle up, I tried to give the server a fifty-sol note (about US$15), as I only had that and a few coins on me at the time. She waved it away, as she lacked the change for such a "huge" amount of money. Instead she said, "Uno sol," pointing to the coins in my hand. The sixteen-ounce glass of chicha de jora had set me back a whopping thirty American cents. Not a bad price to pay for sweet, mildly cider-like afternoon refreshment.

Chile's chicha is decidedly fruitier than Peru's, primarily because the two most common Chilean chicha bases are grapes and apples—a far cry from corn. So, you could say in these cases that chicha has more in common with wine and cider than it does with beer. When you think about it, this makes a great deal of sense since Chile is best known internationally for its wine industry. The grape version of chicha isn't nearly as old as the corn variety, as it was the colonial Spanish who brought grapevines with them and kick-started the wine (and, of course, pisco) industry. Those in the central region of Chile are likely to come across grape-based chicha. In the south, it's all about apples, alone or in combination with other fruits and berries.

So why isn't chicha just called wine? For one thing, it's lower in alcohol and considerably sweeter, as it's made from the most sugar-rich grapes. Moreover, there's no aging. Producers heat the grape juice, but usually not to the boiling point. After they cool it, they pour it into barrels, where it ferments for about a week. It ends up looking like a cross between cranberry and guava juice. Chicha is not necessarily an everyday drink; it reaches peak popularity as the country gets closer to celebrating Fiestas Patrias (commemorating Chilean independence) on September 18.

Bolivia

Bolivia, like Peru and Chile, is brandy country. However, while Peruvians and Chileans duke it out over which country gets to claim the origin of their shared spirit, pisco, no one disputes Bolivia's homegrown proprietary grape-based distilled beverage, singani.

Not surprisingly, singani and pisco have a great deal in common. Both have Spain to thank for their spirits-making heritage, since the invading Spanish brought grapevines and distilling technology with them when they colonized the Americas. But where the two beverages diverge is in the grape varietals they use. Singani, whose original producers were sixteenth-century Jesuit monks, uses only one varietal, Muscat of Alexandria, which is grown at Andean altitudes that can be far upwards of a mile. (By contrast, the Peruvian and Chilean vineyards growing grapes for pisco tend to be lower coastal valleys whose elevations top out at about twelve hundred feet.) The grape gained popularity in Greece, Italy, and, of course, Spain, and the Alexandria in question is the one with the big library in ancient Egypt. It's likely that the varietal originated in North Africa before the Romans spread it across the climatologically compatible parts of Europe.

The ultra-high elevation that the grapes call home results in a number of advantageous characteristics. The combined force of the sun's intensity and radical fluctuations in temperature throughout a typical day produce highly desirable aromatic compounds unique to the varietal and its terroir. After about the three- to four-thousand-foot mark, each additional foot of ascent changes the

283

SINGANI
COCKTAILS

Singani plays quite well with others and can be used as the replacement for many a white spirit in standard cocktails. But there are also some traditionally Singani-based drinks, such as the first one below . . .

☞ CHUFLAY / SHOOFLY

Don't be surprised if you see this drink spelled both ways; you're likely to see the latter in English-speaking countries. The cocktail shares its heritage with the development of railroads across South America. American and British engineers used the term "shoofly" to refer to an atypical line of track used in challenging conditions—in this case the treacherous terrain of the Andes. For the duration of such projects, railroad teams worked in isolation, with no access to their favored libations (for the British, that of course meant gin). But there was an abundance of singani, which became the base ingredient in a cocktail that evolved over time. Locally it came to be known by its Spanglish name, Chuflay (or choo-fly, a slight mispronunciation of shoofly, since the "sh" sound is not part of the Spanish language).

284

⇒ DIRECTIONS ⇐	⇒ INGREDIENTS ⇐
Fill a tall Collins glass, preferably chilled, with ice.	60 ml (2 ounces) singani
	Ginger ale*
Pour in singani, then top off with ginger ale and garnish with lime wedge.	Lime wedge, for garnish

*Go for an artisanal ginger ale, with natural ingredients, and not the mass-marketed kind with little or no actual ginger in it. I recommend Bruce Cost Ginger Ale. You also could substitute Sprite, which has increasingly become the mixer of choice for Bolivian Chuflay drinkers.

☞ YUNGUEÑO

The Yungueño is named after the tropical region from which it emerged, Yungas. So, naturally, this is a good option to help beat the heat, especially the sticky, sweaty heat of the tropics (though it'll certainly help cool you down in the dry heat of a desert, too). Hope you've got a sweet tooth, because it's essentially sugar on top of natural fruit sugar. It's kind of a sweeter, more complex version of a screwdriver; the distinct aromatics of the singani play remarkably well with orange juice.

☞ DIRECTIONS ☜	☞ INGREDIENTS ☜
Pour singani, orange juice, and syrup into a mixing glass and squeeze in lime wedge.	60 ml (2 ounces) singani
Stir with ice, then strain into a rocks glass.	120 ml (4 ounces) fresh-squeezed orange juice (save an orange slice for garnish)
Garnish with orange slice.	10 ml (⅓ ounce) simple syrup
	1 lime wedge

☞ BOLIVIAN 63

This South American twist on the French 75 comes courtesy of Singani 63, Steven Soderbergh's brand (see "Singani, Lies, and Videotape" below). It appears in the cocktail booklet the brand shares with bartenders

☞ DIRECTIONS ☜	☞ INGREDIENTS ☜
Shake singani, lemon juice, and syrup with ice, then strain into a flute glass.	60 ml (2 ounces) Singani 63
Top with Champagne and garnish with lemon twist.	25 ml (¾ ounce) fresh lemon juice
	25 ml (¾ ounce) simple syrup
	Champagne
	Lemon twist, for garnish

☞ SINGANI SOUR

Another recipe from Singani 63, this one is a close cousin of Peru's pisco sour.

☞ DIRECTIONS ☜	☞ INGREDIENTS ☜
Dry-shake singani, lemon juice, agave, and egg white, then shake again with ice.	60 ml (2 ounces) Singani 63
	25 ml (¾ ounce) fresh lemon juice
Strain into a glass and top with bitters.	25 ml (¾ ounce) agave
	1 egg white
	2 dashes Angostura bitters

character of the grape, greatly enhancing its complex aromatics. Muscat grapes are known to have more minerality and to produce a brandy that's more viscous than other similar types.

Many producers also believe that the act of distilling the spirit at such heights also plays a role in the character of the finished product. The higher the altitude, the lower the boiling temperature. Since the producers are distilling at lower temperatures, they may be retaining some of the grapes' subtleties that are lost at hotter temperatures. However, this is all still theoretical.

The Bolivian government granted singani "Controlled Domain of Origin and Geographic Indication" status, establishing the spirit as a unique product of the country, whose grapes must be grown at an elevation of at least 5,250 feet—just thirty feet shy of a proper mile. And singani production is restricted to a few specific "departments"—kind of like states—within Bolivia: Tarija, Cinti, Potosí, and La Paz. There's currently no significant production happening in La Paz, but the government recognizes the department for its potential as a singani producer. The vast majority of the spirit is coming out of Tarija.

It wouldn't be completely inaccurate to call singani "liquid gold." At the very least, the spirit indirectly owes its existence to the precious metal. The city of Potosí—which is now the capital of the Potosí department—was at one time among the richest places in the Americas. The Spanish discovered gold in the region, which brought an influx of settlers to work the mines and ultimately establish a society there. At more than thirteen thousand feet above sea level, Potosí is one of the highest-altitude cities in the world. But that's not necessarily the most comfortable height, so a large number of people began settling in the Cinti Valley just below. That's where most of the food production took place, not to mention where the Jesuits started making wine. They eventually distilled the wine into singani, more out of necessity than anything else. As you can probably imagine, it gets pretty cold at thirteen thousand feet—we're talking nonstop winter cold, à la *Game of Thrones*.

"The cold just runs into your bones," says Ramon Escobar, who imports singani to the United States under the Rujero label, established in Tarija in the eighteenth century. "You don't need a huge jacket or anything because it doesn't help you. You have to warm up from the inside." And that's where Bolivia's native spirit comes in.

Initially, most singani production took place in Cinti, but after the first couple hundred years it shifted to the southern valleys in the Tarija department. Tarija, which shares a border with Argentina, offers larger, more accessible valleys in which to grow Muscat of Alexandria grapes and produce singani. Tarija's terroir is also considered to be superior. The spirits makers at Rujero are particularly known for their vines, some of which were the originals that the Jesuits planted in the eighteenth century. And instead of being trellised, they grow alongside peppercorn trees (experienced tasters with extremely sharp palates swear they can taste some pepper notes, but that may just be the power of suggestion).

Bolivians often drink the clear, unaged spirit neat; someone in a group will pass around a bottle and the others will just pour it into their cups. I'm a fan of drinking it on the rocks. I'd recommend trying it straight first, but then drop a couple of cubes in. A little bit of ice in the glass is nothing short of transformative. It opens up the intense floral notes while keeping a great deal of the alcohol at bay (flavor- and aroma-wise, of course; the booze is still there, so be mindful!).

The other popular way to consume singani is as the core component of the traditional mixed drink, the Chuflay.

⁂ Singani, Lies, and Videotape

Steven Soderbergh—the acclaimed filmmaker behind *Sex, Lies, and Videotape*; *Traffic*; *Out of Sight*; *Erin Brockovich*; and the *Ocean's Eleven* franchise—has become one of the world's biggest non-Bolivian singani fans, having discovered the spirit when he was

287

working on his two-part Che Guevara biopic, *Che*. During the kickoff party for the production—actually in Spain—he received a bottle of singani as a gift. (Seriously, what Bolivian-themed present would you buy for the person who has everything?) So enamored of it was the director that he decided to add "spirits importer" to his résumé. Working with Bolivian distillery Casa Real, he developed his own brand, Singani 63 (the name's a nod to the auteur's birth year).

And he's not merely some pitchman. The guy is truly passionate about his product. I had the opportunity to sit down with him at a New Orleans bar (he is the one who taught me the wonders of the spirit on the rocks). I couldn't imagine him being more animated in a pitch meeting at a movie studio.

⚔ Seco!

Let's say you're hanging out with a bunch of friends at a bar or party, playing cards or what have you. Suddenly, someone yells, "Seco!" No, that person is not ordering the Panamanian spirit that goes by that name (which we'll get to shortly). It's a command—one that all within earshot must heed. Seco, which is Spanish for "dry," is a Bolivian tradition. The moment anyone shouts it, all nearby revelers must "dry" their glasses. In other words, "Down the hatch, everyone!"

"Everybody is obligated culturally," says singani importer Ramon Escobar. "It's very communal; everybody's in on it."

Argentina

There's a very special place reserved in my heart for Argentina's wine country, and it's not because the wine's great (it is) or because the views of the snow-capped Andes in the distance are achingly breathtaking (they are). It's because that's where I heard perhaps the most profound statement anyone has ever uttered about travel and, for that matter, the world itself. It was May 2013, and my wife and I were touring Argentina's most famous wine region, Mendoza. Our driver said something to the effect of (and I'm paraphrasing here), "I think travel will become the new religion. People will see how alike everyone really is."

Let that sink in for a second . . .

And now on to drinking.

Most assume that Argentinian wine is all about Malbec, the deep reddish-purplish varietal known for its intense tannins. And they'd be mostly right. Argentina's cuisine is big on beef, and the Malbec's bold flavor profile pairs phenomenally well with the country's world-famous steaks. (On a side note, I find it interesting that seafood takes a back seat in the cuisine of a country with such a lengthy coastline.) It's not the best place to visit if you're a vegetarian; fortunately, when I went, I had long since abandoned my herbivorous ways.

The winemaking staff at some of Mendoza's major wineries—Bodega Catena Zapata, Piattelli Vineyards, and Norton Vineyards are among my favorites concede that most tourists, especially those from North America and Europe, make a beeline for the Malbec at the tasting bar. But the folks who actually make and serve the wine are just as keen to have visitors try their Cabernet Sauvignon, Chardonnay, Merlot, Torrontés, or Syrah—sometimes even more so. Virtually every producer is making a Malbec; some wineries estimate that it's around 70 percent of their volume. But it's with those other styles that aren't as synonymous with Argentina that the vintners really get to spread their wings, and they're justifiably proud of their efforts. A surefire way to score points with a winery is to say, "I'd really like to try your Cab."

Mendoza's not the easiest place to get to (see "The Road to Mendoza," below), as it's a good seven hundred miles outside of Buenos Aires. But that's no big deal, because you can taste the bounty of the wine region anywhere in Argentina—and in most of the wine-drinking world for that matter. You can't throw a rock

from any corner of the capital's trendy Palermo Soho neighborhood without hitting a wine bar. Like the similar-sounding dis-
tricts in New York and London, that's the place to see and be seen,
albeit with a slightly grungier edge.

The best part of the day, in my opinion, is the mid- to late
afternoon, when we all start to get a little peckish. My wife and
I would find a cozy café or bar and order multiple $2 glasses of
Cabernet, Torrontés, and of course Malbec (it may be cliché at
this point, but it sure is ubiquitous) to drink while devouring pic-
adas—sprawling trays of ham, salami, local cheeses, nuts, olives,
and spreads served with fresh bread. We're talking varsity-level
charcuterie here, people!

To be honest, this was the meal I looked forward to the most,
because after about a day and a half I was completely done with
steak, regardless of the fact that it was often so tender the servers would (very theatrically) slice it with a spoon. And since I've
sipped the truth serum, let me also tell you that it's easy to get
sick of wine after a few days as well. This is not a bad thing at all;
Argentina is about so much more than wine, despite the outsized
publicity and tourist activity generated by oenological pursuits.

Argentina's craft beer scene is among the most developed in
South America, with substantial brewing activity happening in
Patagonia, the southern glacial region it shares with Chile. Even at
the southernmost tip of the continent, within the archipelago of
Tierra del Fuego, there's good beer to be had. There, in the city of
Ushuaia, lies Cerveza Beagle, a brewery named for the adjacent
Beagle Channel (itself named, of course, after Charles Darwin's
ship). Ushuaia is usually the last of the Americas that travelers see
before they embark on a southerly cruise to Antarctica.

But there's no need to go to the ends of the earth (which
Tierra del Fuego pretty much is) to drink good Argentinian beer.
Just as it is with wine, Buenos Aires is replete with beer consumption and educational opportunities. Sommelier Martin Boan is
the local brew guru; he runs Centro de Cata de Cerveza, a training

and certification organization for all things beer, and he presents beer pairing dinners many nights each week.

As for spirits, Argentina is a bit of a cultural melting pot. Buenos Aires, being the cosmopolitan center that it is, has an exploding cocktail scene. However, I wouldn't characterize most of what's being mixed as quintessentially Argentinian. The closest you'll get are drinks based on pisco, from nearby Peru and Chile.

The most curious distilled beverage tradition in Argentina is the country's affinity for Italy's famed herbal liqueur, Fernet Branca. There's a huge population of Italian expats in the country, and Argentinians have kind of made Fernet their own. And not necessarily in the hipster bartender/culinary professional way that it's enjoyed its North American renaissance. For the most part, Argentinians drink it unironically, very often mixed with Coca-Cola in varying proportions. It's not for everyone, trust me.

⋊ The Road to Mendoza

291

The most memorable drinking experience I had in Argentina was not sipping big beefy reds against a mountainous backdrop in the Mendoza Valley. It was the multiple glasses of wine that I enjoyed on a thirteen-hour overnight bus trip from Buenos Aires to Mendoza (a voyage I repeated on the way back a few days later). Sure, thirteen hours on a bus anywhere sounds pretty miserable, but believe it or not, it's the best way to get from the Argentine capital to the heart of its wine country. Domestic airfare has been notoriously cost-prohibitive, so a cottage industry of luxury bus lines started to pop up. The double-decker motor coaches typically seat only twenty-six people—that's because the seats recline into beds, with curtains to provide some level of individual privacy. The seats also feature personal screens with on-demand movie selections in English and Spanish. Crew members lead games of bingo (I won a bottle of Chardonnay!). It felt like, for a short time, the lap of luxury. And it made even the cheapest glasses of Malbec taste like a monarch's private reserve.

Brazil

Think back to August 2016 and the summer Olympics in Rio. The non-sports news stories that got the most play usually had something to do with the dirty water, the sub-par infrastructure, and the Zika virus. Luckily, in my personal newsfeed, the sensationalistic negatives were almost completely drowned out by a flood of spirits-themed features and cocktail recipes—most centering on Brazil's national spirit, cachaça (though eight out of ten times people were pronouncing it "ca-chock-a"—it's "ca-cha-sa"). The Olympics also put the caipirinha—cachaça's most famous cocktail, and more or less the country's official drink—front and center for many. And only good things could come from that.

It's easy to dismiss cachaça as a rum—by definition, that's technically what it is. But it's distilled from raw sugarcane juice, not molasses like most rums, similar to the way the French variant, rhum agricole, is produced.

Cachaça may be ubiquitous these days, but one Brazilian-born beverage that's pretty far off of the international radar is catuaba, a blend of mostly red wines infused with the barks of various trees that grow mostly in the north of the country. It's a traditional drink within the indigenous Tupi population and is most commonly found commercially in bottles labeled Catuaba Taimbé. Since it's mostly wine-based, the alcohol content is a relatively mild 16 percent. Naturally, anything using tree bark is going to have an earthy herbality to it, combined with the sweetness of the wine, but forget about the flavor. This is a beverage better known for its supposed physiological effects. The barks have been called everything from antidepressant to aphrodisiac—which makes the concoction pretty popular among university-age drinkers. It's also historically been at a price point that's attractive to broke college students, but certain hand-crafted varieties that can cost a pretty penny have emerged from restaurants with craft cocktail programs.

When they're not drinking catuaba or cachaça, Brazilians are drinking beer. And they like it very, very cold. It's one of the few places in the world where you're likely to order a bottle of beer at a bar and not want to directly touch it (grab a napkin or, better yet, a dish towel!). More often than not, it's going to be chilled below the freezing point. Even the light lagers of North America usually hit a floor of about 38 degrees Fahrenheit (when Coors Light markets itself as the coldest beer—a pretty meaningless assertion, actually, since that has nothing to do with the beer itself—it's usually around that 38 mark). It's perfectly acceptable to get a mass-marketed lager in the low 40s as well. But it's more than beer's temperature that Brazilians like to control. It's the very world itself.

It wouldn't be an exaggeration to say that Brazil is actually the center of the beer universe—for better or for worse (I know more people who choose the latter, but I digress). At least from a business perspective, that's true. Let's begin with the country's largest beer brands, Brahma and Antarctica, essentially the Budweiser and Miller of Brazil. Each has its own fiercely loyal following, which suits the brands' shared owner just fine: In 1999, their respective breweries merged to form AmBev. But that was only the beginning. Five years later, AmBev merged with Belgium's Interbrew, the already-consolidated owner of such brands as Stella Artois and Hoegaarden, to form InBev. You're probably getting a sense of where this is going. What had been, at the time, considered a colossal transaction, was dwarfed in 2008 when InBev acquired Anheuser-Busch, the St. Louis parent of Budweiser, Michelob, and Busch.

While all this was happening, another conglomerate, South African Breweries, purchased Miller Brewing Company from Philip Morris Companies (the cigarette people) and became SAB-Miller. Then, in 2016, Anheuser-Busch InBev acquired SABMiller, creating a company that controls more than 30 percent of the beer volume in the world—but not the Miller brand itself. Before the

CACHAÇA
COCKTAILS

The team at cachaça brand Leblon, now part of the Bacardi Ltd. portfolio, provided a couple of recipes that go beyond the basic caipirinha.

☞ BRAZILIAN MULE

You can guess by the name that there's going to be ginger beer involved.

⇢ DIRECTIONS ⇠

In a mixing glass, add cachaça, lemonade, and ice.

Shake well and strain over fresh ice in a highball glass.

Top with ginger beer and garnish with lemon or lime wheel.

⇢ INGREDIENTS ⇠

60 ml (2 ounces) cachaça

60 ml (2 ounces) lemonade

30 ml (1 ounce) ginger beer

Lemon or lime wheel, for garnish

☞ BOSSA MANHATTAN

An American classic gets a Bossa Nova makeover. For this one, you'll need an aged cachaça like Leblon Reserva Especial, which is aged for two years in Limousin oak.

⇢ DIRECTIONS ⇠

Combine all ingredients in a mixing glass with ice.

Stir well and strain into a coupe glass.

⇢ INGREDIENTS ⇠

45 ml (1½ ounces) Leblon Reserva Especial cachaça (or similar, oak-aged brand)

30 ml (1 ounce) Cedilla Açai Liqueur

15 ml (½ ounce) agave nectar

2 dashes Angostura bitters

Orange twist, for garnish

☞ STRAWBERRY BASIL CAIPIRINHA

We'll finish with Leblon's complex variation on the caipirinha.

⊸⊨◉ DIRECTIONS ◉⊨⊷

Muddle the lime, strawberries, basil, and sugar in a shaker.

Fill shaker with ice, add cachaça, and shake vigorously.

Serve in a rocks glass and garnish with a strawberry or basil leaf.

⊸⊨◉ INGREDIENTS ◉⊨⊷

¼ of a lime, cut into wedges

3 strawberries

3 basil leaves, torn

2 teaspoons of superfine sugar, or 30 ml (1 ounce) of simple syrup

60 ml (2 ounces) cachaça

Strawberry or basil leaf, for garnish

merger could satisfy anti-trust regulators in the United States, the company had to divest its American business: the 58 percent of the MillerCoors joint venture that it co-owned with Molson Coors Brewing Company (don't even get me started on that one).

Through all the mergers-and-acquisitions milestones since 2004, InBev and all its future iterations maintained a nominal global headquarters in Belgium. I say "nominal" because everyone knew that it was really the Brazilians calling the shots. The top executives, including CEO Carlos Brito, came from the AmBev side. And that's still the case in the wake of the SABMiller purchase. Most of the top board posts went to executives from the Anheuser-Busch InBev side of the deal.

In other words—as far as beer is concerned—as goes Brazil, so goes the world.

Paraguay and Uruguay

Paraguay and Uruguay are wine-producing countries, but they're usually overshadowed by Argentina and Chile—both throughout South America and on the global stage. That wasn't always the case, at least as far as Paraguay is concerned. In the seventeenth century, Chile was already in the upper echelon of South American wine producers, but Paraguay and Peru also occupied that rarefied air (Argentina was up there as well, but it lagged behind the other three). Eventually, Paraguay and Peru's winemaking activities slowed down (most of the latter's grapes went toward production of pisco). Paraguay's wines have gained some attention in recent years, though not much of it is being exported. Uruguay's are rising up the charts and are generally a bit more prominent than Paraguay's. But neither country is likely to be as famous for its wine as for its rum.

Caña paraguaya is Paraguay's sugarcane-based spirit tradition. Like cachaça in Brazil and rums in most of the French Caribbean islands, it's derived from the juice of the cane itself and not from the molasses by-product of cane processing. But caña paraguaya in and of itself isn't the most fascinating aspect of Paraguayan imbibing. It's when the spirit is used as a component of a drink whose consumption is mostly confined to the month of August that it becomes truly interesting.

Caña, lemon, and rue—the latter is a medicinal herb formally known as *Ruta graveolens* and less formally known as "herb of grace"—compose the recipe of carrulín (sometimes spelled carrulím), a beverage that the indigenous Guarani people consume every August 1. The makers squeeze the lemon into the caña and let the leaves of the rue steep in it, usually in bottles that previously housed other beverages.

The Guarani believe that August is the unluckiest month of the year—it's the coldest period, for sure (it's winter down there in the Southern Hemisphere), not to mention the rainiest. The end of the month usually gets downright stormy. To prevent any further calamity, the Guarani drink carrulín to purify and renew the blood and ward off whatever evil entities may be lurking about. They also drink it to fortify themselves against cold and flu symptoms, which makes logical sense since that's the month people are most likely to get sick. Hey, it's worth a try—I've certainly never had success in my own vain attempts to stop the common cold in its tracks.

297

CENTRAL AMERICA

As we leave South America, we head north, toward the aguardiente-soaked land bridge that is Central America.

Panama

Panama is another Latin American country with its own rum-like spirit that's not actually called rum. The Panamanian creation is called seco, and it's considered the national drink of the country with the most famous canal in the world. Most visitors encounter the dominant brand, Seco Herrerano, whose roots date back to 1936. That's when Spanish-born sugar mill magnate Don José Varela Blanco began distilling the sugarcane the Varela family had been harvesting and processing since 1908. Varela Hermanos, as the company is known, is based in the town of Pesé, near an immensely fertile valley in central Panama. It's an industry town, and the industry is sugar. Like cachaça and caña paraguaya, seco is thrice-distilled from pure, unprocessed sugarcane, rather than from molasses. (The Varela family also produces rum made from molasses, the by-product of sugarcane processing.)

Until recently, seco didn't have the greatest reputation, which is a not entirely uncommon phenomenon among indigenous alcohols around the world. Over time, such beverages devolve into commodities and end up being sold very cheaply, losing any shred of cachet they may have once had. However, leave it to the mixologists and culinary pros in the cosmopolitan population centers to rediscover them and find prominent spots for those liquors on their menus. That's pretty much what's happened in Panama City.

In fact, the disrepute that seco has had to overcome parallels that of Panama City itself. Banking was the chief industry in the capital in the 1970s and '80s, but to call most of the commerce of the time "legitimate" would be stretching things a bit. The principal activities of many of the financial institutions weren't as much money management as they were money laundering. After the U.S.-led 1989 invasion and overthrow of General Manuel Noriega, some of the more unsavory elements of the banking industry left. The city and the country have since enjoyed surges in tourism—especially eco-travelers visiting the rain forest adjacent to Panama City.

Today, seco cocktails range from the traditional—like the unofficial national drink, Chichita Panameña—to the more experimental. Seco has a fairly neutral flavor and aroma and therefore makes a good alternative in cocktails that call for vodka.

SECO COCKTAILS

☞ CHICHITA PANAMEÑA

If you have a good juicer or blender, I highly recommend that you get your hands on some fresh grapefruit and pineapple for this drink. Otherwise, canned or bottled juices are fine.

→☟ DIRECTIONS ☜←

Combine ingredients in a cocktail shaker, shake vigorously, and then pour over ice.

If you used fresh fruit and have any pineapple left over, garnish glass with a slice of it.

→☟ INGREDIENTS ☜←

60 ml (2 ounces) seco

60 ml (2 ounces) fresh grapefruit juice

60 ml (2 ounces) fresh pineapple juice

☞ SECO CON VACA

This translates directly to "seco with cow," but don't worry—the recipe calls for milk, not ground beef. It's one of the traditional ways to consume the beverage, particularly on the Atlantic coast of Panama.

→☟ DIRECTIONS ☜←

Pour seco and milk into a glass and stir.

Ice is optional.

→☟ INGREDIENTS ☜←

60 ml (2 ounces) seco

120 ml (4 ounces) milk

The Guaros of Guatemala, Costa Rica, El Salvador, and Nicaragua

Guatemala's aguardiente, Quezalteca (sometimes spelled Quetzalteca), has become the stuff of legends in its country. It takes its name from Guatemala's second-largest city, Quezaltenango, which is where Industria Licorera Quezalteca first produced the stuff some seventy years ago. Quezalteca used to have a rather offensive nickname, "indita," or "little Indian girl"—signifying that it was considered a drink of only the indigenous population. That moniker has, thankfully, fallen out of favor, and most now call it either Quezalteca or guaro, a diminutive of aguardiente. (For those trying to keep score at home: "guaro" and "aguardiente" can be used interchangeably. Quezalteca is a type of guaro or aguardiente native to Guatemala. All Quezalteca is guaro. All guaro is not Quezalteca.)

Quezalteca tends to be slightly lower in alcohol content than traditional rum; rums are usually 40 percent ABV and above, while the Guatemalan spirit has an alcohol content of 36 percent. The flavored versions of Quezalteca are quite popular, often more so than the straight product. Many gravitate toward Quezalteca Rosa de Jamaica—rosa de Jamaica being an alternative name for hibiscus, which has become a trendy ingredient in cocktail and beer circles in the United States as well. There are also tamarind and horchata versions that have a lot of fans. Tamarind has yet to catch on in non–Latin American cultures, but it shows up a great deal across many countries in the region. And sweet, creamy horchata is an institution unto itself in its alcohol-free form, so it makes sense that Guatemala has a decidedly adult version of that refresher.

Guatemalans prefer to drink Quezalteca neat or on the rocks—as is the case with the vast majority of Latino cultures and their native spirits—but it is also the preferred base of a ponche (punch) made with fresh fruits and their juices. Quezalteca is also the ideal accompaniment for traditional Guatemalan culinary fare, as it's known to help release the flavors of the spices used in the local cuisine—such as chicken pepian, considered the national dish of Guatemala. It's chicken in a spicy pumpkin and sesame sauce. Another local favorite is a traditional Mayan turkey soup called kak'ik, spiced with coriander, achiote, and chiles.

Quezalteca and other aguardientes are usually packaged in octavos, or "eighths," meaning that it's an eighth of a liter (similar to the way a "fifth" used to be the common measurement for alcohol volume in the States—in that case, a fifth of a gallon).

Still, in the majority of bars in Guatemala, one is less likely to find Quezalteca than beer or rum. Ron Zacapa, Guatemala's most prominent premium rum, has garnered all sorts of accolades and often makes drinkers' short lists for the best rums in the world. It produces some special bottlings—such as Ron Zacapa Centenario XO Solera Gran Reserva Especial, a blend of six- to twenty-five-year-old rums—that can cost more than a crisp C-note in the United States for a 750-milliliter bottle.

If you ask someone in Costa Rica what the national spirit is, the answer will likely be simply "guaro." Guatemalan Quezalteca and Costa Rican guaro begin their lives in a similar fashion: as sugarcane. Though they're often indistinguishable, the main distinction (if there is one) is that Costa Rica's guaro is distilled to a more neutral flavor. Costa Rica's best seller is Cacique Guaro, whose origins date back to 1853, when Fábrica Nacional de Licores produced its first batch. The sugarcane base makes it not all that dissimilar to rum, but flavor-wise it's worlds apart. Cacique Guaro is a relatively mild 30 percent ABV and frequently enjoyed as a Chili Guaro (often combined as Chiliguaro) shot (recipe below).

When it comes to guaro in any of its native countries, it can be fiery, intense, and generally hard to drink. But you can be sure that locals will defend it and embrace it as a source of national pride. That is certainly true of Tic Tack, which many consider to be the national liquor of El Salvador (but none would recommend trying to freshen your breath with it—sorry, somebody had to say it).

301

Like its Costa Rican and Guatemalan cousins, Tic Tack's alcohol by volume is on the low side for a spirit, usually 36 percent. A black silhouette of a rooster on a yellow background, with large, cartoony letters spelling its name make Tic Tack's label pretty easy to spot on the shelf. Despite its sugarcane base, it's sometimes more closely associated with vodka than rum (it's often nicknamed, by outsiders, as "Salvadorian vodka" or "sugarcane vodka"). The brand prides itself on being "multirrectificado" (multi-rectified—undergoing multiple distillations) so it's closer to a neutral spirit than many of the other guaros (though it's still pretty harsh).

In Nicaragua, when folks have the cash to splurge a little, they'll be drinking Flor de Caña rum, the premium brand produced by Managua-based Compañia Licorera de Nicaragua. The brand has been a staple of Nicaragua's drinking culture since 1890 and has been shepherded by the same distilling family for five generations. Spirits range from the four-year-old Extra Lite white rum (only available in Nicaragua) and Ultra Lite (available in some neighboring countries as well) all the way up to the ultra-premium Flor de Caña 25 Centenario, aged twenty-five years, with a deep amber hue and intense vanilla notes.

Needless to say, a twenty-five-year-old rum isn't exactly an everyday drink. You're more likely to find locals drinking Joyita, one of the country's popular aguardiente brands (Caballito is another). Joyita ("little jewel"), packaged in plastic bottles, earns its place under the aguardiente umbrella, as the first word that comes to mind to most when they drink it is "burn." When a 375-ml bottle costs the equivalent of about 75 U.S. cents, what else would you expect?

⋈ Something to Crow About

Guatemala's most famous and oldest continuously produced beer is Gallo (pronounced "guy-yo"), Spanish for "rooster," a rudimentary illustration of which is featured prominently on the brew's

GUARO COCKTAILS

Aguardientes might be a bit rough around the edges when consumed straight, but they're very approachable when mixed with a variety of ingredients.

☞ MORENITA ESPECIAL

Here's a very simple way to enjoy Quezalteca, provided that you can find tamarind juice.

↦ DIRECTIONS ↤	↦ INGREDIENTS ↤
Stir all ingredients together and serve over ice in a martini glass.	60 ml (2 ounces) white Quezalteca
	210 ml (7 ounces) tamarind juice
	2 ml (½ teaspoon) simple syrup

☞ CHILI GUARO

The Costa Rican Chili Guaro can be made by the pitcher or by the shot. For the former, you're going to need to add tomato juice (otherwise, that's a heck of a lot of hot sauce!)

SHOT

↦ DIRECTIONS ↤	↦ INGREDIENTS ↤
Mix guaro, hot sauce, and a squirt of the lime wedge together and pour into a shot glass.	1 ounce Cacique Guaro
	4–5 (or more!) dashes of hot sauce (most use Tabasco, but I prefer Cholula or a small artisanal brand)
Salt rim of shot glass and garnish with what's left of the wedge.	Lime wedge
	Salt

PITCHER

↦ DIRECTIONS ↤	↦ INGREDIENTS ↤
Mix guaro, tomato juice, hot sauce, and lime juice in a pitcher.	1 cup Guaro Cacique
	2–3 tablespoons hot sauce
Salt rims of shot glasses and garnish each with a lime wedge.	3 cups tomato juice
	½ cup lime juice
Pour and enjoy!	Salt
	Lime wedges, for garnish

label. Produced by Cervecería Americana Sociedad Anonima, it's ubiquitous across its home country. The brand has a visible presence in North America as well, but if you search here for a beer called Gallo, you'll be looking for a very long time, since it doesn't exist under its original name in the States—likely because of the better-known American wine company whose name is spelled the same but pronounced differently. If you're curious about tasting Guatemala's number-one macro lager brand stateside, you'll need to order a Famosa, Spanish for "famous." And though the word for "rooster" is gone, the image of one still graces the Famosa bottle.

Honduras and Belize

Anyone visiting Honduras is likely to encounter at least one of the following beers: Barena, Imperial, Port Royal, or Salva Vida. These are all produced by Cervecería Hondureña, now a business unit of the largest beer maker in the world, Anheuser-Busch InBev (Cervecería Hondureña was among the spoils AB InBev reaped when it acquired its almost-as-gargantuan rival SABMiller in 2016). But macro beer brands in most countries are just corporately owned firewalls blocking people's entry into the more obscure facets of their cultures.

Like much of Latin America, Honduras makes the most of its local flora, producing a diverse range of lively beverages. This being Central America, you might surmise that corn has got to figure into it somewhere. And you'd be right: Honduras is another country where chicha, the beer-like beverage made from fermented corn, is quite popular. And when Hondurans thirst for something a bit stronger, you can bet they'll be drinking guaro.

But along the Caribbean coast of the country, the local Garifuna inhabitants—descended from an array of multinational ancestors, including the indigenous Kalinago and Arawak, as well as African people—consume a strong herbal liquor known as guifiti (sometimes referred to as Garifuna guifiti). It's a combination of herbs and roots steeped in rum or guaro. Recipes vary, and they are usually closely guarded secrets among the makers, but you're likely to find everything from familiar run-of-the-mill botanicals like garlic and cloves to mildly eyebrow-raising plants like cannabis. Guifiti is used to ease a multitude of ailments and foster a sense of well-being; for male drinkers, it "makes you strong." (Whenever you hear the equivalent of that three-word phrase in any language, it usually means "it's natural Viagra." To say guifiti's efficacy on that front is questionable would be putting it lightly. To be sure, if one were to drink too much of anything alcoholic, it likely would have the reverse of the desired effect.)

In nearby Belize—which went by the name of British Honduras until the early 1970s—local entrepreneurs also make the most of indigenous flora, but not in quite the same way. The fact that Belize lacks the ideal climate for grape growing that many South American nations boast hasn't stopped Belizeans from making wine. They just had to get a little creative with it.

Among the fruits that grow in abundance in the region is the soursop, which some have deemed a superfruit—whether or not you buy in to such claims—for its purported but clinically unproven applications as an anti-carcinogen. Belize's Bel-Mer Winery markets a wine made from the fermented juice of the soursop, as well as sister products based on sorrel, blackberry, pineapple, tamarind, and even ginger. As Belize has become a popular Central American tourist destination, you can surmise that more than a few bottles of these products have made it home in travelers' checked luggage.

305

Chapter 9

CARIBBEAN ISLANDS

The Caribbean is all about rum. Anyone who's seen even one Pirates of the Caribbean movie or ridden the Disney ride that inspired the franchise knows that. However, not all rums are created equal—nor do they all spell "rum" the same way, thanks to the fact that so many disparate European empires with different languages colonized the islands.

Sugarcane cultivation was a huge industry across most of the islands from the seventeenth century onward. Unfortunately, that industry depended heavily on the labor of slaves, and rum's legacy is tainted by that abhorrent practice. A common misconception, however, is that rum grew out of the sugar business on the islands. In truth, rum existed long before colonial powers started processing sugar in the Caribbean.

Ed Hamilton is one of the world's foremost experts on the spirit. In addition to running a rum importation business, he created the website The Ministry of Rum, a great educational source for anyone who wants to learn about the spirit. More often than not, Hamilton finds himself dispelling common myths that are largely perpetuated by distillers' marketing departments (and that frequently end up in books and articles written about rum).

One fact he's quick to point out is that what Brazilians call cachaça—essentially a rum made from distilling pressed sugarcane juice—predated the Caribbean sugar industry by about a century. And Puerto Rico, known as one of the great Caribbean rum-producing islands, was distilling spirits as early as 1520. "That was close to a hundred years before sugar took over the islands," Hamilton notes.

Most of the islands developed their own signature styles for rum. However, that doesn't mean there are necessarily any hard-and-fast rules about who's producing what. "Basically, people make what they have a market for," Hamilton says. "They drink what's available. I read articles all the time—from people I respect—they talk about the English rums, the French rums. Throw that all out the window. We've got heavy rums and light rums and people say, 'Oh the demerara rums are heavy rums and they're full of flavor' and all that." Some of them are, Hamilton says, but it's hardly a mandate. "Trying to identify and put all these things in nice little boxes," he argues, "is really a waste of time."

Flavor and stylistic variations notwithstanding, some traditions have developed in some island groups and not in others. Let's look at a few of these.

BRITISH ISLANDS

For a good two hundred years or so, until as late as the 1970s, the biggest market for rum was the British Royal Navy. And for most of that period, Britain controlled Jamaica, which is one of a handful of countries and territories that one immediately associates with rum. (The Brits wrested control of Jamaica from Spain in 1655, and Jamaica achieved independence from Britain in

BRITISH ISLAND COCKTAIL

Though you're more likely to encounter locals drinking their rum neat or with a fruit juice chaser, it's inaccurate to say that the Caribbean islands lack a mixed drink culture. Rum punch, after all, has been a cross-island staple since the 1600s; most eateries, watering holes, and private homes have their own signature punches that are sources of great pride. Since Barbados is better known than most Caribbean islands for having some degree of a cocktail culture, here's a riff on a Barbadian classic.

☞ BARBADIAN RUM PUNCH

Mount Gay Rum, the most prominent of Barbados-produced rums, provided this recipe. Since punches are meant to be scaled up and served from a bowl or other larger vessel and not necessarily meant to be a bespoke drink, everything's measured in imprecise "parts."

309

⇒ DIRECTIONS ⇐

Pour all ingredients into a large pitcher or bowl and stir well.

Add ice.

⇒ INGREDIENTS ⇐

1 part fresh lime juice

2 parts simple syrup

3 parts Barbadian rum (Mount Gay recommends its Black Barrel, a dark rum whose charred oak notes might woo a few bourbon aficionados.)

4 parts water or unsweetened iced tea (I'd strongly suggest the latter, unless you're worried the caffeine will keep you up all night.)

1962. Now an independent country, it remains part of the British Commonwealth.)

Historically, Jamaican rums have been fuller bodied than other islands' output, but again, that's not true of all of them. For instance, one prominent rum producer, Appleton, makes the fairly vodka-esque Appleton White, with a flavor that flirts with neturality. But Appleton and other Jamaican distilleries originally produced more flavor-forward rums (Appleton's Estate rums are among those) because they wanted to compete with the other British-controlled territories for the Navy revenue. It was really a matter of differentiating from the competition. Distillers often achieved greater flavor complexity by using the dunder—leftover liquid—from a previous distillation.

One thing Jamaicans weren't and still aren't big on: cocktails. Sure, if you go to an all-inclusive resort, you're going to find plenty of tropical mixology, but that's for the tourists. "One thing I hear from bartenders all the time," Hamilton says, "is 'What are the great cocktails in the islands?' There are no great cocktails in the islands. In the islands, they don't make cocktails—they make rum. And they mix it with whatever's available."

A traditional Jamaican mixed drink—again, these are not influenced by non-Jamaican cocktail movements—rarely has more than two ingredients. Sometimes that could be just a few dashes of Angostura bitters (a product of Trinidad), sometimes fruit juice (islanders drink whatever's in season), or maybe a few squeezes of lime. "I say all the time, they don't drink overproof Jamaican rum in Jamaica—they shoot it," Hamilton reveals. After shooting it, they chase it with things like the country's national lager brand, Red Stripe (previously owned by Diageo, now owned by Heineken), fruit juice, or, even more simply, water.

On the other hand, Barbados, another former British colony, has more of a pronounced cocktail tradition, using any number of rum brands produced on the island, the biggest of which are Mount Gay and Cockspur. (Interestingly, the per capita consumption of Angostura bitters is greater in Barbados than it is in Trinidad, where it's produced, as it's a common cocktail component.)

FRENCH ISLANDS

The French islands didn't have the luxury of a deep-pocketed navy bankrolling a rum industry. That's mainly because French sailors were drinking brandy, France being a big grape-growing, wine-producing country and all. If their ships happened to run out of brandy, they'd buy some rum from local planters on the islands, but this was nothing on the scale that the British Navy was buying it.

But one spirits-making tradition that has become synonymous with the French-controlled islands, particularly Martinique, is rhum agricole (rhum is the French spelling of rum). Similar to the way cachaça is produced, rhum agricole is distilled from pure sugarcane juice, rather than molasses (which is a by-product of cane processing). In fact, well into the eighteenth century, the American colonies particularly in New England and the mid-Atlantic—were buying up the molasses from Martinique, as colonists were distilling their own rum and making a killing on it. The English islands were also exporting to the northern continent, especially since they were forbidden from sending finished alcohol back to England.

Seeing this, the British Parliament enacted the Molasses Act of 1733, which imposed a tax of six pence per gallon on any molasses being imported to America from non-English colonies. That proved fairly prohibitive for the French, as well as the Dutch and Spanish. However, it also proved difficult to enforce (the higher the tax, the more likely people are going to try to maneuver around it) and in 1764, the British replaced the Molasses Act with the Sugar Act. The tax rate was cut in half, in hopes that more people would actually be willing and able to pay it. It's just one of the onerous taxes that piled up over the next decade and precipitated the American Revolution.

The English also decreed that molasses could be imported only on British ships. The Martinique city of Saint-Pierre had been one of the biggest trading ports in all the Caribbean, and England's actions severely impacted business there. In the nineteenth century, Europeans determined that a product sweet enough to emulate sugarcane could be derived from sugar beets. Since the beets grew on the continent, no one had to worry about the shipping and logistics costs of getting sugarcane from the islands.

Needless to say, by the 1860s the French islands had seen the demand for their sugar decline significantly. Distillers on Martinique realized that they could make rum from sugarcane juice, rather than going through the trouble of processing the cane to get the molasses for distillation. Enter rhum agricole.

Martinique's industry suffered a major setback in 1902, when the volcano Mount Pele erupted and decimated Saint-Pierre, taking a huge chunk of the island's production capacity with it. But rhum agricole distilling ramped up in earnest with the outbreak of World War I. More than half of the distilleries across France were either obliterated or occupied by German forces. French troops needed to get their alcohol from somewhere, so Martinique rose to the challenge. But the boom was short-lived. After the war, alcohol not produced on the European continent faced a stiff tax levy (thanks to the lobbying efforts of continental distillers), which stuck until after World War II.

The most pronounced distinction between molasses-based rum and rhum agricole is that the former's flavor notes tilt toward vanilla, while the latter has some grassy elements. That's because sugarcane is in the grass family. Since rhum agricole uses cane juice, it retains a lot of the plant's vegetal character.

So distinct is the spirit that it's made Martinique the only geographic region in the world with a regional protection designation for rum. And even within Martinique, there are restrictions on exactly what can legally be called rhum agricole. The cane may be grown only in twenty-three specific towns across the island.

Additionally, harvesters are limited to 120 metric tons of cane per hectare. That's primarily a sustainability measure; it discourages excessive use of fertilizer to boost yields. Rhum agricole also must be distilled to between 65 and 75 percent alcohol before dilution to around 40 percent ABV.

Different ages dictate which of the three main rhum agricole grades may be expressed on the label: blanc ("white") is unaged, elévé sous bois (loose translation: "raised in wood") is cask aged, and vieux ("old") is extra aged, usually for more than three years.

In the French Caribbean, the popular way to consume rhum agricole is as the key component of Ti'Punch (derived from petit ponch, meaning "small punch"). Usually, the combination involves about three ounces of overproof rhum agricole (around 110 proof), a tiny squeeze of a lime and about a half teaspoon of sugar or cane syrup. And don't bother adding ice. It's pretty much frowned upon in those parts, despite the sweaty tropical climate.

A rhum agricole brand that you might recognize is Rhum Clément, whose line includes a number of mature sipping rhums Many of those use designations common in Cognac (Martinique was a French colony, after all). For instance, Rhum Clement VSOP is aged for at least four years in virgin Limousin oak and re-charred ex-bourbon casks. The brand also markets an XO that's a rare blend of rhums from the vintage years 1976, 1970, and 1952. There are also six- and ten-year-old Grande Reserves.

Other famous brands include Rhum J.M, also from Martinique, and Rhum Damoiseau, from the Guadeloupe archipelago.

Rhum agricole may have made Martinique famous, but that doesn't mean the island doesn't also produce molasses-based rums. As recently as the 1990s, the volume of molasses rum produced on the island was roughly equivalent to that of rhum agricole. These days, there's considerably less molasses rum being made there, mainly because Martinique's sugar production has fallen off once again.

R(H)UM DRINKS

Cocktail culture may have been imported to most Caribbean islands, but many of these drinks evoke the spirit of those tropical destinations.

☞ AGRICOLE DAIQUIRI

Before the daiquiri was the daiquiri, similar drinks appeared on Martinique with slight variations. But this particular cocktail from Rhum Clément defers to the Cuban creation that made such refreshers famous.

⤞ DIRECTIONS ⤚	⤞ INGREDIENTS ⤚
Shake all ingredients with ice and strain into a chilled cocktail glass.	60 ml (2 ounces) Rhum Clément Premiére Canne
Garnish with lime wheel.	25 ml (¾ ounce) Sirop de Canne (spiced sugarcane syrup)
	60 ml (2 ounces) fresh lime juice
	7 ml (¼ ounce) maraschino liqueur
	Lime wheel, for garnish

314

☞ FRENCH RIVIERA

Rhum Clément recommends using its Select Barrel rhum agricole, aged in previously used French oak.

⤞ DIRECTIONS ⤚	⤞ INGREDIENTS ⤚
Stir all ingredients and strain into an Old Fashioned glass with a large ice cube or sphere, or into a chilled rocks glass.	60 ml (2 ounces) Rhum Clément Select Barrel
Garnish with a strip of orange peel.	15 ml (½ ounce) Bénédictine
	15 ml (½ ounce) dry vermouth
	Orange peel, for garnish

☞ MARY PICKFORD

The original Pickford, named and supposedly created for the legendary silent screen actress, used Cuban rum.

⇥ DIRECTIONS ⇤

Shake all ingredients well with ice and strain into a chilled cocktail glass or Champagne flute.

⇥ INGREDIENTS ⇤

45 ml (1½ ounces) Rhum Clément Premiére Canne

25 ml (¾ ounce) pineapple juice

7 ml (¼ ounce) maraschino liqueur

1 drop Grenadine

☞ LET'S HAVE A TIKI

Rhum agricole has had a presence in tiki cocktails for quite some time. Veteran bartender Kiowa Bryan, the national director of brand advocacy for Spiribam—an importation and marketing joint venture among several rhum agricole distillers (including Rhum Clemént)— created this one, which features a guest appearance by a certain Scandinavian spirit.

315

⇥ DIRECTIONS ⇤

Whip ingredients with a few pieces of crushed ice to emulsify.

Pour over crushed ice in a Collins or hurricane glass.

Lightly swizzle and add more crushed ice to fill.

Top with 3 dashes of Angostura bitters.

Garnish with fresh grated nutmeg and a generous sprig of mint.

⇥ INGREDIENTS ⇤

45 ml (1½ ounces) rhum blanc

15 ml (½ ounce) aquavit

30 ml (1 ounce) pineapple juice

25 ml (¾ ounce) pistachio-lavender orgeat (recipe below)

15 ml (½ ounce) lemon juice

3 dashes Angostura bitters

Grated nutmeg, for garnish

Large mint sprig, for garnish

PISTACHIO-LAVENDER ORGEAT

Take 2 cups whole, shelled pistachios, plus 1 cup of the same lightly ground in a spice grinder, and add 3 cups water and 3 cups granulated sugar in a saucepan. Bring to a boil over medium heat, stirring occasionally. Cover and let sit overnight in a cool, dark place. Double-strain into another saucepan and bring to a boil over low heat. Remove from heat and add 1 tablespoon dried lavender. Stir, then let infuse for ten minutes. Re-strain.

☞ HAPPY ACCIDENT

Kiowa Bryan provided this one as well, which combines some popular Spanish and Italian beverages with rhum.

⇥ DIRECTIONS ⇤	⇥ INGREDIENTS ⇤
Build in a stirring glass, add ice, and stir.	45 ml (1½ ounces) aged agricole
	25 ml (¾ ounce) Palo Cortado sherry
Strain into a stemmed cocktail glass. Express orange peel and discard.	7 ml (¼ ounce) maraschino liqueur
	15 ml (½ ounce) Cynar amaro
	Orange peel

DUTCH ISLANDS

You can probably count on one hand the number of places—be they countries, states, or regions—whose local eponymous beverage is better known than the place itself. Most people have heard of Cognac the drink, but a relatively small minority of non-French travelers have Cognac, France, on their travel bucket lists. The same can be said for Champagne. As a sparkling wine, it's a household word, but most would be hard-pressed to find the region on a map.

And then there's Curaçao, the liqueur that finds its way into many a drink—most often tropical in nature—flavored with the peel of a specific type of orange descended from Valencia oranges. It most often sports a blue hue, but it is possible to get it in orange, yellow, and a couple of other colors (the color is just food coloring and imparts no flavor of its own). It's really just cocktail eye-candy.

Curaçao takes its name from the one place those oranges grow, a small island country about forty miles off the northern coast of Venezuela. It's a mostly autonomous island territory of the Kingdom of the Netherlands, previously part of the Netherland Antilles (which was dissolved in 2010). Aruba, one of its closest neighbors—and fellow Dutch island—usually overshadows Curaçao as a tourist destination. But I would argue that Curaçao has made greater contributions to global drinking than its more famous sister.

The prized oranges—officially called laraha—that give the liqueur its signature citrusy flavor profile developed on the island quite accidentally. Spanish explorers were keen to plant Valencia orange trees, popular on their home turf, on the newly discovered island in the early sixteenth century. Unfortunately, the climate and terrain of their adopted home was incompatible with growing oranges. Instead of sweet, voluptuous Valencias, the soil produced a tiny, bitter fruit that was a shell of its former self.

317

But all was not lost. Planters eventually realized there was some gustatory value in the peels of the barely edible laraha. Drying the peels accentuates much of their fragrant goodness. When they're steeped in a clear spirit (usually a brandy) for several days, the result is a somewhat bitter, orange-like liqueur—sort of a distant cousin of something like Campari or Aperol, but with a completely counterintuitive cerulean tint.

Prior to the liqueur's commercialization, wealthy plantation owners living in mansions known as landhuises would develop their own secret recipes for the stuff. (Unfortunately, the slave trade thrived on Curaçao well into the nineteenth century.) History credits Landhuis Chobolobo with producing the first batch of the liqueur in 1896. N. V. Senior & Co. purchased the plantation about fifty years later, and the Senior family continues to produce the Genuine Curaçao Liqueur to this day. On a visit to the remarkably compact production facility in 2005, I naively thought, "Wow, this is where all the Curaçao is made?!" Well, when it's behind most bars and on most liquor store shelves in America and many other countries around the world, obviously not. The sad thing about Curaçao is that it doesn't enjoy regional protection like Cognac, Champagne, cachaça, and others. Anyone in the world can produce the product, and most of the stuff you're likely to find in your glowing blue tiki drinks comes from a much larger distillery that's part of a much larger global conglomerate. You can still get the real deal—there's just a lot less of it.

Curaçao is a Caribbean island, so there must be rum there, too, right? Naturally. But Curaçao enjoys a distinction that few other tropical paradises can claim: green rum. The cozy Netto Bar in the capital city of Willemstad has become a must-visit destination for thirsty travelers, thanks to the day-glo spirit. The bar, which was a key component of the itinerary on a booze writers group trip I took, is a bit of a shrine to the World Cup, with soccer balls and jerseys hanging from the walls and ceiling. They've been serving the green stuff—Rom Berde—since 1954.

But Netto Bar is engaged in a bit of a local feud with Café Santa Rosa, a bar out in the Willemstad suburbs that also makes a green rum, though not as bright a shade as Netto's Crayola-eight-pack hue. There's a disagreement over who greened their rum first. Café Santa Rosa has been open longer, but that doesn't mean it's been serving the spirit the whole time. Netto Bar has gained global acclaim for its Rom Berde, so I'm going to side with that one, whether I'm right or not.

Locals usually drink their green rum neat or mixed with coconut water. I chose the former. It tastes like rum, but maybe a bit more medicinal (although that could be the power of suggestion, given its color).

SPANISH ISLANDS

There's no way I can talk about rum without talking about the culturally vibrant yet monumentally politically complicated country that is Cuba.

Pick up a bottle of Bacardi. Go ahead, I'll wait. Got it? Great! Now, there's a little band a couple of inches beneath the main label. What does it say? "Puerto Rican rum. Est. 1862." True, it was established in 1862. But it's a bit misleading as to *where* it was established. When Facundo Bacardi Massó established the family business—way back when the United States was in the second year of its Civil War—it was in the city of Santiago de Cuba in (as you can guess from its name) Cuba. Facundo had immigrated to the island ninety miles south of Florida about three decades before he and his brother, José, established the distillery. It was in the 1930s that Bacardi set up operations outside of Cuba, and that turned out to be a decision that ultimately saved the company.

Some of the Bacardi family members had gone to school with a young revolutionary by the name of Fidel Castro, who was initially a friend. However, when the full extent of his power grab became clear, they were friends no longer. By the time Castro's

319

regime had seized control of the country, the Bacardis had had to give up their home base; the Communists had nationalized all business. But because the family also had operations outside of Cuba, including a setup in Puerto Rico, they were able to continue producing their spirits.

Cuba is responsible for two of the most popular rum-based drinks in the world. The first of those is the daiquiri. As with most creations, there remains some dispute about the daiquiri's exact origins, but the consensus is that it was born at the turn of the twentieth century and that Americans had a major hand in it. The prevailing story credits American engineer Jennings Cox as the father of the daiquiri. He was working in Cuba during the Spanish-American War. Daiquiri was the name of a beach near Santiago de Cuba, a hop, skip, and a jump away from the iron mine at which Cox was based.

The daiquiri's creation benefited from the emergence of a lighter style of rum—courtesy of Bacardi—that was eminently mixable. Lemons, sugar, rum, mineral water, and crushed ice were the original ingredients in this famous drink. Its true heyday was the 1920s and '30s, when American writers (especially the likes of Ernest Hemingway and F. Scott Fitzgerald, to drop just a couple of names) rhapsodized about the daiquiri at a time when many Americans were heading to the island to drink legally, since they couldn't do so at home between 1920 and 1933.

Cuba's other super-famous cocktail, the mojito, has even more questionable origins than the daiquiri, but there's little doubt that it predated the latter significantly. Versions of it existed as far back as the late 1500s, though they didn't bear the name mojito. The drink evolved over the course of two to three hundred years before it emerged in a style similar to the modern version in the 1800s. The rum, lime juice, sugar, seltzer, and mint drink has since taken the world by storm.

As awash in rum as the Spanish-speaking Caribbean islands— and much of Latin America—may be, it hasn't always been

CUBAN COCKTAILS

☞ CLASSIC DAIQUIRI

The daiquiri first emerged in nineteenth-century Cuba, and since then, the term has been applied to a loose confederation of fruity drinks, many of them frozen. However, the original was about as simple and straightforward as mixed beverages get.

⇝ DIRECTIONS ⇜

Pour all ingredients into a shaker filled with ice and shake.

Strain into glass (preferably chilled).

⇝ INGREDIENTS ⇜

45 ml (1½ ounces) white rum

25–30 ml (¾ ounce to 1 ounce) lime juice (freshly squeezed, of course)

5–10 ml (1 to 2 teaspoons) simple syrup

☞ CLASSIC MOJITO

I've featured a couple of creative twists on mojitos, swapping out rum in favor of some more offbeat spirits. I'd be remiss if I didn't celebrate the original in all its uncomplicated glory.

321

⇝ DIRECTIONS ⇜

Pour the lime juice in a tall, thick glass.

If you're going the whole wedge route, squeeze the wedges into the glass and then drop them in.

Combine the lime juice with the sugar

Next, squeeze the mint leaves between both of your palms to release their aroma.

Rub the leaves around the rim of the glass (and inside the glass itself, if you desire; use a muddler for this) and drop the mint in when finished.

Fill half of the glass with crushed ice, add the rum, and stir.

Top off with more crushed ice and the soda water and garnish with the mint sprig.

⇝ INGREDIENTS ⇜

45 ml (1½ ounces) light/blanco rum

30 ml (1 ounce) fresh lime juice (or 4 lime wedges)

2 teaspoons sugar (caster, if possible, or as fine as you can get)

10–12 fresh mint leaves, plus a sprig for garnish

Splash of soda water

fashionable to drink it, particularly in the Dominican Republic. (Admittedly, "fashionable" is a relative concept.) Consultant, bartending pro, and cocktail innovator Miguel Lancha worked for several years in the Dominican Republic and observed local drinking habits, while the not-so-local tourists were guzzling sweet tropical cocktails made mostly from fruit juice concentrates (to be fair, fresh fruit is becoming more common in such drinks).

Dominicans generally viewed rum as the spirit of folks living out in rural areas. Aspirational urban dwellers in Santo Domingo sought prestige in a glass of Scotch whisky. Yes, Scotch—the one from Scotland. They haven't been gravitating so much toward the single malts, but to the more prominent blends like Johnnie Walker (Black Label is a particular favorite), Chivas Regal, and Buchanan's. It's a status symbol, consumed by those who want to show they can afford the good stuff. If you're out partying and someone orders a bottle of Scotch for the table, that person very likely wants to impress you.

But those without the means, the access, or, quite frankly, the desire to drink the Scottish imports are perfectly happy to make the most of the country's molasses-based bounty. And naturally, they're drinking that rum neat, whether or not it's considered a "sipping" rum, in the sense that Americans and Europeans think of it. It's common to find a 250-milliliter bottle tucked into a person's pocket during get-togethers and celebrations; they'll sip liberally from it while dancing (the country put merengue on the map) and enjoying the night and life in general.

The cosmopolitan set have also begun to slowly embrace rum once again, as higher-end brands like Brugal and Barceló have gained traction, giving Scotch a run for its money in the prestige game.

Of course the one beverage that unifies everyone, regardless of whether they're trying to impress someone, is beer. And in the Dominican Republic, it's very no-nonsense, macro light lager they'll be drinking. Most likely the brand will be Presidente, on the market since 1935, though it was born as a dark brew before it was reinvented as a pilsner-style lager—the dominant style in the world—in the '60s. Anheuser-Busch InBev now owns a majority stake in Presidente's brewer, Cervecería Nacional Dominica, through AB InBev's Brazilian business unit, AmBev (the mega-brewer paid a cool $1.2 billion for that stake in 2012).

+≈ *Chapter 10* ≈+

NORTH AMERICA

We've explored most of the rest of the world, so it's about time I brought things home. You don't need me to tell you that North America is a patchwork of ethnic influences from many of the other continents we've visited, combined with a couple millennia's worth of indigenous cultures whose presence long predated that of the conquerors and colonists. Everyone from the Mayas and Aztecs to the Europeans and Africans had a hand in shaping North American drinking traditions. Beer-like precursors are rooted in the drinks of the early native populations of Mexico. The stronger stuff mostly has immigrants to thank for bringing distilling technology and expertise from places like Spain, Scotland, and France.

MEXICO

Of all the flora that grows throughout Mexico, agave is the one that's most synonymous with the United States' neighbor to the south. It's no surprise, then, that its most iconic alcohols are derived from various species of the plant. Most people are familiar with tequila and, to a lesser extent, mezcal, both of which are agave-based.

{ AGAVE, IN VARIOUS STAGES OF GROWTH, IN OAXACA }

The two spirits are essentially siblings, but they have their own personality traits. Tequila comes from one species of agave—*Agave tequilana,* or blue agave (sometimes called Weber Blue, after the German botanist who first identified the plant). Meanwhile, mezcal can use any of about thirty different agave species. Moreover, tequila production is limited to the Mexican state of Jalisco (with a few exceptions), whereas mezcal's point of origin within the country is a little more flexible, though the vast majority of it comes from the state of Oaxaca.

That's all very esoteric and probably lost on most casual drinkers. However, what's not lost on them is the prevailing flavor distinction: Mezcal is incredibly smoky. The piñas, or hearts of agave plants, that ultimately become mezcal, are cooked in underground charcoal-fired ovens, giving the finished product that defining component. Tequila agave, on the other hand, is steamed, which doesn't impart any noticeable flavor nuances.

But centuries, perhaps millennia, before the Spaniards brought distilling technology to Mexico and the rest of what would become Central and South America, the ancient peoples of the region were fermenting the fine nectar of the agave into a drink called pulque, a viscous, faintly milky liquid that's about as high in alcohol as a glass of beer. At religious festivals, the Aztecs used to drink the stuff out of fancy jars carved out of translucent onyx marble, often shaped like monkey heads. (Monkeys at the time were considered wickedly immoral beasts and were associated with inebriation and, therefore, pulque.) Pulque remained a staple of the Mexican drinking diet until the late nineteenth century, when most of the population moved on to beer. Most pulquerías shuttered, but they've been enjoying something of a hipster renaissance of late.

But let's not get ahead of ourselves. Let's talk a bit about all that beer.

It's no coincidence that today the number one country of origin for imported beer in the United States is Mexico—and it leads by a considerable margin. About 60 percent of the import beer coming into the United States is of Mexican origin. Corona is the hands-down leader of the pack, followed by another beer from the same brewery, Modelo Especial. Dos Equis (owned by Heineken) is pretty high up there as well, thanks in part to its monstrously successful "Most Interesting Man in the World" ad campaign.

Brewing beer-like beverages—even beyond pulque—has been part of Mexican life since before the Spanish conquest. As in other parts of Latin American, indigenous peoples were fermenting corn into a beer-like precursor to the beverage (remember chicha?). But the real commercial Mexican brewing boom, based on European beer traditions, occurred throughout the nineteenth century. That's largely thanks to a large migration of Germans to the country that began mid-century and continued through much of the rest of it.

There was even a brief period between 1864 and 1867 when Austrian archduke Ferdinand Maximilian Joseph—of the House of Habsburg—ruled as Emperor Maximilian I of Mexico. He wasn't the most beloved character in global history and he was, to be honest, kind of an idiot. His ascension to that role was the result of a rather hare-brained conspiracy between the French and some conservative Mexican politicians who wanted to get rid of their enemy President Benito Juárez. The French had invaded Mexico a few years prior, at the start of what came to be known in Mexico (rather euphemistically) as the Second French Intervention. The Second French Empire, under the leadership of Napoleon III (whose diminutive, megalomaniacal uncle is definitely the more infamous Napoleon in the eyes of history), wanted access to Latin American markets, essentially to plunder its resources. To do so, the French needed a friendly government. Initially, France had the backing of Britain and Spain, but they also wanted to make nice with Austria, which the former had defeated in the Franco-Austrian War a few years earlier. So that's where old Maximilian came in. If you note the dates, you'll understand that Mexico's neighbor to the north was a little too busy with something called the Civil War to notice what was happening down there (the whole affair, was, in fact, counter to the Monroe Doctrine of 1821, in which then President James Monroe told Europe to keep its hands off the Americas).

In 1867, Juárez-loyal guerillas pushed out the French and executed the short-lived Austrian-born emperor of Mexico. But there was still plenty of Germanic influence throughout the country, resulting in a countrywide brewing boom. The lager brands that folks north of the border have come to know and love were all results of the surge in beer-making activity in the nineteenth and early twentieth centuries. Cervecería Cuauhtémoc Moctezuma isn't exactly a household name these days (nor does it roll easily off gringo tongues), but had it not been established in 1890, there would never have been a brand called Dos Equis (not to mention its worldly twenty-first-century pitchman). A more familiar name to most, Modelo, came along thirty-five years later and eventually spawned Corona. (Cuauhtémoc eventually became a component of FEMSA, which is now owned by Heineken; Anheuser-Busch InBev acquired Modelo in 2013, but Constellation Brands retains a perpetual license to import the brand in the United States. Okay, digression into the dynamics of global brewing over.)

As in most beer cultures dominated by one or two brewing behemoths, a small craft sector has emerged in Mexico, luring a new generation of drinkers tired of commoditized macro lagers. But beer doesn't have a monopoly on the concept of "craft" (whatever that means in this day and age). Call it subconscious ethnocentrism, but whenever someone mentioned "craft spirits," I used to associate it with small upstart handcrafted whiskey producers throughout the United States. That was until I went to Oaxaca.

I got to tag along on a trade junket sponsored by ProMéxico, a Mexican government agency whose mission is to boost the country's profile on the global economic stage. I say "tag along," because I was clearly the odd man out on that trip (almost like showing up at a wedding and realizing the invitation you received was addressed to your home's previous occupant). The other thirty or so folks were prominent and semi-prominent mixologists, bar owners, and importers whom ProMéxico and the trade group Mezcales de México wanted to be their conduit for mezcal in the States.

As peripheral as I may have felt during the four-day Oaxacan trek, I wouldn't have traded the experience for anything. We visited a couple of distilleries that were fairly high-tech and industrial, but the vast majority would fall under the heading of "traditional." Now, that's a term that gets kicked around by beverage producers of all sizes trying to gain street cred, particularly with millennial consumers seeking "artisanal" "authenticity." I've been in distilleries, breweries, wineries, meaderies, and cideries on six continents, but I don't think I've ever encountered any operations that are more deserving of such terms than those in Oaxaca.

We first embarked on a steep climb on uneven, dusty terrain in ninety-degree heat. "Now you'll never complain about how expensive mezcal is," one of the guides told us as we hiked next to a pair of donkeys that would be tasked with carrying the wild bounty back down to civilization. At last, we reached the spot where we could witness a couple of machete-wielding harvesters hacking apart an agave plant that had been growing amidst the brush for about a quarter century. (That's about how long it takes for many agave varieties to reach full, fermentable maturity.) But the agave cutters don't just go to town on the plant as soon as they find it. First there's a bit of a harvesting ritual. The lead chopper pours a small cup of mezcal, toasts to God, pours the spirit over the plant's roots, and then slices away. He was also kind enough to share the wealth. He poured a bit of the mezcal—in this case made from the jabalí agave species—into a dried, hollowed-out gourd for each of us, and we made our way back down the treacherous, trail-less hill as we sipped a 90-proof alcoholic beverage with one hand and petted the donkeys with the other. (Don't try this at home, kids. We are professionals.)

The ancestral process for making the agave piñas beverage-ready is equally charming. The artisans smoke the piñas in a pit lined with various woods for three, sometimes four, days. They let the piñas cool for about twenty-four hours, then chop them into smaller pieces, which then have to be crushed. The industrial producers achieve that end through heavy machinery, but the small makers use a piece of technology known as a donkey. Yes, that's right, the distillers aren't quite done with those put-upon beasts of burden. The donkeys (or, sometimes, small horses or ponies) are harnessed to a large wheel-like millstone called a tahona. The makers fill a brick-enclosed circular space with the piña pieces and then lead the donkey or horse around the circle, pulling the one-ton stone over those chunks to pound them into the ground.

Once the sugars are adequately squeezed out, the crushed agave goes into a wooden fermenting vat for several days, or even a week or longer. It's fermented as a solid—there's no water added—and then transferred to a direct-fired still (which looks kind of like an outdoor brick oven) to become the spirit we know and love.

American and European drinkers' increasing embrace of this centuries-old Mexican distilled beverage has done wonders for the Oaxacan tourism and nightlife scene. There's been a surge in the number of upscale mezcal bars that have opened, especially in Oaxaca City. The mezcal boom has made parts of the city look like Brooklyn, with arts and entertainment spaces constructed within repurposed industrial buildings (one such venue, La Calera, reminded me of a slightly larger version of the now-defunct watering hole Rebar in Brooklyn's DUMBO neighborhood). Booze is seriously big business there!

How much you enjoy mezcal depends on your tolerance for smoky beverages. I'll admit that I have to be really in the mood for smoky flavors—whether it's mezcal or a peaty Scotch whisky. But being in the spirit's natural habitat tends to put a person in the mood for the duration of one's stay. And you know what makes mezcal taste even better? Drinking it alongside a plate of traditional Oaxacan barbacoa (barbecue). Not surprisingly, the smokiness of the mezcal plays quite well with the meats and sides cooked in a subterranean brick oven. The cooks separate the meat (during the dinner I attended in the middle of an agave field, it was goat) from the organs and entrails and place them in their own segregated plates and pots, which they cover with aluminum foil. Once all the items are in place, they cover the brick structure with a tin roof and let everything cook for a good four to six hours. When it's ready, servers load the various dinner components onto earthenware plates and let guests dig in, family-style. And right about then is when the mezcal bottles start getting passed around. That evening easily ranks as one of my top ten dining and drinking experiences.

✵ How Sweet It Is

It's perfectly safe to gnaw on the crushed, sugary bits of agave before they go into the fermenter. They've got a chewy, beef-jerky

331

sort of consistency with a flavor that's somewhere between a raisin and a fig. It's with all that sweet goodness that the spirit-making magic happens.

⚔ Peak Pulque

One of the moments I remember most fondly about Oaxaca didn't involve mezcal—for which the state is known—but a pair of artisans ladling homemade pulque from an earthenware pot for what amounted to about a buck a cup. And they were serving it outside a mezcal distillery. I was so charmed I didn't even care that I didn't know the origin of the ice with which they were cooling it. (In general, if you don't see it come out of a bag in Mexico, you don't want it in your drink.)

⚔ A Pox on You!

When it comes to spirits, Mexico, undeniably, is most famous for tequila and mezcal. However, in the Mexican state of Chiapas, you may be just as likely to find people drinking something called Pox. Though to our Anglo eyes it may look like a diseased word, it actually means quite the opposite in the Mayan Tzatzil tongue: "medicine." Made from a combination of sugarcane, corn, and other grains, it's pretty much the Mayan answer to an aguardiente. Sometimes it's infused with fruits, herbs, and other botanicals.

⚔ Tepache

Our international delegation of drinks industry folk had just finished touring the production facilities and lush grounds of the hacienda-like Cemosa Distillery in Oaxaca when our hosts directed us to a sprawling courtyard of tents and tables where a lavish spread of Oaxacan culinary indulgences awaited us. I began to hear enthusiastic murmurs of "tepache" among my tablemates,

MEZCAL COCKTAILS

Marcos Tello, director of mixology for Mezcal El Silencio, contributed the following recipes—one quick and simple, the other far more complex.

☞ CAFÉ NOIR

Hope you like your coffee black.

➺ DIRECTIONS ⤙	➺ INGREDIENTS ⤙
Combine all ingredients in a coffee mug and stir with a cinnamon stick and vanilla bean.	30 ml (1 ounce) Mezcal El Silencio Espadín
	30 ml (1 ounce) Kahlúa (or other coffee liqueur)
	60 ml (2 ounces) espresso
	Cinnamon stick, for garnish
	Vanilla bean, for garnish

☞ ZAPOTEC ZOMBIE

Tiki enthusiasts will be intrigued by this smoky twist on one of the scene's most celebrated cocktails.

➺ DIRECTIONS ⤙	➺ INGREDIENTS ⤙
Build cocktail in a zombie tiki mug and stir well.	60 ml (2 ounces) Mezcal El Silencio Espadín
Garnish with pineapple leaves.	15 ml (½ ounce) aged rum
	15 ml (½ ounce) overproof rum
	25 ml (¾ ounce) passion fruit syrup (1 part demerara sugar to 1 part passion fruit puree)
	25 ml (¾ ounce) demerara syrup (2 parts demerara sugar to 1 part hot water)
	25 ml (¾ ounce) fresh lime juice
	25 ml (¾ ounce) fresh lemon juice
	25 ml (¾ ounce) fresh pineapple juice
	1 dash Angostura bitters
	Pineapple leaves, for garnish

but I was unfamiliar with the term. I was told it would've been a tragedy if I left Mexico without trying a glass of the fermented pineapple-rind beverage so, naturally, I obliged. When poured, it would be easy to mistake it for unfiltered apple juice, or what Americans call apple cider. The flavor is a bit cider-like (the hard kind, though tepache has no alcohol content), tilting toward the sweet, moderately tart side. It tastes like a bizarre hybrid of beer, kombucha, cider, and pineapple juice. A few pinches of cinnamon is the preferred condiment for tepache. Oh, Mexico, you never fail to surprise!

CANADA

My first exposure to Canada's beer culture came at the age of twelve. No, I wasn't breaking any laws, and no, it really wasn't the best representation of such a complex and celebrated heritage. I'm talking, of course, about the film *Strange Brew,* starring (and written and directed by) Rick Moranis and Dave Thomas as their famous SCTV alter egos Bob and Doug McKenzie. It was on heavy rotation on HBO in the summer of '84, and I probably watched it seventeen or eighteen times. I was well into my twenties before I discovered that Canadian beer drinkers aren't all "hosers" who punctuate every sentence with "eh."

There are few people on this earth who know more about Canada's alcohol consumption habits than my friends Davin de Kergommeaux, who lives in the Canadian capital city, Ottawa, and Don Tse, who hangs his hat in Calgary, Alberta. Davin is his country's foremost expert on domestic whisky, and Don kind of knows his way around a pint of beer—he's recorded tasting notes on every brew he's ever drunk. I was on hand in 2013 to witness the ten thousandth, and in 2016 he hit fifteen thousand. By the time you read this, he'll probably be closing in on twenty thousand.

Davin is best known as the author of *Canadian Whisky: The Portable Expert;* he was instrumental in helping me develop the chapter on Canadian whisky in *The Year of Drinking Adventurously*. Most recently, he's teamed up with fellow whisky writer Blair Phillips on a book covering their coast-to-coast journey deep into Canada's diverse drinking cultures, exploring off-the-beaten-path dive bars in big cities and tiny rural towns (where they've hoisted a few with former bootleggers).

One of the lesser-known facts about Canadian whisky is that it has relatively little to do with the Scottish and Irish immigrants who settled in Nova Scotia and Newfoundland, respectively. Well, not directly, anyway. Those new arrivals from across the pond certainly brought with them a wealth of distilling expertise. But they were mostly making rum, which continues to have a presence in Canada's eastern Maritime Provinces today (though there's not much rum distilling happening there; that's mostly coming from the Caribbean). The nearby New England colonies—ultimately states—were also famous for their rum production and consumption, but we'll get to that when we venture south.

The Maritimes—which also include Prince Edward Island and New Brunswick—enjoyed their very strategic location (they don't call them the Maritimes because they're landlocked). The molasses was gushing into the ports, as was finished spirit when the Canadians couldn't make it fast enough themselves. But when you moved west of Quebec, things got a little more complicated. The Lachine Rapids on the St. Lawrence River at Montreal created a natural barrier for ocean-going vessels. Once they reached that point, the water ceased to be navigable, so getting molasses to many points in neighboring Ontario meant traveling by land in horse-drawn conveyances across treacherous terrain.

Luckily for Ontarians, their province—which has gained a reputation as Canada's breadbasket—had an abundance of grain, especially wheat. There was such a surplus that the locals figured they might as well start distilling it. It certainly was a lot simpler and more cost effective than waiting for molasses to reach them. Boats were able to carry grain along the St. Lawrence and through

335

the Great Lakes to other parts of Ontario. In the mid- to late nine-teenth century, some of Canada's most iconic producers set up shop near those routes, particularly Hiram Walker & Sons (maker of Canadian Club, now a wholly owned subsidiary of Pernod Ricard) and Joseph E. Seagram & Sons (whose brands have since been split up and sold off to Pernod Ricard and Diageo).

But today, it's the Prairie Provinces—Manitoba, Saskatche-wan, and Alberta—that are true whisky country, at least from a consumption standpoint. "I don't think there's any place in Can-ada that consumes as much whisky as the little province of Sas-katchewan, right in the heart of the Prairies," de Kergommeaux muses. (He means little in terms of population, not geographic area. Saskatchewan's population is just a touch above one million, or roughly equivalent to that of one of our most desolate states, Montana. Geographically, it's about the size of an entire time zone in the continental United States.)

Saskatchewan's neighbor to the east, Manitoba, is responsible for the best-selling whisky in all Canada, Crown Royal. Gimli, a small town about an hour's drive north of the provincial capital, Winnipeg, is home to the brand's distillery. (After it's barrel-aged in Manitoba, it's shipped to Ontario for blending and bottling.) As famous and widely available as Crown Royal is across Canada and beyond, it's still very much a local beverage for folks in south-ern Manitoba (as in the rest of the Canadian provinces, most of the population resides in the southern portion). If you want an authentic Manitoba experience, believe it or not, drinking the country's biggest whisky brand is it!

In Alberta, just west of Manitoba, folks like to do their own thing as far as aged grain-based spirits are concerned. Don't get the wrong idea; drinkers in Alberta, especially in its largest city, Cal-gary, are completely enamored of whisky. But you're more likely to find them at a bar sipping a Macallan 12 than you are Crown Royal Northern Harvest Rye. "Calgarians are Scotch whisky-mad," says Don Tse, himself a Calgarian and a rabid Scotch fiend.

So serious about their Scotch are drinkers in Calgary that their local retailer, Kensington Wine Market, has been globally recognized as among the best in the world. In 2015, *Whisky Magazine* named it the second-best retailer in the world in its Icons of Whisky (behind only UK retailer Berry Bros & Rudd, which has been peddling fine beverages since 1688). Kensington's owner and resident whisky expert, Andrew Ferguson, is one of a small number of North American retailers to be inducted as a Keeper of the Quaich, an ultra-exclusive international community of individuals recognized for their commitment to Scotch whisky. ("Quaich" evolved from the Gaelic "cuach," a drinking bowl with handles on each side.)

Things get a bit weird when you continue west of Alberta. British Columbia has a bit of a reputation of being an odd duck among provinces (that applies to Quebec on the opposite coast as well and, don't worry, I'll get back there in a minute). The Rocky Mountains provide an immense natural barrier between BC and the rest of the country, cutting it off from its neighbors. It was a late bloomer as far as European settlement goes. The first British colony was set up there in 1858; it became a full-fledged province in 1871 only after it was connected to the transcontinental railroad. Otherwise, getting there and trading would be difficult, if not impossible, by conventional forms of nineteenth-century transportation.

If one were to describe BC's drinking culture, it would be as a hodgepodge of traditions imported from the other provinces. In modern times, there's been a boom in craft brewing and distilling there—likely owing to the influence of its neighbors in America's Pacific Northwest (Oregon and Washington State are hotbeds of artisan brewing and distilling, far outpacing the already robust activity in other parts of the country).

Every once in a while, there are minor rumblings among BC residents about possibly seceding from the rest of the country, much as the topic comes up periodically in Quebec.

Okay, so, back to that French-speaking province in the east: Anyone who's been to Quebec—whether to its biggest city, Montreal, or out in the hinterlands—knows that "iconoclastic" doesn't even begin to describe the province. If you visit Toronto in the neighboring province of Ontario, the vibe is that of a smaller New York City. Go to Montreal and you'll swear you're in Europe. It's hard to believe that you're just across the border from upstate New York. The province also bucks many of the drinking conventions across the rest of Canada, or is at least way ahead of everyone else.

Quebec has long been known to embrace its French-ness, but that identity really reached a fever pitch around the middle of the twentieth century, when the province aggressively promoted the wines of France. Red wine is especially popular throughout the province. Another trait Quebec inherited from France was a foodie culture that predated the culinary revolution in much of the rest of North America. "The thing about Quebec, and it's unknown to much of the rest of the world, is that it's a gourmand's paradise," de Kergommeaux gushes. "They make the most fabulous cheeses there, they make wonderful meats, they really have a very strong culture of making local foods."

I can definitely vouch for that. Montreal has its own version of a pastrami-like delicacy that's called Montreal smoked meat, and it's a source of immense local pride (and spirited debate with New York over whose is better). Cheese-wise—let's just say I have a, umm, friend who shall remain nameless who's smuggled many a portion of local fromage back across the border.

And then there's the beer. I like to say that I began my courtship with beer in the States in 2003. November of that year was when I fell in love with it. And the sparks flew in Montreal. That's where my wife-to-be and I discovered La Fin du Monde, from a Quebecois brewery called Unibroue. La Fin du Monde, which means "the end of the world"—not a reference to the apocalypse, but to the fact that its home province's northernmost points were once referred to as such—is a Belgian tripel style; most of Unibroe's products have a Belgian and/or French orientation. At that moment, it was a completely transformative experience for me (though perhaps it also had something to do with the fact that we got engaged that weekend). Even the fact that Japan's Sapporo ultimately acquired Unibroue demonstrates that Quebec is far ahead of the curve; that was in 2006, long before it became "cool" for multinational brewers to start scooping up craft operations (Anheuser-Busch InBev didn't buy Goose Island Beer Company until a full five years later).

Quebec has also been a bit of a trailblazer in the development of its cider business. In 1994, it created its own style, ice cider, using its frigid winters to its advantage. The process of concentrating the sugars in apples through freezing—both on the tree and in juice form—is similar to that used to make ice wine.

Quebec's alcohol laws are more lenient than those in most other provinces. Quebecois brewers and winemakers can sell their wares in grocery and convenience stores (with some restrictions) throughout the province. And even the places you'd least expect to carry artisanal beers stock them. Walk into a mom and pop corner store in Montreal and you're likely to see a selection somewhere approaching two hundred different bottles of Quebecois beer.

There's been a bit more retail freedom in Alberta, as well, since the province privatized alcohol sales in the mid-1990s. However, government control can be as much of a help as a hindrance for small up-and-coming breweries. Take Alberta's Big Rock Brewing, for instance. Big Rock was a pioneer among craft breweries in Canada—and North America in general, for that matter—having opened in 1985, when the number of breweries in the United States was still under a hundred. Big Rock owes much of its early success to the government retail monopoly that existed in Alberta when the brewery was just getting started. That's because the moment the government-run retail stores agreed to carry Big Rock's products, it meant that virtually every shop run by the province would carry the brand. The brewery achieved a relatively massive distribution footprint in an instant.

On the flip side, though, if the provincial monopoly decides not to carry a small brewery's brand for whatever reason, that brand barely stands a chance. But many of the provincial governments are recognizing the value small brewers are bringing to their provinces and are working to help their homegrown artisans get a leg up. In British Columbia, for instance—which every so often flirts with the notion of privatization—there's an annual revenue threshold the government requires beer suppliers to reach before the stores will even think of carrying them. BC waives that minimum requirement for breweries based within the province.

All provincial idiosyncrasies aside, the development of Canada's beer scene into what it is today mostly paralleled the trajectory in the States. Rapid consolidation throughout the second half of the twentieth century whittled the market down to two dominant players, Labatt and Molson (the former is now part of Anheuser-Busch InBev, and the latter is the Canadian half of the Molson Coors merger). The market essentially had become a duopoly, with its two biggest players hovering around a similar size—a bit different from the U.S. dynamic, where the number-two player was quite a distance behind AB InBev.

And then craft brewing—initially called microbrewing—happened. It enjoyed a strong initial wave in the late '80s into the mid-'90s, then had a bit of a Darwinian shakeout when underperforming players dropped out of the business. The market flattened for a while and then kicked into high gear in the early 2000s, just as it did in the States. And so far, it hasn't looked back. At last count, the number of breweries in Canada was closing in on seven hundred, according to Beer Canada, the trade association for the country's brewers.

There are also a couple of independent, smallish, regional, non-craft brands that have managed to survive outside the portfolios of the mega-conglomerates. The most visible of those is Moosehead, brewed in Saint John, New Brunswick. As you would expect, those in its home province are fiercely loyal to it. And then there are brews that seem local or regional but are actually owned by macro brewers. A perfect example of that is Black Horse, which practically flows like water in Newfoundland—but it's owned by Molson Coors.

My personal favorite Canadian beer would have to be Elsinore. Okay, not really, that brand doesn't exist; it's the fictional brewery in *Strange Brew*. Unfortunately, I'll never be able to dissociate Canadian beer from that flick, but that's okay—the Canadians don't seem to mind. In fact, the movie tends to be on heavy rotation in summer movies-in-the-park screenings throughout the country. "People love that movie," Don Tse tells me. "I think Canadians are kind of self-deprecating in our sense of humor anyway. And like all caricatures, it's false with grains of truth."

The movie also makes Canadians nostalgic for the bulbous little old-school bottle that had been a true symbol of the Canadian drinking heritage. By the late 1980s, the longneck had replaced the stubby, as it had most other retro beer packaging styles. It's been making a comeback with niche brands in Canada, the United States, and beyond (it's been the bottle of choice for Jamaica's Red Stripe for quite some time). "The stubbies were perfect, they were so compact," de Kergommeaux reminisces. "You could fit more beers on the shelf, more beers in the fridge. I don't think people ever really got over losing the stubby." To me, it'll always be the bottle in which Bob and Doug McKenzie grew a mouse from its infancy to scam Elsinore into giving them free beer.

✧ Flirting with Temperance

Canada has never had a national Prohibition, but alcohol has been banned at times throughout the provinces and in local communities. "Except in Quebec," says Davin de Kergommeaux. "To

CANADIAN WHISKY COCKTAILS

David Mitton, the Global Canadian Whisky Ambassador for Pernod Ricard, developed these cocktails using whiskies in the company's portfolio.

☞ RONALD CLAYTON

Mitton created this drink in honor of his late grandfather, Ronald Clayton Mitton, a dairy farmer from Albert County, New Brunswick. When David and the other grandkids would visit, they always enjoyed bowls of vanilla ice cream with maple syrup drizzled over the top. The smell of his granddad's tobacco smoke was also a fond memory of David's childhood, hence the tobacco syrup.

→⊗ DIRECTIONS ⊗←	→⊗ INGREDIENTS ⊗←
Combine all ingredients in a mixing glass, add ice until glass is three-quarters full, and stir 18 to 20 times to chill and blend but not dilute the drink too much.	75 ml (2½ ounces) Lot No. 40 whisky, infused with vanilla*
	15 ml (½ ounce) tobacco syrup (recipe below)
Strain over one large ice cube in a coupe glass.	2 dashes Urban Moonshine Organic Maple Bitters

TOBACCO SYRUP

→⊗ DIRECTIONS ⊗←	→⊗ INGREDIENTS ⊗←
Combine rum and sugar in a saucepan and bring to a simmer over medium heat, stirring until sugar dissolves. If alcohol ignites, place saucepan lid over the flame to extinguish.	1½ cups Havana Club 7-year-old rum
	1 cup raw sugar
	Amphora pipe tobacco
Continue simmering for 10 to 20 minutes, then remove from heat.	
Pour syrup through a sieve packed with pipe tobacco into another saucepan.	* To infuse your Lot No. 40 with vanilla, split a vanilla bean in half lengthwise and scrape out the seeds with the back of a knife. Place the seeds and empty pod in the bottle of whisky. Give it a shake and leave it for about 24 hours.
Repeat several times until you can smell the tobacco in the syrup.	
Let cool, then transfer to a bottle and refrigerate for up to 1 month.	

☞ TRINITY BELLWOODS

Fernet makes a guest appearance in this drink, which Mitton developed using the Gooderham & Worts whisky brand.

☞ DIRECTIONS ☜

Muddle lemon, mint leaves, and syrup in the base of a cocktail shaker, then add remaining ingredients.

Shake well with ice for 5 or 6 seconds, then double-strain over crushed ice.

Garnish with mint sprig.

☞ INGREDIENTS ☜

4 lemon wedges

6 to 8 mint leaves

25 ml (¾ ounce) simple syrup

60 ml (2 ounces) Gooderham & Worts whisky

7 ml (¼ ounce) Fernet Branca

3 dashes Bittered Sling Lem-Marrakech bitters

Mint sprig, for garnish

☞ CHERRY BOMB

The last of Dave Mitton's offerings calls for the Pike Creek whisky brand.

343

☞ DIRECTIONS ☜

Muddle cherries, 1 rosemary sprig, and lemon juice in the base of a cocktail shaker, then add remaining ingredients.

Shake well with ice for 5 or 6 seconds, then fine-strain over crushed ice.

Garnish with the remaining sprig of rosemary.

☞ INGREDIENTS ☜

4 sour cherries

2 rosemary sprigs (reserve 1 sprig for garnish)

25 ml (¾ ounce) fresh lemon juice

45 ml (1½ ounces) Pike Creek whisky

25 ml (¾ ounce) sweet vermouth

15 ml (½ ounce) Cherry Heering

Quebec, it was just sheer nonsense. It never even crossed their minds to prohibit alcohol in Quebec."

Canada actually took a pretty big hit from U.S. Prohibition, thanks to the fact that Canadian distillers suddenly lost most of their customers. They had been doing big business with their southern neighbor, primarily because the population was dramatically larger in the United States.

⋈ Mondial de la Bière

Is it any surprise that a province whose craft beer culture is so distinct from the rest of Canada hosts one of the most revered beer festivals in North America, if not the world? Each year since 1994, Montreal has played host to Mondial de la Bière, which draws nearly two hundred thousand festivalgoers to the city's Palais des Congrès. The five-day event, usually staged in early June, is more than just a beer festival; there's a huge educational component that attracts industry types from all over the world. So successful has the event become that it's launched sister events in France and Brazil.

UNITED STATES OF AMERICA

I saved my home country for late in the book because it's a daunting task to write about a drinking culture to which I'm so close. Not only that, but it's virtually impossible to sum up the soul of American drinking traditions because the United States is such a fragmented place. There's really no such thing as an "American drinking culture." It's a patchwork of many different cultures from many far-flung parts of the country, all influenced in their own way by history and happenstance.

To get to the heart of America, it's best to start with America's native spirit, bourbon. Full disclosure: As I write this section, I'm sitting at the bar at a popular Louisville watering hole, the Silver

Dollar, kind of a hipster hangout with an epic whiskey list. I figured I'd let Kentucky seep into my pores and fill me with some
barrel-aged inspiration.

Bourbon can be produced anywhere in the country (distillers
in other countries can't legally call their products bourbon), but
folks who make it in places like New York and the Pacific Northwest know they're just playing in the Kentucky sandbox. Well, not
sand, per se, but limestone. The Bluegrass State is incredibly rich in
limestone, which gives its water the character many swear is indis-
pensable in the bourbon-making process. It's got a high pH, which
we all know from high school science class means that it's alkaline,
the opposite of acidic. The limestone also adds calcium, giving the
water a high minerality, and filters out less desirable elements such
as iron, which is known to impart an unpleasant taste. Not everyone uses limestone-rich water, not even everyone in Kentucky,
but Maker's Mark is among the limestone devout. Maker's used
to get its water from the limestone spring that also powered its
gristmill, but now it draws it from a lake on its grounds in Loretto,
Kentucky, and fiercely protects the ecosystem surrounding it.

But forget about the water for a minute. The real star of the
bourbon show is corn. (By law, bourbon's mash bill, or grain mix,
must be at least 51 percent corn.) Easy access to the crop and an
affinity for its sweetness are what convinced the early bourbon
makers to start fermenting and distilling it. The first distillers
in the region, around the late eighteenth century, were likely Scottish settlers, who already knew a thing or two about the process.

There's some debate over where the name bourbon came
from. The most obvious assertion, and one to which many a distiller subscribes, is that it comes from Bourbon County, Kentucky.
Seems like a no-brainer, right? Not so fast. According to bourbon
expert and historian Michael Veach, it may have little to do with
Kentucky and everything to do with Louisiana—New Orleans,
to be precise. It seems that after the farmers harvested the corn
and the whiskey makers fermented and distilled it into whiskey,

they'd send it down the two big rivers of the region, the Ohio and the Mississippi, to the Big Easy. Eventually, it gained a reputation as that stuff people drink on Bourbon Street. Hence, "bourbon." Most people believe this tale is the correct one, though there are still those who cling to other origin stories.

Whether or not it's responsible for the name, the journey down the mighty Mississippi played a critical, albeit accidental, role in making bourbon what it is today. There's one ingredient in the spirit that can't be grown, harvested, or drawn from a well: time.

Farmers would harvest corn at the tail end of summer, and distillers would turn it into whiskey in the autumn. Trouble was, they'd have to wait until spring to get it to their intended clientele down in the Crescent City (New Orleans certainly has a lot of nicknames!). Springtime was the rainy season, and the abundant precipitation got the currents flowing incredibly fast, accelerating the southward journey. In the ensuing five or six months between distillation and transportation, the spirit benefited from its repose in oak barrels. The wood started to contribute color and flavor, imparting those lovely vanilla notes we now associate with bourbon. The whiskey continued to age during the trip downriver.

All these factors are now standardized. For starters, there's the corn minimum. The Scots and the Irish weren't distilling with corn; their whiskey was all or mostly barley-based. Corn as the dominant cereal was unique to bourbon.

Another stipulation is that the barrel's innards must be charred. There are many legends associated with how this started. Some say the casks accidentally caught fire and the distiller didn't want to have to shell out for new ones. And the rest is (sort of) history. But the charring has some practical applications beyond the notion that it's just what you're supposed to do. The burned oak acts as a filtering agent—many vodka producers, for instance, filter their spirit through charcoal to get as pure a product as possible. In a barrel, that process happens naturally. It caramelizes some of the sugar in both the oak and the corn whiskey, enhancing the vanilla and candy-like characteristics, as well as adding a bit of peppery spice.

There are also certain aging thresholds as well. Two years in wood is the minimum requirement for a product to be labeled "straight bourbon." However, if the time spent in the barrel is under four years, it must carry an age statement. The age statement is voluntary for anything four years and older—much more mature bourbons often choose to trumpet their advanced ages as a marketing tactic.

Then there's "bottled-in-bond" bourbon, which meets even more stringent criteria. Any whiskey that's labeled "bottled-in-bond" must be the product of one distillation season, made by one distiller at a single distillery. It then must be stored in a bonded warehouse overseen by U.S. government regulators for at least four years. The designation is a result of the 1897 federal Bottle in Bond Act, which was a response to all of the rampant adulteration happening in American spirits at the time.

347

{
SOME WEATHERED
WHISKEY BARRELS
AT THE WILLET
DISTILLERY IN
BARDSTOWN,
KENTUCKY
}

The bourbon renaissance—that's too mild, more like Bourbon Big Bang—has done wonders for much of Kentucky. Many of the top spirits makers in the United States and abroad have been investing heavily in the spirit, and all one needs to do is spend a day in Louisville to see how that is manifesting. The city has been like a mini Dubai, with cranes raising concrete and stone to revitalize long-abandoned distillery operations, as well as to build new condo complexes and hotels to accommodate the whiskey-fueled migration into the city.

Every few months some mainstream media organization publishes a story decrying the coming bourbon shortage. There's always a "sky is falling" element to such articles, but that's not to say those kinds of concerns are unwarranted. The more seasoned distilleries are relying on stocks that require years to age. Some of those were distilled even before the bourbon renaissance. For instance, Diageo, the largest spirits conglomerate in the world, released a line it called Orphan Barrel, with whiskeys that are more than twenty years old—mostly pulled from the warehouses of defunct distilleries whose stocks the company now owns. It's difficult to project what demand will be in two years' time, let alone six to ten. Now that bourbon's hot, the struggle is to keep up with demand without exhausting one's reserves. In 2013, the Maker's Mark distillery made the rather controversial announcement that it was planning to reduce the strength of its 90-proof spirit by a couple of points to stave off a shortage, since slightly more dilution means that much more bourbon to hang on to. It proved an overwhelmingly unpopular decision, and the distillery, owned by international spirits giant Beam Suntory, quickly reversed its decision.

Exploding demand has also led individuals to do some rather stupid things. One of the most highly publicized events within modern whiskey circles occurred in 2013, when sixty-eight cases of Pappy Van Winkle—whose more mature bourbons (seventeen, twenty, and twenty-three years old, for instance) are among the greatest and most expensive of white whales among aficionados of Kentucky's finest—went missing from the Buffalo Trace Distillery in the commonwealth's capital city of Frankfort. The lead culprit, whom police finally nabbed in 2015, was an employee of the distillery who had been liberating bottles from his place of employment for a good five years, hoping no one would notice. His haul was valued at somewhere in the neighborhood of $100,000.

The greater crime occurred in early 2016, when Kentucky law enforcement officials announced that they would not be auctioning off twenty-eight of the bottles, as had been the previous plan, but instead would destroy them. No, this was not a case of police bungling. They were honoring the request of members of the Van Winkle family themselves. (The more paranoid elements among whiskey drinkers accused the Van Winkles of doing it for the publicity and making the brand even rarer than it already is.) Whatever the reason, it's just one more great story to add to the long history associated with America's native spirit.

But America was not built on bourbon alone. Entire libraries' worth of books have been written about the multitude of American drinking traditions old and new—not to mention a certain fourteen-year-period when no one was supposed to be consuming alcohol.

There's rye, of course, another quintessentially American whiskey—and Canadian, too, but the American version very often has far more actual rye in its mash bill than the Canadian. In fact, Canadian producers have no guidelines about how much rye to use; in the States, if you want to call something rye whiskey, its mash bill must be no less than 51 percent rye.

Where bourbon is culturally and historically tethered to Kentucky, the mid-Atlantic states—most notably Pennsylvania and Maryland—were, once upon a time, rye country. This is mainly because the grain—which is in the grass family—is fairly resilient, so it's able to grow in less optimal soil and holds up pretty well against cold temperatures. (I'm from the mid-Atlantic and, while it's not the absolute coldest place in the country, the winters do totally suck.) You could argue that northern Virginia was part of the rye belt, as George Washington famously produced rye whiskey at his Mount Vernon estate during his retirement. That distillery has been restored and is producing whiskey once again, using eighteenth-century technology. And you really pay for the privilege of drinking it; a 375-milliliter bottle of the unaged white rye whiskey will set you back $98; the straight rye version, matured in oak for two years, will run you $188.

Now is probably a good time to mention that President Washington's government was somewhat responsible for nearly obliterating the mid-Atlantic spirits business entirely. You probably have some memory of learning about the Whiskey Rebellion in high school history. As relatively bloodless as it may have been, it did reshape American distilling considerably. The newly formed federal government imposed a tax on spirits production—all spirits, not just whiskey, but it came to be known as the "whiskey tax" because that's what most people were drinking by the late eighteenth century. Western Pennsylvania producers were most active in protesting the tax, a protest that came to be known as a "rebellion." Some of it got violent—much tar-and-feathering of federal employees occurred.

The insurrection stretched from 1791 to 1794, when Washington deployed troops. The rebellion had collapsed by the time they reached Western Pennsylvania.

The tax proved somewhat short-lived, as Thomas Jefferson repealed it after he took office, and distilling activity started to pick up again throughout the nineteenth century (to be ultimately undone by Prohibition, of course).

One of the most recognized and venerable rye brands, Old Overholt, originated in 1810 in Broad Ford, Pennsylvania, just south of Pittsburgh. It was one of a number of whiskeys produced in the Monongahela tradition, named for the western Pennsylvania river and valley. Monongahela rye whiskeys are known to be spicier and more robust than the original Maryland and Pennsylvania ryes due to their higher rye content relative to other grains like wheat and corn. Today, Old Overholt (now owned by Beam Suntory) is produced in the heart of bourbon country, at the Jim Beam distillery in Kentucky. Another iconic brand from rye's mid-Atlantic golden age, Pikesville, was born in the last decade of the nineteenth century in the Maryland town of the same name (just outside Baltimore) and ultimately ended up in the Bluegrass State as well—it's now owned by Bardstown-based Heaven Hill Brands. Heaven Hill also has an erstwhile Monongahela rye in its portfolio, Rittenhouse—another brand that makes many whiskey lovers' short lists of the best on the market.

I'm happy to report, however, that rye production is, slowly but surely, making a comeback in the mid-Atlantic. Among those making whiskey from the venerable grain is Sagamore Spirit, a company founded by Under Armour CEO Kevin Plank. The early batches of Sagamore Rye used sourced whiskey produced in Indiana, but the company opened a distillery of its own in Baltimore's Port Covington neighborhood in the spring of 2017. Whiskeys produced at the new facility likely won't hit the market until around 2020, due to the aging required. In Western Pennsylvania, the Monongahela tradition is back in full swing, led by producers like Pittsburgh Distilling Company, maker of Wigle Whiskey. The brand's namesake, Phillip Wigle, was a key figure in the Whiskey Rebellion. Modern Virginia whiskey makers, like Catoctin Creek Distilling, have been quite active on the rye front as well. Catoctin Creek's products, like Roundstone Rye, attracted the attention of major beer, wine, and spirits corporation Constellation Brands, which bought a minority stake in the small distillery in 2017.

Since I mentioned New Orleans's role in the early American spirits trade, I must also point out NOLA's indisputable role in the history of global imbibing: The Big Easy and cocktails have become synonymous. Many had previously asserted that the cocktail concept was invented there, but historians have, for the most part, debunked that claim. It remains unclear where exactly in the world the cocktail was invented—but New Orleans is as good a place as any, as the city's professional tour guides will try to convince you.

What difference does it make, anyway? There's evidence that folks were consuming mixed drinks in Louisiana's biggest city at least as far back as the immediate post-French period, and people still order many of the same cocktails the locals would've been drinking between the early nineteenth and early twentieth centuries. I'm guilty of throwing around the word "iconic" a bit too much, but in this case, there's no better term to describe something like the Sazerac. NOLA apothecary Antoine Amédée Peychaud—creator of the oft-used Peychaud's bitters—gets the credit for inventing the drink, which consisted primarily of Cognac, his namesake bitters, and sugar. The date of the first Sazerac sip is placed somewhere in the 1830s; by the 1850s it was a full-fledged French Quarter phenomenon. Eventually, absinthe was added to the mix, and at some point in the 1870s, rye whiskey took the place of the Cognac.

It wasn't just a case of changing tastes. We've got pesky little bugs to thank for the switch. By the late 1850s, Europe was in the midst of the great wine blight, caused by an epidemic of a species of aphid commonly known as grape phylloxera. Since Cognac is a type of brandy, and brandy is, more or less, distilled wine, early mixologists—okay, it wasn't a word then, but I'll use it anyway—shifted away from grape-based spirits and used whatever grain-based distillates were readily at their disposal.

Solidifying New Orleans's position in the development and evolution of the American cocktail is the annual Tales of the Cocktail, an event born in 2002 as a small gathering of mixed drinks enthusiasts that has morphed into the world's most prominent cocktail festival. It began relatively modestly as the New Orleans Original Cocktail Tour, a walking tour through the city's drinking history—the brainchild of Ann Rogers Tuennerman. The inaugural attendees all fit into the city's iconic Carousel Bar, attached to the Hotel Monteleone, which is now the conference's official headquarters. In 2007, Tuennerman founded the New Orleans Culinary & Cultural Preservation Society (NOCCPS), the non-profit that organizes and stages the colossal event each year.

Bartenders and bar owners, spirits brand reps and ambassadors, importers and distributors, and plain old lovers of fine drink converge on the Louisiana city each July (oppressive heat and humidity be damned!) for what is, in essence, a five-day, city-wide party—with an educational conference sandwiched in somewhere. It always attracts the biggest guns from the brand world. I've been to some industry parties in my day, but I'd never experienced anything like the epic soirees that Diageo, Beam Suntory, Bacardi, and Pernod Ricard stage at various venues across NOLA. (A warning to anyone planning to visit the Big Easy for non-cocktail reasons in the month of July: If you think the summer's a great time of year to score a cheap hotel because no one in their right minds would be traveling to the city during such a sticky and sweaty time of year, be sure to steer clear of the Tales dates. You will not get a room.) So popular has Tales become that there's now even a Tales road show, having made stops in Buenos Aires, Vancouver, and Mexico City.

Americans also get much of the credit for popularizing the cocktail party. There's some controversy over when and where such gatherings were born. Some say the cocktail party was invented in St. Louis in 1917 when a local socialite invited some fifty people to her house to imbibe—probably one of the last times anyone would be able to do so legally for about a decade and a half. Others have given credit to a Londoner for hosting the first cocktail party, though that particular event supposedly took place some seven years after the Missouri soiree.

But in the drinking world, it's not about the first time something happens, it's about whether it catches on. And there's a good chance cocktail parties wouldn't have become an institution in the United States had alcohol not become illegal. Once

Prohibition was on the books, people couldn't drink in public. Of course there were the speakeasies, but with hidden entrances, passwords, and the very real possibility of ending up in a paddy wagon, most drinkers couldn't be bothered. So alcohol consumption moved into the home. And rather than people huddling on their couches nursing a flask with the drapes closed, it became much more fashionable—and sociable—for hosts to invite guests to sip glasses of mixed contraband.

⋊ Rum Running

Long before whiskey distilling dominated the mid-Atlantic, the area in and around Maryland was all about rum. What would become Baltimore's Inner Harbor was, in the sixteenth and seventeenth centuries, a hotbed of molasses activity. A non-stop succession of ships would bring the sugarcane by-product into the bustling port, which artisans were more than happy to turn into rum. When Britain imposed the molasses and sugar taxes on the colonies in the eighteenth century, rum stopped being such an economical spirit. Distillers eventually turned to the grain that survives best in the region's cold winters: rye.

⋊ Apples of Our Eyes

As ubiquitous as beer has become in the States over the past couple of centuries, there was a time, particularly during the Colonial period, that cider captured more of the public's imagination than its grain-based cousin. The earliest waves of English colonists brought with them huge stocks of apple seeds and planted orchards as far as the eye could see. By the time the *Mayflower* found Plymouth Rock, apples were growing from Virginia to Massachusetts. And since the Brits had many centuries of experience turning the fruit into alcohol, they were able to hit the ground running in the New World.

RYE COCKTAILS

For cocktails made from this truly American spirit, I turned to one of my favorite American bartenders, Ben Paré (aka the "Cocktail Snob"), who ran the beverage program at New York City's Sanctuary T.

☞ BITTER BROWN DERBY

The name is pretty self-explanatory; Paré amps up the bitterness on this classic, named for the famed LA nightspot.

➻ DIRECTIONS ⟀	➻ INGREDIENTS ⟀
Combine all ingredients in a shaker, top with ice, and shake.	60 ml (2 ounces) rosemary-infused rye whiskey*
Pour into a rocks glass and top with fresh ice.	30 ml (1 ounce) Aperol
	15 ml (½ ounce) honey syrup (1 part honey to 1 part water)
Using a lighter or a blowtorch, char a rosemary sprig until it is smoking and lay across top of glass.	15 ml (½ ounce) fresh grapefruit juice
	3 dashes grapefruit bitters
	Rosemary sprig, for garnish

*To make the rosemary-infused rye, macerate 3 or 4 rosemary sprigs in a bottle of rye of your choosing. Let it sit at room temperature for 3 days or so, then remove the rosemary.

355

☞ CLASSIC RYE SMASH

Paré says this is his favorite summer drink. It's pretty simple to make, because who wants to do more work when it's so hot out?

➻ DIRECTIONS ⟀	➻ INGREDIENTS ⟀
In a shaker, combine 2 mint sprigs and lemon wedges.	3 mint sprigs (1 reserved for garnish)
Top with rye, simple syrup, and ice.	½ lemon, cut into wedges
Shake hard, then pour into a rocks glass.	60 ml (2 ounces) Bulleit Rye Whiskey
Serve with julep strainer on top to keep out mint.	25 ml (¾ ounce) simple syrup
Alternatively, you may strain cocktail over fresh (preferably crushed) ice.	
Garnish with fresh mint sprig.	

☞ HONEY BADGER

If you've seen the viral video, you know that the Honey Badger is a beast not to be trifled with.

➳▷ DIRECTIONS ◁↢

Combine all ingredients in a shaker, add ice, and shake.

Strain into a rocks glass and top with fresh ice.

Add preferred garnish.

➳▷ INGREDIENTS ◁↢

60 ml (2 ounces) Bulleit Rye Whiskey

30 ml (1 ounce) spiced apple cider

15 ml (½ ounce) maple syrup

15 ml (½ ounce) fresh lemon juice

3 or 4 dashes aromatic bitters

Cinnamon-coated apple slice, sage sprig, or lemon twist, for garnish

APPLEJACK COCKTAILS

☞ APPLE BADGER

Once you've tried the Honey Badger, it's time to swap out the rye in favor of applejack.

⇥ DIRECTIONS ⇤

Combine all ingredients in a shaker, add ice, and shake.

Strain into a rocks glass and top with fresh ice.

Add preferred garnish.

⇥ INGREDIENTS ⇤

60 ml (2 ounces) Laird's Applejack

30 ml (1 ounce) spiced apple cider

15 ml (½ ounce) maple syrup

15 ml (½ ounce) fresh lemon juice

3 or 4 dashes aromatic bitters

Cinnamon-coated apple slice, sage sprig, or lemon twist, for garnish

☞ APPLE TODDY

This one's great after a long day on the slopes (or shoveling your car out of the snow).

⇥ DIRECTIONS ⇤

Combine applejack, cider, maple syrup, teabag, and cloved lemon in a large mug.

Top with hot water.

Let steep for 5 minutes before consuming.

⇥ INGREDIENTS ⇤

45 ml (1½ ounces) Laird's Applejack

60 ml (2 ounces) apple cider (unfiltered apple juice)

30 ml (1 ounce) maple syrup

1 chai teabag (preferably rooibos)

1 cloved lemon

Hot water

In kindergarten, we all learned the legend of Johnny Appleseed (I recall, in the fall of 1977, having to bring seeds to school for one lucky fellow five-year-old to sprinkle throughout the classroom in honor of this near mythical figure). Well, good old Johnny (real surname, Chapman), in the late eighteenth and early nineteenth centuries, cultivated apple nurseries across what would become the American Rust Belt, not because he loved pies but because Midwesterners wanted their alcohol. When Anheuser-Busch InBev launched its Johnny Appleseed cider brand (which ultimately tanked) in 2014, the company was honoring one of the most important American figures in the history of the beverage.

But even before Johnny took his first steps on this earth, another innovation was happening in my home state, New Jersey. Robert Laird of Colts Neck (near the Central Jersey Shore in Monmouth County) began distilling fermented apple juice into a spirit that became known as applejack. He sold the first commercial batches of the apple brandy in 1780, but he was making the stuff for personal consumption long before that. Laird's descendants frequently cite pre-1760 letters from one General George Washington (a good decade and a half before the Revolution kicked off) requesting Laird's applejack recipe. Laird later served under Washington during the war and supplied troops with ample amounts of the brandy. The Laird family continues to run the operation to this day. Check behind the bar or on your local liquor store's shelf for Laird's Applejack.

$\dashleftarrow$ *Chapter 11* $\dashrightarrow$

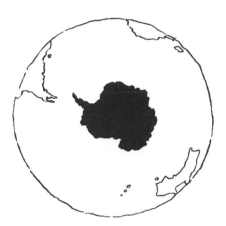

THE END OF THE WORLD
AND BEYOND

I'm not getting all apocalyptic on you here. Antarctica is, technically, the end of the world (okay, let's call it the edge, not the end). You're probably wondering, What could there possibly be to drink in Antarctica? And who's drinking it—penguins?

The icy continent at the bottom of the earth is in fact home to the world's southernmost bar. The scientists working there make many sacrifices, but you can't expect drinking to be one of them! The Ukrainian-run Vernadsky Research Station sits on a pocket-size island just off an Antarctic peninsula about eight hundred miles south of Tierra del Fuego at the southernmost edge of Argentina. Aside from massive parkas, what's really keeping researchers warm, especially during the six months of darkness, is vodka—produced and served at Faraday Bar, the onsite watering hole.

The bar has been at this spot since the mid-'80s, when it was a British base. The Brits sold it to Ukraine about a decade later, and the Ukrainians kept the English name. There are only about a dozen "regulars" at any one time, but Faraday is open to visitors, who can pay $3 for a shot of the homemade spirit. Many commercial vodka producers in more populated, northerly parts of the world duke it out over whose spirit uses the purest water. But they've got nothing on the Antarctic glacial water in Faraday's finest.

So, we've reached the edge of the planet. What else is there? Space, of course. It'll be quite a few years before there's a bar on the moon or a distillery on Mars, but spirits have been a part of the Space Age for nearly as long as there's been a Space Age. I'm a huge fan of sci-fi movies and literature, but when it comes to the actual, infinite expanse of the cosmos (with all sorts of physics and math and stuff), admittedly my expertise doesn't extend much beyond books and films such as *The Right Stuff, Gravity, The Martian, From the Earth to the Moon,* and *Apollo 13.* So I thought it best to consult an expert on the space program, Jeffrey Kluger, senior science writer at *Time* magazine and coauthor, with astronaut Jim Lovell, of the book on which the aforementioned *Apollo 13* film was based.

The rules in the early days of the American space program were somewhat different than they are today. One of them: Expect to drink quite a bit. In the 1940s and 1950s, when manned space flight was but a glimmer in the nation's eye, the test pilots who would light the way for off-world travel enjoyed tossing back a few—okay, more than a few—when they were off-duty and not operating large, flying tanks of combustion. The Happy Bottom Riding Club in the Mojave Desert, a stone's throw from Edwards Air Force Base, was a favorite haunt. A who's who of Earth-leaving, sound barrier–breaching pioneers passed through the saloon's doors—everyone from Chuck Yeager to Alan Shepard frequented the watering hole (which, incidentally, was owned by Florence Leontine Lowe—better known as Pancho Barnes—a trailblazing female pilot in a very male-dominated profession, especially in those days).

"You got drunk there when the sun went down—because the sun went down and you were a pilot, that's what you did," Kluger tells me. "Obviously, when it came time to go to space, your conduct and the things you had access to were much more regulated, as well as when you went into crew isolation before a flight. Alcohol was off-limits, but that hasn't prevented alcohol from finding its way onto spacecrafts at various points in history."

The three astronauts on *Apollo 8* brought bottles of brandy with them to celebrate their Christmas 1968 loop around the moon, but Commander Frank Borman didn't let anyone open them. Killjoy! Also on board was James Lovell, more famous for the "successful failure" that was *Apollo 13*. Lovell later auctioned off his small bottle of brandy. The only documented time that alcohol was consumed during a space mission was when Buzz Aldrin took communion, including sacramental wine, after *Apollo 11* touched down on the surface of the moon.

Sherry was supposed to be allowed on one of the Skylab missions in the early '70s, but when the public got wind of it, it caused an uproar among some people. It's not as though the astronauts were going to be flying through orbit completely tanked—the fortified wine would have been paired with meals. But after that, NASA prohibited alcohol in space for anything other than scientific experiments (sort of like spirits "for medicinal purposes" during Prohibition).

Officially, Russian cosmonauts weren't supposed to drink either, but they came from a culture that was more permissive around imbibing. The marketers behind Stolichnaya vodka frequently point out that theirs was the first vodka in space, part of the 1975 joint U.S.-Soviet *Apollo-Soyuz* mission, where the two superpowers rendezvoused high above the earth. When American astronaut General Thomas Stafford met Soviet cosmonaut Alexei Leonov, Leonov handed Stafford a tube marked with the Stoli logo, telling the American that it was a Russian tradition to drink it in space. Stafford politely declined, noting NASA regulations, but when Leonov opened the metal tube, it contained only borscht, the famous Russian beet soup. Stoli and countless other Russian vodkas have made it into space, but it didn't play quite the role that marketers had hyped (save for the brand's label).

These days it's more than likely that spirits sipping is a semi-regular occurrence on the International Space Station (ISS), especially among the Russian contingent. "On the space station today, there's a Russian segment and an American segment, and obviously all nations move back and forth freely among all segments," Kluger says. "But the Americans tend to bunk down on their end and the Russians bunk down on their end. People inside the Roscosmos, the Russian Space Agency, do concede that when cargo managers are packing a cargo vehicle to be sent up to the station, they will often smuggle bottles of brandy and Cognac between pallets of legitimate cargo."

Stoli did make a bit of semi-cosmic history in 2012 as part of an "experiment" to test the effects of bartending in zero gravity. The brand sent a mixologist decked out in a red Stoli jumpsuit to the edge of the earth's atmosphere to mix a simple concoction the spirits marketer dubbed the Stoli Moonwalk ("3 parts Stoli, 1 part lime juice, zero gravity," with a lime garnish). It made for a dynamic, engaging YouTube marketing video (it's always fun to watch floating globs of neutral spirit), if nothing else.

But vodka's not the only spirit with the right stuff. The global whisky renaissance has proved that the globe is not big enough to contain humankind's excitement for the grain-based distilled beverage. Scotland's Ardbeg Distillery sent samples to the ISS to test the interaction between the compounds found in whisky and charred oak in space at zero gravity versus on Earth—whether whisky matured in orbit tasted any different than it does when it's aged on the Scottish island of Islay. A distillate sample and charred oak shavings were kept separated until they reached the station. They were brought into contact with one another in January 2012 and remained that way for 971 days, orbiting Earth fifteen times a day. The experimental vials returned to Earth (Kazakhstan, to be precise) in September 2014. The experts detected some significant differences—but 99.9 percent of palates probably wouldn't. We'll just have to take their word for it.

And just as the Scottish tradition inspired the Japanese whisky industry, so did the former's out-of-this-world experiments. In the summer of 2015, a Japanese supply spacecraft docked with the ISS, bringing with it five spirited samples from Japan's largest distillery, Suntory. This time, the aim was to determine whether whisky mellows at the same rate in microgravity as it does on Earth. If it happens faster up there, maybe a lot of startup distilleries will finally have a solution to accelerate the process and get their spirits out into the market faster. Of course, the cost of sending whisky into space is probably far more expensive than actually building distilleries. So, you've got to pick your battles.

As a space tourism industry is about to be born, it's pretty much a given that drinking will have a rightful place in space (not among the pilots, of course, but the passengers). You need only look at all the transportation technology that came before rockets. "Read through the sort of alcohol manifest that was aboard the *Titanic* when it sailed," Kluger offers. "As soon as [ocean liners] became big enough and stable enough to have bars, they had bars."

Not to focus entirely on great disasters of the twentieth century, but there was a bar on the *Hindenburg* as well. And as soon as commercial airplane travel became a full-fledged industry, flight attendants poured drinks, free of charge—mostly because the thought of racing through the air in a giant metal tube was a brand-new concept and travelers were understandably a little freaked out about it. I think nervous fliers today should be able to play that card whenever they want to exempt themselves from having to pay $7 for a 50-milliliter bottle of vodka, but so far no airline has taken me up on that.

Now, let's look a few decades (or, more likely, centuries) beyond the birth of the space tourism industry toward more long-term voyages. A few minutes in sub-orbital space or, perhaps, a few hours in orbit, pales in comparison with the time commitment associated with extra-planetary colonization. And don't expect the eight-month journey just to reach the planet to be one big party. If your great-grandchildren happen to be among the red planet's first colonists, they can expect to be rationing any booze they bring with them on the ship. Space flight is all about weight—the less there is, the better. There likely won't be a fully stocked bar, but rather a couple of tiny bottles here and there that passengers will get to crack open at sporadic intervals.

When the craft finally arrives at its destination, the shipmates likely will be there for good. So any alcohol consumed on Mars will have to be of Martian origin. In other words, there'd better be a couple of distillers on board, because the colonists will be making their own tipples. But first they'd have to be farmers, à la Matt Damon in *The Martian*. And while the potatoes that Damon's character, Mark Watney, grew on previously "dead" Martian soil would be perfectly fine as fermentable bases, there's a better chance that the first extraterrestrial spirits would be closer to rums than spud-based vodkas. That's according to Tristan Stephenson, cofounder of the London-based drinks consultancy Fluid Movement. Stephenson has co-presented with Kluger on Space Age–boozing panels. Rum's base, sugarcane, would be ideal, Stephenson says, because it's leafy and grows quite quickly. Hydroponic farming, which would be essential for growing anything on Mars, works especially well with leafier vegetation. The actual act of distillation, Stephenson notes, wouldn't be quite so hard on the fourth planet from the sun. In fact, the frigid, low-pressure environment would be quite conducive to making spirits. Low pressure translates to a lower boiling point, and the deep freeze means it would be easier to cool the vapor to condense it back into liquid. That means less energy would be required.

If the notion of unearthly distillation still sounds weird to you, take heart: There's already an operating still in space. The ISS has one on board—not to make liquor, mind you, but to recycle bodily fluids to make them potable to the astronauts and cosmonauts during their extended stay in orbit. And it is with that image I will leave you.

⊰ Forbidden Fizz

If you're ever lucky enough or rich enough to score a ticket on a commercial space flight, you'll likely have a multitude of drinking options to enhance the experience. And you'll surely be in a celebratory mood, so you'll want to be breaking out the bubbly. I hate to be the bearer of bad news, but you're probably not going to be drinking Champagne—or beer, for that matter. The thing is, you can't burp in space. Burping requires gravity, and if you're in a zero-g environment, the gassy liquids will just sit in your stomach, jumbling into a blob in your gut. It won't be pleasant. So unless you're on a craft like those portrayed in *Interstellar* or *The Martian* that continuously revolve to create centrifugal gravity, you're going to want to stick to whisky and wine.

365

⊰ Space Glass

Whenever humanity does get around to building a cosmic watering hole, the Sam Malone of that space-Cheers won't have to worry about finding the right drinking vessel. The team behind the blended Scotch brand Ballantine's commissioned the Open Space Agency to develop a glass that enables micro- and zero-gravity sipping. The functional component is a magnet embedded in the base that makes imbibing possible, without whisky (or any other drink for that matter) flying all over the place before it gets to the drinker's mouth.

THE WORLD IS
NOT AMERICA

I want to go back to Poland for a minute. It was July 2016, and I was sitting in a hole-in-the-wall vodka shot bar in Warsaw, pondering the state of the drinking world. I had just left a bar call PiwPaw Beer Heaven, which boasts as extensive a craft beer list as one would find in east-central Europe. Tens of thousands of bottle caps representing brews from around the globe adorn the walls and ceiling of this world-class pub, whose international offerings tilt heavily toward those representing Poland's own burgeoning craft brewing scene. Oh, and the place just happens to be open twenty-four hours (so if you're jet-lagged and can't sleep, you can always run out for a couple of pints at 4 A.M.).

367

If it had been 2008, PiwPaw would've been just the type of place I would have refused to ever leave, no matter what city I happened to be in. Such places barely existed outside the major beer cities (a fact that I frequently and vocally lamented), and happening upon one was like locating the lost Ark of the Covenant (sans face melting).

But on the 2016 trip, the time I spent in divey, (ironically) Communism-fetishizing vodka bars was exponentially greater than the few hours I sipped drafts at the malt-and-hops-centric watering holes. Don't get me wrong; I'm thrilled that Poland is among the rapidly growing number of countries across Europe and the rest of the world bitten by the craft bug. But the shot bars are, at least from my point of view, decidedly more Polish. Yes, Polish brewers created most of the beers at PiwPaw. And, yes, a large number of Poles had abandoned vodka in the '90s when foreign spirits started pouring across borders previously closed off to most of the planet. But vodka has since made a comeback as the country starts to re-embrace its spirited heritage. And while they've also been embracing small-batch, artisanal brews, the styles of beer they're making originated outside of Poland and are being produced by brewers in most other craft-loving countries. And those are based, in no small part, on the styles American craft brewers (once called microbrewers) popularized in the preceding decades.

The U.S. trade associations that represent brewers and distillers are always enthusiastically touting the influence that the modern American craft beverage scene is having on international markets. In addition to spurring a worldwide boom in artisanal beer and spirits production, they're also responsible for a surge in exports of American-made craft beer and whiskey—especially bourbon—to those far-flung territories.

It's a beautiful thing, to be sure! But, at the same time, it's also . . . not.

For a clearer illustration of my point, let's leave Poland and head to Great Britain. When I mention English beer, people immediately think of pale ales, India pale ales, porters, and the like. And those classics are still prevalent and available on tap, the way they were meant to be enjoyed. However, a new wave of British breweries are eschewing casks and the styles deeply rooted in their rich history and serving up their offerings with an unmistakable American accent. They're still making pales, but they're American-style pales. They're still making IPAs (a lot of them, in fact), but they're American-style IPAs. What's bizarre is that IPA wouldn't have even caught on in the United States without the centuries of British brewing tradition that put the style on the map. (If you're wondering what the difference is between an American IPA and an English IPA, it's all about the hops. American-grown hop varieties tend to be "louder" and more robustly citrusy than the species traditionally grown on British soil—or on German, Belgian, French, and Czech soil, for that matter.)

Sure, I'm excited to try the latest stout or Belgian-style amber from that new brewery in Osaka that's been winning a stack of awards, but at the end of the day, those are still Japanese adaptations of styles popularized in other parts of the world. Even brewers in Belgium, the country that made me fall in love with beer (and alcohol in general), have been hopping up their products to capitalize on the world's love affair with American flavors. The fact that there's now such a thing as a Belgian-style IPA speaks volumes about just how upside-down the world has become.

The dynamic's a bit different with regard to spirits, but not radically so. An overseas distiller can't call a whisky "bourbon" if it's not made in America (though some do, depending on how strict their local regulatory situation might be). But non-U.S. distillers are finding any legal way they can to put the word "bourbon" on their logos—usually it's in relation to the cask in which the spirit was finished (for instance, "bourbon-barrel finished" or "bourbon-barrel matured"). And it always floors me when I'm in a place like Scotland, Australia, or Japan and I see a low-volume American brand behind the bar. On more than one recent occasion, I've had bartenders fourteen or fifteen time zones away try to pour me a glass of Hudson Whiskey Baby Bourbon when I asked for a recommendation. I am in no way bashing Baby Bourbon— it's one of my all-time favorite whiskeys. Eight out of ten times that I see it on a bar menu, I order it—in the States, that is. It's a truly American product, and I like drinking it in America. I didn't just spend twenty hours on a plane (in an economy-class seat, mind you) so I could sip a spirit that's distilled in upstate New York.

I want to be completely clear on one thing: My sentiment is coming from a place of ambivalence, not stridency. While I'm thrilled that better, thoughtful drinking is an international phenomenon, I'm a tad mournful that worldwide imbibing marches slowly but steadily toward homogenization.

So as I leave you, I'm making one final appeal: If you're in Japan, drink shochu and nihonshu. If you're in Korea, make it makgeolli.

369

West Africa? Try to track down some sodabi or akpeteshie. Don't even think of going anywhere near Bolivia without sipping singani until your glass is seco. And, yes, if you visit Poland, it would be a crime not to enjoy straight vodka.

That being said, even if you don't leave your own city, you can still allow yourself to be transported. Next time you're strolling the aisles of your local liquor store, don't pass the lone bottle of that odd, unpronounceable spirit from another land. If you're enjoying an evening out, ask the bartender for a taste of that strange liquid behind the label with the East Asian or Cyrillic letters. It's an absolute gift that any of these beverages continue to exist. Always be curious about how the rest of the world tastes. Our greatest cultural and geographical educational tools are our own gustatory and olfactory systems. So let's always be honing them as we explore the drinkable globe.

Happy sipping!

ACKNOWLEDGMENTS

This always manages to be both my favorite and least-favorite section of a book to write. On one hand, I love giving much-deserved shout-outs to those who have helped me along the way and without whose insight or inspiration these projects wouldn't exist. On the other hand, more and more names get added to the list over the years and I'm deathly afraid of neglecting to include someone. Trust me, if you don't make these pages, it's nothing personal. It's just my usual absentmind-edness, for which I apologize in advance.

First off, I'm thrilled to be once again working with the good folks at Turner Publishing, especially Todd Bottorff, Jon O'Neal, Stephanie Bowman, Maddie Cothren, and Caroline Herd. And thanks to Karen Wise for her thorough line edit.

I'm also grateful for the continued support and tenacity of my agent, John Willig, who's been helping me get my words out to the world since the very beginning of the book-writing phase of my career.

Now, for the people and places who've helped me in the, umm, drinking phase of my career, in no particular order: Reno's Appliance, Jim & Clarissa Cioletti (hi, mom & dad!), Marty & Temple Moore, Don Tse, Davin de Kergommeaux (coincidental that I put the two Canadians next to each other, but I couldn't get the Canada section done without them!), Stephen Lyman, Noriyuki Yamashita (and Glocal Bar Imo Vibes!), Ken Kajihara and the Japanese Sake & Shochu Makers Association, Bill Gunther, Jesse Falowitz, Mai Kumagami, Nat West, Lew Bryson, Emily Sauter, Leila Hamdan, Karen Auerbach, Roland Ottewell, Jim & Lisa Flynn, Julia Herz, Sarah & Giancarlo Annese, Jeff & Joanna Bauman, Peter Barrett, Arek Stan, Myriam Hendrickx, Laura Schacht, Wouter Bosch, Thomas Datema, Mike & Kristina Mansbridge, Jamie Graves, Felicity Cloake, Adam Levy, Amanda Schuster, Tom & Amanda Cioletti, Mike Gemmell, Christine & Daniel Cooney, Bartholomew Broadbent, Lionel Bokobsa, Madeleine Andrews, Alexandra Sklansky,

Margie Lehrman, Bryan Roth, Erika Bolden, Maureen Ogle, Kiowa Bryan, Jimmy Carbone, Augie Carton, Justin Kennedy, John Kleinchester, Natasha Bahrs, April Darcy, Christine Deussen, Shannon Fischer, Colin Asare-Appiah, Harry Kloman, Craig Hartinger, Schuyler Deming, Farshad Aduli, Emily Pennington Hood, Preston & Allen O'Neill, Ben Paré (my go-to cocktail consultant!), Marty Duffy, Dave Schmier, Darek Bell, Michael Flannery's and Nancy Blake's in Limerick, the folks at Emma's Espresso and Wine Bar in Alexandria, Virginia (who have no idea that I wrote about 60 percent of this book there, hopped up on Arnold Palmers—and they thought I was just being aloof and antisocial), Gin Festival, the Gin Joint in Charleston, Pernod Ricard and the team at the New Midleton Distillery, Diageo, Beam Suntory, Bacardi Ltd., Lisa Hawkins and everyone at the Distilled Spirits Council, Ali Dedianko and everyone at Belvedere, Alex Luboff, Jordan Wicker and "Silent" Tyler Lloyd of Speaking Easy Podcast (listen on iTunes now!), Lizzie and Melanie Asher, Sake Bar Decibel and Umi No Ie in New York and Bar Gen in Tokyo.

I also want to express my gratitude to all of the extremely helpful industry people—bars, bartenders, beverage companies, etc.—who provided cocktail recipes for this book. Thanks to all of them, everyone gets a chance to taste the world.

Extra special thanks to all of the people who continue to give me writing assignments and edit said assignments for their magazines and websites, especially Erika Rietz, Kate Bernot and Zach Fowle of Draft. Big shout-out to John Holl and his bowtie collection, Erica Duecy of Seven-Fifty Daily, Jon Page and Ken Weaver of various beer-related pubs, Connie Gentry and Danny Klein of FSR Magazine, Jess Baker of CraftBeer.com, and William Tish of Beverage Media.

I'd like to dedicate this book to the memory of Simon Fenton.

I've probably left far too many people out; if I did, I'll thank you in person! Oh yeah, I probably shouldn't finish this without thanking my wife, Craige Moore, whose love is my favorite intoxicant!

Speaking of which, it's time for a drink. Cheers!

THE DRINKABLE GLOSSARY

ABV Alcohol by volume, given as a percentage. If a beverage is 10 percent ABV, it contains 10 percent alcohol.

aguardiente A generic term for many types of spirits produced throughout Latin America. The term loosely translates to "fiery water." Sometimes it's known by the diminutive, "guaro."

airag A Mongolian fermented milk beverage (see also **kumyss**).

amaro The term for a wide group of herbal liqueurs with varying levels of bitterness (amaro means "bitter" in Italian) that originated in Italy.

Amarula cream A cream liqueur produced in South Africa with a base distilled from the fruit of the indigenous marula tree. It's also available in its naked, non-cream spirit form.

akpeteshie A spirit made from distilled palm wine in Ghana (see also **sodabi**).

aquavit A Scandinavian spirit whose prevailing flavors come from caraway and/or dill.

arak/arack/arrack A spirit of Middle Eastern origin whose dominant flavor is anise.

baijiu A strong spirit distilled in China, made from a base of sorghum and other grains.

Batavia arrack Not to be confused with the anise-flavored spirit arak, Batavia arrack is a rum-like spirit distilled mostly from sugarcane in Indonesia.

Becherovka An herbal liqueur first produced in the nineteenth century in what is now the Czech Republic.

Beirão/Licor Beirão A Portuguese liqueur with nineteenth-century origins, made from a proprietary blend of herbs and roots.

boukha A fig-based brandy that originated in Tunisia.

brandy A spirit distilled from a fruit base, usually grapes. A brandy distilled from a non-grape base is often called eau-de-vie (water of life), though that term frequently applies to all unaged brandies. Cognac is a specific form of brandy produced in Cognac, France.

brennivín A Nordic spirit (it translates to "burned wine") flavored with caraway, most closely associated with Iceland.

cachaça The national spirit of Brazil, this rum-like beverage is distilled from pure sugarcane juice.

chacha A grape-pomace-based brandy from the Eastern European country of Georgia .

chang'aa Kenyan moonshine.

chicha de jora A mildly alcoholic (around 5 percent ABV) fermented corn beverage popular in South America.

distillation The process of boiling a fermented liquid and re-condensing the vapor into a liquid with a higher concentration of alcohol—referred to as a spirit. The bases of whisky, vodka, brandy, tequila, shochu, and so on are first fermented before they're distilled. Beer, wine, mead, sake, and cider all are fermented but not distilled. The distilling apparatus is referred to as a still.

eau-de-vie See **brandy**.

feni A spirit distilled from cashew fruit, native to Goa, India.

fermentation The process of yeast converting sugar into alcohol. Often the starches from the base ingredients—particularly grains—must be converted to fermentable sugar. The more sugars the microorganisms consume, the drier the beverage is going to be. Wines that are on the sweeter side tend to contain more residual sugars. All alcoholic beverages are fermented, but not all are distilled.

Fernet A popular Italian liqueur, made from a blend of spices and herbs.

ginjinha A Portuguese sour cherry liqueur, frequently known as "ginja."

kumyss A fermented milk beverage popular in Mongolia and Central Asia.

kvass An Eastern European beverage, typical in countries like Ukraine and Belarus, made by steeping and fermenting dark bread.

hops Green flowers used as the flavoring, aroma, and bittering agents in beer.

jenever/genever A Dutch and Belgian spirit that was a forerunner of gin. The key distinction is that much of jenever's flavor comes from malt wine, a malted grain-based distillate that makes up a varying percentage of jenever's spirit base. Gin's flavor tends to derive mostly from its added botanicals, as the spirit base is usually neutral, unlike malt wine. Though gin and jenever both contain juniper, the botanical's presence usually is far less pronounced in jenever.

lakka The Finnish word for cloudberry, a popular liqueur flavor in Finland.

lotoko Congolese moonshine, usually distilled from a cassava base.

malt Usually refers to malted barley, or barley that has undergone germination in water and is then dried with hot air. In this process, enzymes emerge that facilitate the conversion of starch into fermentable sugar.

mastiha A tree native to Greece whose sap is used to flavor a liqueur.

mezcal A Mexican spirit distilled from any of around thirty different species of agave. The state of Oaxaca is the epicenter of mezcal production. A key flavor element that distinguishes it from tequila is its smokiness. The agave hearts used in mezcal are baked in stone ovens dug in the ground, imparting the smoky flavor. Tequila hearts are steamed, a process that doesn't result in the same smokiness.

nihonshu See **sake**.

ogogoro A Nigerian spirit distilled from palm sap, similar to akpeteshie and sodabi.

ouzo An anise-flavored spirit native to Greece.

pálinka A fruit brandy from Eastern Europe, particularly Hungary.

peket A Belgian nickname for jenever.

poitin An often strong spirit traditionally distilled in Ireland from available grains, fruits, and/or vegetables; it's the Irish equivalent of moonshine.

pomace The unpressed skins, seeds, stems, and other leftovers from winemaking, used to make grappa, among other spirits.

port A fortified wine produced only in northern Portugal's Douro Valley.

proof The alcoholic strength of a spirit. The number is double that of the ABV. An 80-proof vodka is, therefore, 40 percent ABV.

punsch A Swedish spirit that consists of Batavia arrack mixed with sugar, spices, citrus juice, and, sometimes, tea.

Quezalteca An aguardiente (or guaro) native to Guatemala.

raki An anise-flavored spirit native to Turkey (similar to Greece's ouzo).

Riga Black Balsam An herbal liqueur popular in Latvia.

rhum agricole A rum style that originated in the French Caribbean. Unlike most rums, which are distilled from molasses, rhum agricole is distilled from pure cane juice (a base similar to that of Brazil's cachaça).

rum A spirit distilled from molasses (a by-product of sugarcane processing) or from the raw cane juice itself.

sake A generic term for an alcoholic beverage in Japan, it most commonly refers to the brewed, fermented rice beverage that's typically clear or, in the case of the roughly filtered variety nigori, cloudy white. Alcohol percentage usually ranges from 15 to 19 percent. It's also known as nihonshu.

schnaps A spirit made from distilled fruit (aka eau-de-vie), common in German-speaking countries.

sherry A fortified wine produced only in the town of Jerez de la Frontera, Spain.

shochu A Japanese spirit, usually clear, derived from any of more than fifty possible bases. The most common bases are sweet potatoes, rice, barley, brown or black sugar, and buckwheat. Most brands are around 25 percent ABV. Finer examples of the spirit are distilled only once and thus retain character from the base ingredient. And, as in sake, shochu uses koji, the mold that produces enzymes to break down starches into fermentable sugar. Koji imparts additional character.

slivovitz An Eastern European eau-de-vie, often distilled from plums (sljivovica, from which the name derives, is Serbian for "plum").

sodabi A spirit made from distilled palm wine in Benin.

soju Korea's national spirit, not to be confused with Japan's shochu. Soju tends to have a more neutral flavor than shochu.

tahona A two-ton stone wheel, often pulled by a donkey or horse, that crushes agave to release its fermentable juices. It's an old method used only in the most traditional tequila and mezcal distilleries.

t'ej Ethiopian honey wine.

tongba A beer-like beverage from the Himalayan region, sometimes called chhaang. It's typically made from millet, often incorporating other grains like barley and rice and served hot.

umquombothi A vaguely beer-like beverage produced in southern Africa from corn, millet, and other available grains.

vermouth An aromatized wine flavored with a combination of roots and herbs; its name is derived from one of those, wormwood, or "Wermuth" in German.

vodka A spirit distilled from grain, potatoes, or many other possible bases. It is distilled to neutrality and unaged and therefore has no discernible color, flavor, or aroma (beyond the whiff of ethanol you're likely to get). It's diluted to about 40 percent alcohol (80 proof) before bottling.

witblits South African moonshine.

whisky A spirit distilled from a cereal or grain, such as corn, malted barley, wheat, rye, or any combination of those. It is typically not distilled to neutrality, so it retains some of the character of the base grain, and is usually aged in wooden barrels (though unaged versions have been sold as "white whisky," "white dog," or even "moonshine"). You might sometimes see the spelling "whiskey"; that's the preferred spelling in Ireland and the United States (though American bourbon brand Maker's Mark opted for the e-less spelling).

377

BIBLIOGRAPHY

Australia and New Zealand

Korff, Jens. "Aboriginal Alcohol Consumption." Creative Spirits. May 8, 2016. www.creativespirits.info/aboriginalculture/health /aboriginal-alcohol-consumption#axzz3wDrehXRu.

"The Spirit of New Zealand Whisky." Southern Distilleries Ltd. www.hokonuiwhiskey.com/spirit.html.

Thomson, Mathew. Personal interview; March 10, 2015. Phone interview; August 15, 2016.

Clark, Jason. "The Label Reviving New Zealand's Whisky Tradition." Stuff: Food & Wine. April 18, 2015. www.stuff.co.nz/life-style /food-wine/drinks/67672902/the-label-reviving-new-zealands-whisky-tradition.

"A Brief History of Emigration and Immigration in Scotland: Research Guide 2." John Gray Centre. www.johngraycentre.org/about/archives/ brief-history-emigration-immigration-scotland-research-guide-2.

Duckett, Tim. Personal interview. February 25, 2015.

Bignall, Peter. Personal interview. February 27, 2015.

Kudelka, Jon, and Andrew Marlton. *Kudelka and First Dog's Spiritual Journey: In Which Two Cartoonists Bravely Tour the Dangerous Tasmanian Whisky Trail.* South Hobart, Australia: Kudelka Productions, 2014.

Southeast Asia

Santos, Lean. "Filipinos Are the World's Biggest Gin Drinkers." Rappler. June 18, 2013. www.rappler.com/business/industries /176-food-and-beverage/31582-filipinos-are-biggest-gin-drinkers.

Umpleby, Craig. "Lao Lao Whiskey aka Sticky Rice Moonshine." A World of Drinks (message board). April 2, 2014. http://drinks1405.rssing.com/chan-28354550/all_p1.html.

"Thai Whiskey: Mekhong v. Sang Som." Intoxicated Abroad. February 3, 2011. www.intoxicatedabroad.com/2011/02/thai-whiskey-mekhong-v-sang-som.html.

McMah, Lauren. "The Party Could Be Over in Bali as Indonesia Considers Banning Alcohol." News.com.au. August 17, 2016. www.news.com.au/travel/world-travel/asia/the-party-could-be-over-in-bali-as-indonesia-considers-banning-alcohol/news-story/a89cf26b94c2d2377216f9e6f1acb6ca.

Nazarudin, Harry. "Making 'Brem' and 'Arak' in Bali." *Jakarta Post.* January 26, 2013. www.thejakartapost.com/news/2013/01/26/making-brem-and-arak-bali.html.

Nur Zuhra, Wan Ulfa. "Enjoying 'Tuak' in Batak Country." *Jakarta Post.* January 21, 2013. www.thejakartapost.com/news/2013/01/21/enjoying-tuak-batak-country.html.

Sophanna, Khim. "Beer and Development." Trustbuilding's Blog. September 2, 2012. https://trustbuilding.wordpress.com/2012/09/02/beer-and-development.

Bray, Adam. "The Intoxicating World of Vietnam's Rice Wine Culture." CNN Travel. March 10, 2010. http://travel.cnn.com/explorations/none/vietnams-rice-wine-culture-223868.

Hiếu Trần Trung. "Ben Tre Coconut Wine." Vietnam-online.org. October 21, 2014. Available at https://web.archive.org/web/20160909164705/http://vietnam-online.org/index.php/ben-tre-coconut-wine.

East Asia

"Airag." Mongol Food. www.mongolfood.info/en/recipes/airag.html.

Evans, Caroline. "Airag—Getting Loose on the Mongolian Horse Juice." On the Gas. May 6, 2013. http://onthegas.org/drink/airag-getting-loose-on-the-mongolian-horse-juice.

"Isgelen-Tarag." Mongol Food. www.mongolfood.info/en/recipes/isgelen-tarag.html.

Dinkins, Dominic. Phone interview. June 9, 2016.

Dinkins, Dominic, and HyoSun Kwon. Learn Basic Korean Words & Vocabulary with Dom & Hyo. https://domandhyo.com.

Florcruz, Michelle. "China's Wine Industry Explodes, but Not Yet on the World Stage." *International Business Times.* May 3, 2015. www.ibtimes.com/chinas-wine-industry-explodes-not-yet-world-stage-1902284.

Finkenbinder, Joe. Phone interview. September 28, 2016.

South Asia, Central Asia, and the Middle East

"Foreign Travel Advice: United Arab Emirates." Gov.uk. www.gov.uk /foreign-travel-advice/united-arab-emirates/local-laws-and-customs.

Kantaria, Annabel. "Drinking in the UAE—What You Need to Know." May 9, 2013. *Telegraph* blog. Available at https://web.archive.org/web /20160312002125/http://my.telegraph.co.uk/expat/annabelkantaria /10150455/drinking-in-the-uae-what-you-need-to-know.

"Arak." Eagle Distilleries Co. www.eagledis.com/arak.html.

"Lebanon Demographics Profile 2016." Index Mundi. Last updated October 8, 2016. www.indexmundi.com/lebanon/demographics _profile.html.

Wood, Josh. "Militants Set Their Attacks on Alcohol in Lebanon." *New York Times.* January 25, 2012. www.nytimes.com/2012/01 /26/world/middleeast/militants-set-their-attacks-on-alcohol- in-lebanon.html.

"Can You Drink Alcohol in Saudi Arabia?" Living in Saudi Arabia. August 1, 2012. http://livinginsaudiarabia.org/268/can-you- drink-alcohol-in-saudi-arabia.

Cacciottolo, Mario. "Saudi Arabia Drinking: The Risks Expats Take for a Tipple." *BBC News.* October 13, 2015. www.bbc.com/news /uk-34516143.

Broadbent, Bartholomew. Phone interview. April 11, 2016.

Hochar, Marc. Phone interview. April 12, 2016.

"The Incredible Story of Feni That Butler Didn't Tell You." Goa.Life. http://goa.life/the-incredible-story-of-feni-that-butler-didnt- tell-you.

Bojha, Ajay. Personal interview. September 21, 2016.

Sayej, Alaa. Personal interview. October 27, 2016.

"Iraq's Parliament Passes Law Banning Alcohol." *Guardian.* October 23, 2016. www.theguardian.com/world/2016/oct/23 /iraqs-parliament-passes-law-banning-alcohol.

Braun, Robert. Phone interview. November 21, 2016.

Africa

Slater, Murray. "Umqombothi: Africa's Original Sorghum Beer." Beer House. October 30, 2014. www.beerhouse.co.za /2014/10/30/umqombothi-africas-original-sorghum-beer.

Musambachime, Mwelwa C. *One Zambia, One Nation, One Country.* Bloomington, IN: Xlibris, 2016.

"In Defence of the Kachasu Industry." *Zambian Economist.* June 10, 2008. www.zambian-economist.com/2008/06/in-defence-of-kachasu-industry.html.

"Would You Like Some ARVs with Your Kachasu?" African Science Heroes. November 22, 2009. https://afrisciheroes.wordpress.com /tag/kachasu.

"Kill Me Quick." *Economist.* April 29, 2010. www.economist.com /node/16018262.

Aarhus, Paige. "Really Strange Brew." *Vice.* October 13, 2011. www.vice.com/read/really-strange-brew-0000009-v18n10.

Pullman, Nina. "Lychees: An Exotic Fruit That Provides a Lifeline for Madagascar." *Guardian.* January 28, 2016. www.theguardian.com /sustainable-business/2016/jan/28/lychees-madagascar-exotic-fruit-lifeline-farmers-poverty.

Kroll, David. "Did Crocodile Bile Really Kill 75 People in Mozambique?" *Forbes.* January 12, 2015. www.forbes.com/sites/davidkroll /2015/01/12/what-is-crocodile-bile-and-is-it-really-poisonous /#3e83aeecfd02.

"Mozambique: Mass Poisoning Caused by Bacterial Contamination." AllAfrica. November 4, 2015. http://allafrica.com/stories /201511050128.html.

Morton, Julia F. "Cashew Apple." In *Fruits of Warm Climates.* Miami: Julia F. Morton, 1987. Available at www.hort.purdue.edu /newcrop/morton/cashew_apple.html.

Rigney, Todd. "Poisoned Alcohol Death Toll Rises in Libya." Inquistr. March 13, 2013. www.inquisitr.com/569823/poisoned-alcohol-death-roll-rises-in-libya.

Olivesi, Marine, and Bradley Campbell. "Libyans Risk Poisoning for a Sip of Illegal Hooch in Their Dry Nation." *The World* (radio program). March 19, 2014. www.pri.org/stories/2014-03-19 /libyans-risk-poisoning-sip-illegal-hooch-their-dry-nation.

Musasizi, Simon. "Jakana's Dream Is to Immortalize Mubisi, Tonto." *Kampala Observer.* July 15, 2014. Available at http://allafrica.com /stories/201407160280.html.

Bendana, Christoper. "Banana Beer: Has Tonto Lost the War?" New Vision (Uganda). November 22, 2014. www.newvision.co.ug /new_vision/news/1315612/banana-beer-tonto-lost-war.

Motlhanka, D. M. T., and S. Ngwako. "Notes on Chetopoti: A Traditional Botswana Fermented Alcoholic Beverage from Water Melons." *Botswana Notes and Records,* vol. 41 (2009): 133–35. Available at www.jstor.org/stable/23237935.

Valussi, Roberto. "Ghana's Anti-Colonial Beverage Gets Rehabilitated." *Al Jazeera.* June 17, 2015. www.aljazeera.com/indepth /features/2015/06/ghana-anti-colonial-beverage-rehabilitated-150616073107080.html.

Hill, J. "Beer in Ancient Egypt," Ancient Egypt Online. www.ancientegyptonline.co.uk/beer.html.

"Morocco's King Mohammed V Honored for Protecting Jews from Nazis during World War II." Moroccan American Center for Policy. December 23, 2015. Available at www.marketwired.com /press-release/moroccos-king-mohammed-v-honored-for-protecting-jews-from-nazis-during-world-war-ii-2084452.htm.

"Food." Embassy of Equatorial Guinea in the United Kingdom. http://embassyofequatorialguinea.co.uk/food.

Bokobsa, Lionel. Personal interview. September 9, 2016.

Abdoulaye, Leila. Personal interview. September 9, 2016.

Maasho, Aaron, and Edmund Blair. "Foreign Brewers Battle for Ethiopia's Beer Drinkers." Reuters. April 1, 2015. www.reuters.com /article/us-ethiopia-beverages-idUSKBN0MS49820150401.

Kloman, Harry. Personal interview. October 6, 2016.

Fenton, Simon. Phone interview. November 14, 2016.

383

Eastern and Central Europe and the Balkans

Kamenev, Marina. "Russia's Artisanal Moonshine Boom." *Time*. February 15, 2009. http://content.time.com/time/world/article /0,8599,1879572,00.html.

Jenssen, Jeff. "Croatian Wine on the Rise." *Wine Enthusiast*. March 19, 2014. www.winemag.com/gallery/croatian-wine-on-the-rise.

"Cviček." In Your Pocket. December 13, 2016. Available at https://web.archive.org/web/20160229195130 /http://www.inyourpocket.com/Slovenian-Wine/Cvicek_72985f.

Haviaris, Monolis. Phone interview. August 20, 2016.

Kalnins, Maris. Phone interview. November 7, 2016.

"Georgian Qvevri Wine-Making Method Added to UNESCO Heritage List." Georgian Recipes. January 15, 2014. https://georgianrecipes.net/2014/01/15/georgian-qvevri-wine-making-method-added-to-unesco-heritage-list.

Gal, Helga. Phone interview. November 21, 2016.

Dudova, Zuzana. Phone interview. November 22, 2016.

Northern and Western Europe

Associated Press. "Beer (Soon) for Icelanders." *New York Times*. May 11, 1988. www.nytimes.com/1988/05/11/world/beer-soon-for-icelanders.html.

"Why Iceland Banned Beer." *BBC News*. March 1, 2015. www.bbc.com /news/magazine-31622038.

Dietsch, Michael. "The Serious Eats Guide to Genever." Serious Eats. http://drinks.seriouseats.com/2012/06/serious-eats-guide-to-genever-what-is-jenever-history-production-bols.html.

"18th Century Gin Craze." History Channel. www.history.co.uk /history-of-london/18th-century-gin-craze.

"The Gin Act 1751 Is a Reminder That Drunkenness on the Streets Is Nothing New." Intriguing History. www.intriguing-history.com /gin-act-1751.

Bachman, Alex. "A Guide to Amaro, Italy's Bittersweet Export." Eater. April 17, 2015. www.eater.com/drinks/2015/4/17/8431759 /a-guide-to-amaro-italys-unruly-bittersweet-export.

"France, the World's Leading Wine Producer." France Diplomatie. www.diplomatie.gouv.fr/en/french-foreign-policy/economic-diplomacy-foreign-trade/facts-about-france/one-figure-one-fact/article/france-the-world-s-leading-wine.

"Sémillon." Wine Searcher. www.wine-searcher.com/grape-446 -semillon.

Vekkilä, Juuli. Phone interview. August 24, 2016.

Kasula-Sainio, Salla. Phone interview. August 24, 2016.

Cooney, Christine. Phone interview. June 6, 2016.

Bonoli, Matteo. Personal interview. July 20, 2016.

Collia, Luca. Phone interview. August 5, 2016.

"Greenland to Ration Alcohol." *St. Petersburg Times.* July 31, 1979.

"Greenland on a Binge Since Rationing End." *Kentucky New Era.* July 2, 1982.

Robert Petersen. "Colonialism as Seen from a Former Colonized Area." *Arctic Anthropology* vol. 32, no. 2 (1995): 118–26. Available at http://arcticcircle.uconn.edu/HistoryCulture/petersen.html.

Monti, François. Phone interview. September 1, 2016.

Kroth, Maya. "In Barcelona, Vermouth Enjoys a Spirited Revival." *Washington Post.* March 13, 2014. www.washingtonpost.com/lifestyle/travel/in-barcelona-vermouth-enjoys-a-spirited-revival/2014/03/13/17545992-a870-11e3-8599-ce7295b6851c_story.html.

Rocha, Nuno. Phone interview. October 31, 2016.

Facile, Henrik. Phone interview. November 4, 2016.

Pimpão, Marta. Phone interview. November 7, 2016.

Kragelund, Lars. Phone interview. November 22, 2016.

Jónsson, Óli Runar. Phone interview. November 23, 2016.

Jackson, Michael. *Michael Jackson's Great Beers of Belgium.* Boulder, CO: Brewers Publications, 2008.

Central and South America

Ebner, Tim. "Where to Drink Singani, a Bolivian Spirit New to DC." Eater: Washington, DC. October 1, 2015. http://dc.eater.com/maps/singani-rujero-bolivian-lupo-verde-compass-rose-jack-rose.

Uyehara, Mari. "Steven Soderbergh's Singani 63." *Saveur.* April 7, 2015. www.saveur.com/article/wine-and-drink/steven-soderberghs-singani-63.

Escobar, Ramon. Phone interview. June 22, 2016.

Soderbergh, Steven. Personal interview. July 22, 2016.

Gemmell, Michael K. Phone interview. August 13, 2016.

Leon, Mario. E-mail interview. June 22, 2016.

LaMonica, Sophia. "Cacique Guaro Is Costa Rica's Original Distilled Spirit." *USA Today.* January 29, 2012. www.10best.com/interests /foodie/cacique-guaro-is-costa-ricas-original-distilled-spirit.

Yeamans-Irwin, Becca. "Boozing in Belize." Alcohol Professor. October 14, 2014. www.alcoholprofessor.com/blog/2014/10/10 /boozing-in-belize.

Asher, Elizabeth. Phone interview. November 7, 2016.

Asher, Melanie. Phone interview. November 7, 2016.

Stuart, Jim. "Chilean Chicha." Eating Chile blog. September 18, 2011. http://eatingchile.blogspot.com/2011/09/chilean-chicha.html.

Caribbean Islands

Hamilton, Ed. Phone interview. July 12, 2016.

"AOC Rhum Martinique description." Rhum-Agricole.net. www.rhum-agricole.net/site/en/aoc_described.

Booton, Jennifer. "Anheuser-Busch pays $1.2B for Dominican Presidente Brewer." Fox Business. April 16, 2012. www.foxbusiness.com /features/2012/04/16/anheuser-busch-pays-12b-to-devour-dominican-presidente-brewer.html.

Appiah, Colin. Phone interview. November 15, 2016.

Caribbean Premier Products. www.coooldelight.com.

North America

Bragg, Meredith. "Did New Orleans Invent the Cocktail?" (video). *Smithsonian Magazine.* www.smithsonianmag.com/videos /category/arts-culture/did-new-orleans-invent-the-cocktail.

Lancha, Miguel. Phone interview. August 22, 2016.

Dikty, Alan, and Bill Owens, eds. *The Art of Distilling Whiskey and Other Spirits.* Beverly, Massachusetts: Quarry Books, 2011.

Bryson, Lew. *Tasting Whiskey: An Insider's Guide to the Unique Pleasures of the World's Finest Spirits.* New York: Storey, 2014.

The End of the World and Beyond

"Stoli Zero-G" video. YouTube. October 4, 2012. www.youtube.com /watch?v=7pduLVyxOyc.

Kiefaber, David. "Stoli Goes to Space, the Final Frontier of Drinking." AdWeek. October 26, 2012. www.adweek.com/adfreak /stoli-goes-space-final-frontier-drinking-144814.

Lumsden, Bill. "The Impact of Micro-Gravity on the Release of Oak Extractives into Spirit." Ardbeg.com. www.ardbeg.com/CDN /ardbeg-media/ardbeg/supernova/ARD9109SupernovaWhite-PaperA4.pdf.

Kluger, Jeffrey. Phone interview. September 15, 2016.

Stephenson, Tristan. Phone interview. November 10, 2016.

INDEX

389